Mometrix
TEST PREPARATION

Secrets of the

National Board Certification
Generalist: Early Childhood
Exam Study Guide

Disclaimer: Mometrix Media LLC is not affiliated with the National Board for Professional Teaching Standards (NBPTS), nor are Mometrix products and publications endorsed by or approved by NBPTS. Mometrix has not received confidential information or assistance from NBPTS, its assessors, or National Board Certified Teachers in developing its products and publications.

DEAR FUTURE EXAM SUCCESS STORY

First of all, **THANK YOU** for purchasing Mometrix study materials!

Second, congratulations! You are one of the few determined test-takers who are committed to doing whatever it takes to excel on your exam. **You have come to the right place.** We developed these study materials with one goal in mind: to deliver you the information you need in a format that's concise and easy to use.

In addition to optimizing your guide for the content of the test, we've outlined our recommended steps for breaking down the preparation process into small, attainable goals so you can make sure you stay on track.

We've also analyzed the entire test-taking process, identifying the most common pitfalls and showing how you can overcome them and be ready for any curveball the test throws you.

Standardized testing is one of the biggest obstacles on your road to success, which only increases the importance of doing well in the high-pressure, high-stakes environment of test day. Your results on this test could have a significant impact on your future, and this guide provides the information and practical advice to help you achieve your full potential on test day.

Your success is our success

We would love to hear from you! If you would like to share the story of your exam success or if you have any questions or comments in regard to our products, please contact us at **800-673-8175** or **support@mometrix.com**.

Thanks again for your business and we wish you continued success!

Sincerely,
The Mometrix Test Preparation Team

> **Need more help? Check out our flashcards at:**
> **http://MometrixFlashcards.com/NBPTS**

Copyright © 2022 by Mometrix Media LLC. All rights reserved.
Written and edited by the Mometrix Exam Secrets Test Prep Team
Printed in the United States of America

TABLE OF CONTENTS

Introduction

Thank you for purchasing this resource! You have made the choice to prepare yourself for a test that could have a huge impact on your future, and this guide is designed to help you be fully ready for test day. Obviously, it's important to have a solid understanding of the test material, but you also need to be prepared for the unique environment and stressors of the test, so that you can perform to the best of your abilities.

For this purpose, the first section that appears in this guide is the **Secret Keys**. We've devoted countless hours to meticulously researching what works and what doesn't, and we've boiled down our findings to the five most impactful steps you can take to improve your performance on the test. We start at the beginning with study planning and move through the preparation process, all the way to the testing strategies that will help you get the most out of what you know when you're finally sitting in front of the test.

We recommend that you start preparing for your test as far in advance as possible. However, if you've bought this guide as a last-minute study resource and only have a few days before your test, we recommend that you skip over the first two Secret Keys since they address a long-term study plan.

If you struggle with **test anxiety**, we strongly encourage you to check out our recommendations for how you can overcome it. Test anxiety is a formidable foe, but it can be beaten, and we want to make sure you have the tools you need to defeat it.

Copyright © Mometrix Media. You have been licensed one copy of this document for personal use only. Any other reproduction or redistribution is strictly prohibited. All rights reserved.

Secret Key #1 – Plan Big, Study Small

There's a lot riding on your performance. If you want to ace this test, you're going to need to keep your skills sharp and the material fresh in your mind. You need a plan that lets you review everything you need to know while still fitting in your schedule. We'll break this strategy down into three categories.

Information Organization

Start with the information you already have: the official test outline. From this, you can make a complete list of all the concepts you need to cover before the test. Organize these concepts into groups that can be studied together, and create a list of any related vocabulary you need to learn so you can brush up on any difficult terms. You'll want to keep this vocabulary list handy once you actually start studying since you may need to add to it along the way.

Time Management

Once you have your set of study concepts, decide how to spread them out over the time you have left before the test. Break your study plan into small, clear goals so you have a manageable task for each day and know exactly what you're doing. Then just focus on one small step at a time. When you manage your time this way, you don't need to spend hours at a time studying. Studying a small block of content for a short period each day helps you retain information better and avoid stressing over how much you have left to do. You can relax knowing that you have a plan to cover everything in time. In order for this strategy to be effective though, you have to start studying early and stick to your schedule. Avoid the exhaustion and futility that comes from last-minute cramming!

Study Environment

The environment you study in has a big impact on your learning. Studying in a coffee shop, while probably more enjoyable, is not likely to be as fruitful as studying in a quiet room. It's important to keep distractions to a minimum. You're only planning to study for a short block of time, so make the most of it. Don't pause to check your phone or get up to find a snack. It's also important to **avoid multitasking**. Research has consistently shown that multitasking will make your studying dramatically less effective. Your study area should also be comfortable and well-lit so you don't have the distraction of straining your eyes or sitting on an uncomfortable chair.

The time of day you study is also important. You want to be rested and alert. Don't wait until just before bedtime. Study when you'll be most likely to comprehend and remember. Even better, if you know what time of day your test will be, set that time aside for study. That way your brain will be used to working on that subject at that specific time and you'll have a better chance of recalling information.

Finally, it can be helpful to team up with others who are studying for the same test. Your actual studying should be done in as isolated an environment as possible, but the work of organizing the information and setting up the study plan can be divided up. In between study sessions, you can discuss with your teammates the concepts that you're all studying and quiz each other on the details. Just be sure that your teammates are as serious about the test as you are. If you find that your study time is being replaced with social time, you might need to find a new team.

2

Copyright © Mometrix Media. You have been licensed one copy of this document for personal use only. Any other reproduction or redistribution is strictly prohibited. All rights reserved.

Secret Key #2 – Make Your Studying Count

You're devoting a lot of time and effort to preparing for this test, so you want to be absolutely certain it will pay off. This means doing more than just reading the content and hoping you can remember it on test day. It's important to make every minute of study count. There are two main areas you can focus on to make your studying count.

Retention

It doesn't matter how much time you study if you can't remember the material. You need to make sure you are retaining the concepts. To check your retention of the information you're learning, try recalling it at later times with minimal prompting. Try carrying around flashcards and glance at one or two from time to time or ask a friend who's also studying for the test to quiz you.

To enhance your retention, look for ways to put the information into practice so that you can apply it rather than simply recalling it. If you're using the information in practical ways, it will be much easier to remember. Similarly, it helps to solidify a concept in your mind if you're not only reading it to yourself but also explaining it to someone else. Ask a friend to let you teach them about a concept you're a little shaky on (or speak aloud to an imaginary audience if necessary). As you try to summarize, define, give examples, and answer your friend's questions, you'll understand the concepts better and they will stay with you longer. Finally, step back for a big picture view and ask yourself how each piece of information fits with the whole subject. When you link the different concepts together and see them working together as a whole, it's easier to remember the individual components.

Finally, practice showing your work on any multi-step problems, even if you're just studying. Writing out each step you take to solve a problem will help solidify the process in your mind, and you'll be more likely to remember it during the test.

Modality

Modality simply refers to the means or method by which you study. Choosing a study modality that fits your own individual learning style is crucial. No two people learn best in exactly the same way, so it's important to know your strengths and use them to your advantage.

For example, if you learn best by visualization, focus on visualizing a concept in your mind and draw an image or a diagram. Try color-coding your notes, illustrating them, or creating symbols that will trigger your mind to recall a learned concept. If you learn best by hearing or discussing information, find a study partner who learns the same way or read aloud to yourself. Think about how to put the information in your own words. Imagine that you are giving a lecture on the topic and record yourself so you can listen to it later.

For any learning style, flashcards can be helpful. Organize the information so you can take advantage of spare moments to review. Underline key words or phrases. Use different colors for different categories. Mnemonic devices (such as creating a short list in which every item starts with the same letter) can also help with retention. Find what works best for you and use it to store the information in your mind most effectively and easily.

Copyright © Mometrix Media. You have been licensed one copy of this document for personal use only. Any other reproduction or redistribution is strictly prohibited. All rights reserved.

Secret Key #3 – Practice the Right Way

Your success on test day depends not only on how many hours you put into preparing, but also on whether you prepared the right way. It's good to check along the way to see if your studying is paying off. One of the most effective ways to do this is by taking practice tests to evaluate your progress. Practice tests are useful because they show exactly where you need to improve. Every time you take a practice test, pay special attention to these three groups of questions:

- The questions you got wrong
- The questions you had to guess on, even if you guessed right
- The questions you found difficult or slow to work through

This will show you exactly what your weak areas are, and where you need to devote more study time. Ask yourself why each of these questions gave you trouble. Was it because you didn't understand the material? Was it because you didn't remember the vocabulary? Do you need more repetitions on this type of question to build speed and confidence? Dig into those questions and figure out how you can strengthen your weak areas as you go back to review the material.

 Additionally, many practice tests have a section explaining the answer choices. It can be tempting to read the explanation and think that you now have a good understanding of the concept. However, an explanation likely only covers part of the question's broader context. Even if the explanation makes perfect sense, **go back and investigate** every concept related to the question until you're positive you have a thorough understanding.

As you go along, keep in mind that the practice test is just that: practice. Memorizing these questions and answers will not be very helpful on the actual test because it is unlikely to have any of the same exact questions. If you only know the right answers to the sample questions, you won't be prepared for the real thing. **Study the concepts** until you understand them fully, and then you'll be able to answer any question that shows up on the test.

It's important to wait on the practice tests until you're ready. If you take a test on your first day of study, you may be overwhelmed by the amount of material covered and how much you need to learn. Work up to it gradually.

On test day, you'll need to be prepared for answering questions, managing your time, and using the test-taking strategies you've learned. It's a lot to balance, like a mental marathon that will have a big impact on your future. Like training for a marathon, you'll need to start slowly and work your way up. When test day arrives, you'll be ready.

Start with the strategies you've read in the first two Secret Keys—plan your course and study in the way that works best for you. If you have time, consider using multiple study resources to get different approaches to the same concepts. It can be helpful to see difficult concepts from more than one angle. Then find a good source for practice tests. Many times, the test website will suggest potential study resources or provide sample tests.

Practice Test Strategy

If you're able to find at least three practice tests, we recommend this strategy:

UNTIMED AND OPEN-BOOK PRACTICE

Take the first test with no time constraints and with your notes and study guide handy. Take your time and focus on applying the strategies you've learned.

4

Copyright © Mometrix Media. You have been licensed one copy of this document for personal use only. Any other reproduction or redistribution is strictly prohibited. All rights reserved.

TIMED AND OPEN-BOOK PRACTICE

Take the second practice test open-book as well, but set a timer and practice pacing yourself to finish in time.

TIMED AND CLOSED-BOOK PRACTICE

Take any other practice tests as if it were test day. Set a timer and put away your study materials. Sit at a table or desk in a quiet room, imagine yourself at the testing center, and answer questions as quickly and accurately as possible.

Keep repeating timed and closed-book tests on a regular basis until you run out of practice tests or it's time for the actual test. Your mind will be ready for the schedule and stress of test day, and you'll be able to focus on recalling the material you've learned.

Copyright © Mometrix Media. You have been licensed one copy of this document for personal use only. Any other reproduction or redistribution is strictly prohibited. All rights reserved.

Secret Key #4 – Pace Yourself

Once you're fully prepared for the material on the test, your biggest challenge on test day will be managing your time. Just knowing that the clock is ticking can make you panic even if you have plenty of time left. Work on pacing yourself so you can build confidence against the time constraints of the exam. Pacing is a difficult skill to master, especially in a high-pressure environment, so **practice is vital**.

Set time expectations for your pace based on how much time is available. For example, if a section has 60 questions and the time limit is 30 minutes, you know you have to average 30 seconds or less per question in order to answer them all. Although 30 seconds is the hard limit, set 25 seconds per question as your goal, so you reserve extra time to spend on harder questions. When you budget extra time for the harder questions, you no longer have any reason to stress when those questions take longer to answer.

Don't let this time expectation distract you from working through the test at a calm, steady pace, but keep it in mind so you don't spend too much time on any one question. Recognize that taking extra time on one question you don't understand may keep you from answering two that you do understand later in the test. If your time limit for a question is up and you're still not sure of the answer, mark it and move on, and come back to it later if the time and the test format allow. If the testing format doesn't allow you to return to earlier questions, just make an educated guess; then put it out of your mind and move on.

On the easier questions, be careful not to rush. It may seem wise to hurry through them so you have more time for the challenging ones, but it's not worth missing one if you know the concept and just didn't take the time to read the question fully. Work efficiently but make sure you understand the question and have looked at all of the answer choices, since more than one may seem right at first.

Even if you're paying attention to the time, you may find yourself a little behind at some point. You should speed up to get back on track, but do so wisely. Don't panic; just take a few seconds less on each question until you're caught up. Don't guess without thinking, but do look through the answer choices and eliminate any you know are wrong. If you can get down to two choices, it is often worthwhile to guess from those. Once you've chosen an answer, move on and don't dwell on any that you skipped or had to hurry through. If a question was taking too long, chances are it was one of the harder ones, so you weren't as likely to get it right anyway.

On the other hand, if you find yourself getting ahead of schedule, it may be beneficial to slow down a little. The more quickly you work, the more likely you are to make a careless mistake that will affect your score. You've budgeted time for each question, so don't be afraid to spend that time. Practice an efficient but careful pace to get the most out of the time you have.

Copyright © Mometrix Media. You have been licensed one copy of this document for personal use only. Any other reproduction or redistribution is strictly prohibited. All rights reserved.

Secret Key #5 – Have a Plan for Guessing

When you're taking the test, you may find yourself stuck on a question. Some of the answer choices seem better than others, but you don't see the one answer choice that is obviously correct. What do you do?

The scenario described above is very common, yet most test takers have not effectively prepared for it. Developing and practicing a plan for guessing may be one of the single most effective uses of your time as you get ready for the exam.

In developing your plan for guessing, there are three questions to address:

- When should you start the guessing process?
- How should you narrow down the choices?
- Which answer should you choose?

When to Start the Guessing Process

Unless your plan for guessing is to select C every time (which, despite its merits, is not what we recommend), you need to leave yourself enough time to apply your answer elimination strategies. Since you have a limited amount of time for each question, that means that if you're going to give yourself the best shot at guessing correctly, you have to decide quickly whether or not you will guess.

Of course, the best-case scenario is that you don't have to guess at all, so first, see if you can answer the question based on your knowledge of the subject and basic reasoning skills. Focus on the key words in the question and try to jog your memory of related topics. Give yourself a chance to bring the knowledge to mind, but once you realize that you don't have (or you can't access) the knowledge you need to answer the question, it's time to start the guessing process.

It's almost always better to start the guessing process too early than too late. It only takes a few seconds to remember something and answer the question from knowledge. Carefully eliminating wrong answer choices takes longer. Plus, going through the process of eliminating answer choices can actually help jog your memory.

Summary: Start the guessing process as soon as you decide that you can't answer the question based on your knowledge.

Copyright © Mometrix Media. You have been licensed one copy of this document for personal use only. Any other reproduction or redistribution is strictly prohibited. All rights reserved.

How to Narrow Down the Choices

The next chapter in this book (**Test-Taking Strategies**) includes a wide range of strategies for how to approach questions and how to look for answer choices to eliminate. You will definitely want to read those carefully, practice them, and figure out which ones work best for you. Here though, we're going to address a mindset rather than a particular strategy.

Your odds of guessing an answer correctly depend on how many options you are choosing from.

Number of options left	5	4	3	2	1
Odds of guessing correctly	20%	25%	33%	50%	100%

You can see from this chart just how valuable it is to be able to eliminate incorrect answers and make an educated guess, but there are two things that many test takers do that cause them to miss out on the benefits of guessing:

- Accidentally eliminating the correct answer
- Selecting an answer based on an impression

We'll look at the first one here, and the second one in the next section.

To avoid accidentally eliminating the correct answer, we recommend a thought exercise called **the $5 challenge**. In this challenge, you only eliminate an answer choice from contention if you are willing to bet $5 on it being wrong. Why $5? Five dollars is a small but not insignificant amount of money. It's an amount you could afford to lose but wouldn't want to throw away. And while losing $5 once might not hurt too much, doing it twenty times will set you back $100. In the same way, each small decision you make—eliminating a choice here, guessing on a question there—won't by itself impact your score very much, but when you put them all together, they can make a big difference. By holding each answer choice elimination decision to a higher standard, you can reduce the risk of accidentally eliminating the correct answer.

The $5 challenge can also be applied in a positive sense: If you are willing to bet $5 that an answer choice *is* correct, go ahead and mark it as correct.

Summary: Only eliminate an answer choice if you are willing to bet $5 that it is wrong.

Copyright © Mometrix Media. You have been licensed one copy of this document for personal use only. Any other reproduction or redistribution is strictly prohibited. All rights reserved.

Which Answer to Choose

You're taking the test. You've run into a hard question and decided you'll have to guess. You've eliminated all the answer choices you're willing to bet $5 on. Now you have to pick an answer. Why do we even need to talk about this? Why can't you just pick whichever one you feel like when the time comes?

The answer to these questions is that if you don't come into the test with a plan, you'll rely on your impression to select an answer choice, and if you do that, you risk falling into a trap. The test writers know that everyone who takes their test will be guessing on some of the questions, so they intentionally write wrong answer choices to seem plausible. You still have to pick an answer though, and if the wrong answer choices are designed to look right, how can you ever be sure that you're not falling for their trap? The best solution we've found to this dilemma is to take the decision out of your hands entirely. Here is the process we recommend:

Once you've eliminated any choices that you are confident (willing to bet $5) are wrong, select the first remaining choice as your answer.

Whether you choose to select the first remaining choice, the second, or the last, the important thing is that you use some preselected standard. Using this approach guarantees that you will not be enticed into selecting an answer choice that looks right, because you are not basing your decision on how the answer choices look.

This is not meant to make you question your knowledge. Instead, it is to help you recognize the difference between your knowledge and your impressions. There's a huge difference between thinking an answer is right because of what you know, and thinking an answer is right because it looks or sounds like it should be right.

Summary: To ensure that your selection is appropriately random, make a predetermined selection from among all answer choices you have not eliminated.

Copyright © Mometrix Media. You have been licensed one copy of this document for personal use only. Any other reproduction or redistribution is strictly prohibited. All rights reserved.

Test-Taking Strategies

This section contains a list of test-taking strategies that you may find helpful as you work through the test. By taking what you know and applying logical thought, you can maximize your chances of answering any question correctly!

It is very important to realize that every question is different and every person is different: no single strategy will work on every question, and no single strategy will work for every person. That's why we've included all of them here, so you can try them out and determine which ones work best for different types of questions and which ones work best for you.

Question Strategies

☑ READ CAREFULLY

Read the question and the answer choices carefully. Don't miss the question because you misread the terms. You have plenty of time to read each question thoroughly and make sure you understand what is being asked. Yet a happy medium must be attained, so don't waste too much time. You must read carefully and efficiently.

☑ CONTEXTUAL CLUES

Look for contextual clues. If the question includes a word you are not familiar with, look at the immediate context for some indication of what the word might mean. Contextual clues can often give you all the information you need to decipher the meaning of an unfamiliar word. Even if you can't determine the meaning, you may be able to narrow down the possibilities enough to make a solid guess at the answer to the question.

☑ PREFIXES

If you're having trouble with a word in the question or answer choices, try dissecting it. Take advantage of every clue that the word might include. Prefixes and suffixes can be a huge help. Usually, they allow you to determine a basic meaning. *Pre-* means before, *post-* means after, *pro-* is positive, *de-* is negative. From prefixes and suffixes, you can get an idea of the general meaning of the word and try to put it into context.

☑ HEDGE WORDS

Watch out for critical hedge words, such as *likely, may, can, sometimes, often, almost, mostly, usually, generally, rarely,* and *sometimes*. Question writers insert these hedge phrases to cover every possibility. Often an answer choice will be wrong simply because it leaves no room for exception. Be on guard for answer choices that have definitive words such as *exactly* and *always*.

☑ SWITCHBACK WORDS

Stay alert for *switchbacks*. These are the words and phrases frequently used to alert you to shifts in thought. The most common switchback words are *but, although,* and *however*. Others include *nevertheless, on the other hand, even though, while, in spite of, despite,* and *regardless of*. Switchback words are important to catch because they can change the direction of the question or an answer choice.

☑ FACE VALUE

When in doubt, use common sense. Accept the situation in the problem at face value. Don't read too much into it. These problems will not require you to make wild assumptions. If you have to go beyond creativity and warp time or space in order to have an answer choice fit the question, then you should move on and consider the other answer choices. These are normal problems rooted in reality. The applicable relationship or explanation may not be readily apparent, but it is there for you to figure out. Use your common sense to interpret anything that isn't clear.

Copyright © Mometrix Media. You have been licensed one copy of this document for personal use only. Any other reproduction or redistribution is strictly prohibited. All rights reserved.

Answer Choice Strategies

☑ ANSWER SELECTION

The most thorough way to pick an answer choice is to identify and eliminate wrong answers until only one is left, then confirm it is the correct answer. Sometimes an answer choice may immediately seem right, but be careful. The test writers will usually put more than one reasonable answer choice on each question, so take a second to read all of them and make sure that the other choices are not equally obvious. As long as you have time left, it is better to read every answer choice than to pick the first one that looks right without checking the others.

☑ ANSWER CHOICE FAMILIES

An answer choice family consists of two (in rare cases, three) answer choices that are very similar in construction and cannot all be true at the same time. If you see two answer choices that are direct opposites or parallels, one of them is usually the correct answer. For instance, if one answer choice says that quantity x increases and another either says that quantity x decreases (opposite) or says that quantity y increases (parallel), then those answer choices would fall into the same family. An answer choice that doesn't match the construction of the answer choice family is more likely to be incorrect. Most questions will not have answer choice families, but when they do appear, you should be prepared to recognize them.

☑ ELIMINATE ANSWERS

Eliminate answer choices as soon as you realize they are wrong, but make sure you consider all possibilities. If you are eliminating answer choices and realize that the last one you are left with is also wrong, don't panic. Start over and consider each choice again. There may be something you missed the first time that you will realize on the second pass.

☑ AVOID FACT TRAPS

Don't be distracted by an answer choice that is factually true but doesn't answer the question. You are looking for the choice that answers the question. Stay focused on what the question is asking for so you don't accidentally pick an answer that is true but incorrect. Always go back to the question and make sure the answer choice you've selected actually answers the question and is not merely a true statement.

☑ EXTREME STATEMENTS

In general, you should avoid answers that put forth extreme actions as standard practice or proclaim controversial ideas as established fact. An answer choice that states the "process should be used in certain situations, if..." is much more likely to be correct than one that states the "process should be discontinued completely." The first is a calm rational statement and doesn't even make a definitive, uncompromising stance, using a hedge word *if* to provide wiggle room, whereas the second choice is far more extreme.

☑ BENCHMARK

As you read through the answer choices and you come across one that seems to answer the question well, mentally select that answer choice. This is not your final answer, but it's the one that will help you evaluate the other answer choices. The one that you selected is your benchmark or standard for judging each of the other answer choices. Every other answer choice must be compared to your benchmark. That choice is correct until proven otherwise by another answer choice beating it. If you find a better answer, then that one becomes your new benchmark. Once you've decided that no other choice answers the question as well as your benchmark, you have your final answer.

☑ PREDICT THE ANSWER

Before you even start looking at the answer choices, it is often best to try to predict the answer. When you come up with the answer on your own, it is easier to avoid distractions and traps because you will know exactly what to look for. The right answer choice is unlikely to be word-for-word what you came up with, but it

Copyright © Mometrix Media. You have been licensed one copy of this document for personal use only. Any other reproduction or redistribution is strictly prohibited. All rights reserved.

should be a close match. Even if you are confident that you have the right answer, you should still take the time to read each option before moving on.

General Strategies

⊘ Tough Questions

If you are stumped on a problem or it appears too hard or too difficult, don't waste time. Move on! Remember though, if you can quickly check for obviously incorrect answer choices, your chances of guessing correctly are greatly improved. Before you completely give up, at least try to knock out a couple of possible answers. Eliminate what you can and then guess at the remaining answer choices before moving on.

⊘ Check Your Work

Since you will probably not know every term listed and the answer to every question, it is important that you get credit for the ones that you do know. Don't miss any questions through careless mistakes. If at all possible, try to take a second to look back over your answer selection and make sure you've selected the correct answer choice and haven't made a costly careless mistake (such as marking an answer choice that you didn't mean to mark). This quick double check should more than pay for itself in caught mistakes for the time it costs.

⊘ Pace Yourself

It's easy to be overwhelmed when you're looking at a page full of questions; your mind is confused and full of random thoughts, and the clock is ticking down faster than you would like. Calm down and maintain the pace that you have set for yourself. Especially as you get down to the last few minutes of the test, don't let the small numbers on the clock make you panic. As long as you are on track by monitoring your pace, you are guaranteed to have time for each question.

⊘ Don't Rush

It is very easy to make errors when you are in a hurry. Maintaining a fast pace in answering questions is pointless if it makes you miss questions that you would have gotten right otherwise. Test writers like to include distracting information and wrong answers that seem right. Taking a little extra time to avoid careless mistakes can make all the difference in your test score. Find a pace that allows you to be confident in the answers that you select.

⊘ Keep Moving

Panicking will not help you pass the test, so do your best to stay calm and keep moving. Taking deep breaths and going through the answer elimination steps you practiced can help to break through a stress barrier and keep your pace.

Copyright © Mometrix Media. You have been licensed one copy of this document for personal use only. Any other reproduction or redistribution is strictly prohibited. All rights reserved.

Final Notes

The combination of a solid foundation of content knowledge and the confidence that comes from practicing your plan for applying that knowledge is the key to maximizing your performance on test day. As your foundation of content knowledge is built up and strengthened, you'll find that the strategies included in this chapter become more and more effective in helping you quickly sift through the distractions and traps of the test to isolate the correct answer.

Now that you're preparing to move forward into the test content chapters of this book, be sure to keep your goal in mind. As you read, think about how you will be able to apply this information on the test. If you've already seen sample questions for the test and you have an idea of the question format and style, try to come up with questions of your own that you can answer based on what you're reading. This will give you valuable practice applying your knowledge in the same ways you can expect to on test day.

Good luck and good studying!

Copyright © Mometrix Media. You have been licensed one copy of this document for personal use only. Any other reproduction or redistribution is strictly prohibited. All rights reserved.

170 pgs.
I. will. survive,

Copyright © Mometrix Media. You have been licensed one copy of this document for personal use only. Any other reproduction or redistribution is strictly prohibited. All rights reserved.

Piaget

Child Development, Equity, Fairness, and Appreciation of Diversity

Childhood Development Stages

Pee-aget

Bark

MAJOR CHARACTERISTICS OF PIAGET'S THEORY OF COGNITIVE DEVELOPMENT

According to Piaget's theory, infants are in the Sensorimotor stage of cognitive development. This means they learn through sensory input they get from the environment, motor actions they perform, and environmental feedback they receive from those actions. They also eventually coordinate their actions and reactions. For example, babies hear and attend to sounds; visually locate sound sources; and learn that some objects make sounds, like rattles. They learn to reach for, grasp, and manipulate objects. They learn when they shake a rattle, it makes a sound, and then repeat this action purposefully to generate the sound. Adults knowing these characteristics will provide infants with many toys they can manipulate, including toys that make noises/music, spin/twirl, or roll/bounce/fly; experiences affording input through all sensory modalities; and positive reinforcement when babies discover new body parts, objects, sights, sounds, textures, smells, and tastes; and demonstrate new behaviors interacting with these. They will not punish repetitious behaviors, like repeatedly throwing items from cribs/high-chair trays, which are part of learning in this stage. → *toys! throwing shit! = learning*

SENSORIMOTOR STAGE OF PIAGET'S THEORY OF COGNITIVE DEVELOPMENT

birth - age 2

From birth until about 2 years of age, infants are in what Piaget termed the Sensorimotor stage of cognitive development. They learn through environmental input they receive through their senses; motor actions they engage in; and through feedback they receive from their bodies and the environment ★ about their actions. For example, a baby kicks his legs, sees his feet moving, and reaches for them. He sees objects, reaches for them, and grasps them. Eventually, babies learn they can make some objects move by touching or hitting them. They learn through repeated experiences that when they throw objects out of their cribs, their parents retrieve them. They will seem to make a game of this, not to annoy parents, but as a way of learning rules of cause and effect by repeating actions to see the same results. They also enjoy their ability to be causal agents and their power to achieve effects through their actions.

FIRST THREE SUBSTAGES OF THE SENSORIMOTOR STAGE

① primary circular *birth - age 1 : learn through reflexes (suck) (+ look)*
1-4 mos. : coordinate physical sensations w/ new schemas.

From birth to 1 month old, infants learn to comprehend their environment through their inborn reflexes, such as the sucking reflex and the reflex of looking at their surroundings. From 1–4 months old, babies begin to coordinate their physical sensations with new schemas, i.e. mental constructs/concepts they form to represent elements of reality. For example, an infant might suck her thumb by chance and feel pleasure from the activity; in the future, she will repeat thumb-sucking because the pleasure is rewarding. Piaget called this second substage "Primary Circular Reactions." In the third substage, around 4–8 months, which he called "Secondary Circular Reactions," children also repeat rewarding actions, but now they are focused on things in the environment that they can affect, rather than just the child's own person. For example, once a baby learns to pick up an object and mouth it, s/he will repeat this. Thus, babies learn an early method of environmental exploration through their mouths, an extension of their initial sucking reflex.

4-8 mos. ③ Secondary circular reactions!
Children repeat rewarding actions

LAST THREE SUBSTAGES OF THE SENSORIMOTOR STAGE

8-12 mo: Coordination of reactions

According to Piaget, babies about 8–12 months are in the "Coordination of Reactions" substage of the Sensorimotor stage. Having begun repeating actions purposely to achieve environmental effects during the previous substage of Secondary Circular Reactions, in Coordination of Reactions, infants begin

1 2 3

Copyright © Mometrix Media. You have been licensed one copy of this document for personal use only. Any other reproduction or redistribution is strictly prohibited. All rights reserved.

8-12 mo. , 12-18 mo : trial and error   imitation   18-24 : early rep. using chang symbols

further exploring their surroundings. They frequently imitate others' observed behaviors. They more obviously demonstrate intentional behaviors. They become able to combine schemas (mental constructs) to attain certain results. They develop object permanence, the understanding that unseen objects still exist. They learn to associate certain objects with their properties. For example, once a baby realizes a rattle makes a noise when shaken, s/he will deliberately shake it to produce the sound. In "Tertiary Circular Reactions," at about 12–18 months, children begin experimenting through trial-and-error. For instance, a child might test various actions or sounds for getting parents' attention. From 18–24 months, in the substage of "Early Representational Thought," children begin representing objects and events with symbols. They begin to understand the world via not only actions, but mental operations.

OBJECT PERMANENCE

One of the landmarks of infant cognitive development is learning that concrete objects are not "out of sight, out of mind"; in other words, things still continue to exist even when they are out of our sight. Babies generally develop this realization around 8–9 months old, though some may be earlier or later. Some researchers after Piaget have found object permanence in babies as young as 3½ months. Younger infants typically attend to an object of interest only when they can see it; if it is removed or hidden, they are upset/confused at its disappearance and/or shift their attention to something else. A sign that they have developed object permanence is if they search for the object after it is moved or hidden. Babies only become interested in "hide and seek" types of games once they have developed this understanding that the existence of objects and people persist beyond their immediate vision or proximity. Another example of emerging object permanence is the delight babies begin to take in "peek-a-boo" games.

SCHEMA AND SCHEMATA DEVELOPMENT IN INFANTS

Piaget proposed we form mental constructs or concepts that he called schemata, representing elements of the environment, beginning in infancy. A schema does not represent an individual object, but a category or class of things. For example, a baby might form a schema representing "things to suck on," initially including her bottle, her thumb, and her pacifier. Piaget said assimilation is when we can fit something new into an existing schema: the child in this example assimilates "Daddy's knee" into her schema of things she can suck on when she discovers this action. When something new cannot be assimilated into an existing schema, we either modify that schema or form a new schema, which both constitute accommodation. The baby in our example, becoming a toddler, might modify her schema of things to suck to include straws, which require a different sucking technique. Piaget said assimilation and accommodation combined constitute the process of adaptation, i.e. adjusting, to our environment through interacting with it.

Schema = class or category

knee

(straw)   to suck on

pacifier

adaptation / assimilation + accommodation

PIAGET'S SCHEMA EXAMPLES

A toddler on an airplane sees a nearby stranger who is male, about 5'8", with white hair and eyeglasses. Both of his grandfathers have these same general appearances. He murmurs to himself, "Hi, Granddaddy." Explain this according to Piaget's concept of the schema in his cognitive-developmental theory.

The toddler in this example did not actually mistake a complete stranger for either one of his grandfathers. Notice that he did not directly address the stranger as "Granddaddy" with conversational loudness, but murmured it to himself. He recognized this man was not someone he knew. However, he recognized common elements with his grandfathers in the man's appearance. According to Piaget's theory of cognitive development, the explanation for this is that the child had formed a schema, i.e. a mental construct, to represent men about 5'8" with white hair and eyeglasses, based initially on his early knowledge of two such men he knew, his grandfathers, and then extending to include other similar-appearing men, through the process of assimilation of new information into an existing schema. His description did not mean he thought the stranger was named "Granddaddy." Rather, the word "Granddaddy" was not only the name he called

16

Copyright © Mometrix Media. You have been licensed one copy of this document for personal use only. Any other reproduction or redistribution is strictly prohibited. All rights reserved.

one grandfather, but also the word he used to label his schema for all men who appeared to fit into this category.

A toddler sees a large, brown dog through the window and says, "Moo." Explain this according to Piaget's theory of cognitive development.

Piaget found that forming schemas, or mental constructs to represent objects and actions, is how babies and children learn about themselves and the world through their interactions with their bodies and the environment. If they can fit a new experience into an existing schema, they assimilate it; or when necessary, they change an existing schema or form a new one to accommodate a new stimulus. Therefore, in this example, the toddler had seen cows in picture books, photos, or on a farm, and learned to associate the sound "Moo" with cows, reinforced by the teaching of toys, books, and adults. She had formed a schema for large, brown, four-legged, furry animals. Because the dog she saw fit these properties, she assimilated the dog into her cow schema. If she were then told this was a dog that says "Bow-wow," she would either form a new schema for dogs; or, if she had previously only seen smaller dogs, accommodate (modify) her existing dog schema to include larger dogs.

PREOPERATIONAL STAGE OF PIAGET'S THEORY OF COGNITIVE DEVELOPMENT

Children between (roughly) two and six years old are in Piaget's Preoperational stage of cognitive development. Having begun to use objects to represent other things, i.e. symbolic representation, near the end of the previous Sensorimotor stage, children now further develop this ability during pretend/make-believe play. They may pretend a broom is a guitar or a horse; or talk using a block as a phone. Toddlers begin to play "house," pretending they and their playmates are the mommy, the daddy, the mailman, the doctor, etc. The reason Piaget called this stage Preoperational is that children are not yet capable of performing mental "operations," including following concrete logic or manipulating information mentally. Their thinking is intuitive rather than following logical steps. Piaget termed Preoperational children "egocentric" in that they literally cannot adopt another's point of view, even concretely: in experiments, after seeing pictures of a scene as viewed from different positions, children could not match a picture to another person's position, selecting the picture showing the scene from their own viewpoint.

ANIMISM AND MAGICAL THINKING

Piaget found that children in the Preoperational stage are not yet able to perform logical mental operations. Their thinking is intuitive during the toddler and preschool years. One characteristic of the thinking of young children is animism, or assigning human qualities, feelings, and actions to inanimate objects. For example, a child seeing an autumn leaf fall off of a tree might remark, "The tree didn't like that leaf and pushed it off of its branch." Or a child with a sunburn might say, "The sun was angry at me and burned me." A related characteristic is magical thinking, which is attributing cause and effect relationships between their own feelings and thoughts and environmental events where none exists. For example, if a child says "I hate you" to another person or secretly dislikes and wishes the other gone, and something bad then happens to that person, the child is likely to believe what s/he said/felt/thought caused the other's unfortunate event. This is related to egocentrism—seeing everything as revolving around oneself.

PIAGET'S EGOCENTRISM AND ANIMISM CONCEPTS OF PREOPERATIONAL CHILDREN

Preoperational children are egocentric, i.e. they view everything as revolving around themselves. Adults aware of this understand that most two-year-olds, for example, neither want to share with others nor understand why they should. Egocentrism also means being unable to see others' perspectives. Adults who take this ability for granted may not realize the simplicity of both some early childhood problems and their solutions. For example, when a preschooler does something physically or emotionally hurtful

17

Copyright © Mometrix Media. You have been licensed one copy of this document for personal use only. Any other reproduction or redistribution is strictly prohibited. All rights reserved.

to another, adults can guide identification of consequences: "Look at her face now. How do you think she feels?" and then guide perspective-taking: "How would you feel if somebody hit you like you just hit Sally?" This has not occurred to the preschooler, but once s/he is guided to think of it, it can be a revelation. Animism is Preoperational children's attributing human qualities to inanimate objects. Many children's books and TV shows accordingly appeal to young children by animating letters, numbers, or objects (e.g. SpongeBob SquarePants).

MAGICAL THINKING CONCEPT OF PIAGET'S THEORY OF COGNITIVE DEVELOPMENT

According to Piaget, magical thinking is the belief that one's thoughts make external events happen. He identified this as a common characteristic of the way children in his Preoperational stage think. Piaget said that preschool children have not yet developed the cognitive ability to perform mental operations. Because they cannot follow or apply logical thought processes, their thinking is irrational and intuitive rather than organized and based on real-world, empirical observations. For example, a Preoperational child may believe that something good happened because s/he wished hard enough for it. Preschoolers also commonly believe their saying/thinking/feeling/wishing something bad toward another caused the other's misfortune. They often blame themselves for divorce or death in the family, thinking these happened because they were "bad." Adults should explain to young children that what they wished, thought, felt, or said did not cause good or bad events, and reassign causes external to the child, e.g. "Mommy and Daddy were not getting along with each other"/"Grandpa was sick"/"It was an accident, not anybody's fault."

SALIENT CHARACTERISTICS OF PIAGET'S SECOND STAGE OF CHILD COGNITIVE DEVELOPMENT

Piaget's second cognitive-developmental stage is Preoperational. Toddlers and preschoolers in this stage typically begin to recognize rudimentary symbolic representation, i.e. that some objects represent other things. This understanding of symbols allows them to begin using words to represent things, people, feelings, and thoughts. Adults can support early childhood language development by frequently conversing with young children, reading books to them, introducing and explaining new vocabulary words, and playing games involving naming and classifying things. Children in this stage also begin pretend/make-believe play through understanding symbols; adults can encourage and support this play, which develops imagination and planning abilities. Preoperational children's thinking is intuitive, not logical; adults understanding this will not expect them to follow/use logical sequences such as doing arithmetic, as they cannot yet perform mental operations. Adults familiar with Piaget's concept of egocentrism realize Preoperational children cannot see others' viewpoints. They thus engage children's attention/interest by beginning from topics related to children's personal selves and activities.

PREOPERATIONAL VERSUS CONCRETE OPERATIONAL STAGES

Piaget called the stage of most children aged 2–6 years Preoperational because children these ages cannot yet perform mental operations, i.e. manipulate information mentally. At around 6–7 years old, children begin to develop Concrete Operations. A key aspect of this stage is the ability to think logically. This ability first develops relative to concrete objects and events. Concrete Operational children still have trouble understanding abstract concepts or hypothetical situations, but they can apply logical sequences and cause and effect to things they can see, feel, and manipulate physically. For example, Concrete Operational children develop the understanding that things have the same amount or number regardless of their shape or arrangement, which Piaget termed conservation. They develop proficiency in inductive logic, i.e. drawing generalizations from specific instances. However, deductive logic, i.e. predicting specific results according to general principles, is not as well-developed until the later stage of Formal Operations involving abstract thought. Another key development of Concrete Operations is reversibility, i.e. the ability to reverse an action or operation.

The different thinking found between Piaget's Preoperational and Concrete Operations stages is exemplified in experiments he and others conducted to prove his theory. For example, the

Copyright © Mometrix Media. You have been licensed one copy of this document for personal use only. Any other reproduction or redistribution is strictly prohibited. All rights reserved.

absence/presence of ability to conserve liquid volume across shape/appearance has been shown in experiments with differently aged children. A preschooler is shown a tall, thin beaker and a short, wide one. The experimenter also shows the child two identically sized and shaped containers with identical amounts of liquid in each. The experimenter then pours the equal amounts of liquid into the two differently shaped beakers. The preschooler will say either the thin beaker holds more liquid because it is taller or the short beaker holds more because it is wider. Piaget termed this "centration"—focusing on only one property at a time. An older child "decentrates," can "conserve" the amount, and knows both beakers hold identical amounts. Older children also use reversibility and logic, e.g. "I know they are still equal, because I just saw you pour the same amount into each beaker."

PIAGET'S NEW DEVELOPMENTS OF THE CONCRETE OPERATIONS STAGE VERSUS PREVIOUS PREOPERATIONAL STAGE

Piaget said that while preschoolers are in the Preoperational stage and do not think logically because they cannot yet perform mental operations, this ability emerges in the Concrete Operations stage, which tends to coincide with elementary school ages. Concrete Operational children can follow and apply logical sequences to concrete objects they can see and manipulate. This is why they can begin learning mathematical concepts and procedures like addition and subtraction, and grammatical paradigms like verb conjugations. While Preoperational children "centrate" or focus on one attribute of an object, like its appearance, Concrete Operational children "decentrate," accommodating multiple attributes, and can perform and reverse mental operations. Piaget found elementary school-age Concrete Operational children develop conservation—the understanding that an object or substance conserves, or retains, its essential properties despite changes in appearance or configuration. For example, a Preoperational child can count pennies, but not understand ten pennies spread into a long row equal ten pennies clustered together. Children in Concrete Operations, instead of focusing on appearance, will use logic and simply count the pennies, showing that each group has the same number regardless of how they look.

CONSERVATION

Conservation is the cognitive ability to understand that objects or substances retain their properties of numbers or amounts even when their appearance, shape, or configuration changes. Piaget found from his experiments with children that this ability develops around the age of five years. He also found children develop conservation of number, length, mass, weight, volume, and quantity respectively at slightly different ages. One example of a conservation experiment is with liquid volume: the experimenter pours the same amount of liquid into a short, wide container and a tall, thin one. Children who have not developed conservation of liquid volume typically say one container has more liquid, even though they saw both amounts were equal, based on one container's looking fuller. Similarly, children who have not developed conservation of number, shown equal numbers of beads, usually say a group arranged in a long row has more beads than a group clustered together. Children having developed conservation recognize the amounts are the same regardless of appearance. A universal phenomenon is that after developing conservation, we take it for granted and cannot remember or believe our earlier Preoperational thinking.

ABILITIES IN PERCEPTUAL DEVELOPMENT OCCURRING IN INFANCY

In normal development, babies have usually established the ability to see, hear, smell, taste, and feel and also the ability to integrate such sensory information by the age of six months. Additional perceptual abilities, which are less obvious and more complex, continue to emerge throughout the early childhood years. For instance, young children develop increasing precision in recognizing visual concepts like size and shape. This development allows children to identify accurately the shape and size of an object no matter from what angle they perceive it. Infants have these capacities in place, but have not yet developed accuracy in using them. For example, a baby might realize that objects farther away occupy less of their visual fields than nearer objects; however, the baby has yet to learn just how much less of the visual field is taken up by the farther object. Young children attain this and similar kinds of learning

Copyright © Mometrix Media. You have been licensed one copy of this document for personal use only. Any other reproduction or redistribution is strictly prohibited. All rights reserved.

by actively, energetically exploring their environments. Such activity is crucial for developing accurate perception of size, shape, and distance.

VISUAL PERCEPTUAL ASPECTS OF INTERPRETING PICTURES AND EYE MOVEMENTS

As adults, our ability to look at pictures of people and things in the environment is something we usually take for granted. Researchers have established that 3-year-old children's responses indicate their ability to recognize shading, line convergence, and other cues of depth in two-dimensional pictures. However, scientists have also found that children's sensitivity to these kinds of visual cues increases as they grow older. The eye movements and eye fixation patterns of young children affect their ability to get the most complete and accurate information from pictorial representations of reality. When viewing pictures, adults sweep the entire picture to see it as a whole, their eye movements leaping around; to focus on specific details, adults use shorter eye movements. Preschool children differ from adults in using shorter eye movements overall, and focusing on small parts of the picture near the center or an edge. They therefore disregard, or do not see, a lot of the picture's available information.

ACTIVITIES ASSISTING CHILDREN DEVELOP COGNITIVE ABILITIES

As shown by Piaget, young children have difficulty reversing operations. Adults can ask them to build block structures, for example, and then dismantle them one block at a time to reverse the construction. They can ask children to retell rhymes or stories backward. They can take small groups of children for walks and ask them if they can return by the same route as they came. Young children often assume causal relationships where none exist. Adults can provide activities to produce and observe results, e.g. pouring water into different containers; knocking over bowling pins by swinging a pendulum; rolling wheeled toys down ramps; or blowing balls through mazes, and then asking them, "What happened when you did this? What would happen if you did this? What could you do to make this happen?" Young children are also often egocentric, seeing everything from their own viewpoint. Adults can help them take others' perspectives through guessing games wherein they must give each other clues to guess persons/objects and dramatic role-playing activities, where they pretend to be others.

LEARNING STYLES AND IMPLICATIONS FOR EARLY CHILDHOOD EDUCATION

Young children with normal development learn in the same chronological sequences and learn the same types of skills. Even those with delayed development, as with intellectual disabilities, learn the same things in the same order, but simply at a slower rate and hence at later ages; and those with severe/profound impairment may never achieve certain developmental milestones. However, one aspect of learning that varies is learning style. For example, some children approach learning in a primarily visual manner. They focus on what they see and how things look. They learn best given visual stimuli, like colorful objects, pictures, and graphics. They understand abstract concepts and relationships better when these are illustrated visually. Other children approach learning in a primarily haptic or tactile way. They focus on textures and movements, learning through touch and kinesthetic senses. They learn best given concrete things to explore and manipulate, and physical activities to perform. They learn abstract concepts and relationships better through handling materials and engaging in physical movements and actions.

STAGES OF GROWTH AND DEVELOPMENT IN ART

Austrian and German art scholars established six stages in art. (1) The Scribble stage: from 2–4 years, children first make uncontrolled scribbles; then controlled scribbling; then progress to naming their scribbles to indicate what they represent. (2) The Preschematic stage: from ages 4–6, children begin to develop a visual schema. Schema, meaning mental representation, comes from Piaget's cognitive-developmental theory. Without complete comprehension of dimensions and sizes, children may draw people and houses the same height; they use color more emotionally than logically. They may omit or exaggerate facial features, or they might draw sizes by importance, e.g. drawing themselves as largest among people or drawing the most important feature, e.g. the head, as the largest or only body part. (3) The Schematic stage: from 7–9 years, drawings more reflect actual physical proportions and colors. (4)

Copyright © Mometrix Media. You have been licensed one copy of this document for personal use only. Any other reproduction or redistribution is strictly prohibited. All rights reserved.

Dawning Realism: from ages 9-11, drawings become increasingly representational. (5) Children aged 11–13 are in the Pseudorealistic stage, reflecting their ability to reason. (6) Children 14+ are in the Period of Decision stage, reflecting the adolescent identity crisis.

VIKTOR LOWENFELD

Viktor Lowenfeld (1903–1960) taught art to elementary school students and sculpture to blind students. Lowenfeld's acquaintance with Sigmund Freud, who was interested in his work with people with visual impairments, motivated Lowenfeld to pursue scientific research. He published several books on using creative arts activities therapeutically. Lowenfeld was familiar with six stages previously identified in the growth of art. He combined these with principles of human development drawn from the school of psychoanalytic psychology founded by Freud. In his adaptation, he named the six stages reflecting the development of children's art as Scribble, Preschematic, Schematic, Dawning Realism, Pseudorealistic, and Period of Decision. Lowenfeld identified adolescent learning styles as haptic, focused on physical sensations and subjective emotional experiences, and as visual, focused on appearances, each demanding corresponding instructional approaches. Lowenfeld's book Creative and Mental Growth (1947) was the most influential text in art education during the later 20th century. Lowenfeld's psychological emphasis in this text gave scientific foundations to creative and artistic expression, and identified developmentally age-appropriate art media and activities.

CHARACTERISTICS IN ART REFLECTING PERCEPTUAL, COGNITIVE, AND MOTOR DEVELOPMENT

Observations of young children find that while a 2½-year-old can grasp a crayon and scribble with it, by the age of 4 years, s/he can draw a picture we recognize as human. The typical 4-year-old drawing of a human being is called the "tadpole person" because it has no body, a large head, and stick limbs. Between the ages of 3 and 4 years, children typically make a transition from scribbling to producing tadpole person drawings. This development is enabled by greater development in motor control and eye-hand coordination, among other variables. Between the ages of 4 and 5 years, children make another transition by progressing from drawing tadpole persons to drawing complete figures with heads and bodies. Howard Gardner, psychologist and author of the Multiple Intelligences theory, stated that children achieve a "summit of artistry" by the end of their preschool years. He describes their drawings as "characteristically colorful, balanced, rhythmic, and expressive, conveying something of the range and…vitality associated with artistic mastery." (1980)

INVOLVEMENT OF MUSIC IN THE DEVELOPMENT OF INFANTS AND YOUNG CHILDREN

Long before they can speak, and before they even comprehend much speech, infants respond to the sounds of voices and to music. These responses are not only to auditory stimulation, but moreover to the emotional content in what they hear. Parents sing lullabies to babies; not only are these sounds pleasant and soothing, but they also help children develop trust in their environment as secure. Parents communicate their love to children through singing and introduce them to experiences of pleasure and excitement through music. As children grow, music progresses to be not only a medium of communication but also one of self-expression as they learn to sing/play musical sounds. Music facilitates memory, as we see through commercial jingles and mnemonic devices. Experiments find music improves spatial reasoning. Children's learning of perceptual and logical concepts like beginning/ending, sequences, cause-and-effect, balance, harmony/dissonance and mathematical number and timing concepts is reinforced by music. Music also promotes language development. Children learn about colors, counting, conceptual relationships, nature, and social skills through music.

ENHANCING THE EMOTIONAL, SOCIAL, AESTHETIC, AND SCHOOL READINESS SKILLS WITH MUSIC

Young children who are just learning to use spoken language often cannot express their emotions very well verbally. Music is a great aid to emotional development in that younger children can express happiness, sadness, anger, etc., through singing and/or playing music more easily than they can with words. Children of preschool ages not only listen to music and respond to what they hear, they also learn

Copyright © Mometrix Media. You have been licensed one copy of this document for personal use only. Any other reproduction or redistribution is strictly prohibited. All rights reserved.

to create music through singing and playing instruments together with other children. These activities help them learn crucial social skills for their lives, like cooperating with others, collaborating, and making group or team efforts to accomplish something. When children are given guided musical experiences, they learn to make their own judgments of what is good or bad music; this provides them with the foundations for developing an aesthetic sense. Music promotes preliteracy skills by enhancing phonemic awareness. As growing children develop musical appreciation and skills, these develop fundamental motor, cognitive, and social skills they need for language, school readiness, literacy, and life.

PREMATHEMATICAL LEARNING EXPERIENCES

Preschool children do not think in the same ways as older children and adults do, as Piaget observed. Their thinking is strongly based upon and connected to their sensory perceptions. This means that in solving problems, they depend mainly on how things look, sound, feel, smell, and taste. Therefore, preschool children should always be given concrete objects that they can touch, explore, and experiment with in any learning experience. They are not yet capable of understanding abstract concepts or manipulating information mentally, so they must have real things to work with to understand premath concepts. For example, they will learn to count solid objects like blocks, beads, or pennies before they can count numbers in their heads. They cannot benefit from rote math memorization, or "sit still and listen" lessons. Since young children "centrate" on one characteristic/object/person/event at a time, adults can offer activities encouraging decentration/incorporating multiple aspects, e.g. not only grouping all triangles, but grouping all red triangles separately from blue triangles.

SALIENT ASPECTS OF TYPICAL EARLY CHILDHOOD PHYSICAL DEVELOPMENT

Early childhood physical growth, while significant, is slower than infant growth. From birth to 2 years, children generally grow to four times their newborn weight and 2/3 their newborn length/height. From 2–3 years, however, children usually gain only about 4 lbs. and 3.5 inches. From 4–6 years, growth slows more; gains of 5–7 lbs. and 2.5 inches are typical. Due to slowing growth rates, 3- and 4-year-olds appear to eat less food, but do not; they actually just eat fewer calories per pound of body weight. Brain growth is still rapid in preschoolers: brains attain 55 percent of adult size by 2 years, and 90 percent by 6 years. The majority of brain growth is usually by 4–4.5 years, with a growth spurt around 2 years and growth rates slowing significantly between 5 and 6 years. Larger brain size indicates not more neurons, but larger sizes; differences in their organization; more glial cells nourishing and supporting neurons; and greater myelination (development of the sheath protecting nerve fibers and facilitating their efficient intercommunication).

NATURE-NURTURE INTERACTION IN EARLY CHILDHOOD PHYSICAL DEVELOPMENT

The physical development of babies and young children is a product of the interactions between genetic and environmental factors. Also, a child's physical progress is equally influenced by environmental and psychological variables. For the body, brain, and nervous system to grow and develop normally, children must live in healthy environments. When the interaction of hereditary and environmental influences is not healthful, this is frequently reflected in abnormal patterns of growth. Failure to thrive syndrome is a dramatic example. When children are abused or neglected for long periods of time, they actually stop growing. The social environments of such children create psychological stress. This stress makes the child's pituitary gland stop releasing growth hormones, and growth ceases. When such environmental stress is relieved and these children are given proper care, stimulation, and affection, they begin growing again. They often grow rapidly enough to catch up on the growth they missed earlier. Normal body and brain growth—as well as psychological development—depend upon the collaboration of nature and nurture.

SIGNS OF PROGRESS IN TYPICAL MOTOR DEVELOPMENT

Genetics, physiological maturation, nutrition, and experience through practice combine to further preschoolers' motor skills development. Newborns' reflexive behaviors progress to preschoolers'

Copyright © Mometrix Media. You have been licensed one copy of this document for personal use only. Any other reproduction or redistribution is strictly prohibited. All rights reserved.

voluntary activities. Also, children's perception of the size, shape, and position of the body and body parts becomes more accurate by preschool ages. In addition, increases in bilateral coordination of the body's two sides enhance preschoolers' motor skills. Motor skills development entails both learning new movements and gradually integrating previously learned movements into smooth, continuous patterns, as in learning to throw a ball with skill. Both large muscles, for gross-motor skills like climbing, running, and jumping, and small muscles, for fine-motor skills like drawing and tying knots, develop. Eye-hand coordination involves fine-motor control. Preschoolers use visual feedback, i.e. seeing whether they are making things go where and do what they want them to, in learning to manipulate small objects with their hands and fingers.

GENDER DIFFERENCES IN MOTOR DEVELOPMENT

On average, preschool boys have larger muscles than preschool girls, so they can run faster, climb higher, and jump farther. Boys at these ages tend to be more muscular physically. Preschool girls, while less muscular, are on the average more mature physically for their ages than boys. While boys usually exceed girls in their large-muscle, gross-motor abilities like running, jumping, and climbing, girls tend to surpass boys in small-muscle, fine-motor abilities like buttoning buttons, using scissors, and similar activities involving the manipulation of small tools, utensils, and objects. While preschool boys exhibit more strength in large-muscle, gross-motor actions, preschool girls are more advanced than preschool boys in large-muscle, gross-motor skills that do not demand strength so much as coordination, like hopping, balancing on one foot, and skipping. While these specific gender differences in preschoolers' physical and motor development have been observed consistently in research, it is also found that preschool girls' and boys' physical and motor development patterns are generally more similar than different overall.

BASIC TEMPERAMENT TYPES INFLUENCING PERSONALITIES OF CHILDREN

Psychologists studied the behavior of infants and classified their characteristics into three types of temperaments: easy, difficult, and slow to warm up. The majority of infants are easy babies. When they cry from hunger/needing changing/being tired/feeling discomfort/needing cuddling/attention, they are easily soothed by having these needs met. They typically sleep well. While they experience normal negative emotions, their predominant mood is good. Other than normal stranger anxiety at applicable ages, they respond positively to meeting people. In contrast, difficult babies are more likely to cry longer and be much harder to soothe. It is often hard to get them to sleep, and they may sleep fitfully, with many interruptions and/or for shorter times. They are more easily frightened by strange/new people and things, and more easily upset overall. Slow to warm up babies can initially seem difficult by not being as immediately responsive to people other than their parents like easy babies. However, given some time to adjust, they eventually "warm up" to new people and situations.

SELF-CONCEPT AND SELF-ESTEEM

Young children's self-concepts are founded on observable, readily defined, mainly concrete factors. Many young children also experience much adult encouragement. Because their self-concepts are more simple and concrete than those of older children and adults and because they typically receive abundant encouragement and positive reinforcement, preschoolers often have fairly high self-esteem, i.e. judgment regarding their own value. In general, young children tend to have positive, optimistic attitudes that they can learn something new, finish tasks, and succeed if they persist in their attempts. Self-esteem related specifically to one's ability to perform a given task is sometimes called "achievement-related attribution." Albert Bandura called it "self-efficacy." Young children derive self-esteem from multiple sources, including their relationships with their parents; their friendships; their abilities and achievements in tasks involving playing and helping others; their physical/athletic abilities; and their achievements in preschool/school.

Copyright © Mometrix Media. You have been licensed one copy of this document for personal use only. Any other reproduction or redistribution is strictly prohibited. All rights reserved.

INTERNAL VARIABLE INFLUENCING SELF-CONCEPTS, SELF-ESTEEM, AND SELF-EFFICACY

One major internal influence on self-concept is a child's basic temperament. Easy, difficult, and slow-to-warm-up temperaments in babies continue into early childhood (and throughout life). For example, children having easy temperaments are better prepared for coping with challenges and frustration. When they encounter difficulty attempting new tasks, they do not give up as easily and are more persistent. They are thus more likely to develop self-concepts of being good, valuable, and successful and hence have higher self-esteem. Since they experience more success through persistence, they develop greater self-efficacy, i.e. belief in their competence to perform specific tasks. Children with more difficult temperaments become frustrated more easily, after fewer attempts, and give up trying in discouragement or require extra help to perform new or challenging tasks. They are more at risk for believing they cannot succeed and hence are not valuable, leading to their developing lower self-esteem. This also affects self-efficacy: they are more likely to doubt their ability to perform a specific proposed task.

EXTERNAL VARIABLES INFLUENCING SELF-CONCEPTS, SELF-ESTEEM, AND SELF-EFFICACY

The way young children see themselves is affected by the feedback they receive from other people. When adults like parents, caregivers, and teachers give young children positive responses to their efforts—whether they succeed initially or not—the children are more likely to develop positive self-concepts, engendering higher self-esteem, and greater self-efficacy, the belief that they have the competency to succeed at a specific task or activity. On the other hand, when adults frequently give punitive/judgmental/indifferent/otherwise negative responses to young children's efforts, children develop poorer self-images. They feel they are not valued/good/important/worthy. They develop lower self-esteem, and their self-efficacy is weaker; they come to expect failure when they attempt tasks and may not even try. Peers also affect young children's self-concepts and self-esteem. When friends and classmates include a child in activities, this promotes a positive self-image and higher self-esteem and self-efficacy. If peers exclude, tease, or bully a young child, this can cause low self-esteem, make their self-concepts more negative, and lower their self-efficacy.

LOCUS OF CONTROL

Psychologist Julian Rotter originated the term and concept of locus of control. It refers to the place (locus) where we attribute causes for outcomes we experience, either externally or internally. An external locus control is something outside of us—another person and/or his/her actions; an environmental event; or an unknown but exterior influence, like good/bad luck or random chance. An internal locus of control is something inside of us—our native ability, our motivation, or our effort. For example, blaming another for failing—"The teacher gave me something too hard/wouldn't help me/didn't tell me how to do it" or "Johnny was bothering me" are examples of external locus of control. Blaming conditions, e.g. "It was too dark/hot/cold/noisy/the sun was in my eyes" is also external. Individuals may also attribute successes externally: "The teacher helped me" or "Johnny showed me how" or "I was lucky." Blaming/crediting oneself for failure/success is internal locus of control: "I didn't study the new words" or "I'm stupid" with failures or "I worked hard"/"I'm smart" with successes.

FUNCTIONS OF THE BASIC PERSONALITY STRUCTURES IN FREUD'S DEVELOPMENTAL THEORY

Freud proposed that the personality is governed by three structures or forces: the Id, the Ego, and the Superego. The Id, the "pleasure principle," represents the source of our powerful, instinctual urges, such as sexual and aggressive impulses. It is necessary as it energizes us to act, but cannot go unrestrained. The Ego, the "reality principle," represents our sense of self within reality. It is necessary for telling us what will happen if we act on the Id's impulses and knowing how to control them to protect ourselves. The Superego, the "conscience," represents our sense of morality. It is necessary when Ego protects ourselves but not others, so we also control our social interactions to be ethical and nonharmful to others. For example, when a young child sees a cookie or a toy belonging to someone else, his Id says, "I

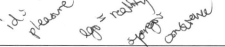

24

Copyright © Mometrix Media. You have been licensed one copy of this document for personal use only. Any other reproduction or redistribution is strictly prohibited. All rights reserved.

want that." His Ego says, "If I take that and get caught, I will be in trouble." His Superego says, "Whether I get caught or not, stealing is wrong."

FIRST STAGE OF FREUD'S PSYCHOANALYTIC THEORY OF PERSONALITY DEVELOPMENT

Freud's orientation toward personality development was psychosexual. He believed the most important factors were the focus of erotic energy, which shifted in each developmental stage, and the child's early relationship with parents. Freud formulated five stages of development: Oral, Anal, Phallic, Latency, and Genital. He found if infants and children successfully complete each stage, they are well-adjusted; if not, they become fixated on one stage. Freud said infants from birth to 18 months are in the first Oral stage: their focus of pleasure is on the mouth as they suck to nurse. If a baby's oral need to nurse is met appropriately, s/he will progress to the following stage. However, if an infant's feeding needs are met either inadequately or excessively, s/he can develop an oral fixation. Signs of this in later life include tendencies to overeat, drink too much, smoke, bite one's nails, talk excessively, and other orally focused activities. Oral personalities either become overly dependent and gullible; or, when resisting oral compulsions, become pessimistic and aggressive to others.

SECOND STAGE OF FREUD'S PSYCHOANALYTIC THEORY OF PERSONALITY DEVELOPMENT

Freud's theory divided personality development into five stages, each based on the corresponding erogenous zone: Oral, Anal, Phallic, Latency, and Genital. Infants 0–18 months are in the Oral stage as the focus is on nursing. Children 18–36 months are in the second Anal stage. The focus of pleasure sensations is on the anus as they are engaged in toilet training. Society and parents demand they control retaining/expelling waste; they must learn to control anal stimulation. This can be a power struggle between child and parents. Children this age are also learning to assert their individual independence and will, mirroring the battle of wills over toileting. Success contributes to healthy development; when unsuccessful, individuals develop anal fixation. Signs of this in later life take two extremes: those who resisted parental control and asserted personal control by retaining their feces develop anal-retentive personalities, becoming rigid, controlling, and overly preoccupied with neatness and cleanliness. Conversely, those who asserted themselves by expelling their feces develop anal-expulsive personalities, with sloppy, messy, disorganized, defiant behavior.

THIRD STAGE OF FREUD'S PSYCHOANALYTIC THEORY OF PERSONALITY DEVELOPMENT

Freud described developmental stages as focusing on particular erogenous zones. Nursing infants are in his Oral stage; toilet-training toddlers are in his Anal stage. His third stage, when children are aged 3–6 years, is the Phallic stage. Pleasure is focused on the genitals as children discover these. Freud focused his theory on males, proposing that at this age, boys develop unconscious sexual desires for their mothers and corresponding unconscious rivalries with their fathers for mother's attention. The rivalry represents aggression toward the father. Therefore, they also unconsciously fear retaliation by the father in the form of castration. Freud named this the Oedipal conflict after the Greek tragic hero Oedipus, who unwittingly slew his father and married his mother. Since these unconscious impulses are socially unacceptable, boys resolve the conflict through a process Freud called "identification with the aggressor." This explains the common behavior of boys around ages 4–5, imitating and wanting to be "just like Daddy." They repress desires for mother and adopt masculine characteristics. Unsuccessful conflict resolution/fixation leads to later confusion/weakness of sexual identity, and either excessive or insufficient sexual activity.

APPLICATION OF FREUD'S THIRD STAGE OF PSYCHOANALYTIC THEORY

According to Freud's theory, preschoolers are in his Phallic stage of psychosexual development. This is the time when they discover their own genitals, so caregivers and educators knowing this will not be distressed at young children's attention to and manipulation of their genitals, and their curiosity and interest in others' genitals as these are not abnormal (unless excessive). Adults who are also aware of Freud's Oedipal conflict in boys and other Neo-Freudian psychologists' corresponding Electra conflict in girls should be neither surprised nor upset when little boys first focus more attention on

25

Copyright © Mometrix Media. You have been licensed one copy of this document for personal use only. Any other reproduction or redistribution is strictly prohibited. All rights reserved.

mothers/female caregivers, and later abandon these attentions to focus on imitating fathers/male caregivers. Freud would say they are demonstrating the Oedipal desire for the mother, which includes fear of castration by the father, and then resolving this conflict through identification with the aggressor/father. Neo-Freudians would say little girls are undergoing a similar process in favoring their fathers and subsequently identifying with their mothers. They pointed out how girls at the same ages become "Daddy's girls," often rejecting their mothers, and then around ages 4–5 want to be "just like Mommy," adopting feminine behaviors, paralleling male development. Freud rejected this notion.

FOURTH STAGE OF PSYCHOSEXUAL DEVELOPMENT OF FREUD'S PSYCHOANALYTIC THEORY OF PERSONALITY DEVELOPMENT

Freud theorized that children are in his fourth Latency stage of development at around the same ages when they begin to attend formal schooling. Since Freud's emphasis on development was psychosexual, he identified an erogenous zone where pleasure was focused in each stage of development. The mouth, anus, and genitals are erogenous zones central to Freud's other developmental stages. However, in the stage he termed Latency, there is no erogenous zone of focus. This is because Freud believed that children's sexuality is repressed or submerged during this period. The child's attention is occupied at this time with learning new social and academic skills in the new environment of the school setting. Adults familiar with Freud's basic psychoanalytic concepts realize that children's focus shifts from their relationships with parents to their relationships with friends, classmates, teachers, and other adults during the Latency stage. Children are not rejecting/abandoning parents, but responding to widening social environments. They are more able to learn academic concepts and structures and more complex social interactions and behaviors.

FOURTH AND FIFTH STAGES OF FREUD'S PSYCHOANALYTIC THEORY OF PERSONALITY DEVELOPMENT

Each of the stages in Freud's theory centered on an erogenous zone. Infants are in the Oral stage as they nurse; toddlers in the Anal stage as they are toilet-trained; preschoolers are in the Phallic stage as they focus on genital discovery, unconscious sexual impulses toward their opposite-sex parent, and unconscious aggressive impulses toward their same-sex parent, and resolving conflicts over these urges. Freud labeled the stage when children are six years old to puberty the Latency stage. During this time, children begin school. They are occupied with making new friends, developing new social skills; participating in learning, developing new academic skills; and learning school rules, developing acceptable societal behaviors. Freud said that children in the Latency stage repress their sexual impulses, deferring them while developing their cognitive and social skills takes priority. Thus, sexuality is latent. From puberty on, children are in Freud's Genital stage, when sexuality reemerges with physical maturation and adolescents are occupied with developing intimate relationships with others.

EGO DEFENSE MECHANISMS OF FREUD'S PSYCHOANALYTIC THEORY OF PERSONALITY DEVELOPMENT

Freud identified and described many ego defense mechanisms in his theory. He said these are ways the ego finds to cope with impulses threatening it, and hence the person. Just a few of these that can be apparent in young children's behavior include the following. Regression—for example, if a child has received parental attention exclusively for four years, but then the parents introduce a new baby, not only is parental attention divided between two children, but the baby naturally needs and gets more attention by being a helpless infant. If the child feels displaced/threatened by the younger sibling, s/he may regress from normal four-year-old behaviors to more infantile ones in a bid for similar attention. Projection—if a child feels threatened by experiencing inner aggressive impulses, e.g. hating another person, s/he may project these feelings onto that person, accusing, "You hate me!" Denial—if a child cannot accept feelings triggered by losing a loved one through divorce or death, s/he may deny reality: "S/he will come back."

Copyright © Mometrix Media. You have been licensed one copy of this document for personal use only. Any other reproduction or redistribution is strictly prohibited. All rights reserved.

CONTRIBUTION OF PSYCHOANALYTIC THEORY TO EARLY CHILDHOOD CARE AND EDUCATIONAL PRACTICES

In his development of psychoanalytic theory, Freud (a physician) identified stages of childhood development according to the particular bodily zones where pleasure is focused during each age period. This identification still regularly informs early childhood care and educational practices. For example, infants are in the Oral stage, when nursing provides pleasure as well as nutrition and satisfying hunger. Knowing this, caregivers recognize that babies begin exploring their environments through oral routes. They thus will not punish mouthing of objects; will anticipate and prevent mouthing of unsafe/unsanitary objects; provide suitable objects and activities for oral inspection and orally oriented rewards. Toddlers engaged in toilet-training are in Freud's Anal stage. As they learn to control their bladders and bowels, they also learn to control their impulses and behaviors. Adults knowing this recognize toddlers' willful, stubborn behaviors as normal parts of the process of establishing individual identities and asserting their wishes. Thus, they will not punish these behaviors harshly/inappropriately, but strike a balance between permitting exploration and providing limits, guidance, and support.

KEY DIFFERENCES BETWEEN FREUD'S AND ERIKSON'S DEVELOPMENTAL THEORIES

Erikson's theory was based on Freud's, but whereas Freud's focus was psychosexual, Erikson's was psychosocial. Both emphasized early parent-child relationships. Freud believed the personality was essentially formed in childhood and proposed five stages through puberty and none thereafter; Erikson depicted lifelong development through nine stages. Each stage centers on a "nuclear conflict" to resolve, with positive/negative outcomes of successful/unsuccessful resolutions. Erikson's first, infancy stage (birth—18 months) is Basic Trust vs. Mistrust. When an infant's basic needs—such as being fed, changed, bathed, held/cuddled, having discomfort relieved, and receiving attention, affection, and interaction are met sufficiently and consistently, the baby develops basic trust in the world, gaining a sense of security, confidence, and optimism. The positive outcomes are hope and drive; negative outcomes are withdrawal and sensory distortion. If infant needs are inadequately and/or inconsistently met, the baby develops basic mistrust, with a sense of insecurity, worthlessness, and pessimism.

HOW ERIKSON'S FIRST STAGE INFORMS EARLY CHILDHOOD CAREGIVING

Erikson's theory is based on Freud's, but focuses on psychosocial rather than psychosexual development. Erikson proposed infants are in his first stage, named for its nuclear conflict of Basic Trust vs. Mistrust. Erikson found if an infant's needs are met adequately and consistently, the baby will form a sense of trust in the world; but if they are not fully and/or regularly met, the baby will form a sense of mistrust in the environment and people. Erikson proposed a positive outcome for resolving the nuclear crisis in each stage; in this stage it is Hope. Caregivers understanding this theory and stage will feed a baby on a regular schedule and not leave the child crying from hunger for long times. They will change the baby's diaper timely when needed rather than letting him/her experience discomfort and cry too long. Moreover, caregivers will meet infant needs for interaction, especially holding and cuddling. Making care/nurturing predictable for babies establishes optimism. The negative outcome of Mistrust is linked to worthless feelings, even suicide.

SECOND STAGE IN ERIKSON'S PSYCHOSOCIAL THEORY OF HUMAN DEVELOPMENT

In each of Erikson's developmental stages, a central conflict must be resolved; success/failure dictates outcomes. Babies first develop basic trust or mistrust in the world during the first stage. Toddlers are in Erikson's second stage of Autonomy vs. Shame and Self-Doubt. In this stage, children 18 months—3 years are learning muscular control (walking, toilet-training) and developing moral senses of right/wrong. As they gain skills, they want to do more things independently, and they begin to assert their individual wills. Parents are familiar with the associated tantrums, "No!" and other common "Terrible Twos" behaviors. Children receiving appropriate parenting during this stage develop a sense of autonomy through being allowed to attempt tasks realistic for them; to fail and try again; and eventually

27

Copyright © Mometrix Media. You have been licensed one copy of this document for personal use only. Any other reproduction or redistribution is strictly prohibited. All rights reserved.

to master them. Positive outcomes are will/willpower and self-control; negative outcomes are impulsivity and compulsion. Children with parenting at either extreme—being ignored and given no guidance or support; or overly controlled/directed, having everything done for them and never allowed freedom—develop shame, doubting their abilities.

HOW ERIKSON'S SECOND STAGE INFORMS EARLY CHILDHOOD CAREGIVING

Erikson's second stage of psychosocial development centers on the nuclear conflict of Autonomy vs. Shame and Doubt. Toddlers in this stage are engaged in learning to walk and toilet-training, involving motor control and self-control. They are also learning to assert themselves. This is one reason for tantrums characteristic of this age group. Toddlers who begin loudly saying "No!" are not merely obstinate or difficult, but are learning to express their wills. Erikson designated Will as the positive outcome of resolving the conflict in this stage, as well as self-control and courage. Children allowed to use their emerging skills to try things on their own become more independent, developing autonomy. Those not allowed to practice and progress in making choices and/or are made to feel ashamed during toilet-training/while learning other new skills, learn to doubt themselves and their abilities instead of developing independence. Adults appreciating this theory and stage let children express preferences and practice new skills, supplying needed encouragement, support, and positive reinforcement without overly restricting, controlling, or punishing them.

THIRD STAGE IN ERIKSON'S PSYCHOSOCIAL THEORY OF HUMAN DEVELOPMENT

Each of Erikson's nine developmental stages involves a "nuclear crisis" the individual must resolve; success or failure results in positive or negative outcomes. Babies develop basic trust or mistrust; toddlers develop autonomy or shame and self-doubt. Erikson's third stage, Initiative vs. Guilt, involves preschoolers. At this age, young children are exploring the environment further commensurately with their increasing physical/motor, cognitive, emotional, and social skills. They exercise imagination in make-believe/pretend play and pursue adventure. Having gained some control over their bodies in the previous stage, they now attempt to exercise control over their environments. When they succeed in this stage, the positive outcomes are purpose and direction. Children who receive adult disapproval for exerting control over their surroundings—either because they try to use too much control or because parents are overly controlling—feel guilt. Negative outcomes include excessive inhibition against taking action or ruthless, inconsiderate behavior at the opposite extreme.

RELATION OF ERIKSON'S THIRD STAGE TO EARLY CHILDHOOD EDUCATION

In his theory of psychosocial development, Erikson proposed his third stage revolves around the nuclear conflict of Initiative vs. Guilt. Erikson described 3- to 5-year-olds in this stage as being at the "play age." Having developed the ability for make-believe/pretend play, children imitate parents and other adults in their activities. At these ages, children begin taking the initiative to plan and enact scenarios wherein they play roles and use objects to symbolize other things. Through creating situations and stories, they experiment and identify socially with adult roles and behaviors. They are also more actively exploring their environments. Relationships expand from parents to family. The positive outcome/strength of this stage is Purpose. Children thwarted in fulfilling their natural goals and desires develop the negative outcome of Guilt through adults' punishing them for trying to control their environments and/or adults' controlling them too much. Adults understanding this encourage and support pretend play. They encourage and approve children for initiating activities rather than inhibiting or always directing their actions.

FOURTH STAGE IN ERIKSON'S PSYCHOSOCIAL THEORY OF HUMAN DEVELOPMENT

Erikson formulated nine stages encompassing the entire human lifespan. The fourth stage corresponds to the end of the early childhood years, when children begin formal schooling. Erikson named this stage, which lasts from around ages 5–6 to puberty, Industry vs. Inferiority. Children in this stage are primarily occupied with learning new academic and social competencies as they attend school, meet more peers and adults, make new friends, and learn to interact in a wider environment. Whereas the focus of Stage

28

Copyright © Mometrix Media. You have been licensed one copy of this document for personal use only. Any other reproduction or redistribution is strictly prohibited. All rights reserved.

2, Autonomy vs. Shame and Doubt, was self-control and parents were the main relationship; and the focus of Stage 3, Initiative vs. Guilt, was environmental exploration and family was the main relationship; in Stage 4, Industry vs. Inferiority, the focus is on achievements and accomplishments. Friends, neighbors, school, and teachers are the most important relationships. Children's successful resolutions bring positive outcomes of competence and method; negative outcomes are narrowness of abilities and inertia (lack of activity).

RELATION OF ERIKSON'S FOURTH STAGE TO EARLY CHILDHOOD EDUCATION

Erikson termed the fourth stage of his psychosocial theory of development as centering on the nuclear conflict of Industry vs. Inferiority. Children commonly enter this stage around the years beginning school, also coinciding with the close of the early childhood years. Children at elementary school ages acquire a great many new skills and much new knowledge. This enables them to attempt and accomplish many more things, which they are expected to do in school. Their increased ability and accomplishment engender a positive sense of Industry. Children's most important relationships are no longer only with their parents and family, but with friends, neighbors, classmates, teachers, and other school staff. Hence social interactions are central during this stage. Children feeling unequal to new tasks develop a sense of Inferiority compared to peers. Parents and educators who encourage and reinforce children's desires and attempts to learn and practice new skills and perform tasks help them develop senses of method and competence. Unsupportive/punitive adult responses result in restricted competencies and/or lack of motivation.

FUNDAMENTAL PRINCIPLES OF BEHAVIORIST OR LEARNING THEORY

Major principles of behaviorism include these: Organisms learn through interacting with the environment. Environmental influences shape behavior. Environmental stimuli elicit responses from organisms. Hypothetical constructs like the mind and/or inner physiological changes are unnecessary for scientifically describing behaviors—everything organisms do, including feeling and thinking. Learning and behavior change are achieved through arranging the learner's environment to elicit certain responses, increasing the probability of repeating those responses by rewarding them (positive reinforcement) and decreasing repetition of unwanted behaviors by punishing (positive punishment) or ignoring them (extinction). Just as Thorndike previously found all animals including humans learn the same way, Skinner also found his principles applied equally to rats, pigeons, and people. His methods have become so popular that early childhood educators routinely give positive reinforcement—verbal praise, treats, and privileges—for performing new skills and demonstrating socially desirable behaviors; teach young children complex tasks in steps (shaping/chaining/task analysis); take away privileges to punish unwanted behaviors (negative punishment); and remove aversive stimuli for complying (negative reinforcement).

CHILDREN'S DEVELOPMENT OF SEXUAL/GENDER IDENTIFICATION
FREUD'S VIEW OF CHILDREN'S DEVELOPMENT OF SEXUAL/GENDER IDENTIFICATION

While different psychological theories/schools of thought agree that sex as a social identity develops through the process of identification, they have different views and explanations for how children develop their social identities as boys or girls. In Freud's view, gender identity develops through processes of differentiation and affiliation. He said once children observe that certain other people have characteristics in common with themselves, they "endeavor to mold the ego after one that had been taken as a model." In other words, they identify with similar other people and try to attain the same attributes. Freud proposed that boys resolve their Oedipal conflicts through identification with the aggressor, i.e. adopting their fathers' characteristics and suppressing sexual impulses toward their mothers. While he focused exclusively on males in this respect, Neo-Freudian psychologists later proposed a female counterpart, the Electra conflict, wherein girls resolve desires for fathers by identifying with mothers and adopting their characteristics. In either case, children differentiate from their opposite-sex parent and identify/affiliate with their same-sex parent.

Copyright © Mometrix Media. You have been licensed one copy of this document for personal use only. Any other reproduction or redistribution is strictly prohibited. All rights reserved.

EXPLANATION OF SOCIAL LEARNING AND BEHAVIORIST THEORIES

Albert Bandura and other proponents of social learning theory maintain that children learn through a process of observing other people's behavior, observing certain behaviors of others that are rewarded, and then imitating those behaviors to obtain similar rewards. The concept of rewards reinforcing behaviors, i.e. increasing the probability of repeating them, comes from behaviorism or learning theory. Social learning theory is based on behaviorism, but includes additional emphasis on the ideas that learning occurs within a social context and that social interactions are primary influences on learning. According to social learning theory, children observe that males and females engage in different behaviors. They additionally observe that boys and girls receive different rewards for their behaviors. Based on these observations, children then imitate the behaviors appropriate to their own sex that they have seen rewarded in others of their sex to obtain the same rewards. Both behaviorist and social learning theories view gender identity development as being environmentally shaped by consequences; social learning theory focuses on the social environment.

KOHLBERG'S COGNITIVE-DEVELOPMENTAL THEORY

Kohlberg had developed a cognitive theory of moral development, based upon and expanding the concepts of morality Piaget included in his theory of cognitive development. Kohlberg also proposed a cognitive-developmental approach to children's acquisition of sex/gender roles. Piaget and Kohlberg discussed classification or categorization as one of the cognitive abilities that children develop. Just as they learn to categorize various things, e.g. foods, animals, people, etc., they learn that people include female and male categories. They then learn to categorize themselves as either female/girls or male/boys. When children are around 2 years old, they each begin to develop their distinctive sense of self. Once they have differentiated self from the rest of the world, they also begin to be able to develop complex mental concepts. These abilities enable them to develop self-concepts of gender. According to the cognitive-developmental view, once children have developed concepts of their sex/gender, these are maintained despite social contexts and are difficult to change.

KEY CONCEPTS OF BANDURA'S SOCIAL LEARNING THEORY

Psychologist Alfred Bandura developed the primary theory of social learning. While his theory incorporates elements of behaviorism in that environmental rewards and punishments that shape the behaviors and learning of children, Bandura focused more on the social dimension of learning in that he found the context of social interactions the most important medium and influence for learning. Bandura's theory also incorporates elements of cognitive theory by emphasizing the roles played by the cognitive processes of attention, memory, and motivation in learning. Bandura found children learn by observing and imitating the behaviors of models, including adults, older children, and peers. He proposed four conditions required for this learning: Attention, Retention, Reproduction, and Motivation. Adults understanding Bandura's theory realize children can learn new behaviors by seeing others be rewarded for performing these, and then imitating them; this greatly expands children's learning potential. Bandura also proved that children viewing violent video content engage in more aggressive behaviors, informing adults of the importance of monitoring and controlling children's exposure to media influences.

HIERARCHY OF NEEDS IN MASLOW'S HUMANISTIC THEORY OF SELF-ACTUALIZATION

Maslow proposed humans are driven by needs, and meeting the most basic needs is prerequisite to meeting more advanced needs. Maslow's needs hierarchy is depicted as a pyramid, with the most fundamental needs at the base. Its five levels are (1) physiological needs: air, water, sleep, and food necessary for survival; (2) security needs: shelter and a safe environment; (3) social needs: feeling loved, receiving affection, and belonging to a family and/or group; (4) esteem needs: feeling personal value, accomplishment, and social recognition; and (5) self-actualizing needs: achieving optimal personal growth and realizing one's full potential. For example, babies and young children must have clean air to breathe and be fed and rested to survive before other needs can be addressed. Children must have safe places to live, then their needs for love and belonging can be met. Once a child feels loved and

30

Copyright © Mometrix Media. You have been licensed one copy of this document for personal use only. Any other reproduction or redistribution is strictly prohibited. All rights reserved.

part of a family/group, s/he can develop self-esteem through accomplishments and feeling valued by society. After satisfying these, children can self-actualize.

ORGANISMIC VALUING, CONDITIONS OF WORTH, THE REAL SELF, THE IDEAL SELF, AND INCONGRUENCE IN CARL ROGERS' THEORY

Rogers said all organisms naturally pursue a tendency to actualize or make the best of life. Organismic valuing is the natural tendency to value what is healthy, e.g. avoiding bad-tasting foods, which can be poisonous or rotten. Organismic valuing leads to positive regard/esteem, engendering positive self-regard/self-esteem, reflecting what Rogers called the real self—the person one becomes under optimal conditions. Rogers observed society substitutes conditions of worth for organismic valuing, giving us things based not on our needs but on meeting society's required conditions. Children are taught early they will receive something they want on the condition they do what adults want. This establishes conditional positive regard, meaning children only feel esteemed by others on others' conditions; this develops conditional positive self-regard, or self-esteem dependent on others' esteem. This creates an unattainable ideal self-based on others' standards rather than the real self. For Rogers, incongruence between real and ideal self-causes neurosis. Rogers' required qualities for effective therapists—congruence/genuineness, empathy, and respect—are equally effective in early childhood education.

Rogers believed in actualization or realizing one's full potential as did fellow humanist Abraham Maslow. While Maslow applied self-actualization to humans, Rogers applied the "actualization tendency" to all life forms. Rogers gave the name "conditions of worth" to the process he observed whereby others give individuals things based not on need but worthiness. For example, while babies usually receive care based on need, as they grow older, adults establish conditions of worth: children get dessert if they finish dinner/vegetables; they get drinks or snacks after finishing a task/activity/lesson/class; and most significantly, they often get affection on condition of acceptable/desirable behavior. In behaviorism, this is called contingencies of reinforcement: rewards are given contingent on desired behaviors. Rogers would likely disagree with this practice, which he called conditional positive regard. He felt it makes children do what others want, not what they want or need, and teaches them conditional positive self-regard, i.e. self-esteem dependent on external standards. Rogers' remedy was unconditional positive regard—unconditional love and acceptance.

Copyright © Mometrix Media. You have been licensed one copy of this document for personal use only. Any other reproduction or redistribution is strictly prohibited. All rights reserved.

Language and Literacy Development

COMMUNICATION DEVELOPMENT NORMALLY OCCURRING WITHIN A CHILD'S FIRST FIVE YEARS OF LIFE

Language and communication development depend strongly on the language a child develops within the first five years of life. During this time, three developmental periods are observed. At birth, the first period begins. This period is characterized by infant crying and gazing. Babies communicate their sensations and emotions through these behaviors, so they are expressive; however, they are not yet intentional. They indirectly indicate their needs through expressing how they feel, and when these needs are met, these communicative behaviors are reinforced. These expressions and reinforcement are the foundations for the later development of intentional communication. This becomes possible in the second developmental period, between 6 and 18 months. At this time, infants become able to coordinate their attention visually with other people relative to things and events, enabling purposeful communication with adults. During the third developmental period, from 18 months on, children come to use language as their main way of communicating and learning. Preschoolers can carry on conversations, exercise self-control through language use, and conduct verbal negotiations.

MILESTONES OF NORMAL LANGUAGE DEVELOPMENT BY THE 2 YEARS OLD

By the time most children reach the age of 2 years, they have acquired a vocabulary of about 150 to 300 words. They can name various familiar objects found in their environments. They are able to use at least two prepositions in their speech, for example in, on, and/or under. 2-year-olds typically combine the words they know into short sentences. These sentences tend to be mostly noun-verb or verb-noun combinations (e.g. "Daddy work," "Watch this"). They may also include verb-preposition combinations (e.g. "Go out," "Come in"). By the age of 2 years, children use pronouns, such as I, me, and you. They typically can use at least two such pronouns correctly. A normally developing 2-year-old will respond to some commands, directions, or questions, such as "Show me your eyes" or "Where are your ears?"

SALIENT GENERAL ASPECTS OF HUMAN LANGUAGE ABILITIES FROM BEFORE BIRTH TO 5 YEARS OF AGE

Language and communication abilities are integral parts of human life that are central to learning, successful school performance, successful social interactions, and successful living. Human language ability begins before birth: the developing fetus can hear not only internal maternal sounds, but also the mother's voice, others' voices, and other sounds outside the womb. Humans have a natural sensitivity to human sounds and languages from before they are born until they are about 4½ years old. These years are critical for developing language and communication. Babies and young children are predisposed to greater sensitivity to human sounds than other sounds, orienting them toward the language spoken around them. Children absorb their environmental language completely, including vocal tones, syntax, usage, and emphasis. This linguistic absorption occurs very rapidly. Children's first 2½ years particularly involve amazing abilities to learn language including grammatical expression.

6 MONTHS, 12 MONTHS, AND 18 MONTHS

Individual differences dictate a broad range of language development that is still normal. However, parents observing noticeably delayed language development in their children should consult professionals. Typically, babies respond to hearing their names by 6 months of age; turn their heads and eyes toward the sources of human voices they hear; and respond accordingly to friendly and angry tones of voice. By the age of 12 months, toddlers can usually understand and follow simple directions, especially when these are accompanied by physical and/or vocal cues. They can intentionally use one or more words with the correct meaning. By the age of 18 months, a normally developing child usually has acquired a vocabulary of roughly 5 to 20 words. 18-month-old children use nouns in their speech most of the time. They are very likely to repeat certain words and/or phrases over and over. At this age,

32

Copyright © Mometrix Media. You have been licensed one copy of this document for personal use only. Any other reproduction or redistribution is strictly prohibited. All rights reserved.

children typically are able to follow simple verbal commands without needing as many visual or auditory cues as at 12 months.

THREE YEARS

By the time they are 3 years old, most normally developing children have acquired vocabularies of between 900 and 1,000 words. Typically they correctly use the pronouns I, me, and you. They use more verbs more frequently. They apply past tenses to some verbs and plurals to some nouns. 3-year-olds usually can use at least three prepositions; the most common are in, on, and under. The normally developing 3-year-old knows the major body parts and can name them. 3-year-olds typically use 3-word sentences with ease. Normally, parents should find approximately 75 to 100 percent of what a 3-year-old says to be intelligible, while strangers should find between 50 and 75 percent of a 3-year-old's speech intelligible. Children this age comprehend most simple questions about their activities and environments and can answer questions about what they should do when they are thirsty, hungry, sleepy, hot, or cold. They can tell about their experiences in ways that adults can generally follow. By the age of 3 years, children should also be able to tell others their name, age, and sex.

FOUR YEARS

When normally developing children are 4 years old, most know the names of animals familiar to them. They can use at least four prepositions in their speech (e.g. in, on, under, to, from, etc.). They can name familiar objects in pictures, and they know and can identify one color or more. Usually they are able to repeat four-syllable words they hear. They verbalize as they engage in their activities, which Vygotsky dubbed "private speech." Private speech helps young children think through what they are doing, solve problems, make decisions, and reinforce the correct sequences in multistep activities. When presented with contrasting items, 4-year-olds can understand comparative concepts like bigger and smaller. At this age, they are able to comply with simple commands without the target stimuli being in their sight (e.g. "Put those clothes in the hamper" [upstairs]). 4-year-old children will also frequently repeat speech sounds, syllables, words, and phrases, similar to 18-month-olds' repetitions but at higher linguistic and developmental levels.

FIVE YEARS

Once most children have reached the age of 5 years, their speech has expanded from the emphasis of younger children on nouns, verbs, and a few prepositions, and is now characterized by many more descriptive words, including adjectives and adverbs. 5-year-olds understand common antonyms, e.g. big/little, heavy/light, long/short, hot/cold. They can now repeat longer sentences they hear, up to about nine words. When given three consecutive, uninterrupted commands, the typical 5-year-old can follow these without forgetting one or two. At age 5 most children have learned simple concepts of time like today, yesterday, tomorrow; day, morning, afternoon, night; and before, after, and later. 5-year-olds typically speak in relatively long sentences, and normally should be incorporating some compound sentences (with more than one independent clause) and complex sentences (with one or more independent and dependent clauses). 5-year-old children's speech is also grammatically correct most of the time.

PERSONAL NARRATIVES

Personal narratives are the way that young children relate their experiences to others by telling the stories of what happened. The narrative structure incorporates reporting components such as: who was involved; where the events took place; and what happened. Understanding and using this structure is crucial to young children for their communication; however, many young children cannot follow or apply this sequence without scaffolding (temporary support as needed) from adults. Adults can ask young children guiding questions to facilitate and advance narratives. They can also provide learning tools that engage children's visual, tactile (touch), and kinesthetic (body position and movement) senses. This reinforces narrative use, increases the depth of scaffolding, and motivates children's participation. Children learn to play the main character; describe the setting; sequence plot actions; and use words and

Copyright © Mometrix Media. You have been licensed one copy of this document for personal use only. Any other reproduction or redistribution is strictly prohibited. All rights reserved.

body language to express emotions. Topic-related action sequences or "social stories" are important for preschoolers to comprehend and express to promote daily transitions and self-regulation. Such conversational skills attainment achieves milestones in both linguistic and emotional-social development.

ACHIEVEMENTS OR PROCESSES ENABLED BY ORAL LANGUAGE SKILLS DEVELOPMENT

Crucial oral language development skills enable children to (1) communicate by listening and responding to others' speech; (2) comprehend meanings of numerous words and concepts encountered in their listening and reading; (3) acquire information on subjects they are interested in learning about; and (4) use specific language to express their own thoughts and ideas. Research finds young children's ability to listen to, understand, and use spoken and written language is associated with their later reading, spelling, and writing literacy achievement. Infants typically begin developing oral language skills, which continue developing through life. Babies develop awareness of and attend to adult speech, and soon begin communicating their needs via gestures and speech sounds. Toddlers express emotions and ideas and solicit information via language. They start uttering simple sentences, asking questions, and giving opinions regarding their likes and dislikes. Young preschoolers expand their vocabularies from hearing others' speech and from books. They describe past and possible future events and unseen objects; tell fictional/"make-believe" stories; and use complete sentences and more complex language.

BENEFITS OF PLAY-BASED ACTIVITIES

When young children play, they often enact scenarios. Play scenarios tell stories that include who is involved, where they are, what happens, why it happens, and how the "actors" feel about it. Children engage in planning when they decide first what their playing will be about; which children are playing which roles; and who is doing what. This planning and the thought processes involved reflect narrative thinking and structure. Children who experience difficulties with planning play are more likely to avoid participating or to participate only marginally. Since playing actually requires these thought and planning processes, children who do not play spontaneously can be supported in playing by enabling them to talk about potential narratives/stories as foundations for play scenarios. When conflicts emerge during play, conversation is necessary to effect needed change. Narrative development constitutes gradual plot development; play conflicts are akin to fictional/personal narrative problems and result in changed feelings. Adults can help young children discuss problems, identify the changed feeling they cause, and discuss plans/actions for resolution.

CONVERSATION OF ADULTS WITH YOUNG CHILDREN

Adults should converse with young children so the children get practice with: hearing and using rich and abstract vocabulary and increasingly complex sentences; using language to express ideas and ask questions for understanding; and using language to answer questions about past, future, and absent things rather than only about "here-and-now" things. To ensure they incorporate these elements in their conversations, adults can consider the following: in the home, care setting, or classroom, whose voices are heard most often and who does the most talking; the child, not the adult, should be talking at least half of the time. Adults should be using rich language with complex structures when conversing with young children. Adults should be talking with, not at children; the conversation should be shared equally rather than adults doing all the talking while children listen to them. Adults should also ask young children questions, rather than just telling them things. Additionally, adult questions should require that children use language to formulate and communicate abstract ideas.

NATURAL VS. INTENTIONAL

Children enjoy conversing with significant adults, including parents, caregivers, and teachers; and they require practice with doing so. Caregivers tend to talk with young children naturally, sometimes even automatically, throughout the day, which helps children develop significant language skills. However, caregivers can enhance young children's oral language development further through intentional conversations. One element of doing this is establishing an environment that gives the children many

34

Copyright © Mometrix Media. You have been licensed one copy of this document for personal use only. Any other reproduction or redistribution is strictly prohibited. All rights reserved.

things to talk about and many reasons to talk. Another element of intentionally promoting oral language skills development is by engaging in shared conversations. When parents and caregivers share storybook reading with young children, this affords a particularly good springboard for shared conversations. Reading and conversing together are linguistic interactions supplying foundations for children's developing comprehension of numerous word meanings. Researchers find such abundant early word comprehension is a critical basis for later reading comprehension. Asking questions, explaining, requesting what they need, communicating feelings, and learning to listen to others talk are some important ways whereby children build listening, understanding, and speaking skills.

1:1 CONVERSATIONS WITH CHILDREN

When parents, caregivers, or teachers converse 1:1 with individual children, children reap benefits not as available in group conversations. Caregivers should therefore try to have such individual conversations with each child daily. In daycare and preschool settings, some good times for caregivers to do this include when children arrive and leave; during shared reading activities with one or two children; and during center time. 1:1 talk allows the adult to repeat what the child says for reinforcement. It allows the adult to extend what the child said by adding more information to it, like new vocabulary words, synonyms, meanings, or omitted details. It allows the adult to revise what the child said by restating or recasting it. It allows the child to hear his or her own ideas and thoughts reflected back to them when the adult restates them. Moreover, 1:1 conversation allows adults to contextualize the discussion accordingly with an individual child's understanding. It also allows adults to elicit children's comprehension of abstract concepts.

EXTENDED CONVERSATIONS AND TURN-TAKING

When adults engage young children in extended conversations including taking many "back-and-forth" turns, these create the richest dialogues for building oral language skills. Adults make connections with and build upon children's declarations and questions. Adults model richer descriptive language by modifying/adding to children's original words with new vocabulary, adjectives, adverbs, and varying sentences with questions and statements. For example, a child shows an adult his/her new drawing, saying: "This is me and Gran in the garden," the adult can build on this/invite the child to continue: "What is your gran holding?" The child identifies what they planted: "Carrot seeds. Gran said to put them in the dirt so they don't touch." The adult can then encourage the child's use of language to express abstract thoughts: "What could happen if the seeds were touching?" The adult can then extend the conversation through discussion with the child about how plants grow or tending gardens. This introduces new concepts, builds children's linguistic knowledge, and helps them learn to verbalize their ideas.

IN-DEPTH COMPREHENSION OF WORD MEANINGS

To support deeper word-meaning comprehension, teachers can give multiple definitions and examples for the same word and connect new vocabulary with children's existing knowledge. For example, a teacher conducting a preschool classroom science experiment incorporates new scientific concepts with new vocabulary words and conversational practice: pouring water on a paper towel, the teacher asks children what is happening to the water. A child answers, "It's going into the paper." The teacher asks how. Another child says, "The paper's soaking it up." The teacher confirms this, teaches the word "absorb," compares the paper to a sponge, and asks how much more water will be absorbed. A child responds probably no more since water is already dripping out. The teacher pours water on a plastic lid, asking if it absorbs. Children respond, "No, it slides off." Confirming, the teacher teaches the word "repel." This teacher has introduced new science concepts and new vocabulary words; engaged the children in conversation; related new concepts and words to existing knowledge; and added information to deepen comprehension.

Copyright © Mometrix Media. You have been licensed one copy of this document for personal use only. Any other reproduction or redistribution is strictly prohibited. All rights reserved.

ADULTS' NARRATION OF CHILD ACTIVITIES AND ACTIONS

One oral language development technique adults can use is to narrate, i.e. describe what a child is doing as s/he does it. For example, a caregiver can say, "I see you're spreading paste on the back of your paper flower—not too much so it's lumpy, but not too little so it doesn't stick. Now you're pressing the flower onto your poster board. It sticks—good work!" Hence narration can be incorporated as prelude and segue to verbal positive reinforcement. This promotes oral language development by introducing and illustrating syntaxes. Communicating locations and directionality employs verbs and prepositions. Describing intensity and manner employs adverbs. Labeling objects/actions that are currently present/taking place with new vocabulary words serves immediately to place those words into natural contexts, facilitating more authentic comprehension of word meanings and better memory retention. Caregivers/teachers can narrate children's activities during formal instructional activities and informal situations like outdoor playtime, snack time, and cleanup time, and subsequently converse with them about what they did.

TOPICS THAT YOUNG CHILDREN ENJOY TALKING ABOUT

Personal content is important with young children, who enjoy talking about themselves; e.g., what their favorite color is or where they got their new shirt; about their activities, like what they are constructing with Legos or shaping with Play-Doh; or about familiar events and things that access their knowledge, like their family activities and experiences with neighbors and friends. Here is an example of how a teacher can make use of children's conversation to reinforce it, expand it, and teach new vocabulary and grammar. The teacher asks a child what s/he is building and the child answers, "A place for sick animals." The teacher asks, "You mean an animal hospital [or vet clinic]?" and the child confirms. When a child says someone was taken to a hospital "in the siren," the teacher corrects the usage: "They took him to the hospital in the ambulance with the siren was sounding?" This recasts "siren" with the correct word choice, "ambulance." It incorporates "siren" correctly and extends the statement to a complete sentence.

STORYTELLING

Young children like to communicate about their personal life experiences. When they can do this through narrative structure, it helps them use new words they are learning, organize their thoughts to express them coherently, and engage their imaginative powers. Teachers/caregivers can supply new words they need; model correct syntax for sentences by elaborating on or extending child utterances and asking them questions; and build further upon children's ideas. For example, a teacher asks a child what they did at her sister's birthday party. When the child describes the cake and makes gestures for a word she doesn't know, the teacher supplies "candles," which the child confirms and repeats. When the child then offers, "Mom says be careful with candles," the teacher asks what could happen if you're not careful, the child replies that candles can start a fire. In this way, teachers give young children models of sentence structure, teach vocabulary, and guide children in expressing their thoughts in organized sequences that listeners can follow.

SHARED BOOK READING

When teachers share books with preschoolers, they can ask questions and discuss the content, giving great opportunities for building oral language through conversation. Books with simple text and numerous, engaging illustrations best invite preschoolers to talk about the characters and events in the pictures, and the plotlines they hear. Children's listening and speaking skills develop; they learn new information and concepts; their vocabularies increase; and their ability to define words and explain their meanings is enhanced through shared reading. Many children's books include rich varieties of words that may not occur in daily conversation, used in complete-sentence contexts. Teachers should provide preschoolers with fictional and nonfictional books; poetry and storybooks; children's reference books like picture dictionaries/encyclopedias; and "information books" covering single topics like weather, birds, reptiles, butterflies, or transportation whereby children can get answers to questions or learn topical information. Detailed illustrations, engaging content, and rich vocabulary are strong

36

Copyright © Mometrix Media. You have been licensed one copy of this document for personal use only. Any other reproduction or redistribution is strictly prohibited. All rights reserved.

elements motivating children to develop oral language and understand how to form sentences, how to use punctuation, and how language works.

Abstract thought is stimulated by asking young children to think about things not observed and/or current. During/after sharing books, teachers can ask children what else might happen in the story; what they imagine the story's characters could be feeling or thinking—which also engages their imaginations; and ask them the meaning of the story's events using questions necessitating children's use of language to analyze this meaning. Teachers can ask younger children vocabulary words: "What did we call this animal?" and encourage them to use language by asking them to describe story details, like "How do the firemen reach people up high in the building?" Once younger children are familiar with a story, teachers can activate and monitor their retention and recall: "Do you remember what happened to Arthur the day before that?" Teachers can ask older children to predict what they think will happen next in a story; to imagine extensions beyond the story ("What would you do if...?"); and make conclusions regarding why characters feel/behave as they do.

ENHANCING THE EFFECTS OF SHARED READING

According to researchers' findings, the effectiveness of shared reading experiences is related to the ways that adults read with young children. Rather than merely labeling objects or events with vocabulary words, teachers should ask young children to recall the shared reading, which monitors their listening comprehension and retention abilities. They should ask children to predict what will happen next based on what already happened in a book; speculate about what could possibly happen; describe characters, actions, events, and information from the shared reading; and ask their own questions about it. Shared reading with small groups of 1–3 children permits teachers to involve each child in the book by questioning and conversing with them about the pictures and plots. To teach vocabulary, teachers can tell children word meanings; point to illustrations featuring new words; relate new words to words the children already know; give multiple, varied examples of new words; and encourage children to use new words they learn in their conversations.

REPEATING SHARED READING

Young children develop preferences for favorite books. Once they know a story's plot, they enjoy discussing their knowledge. Teachers can use this for extended conversations. They can ask children who the characters are; where the story takes place; and why characters do things and events occur. They can ask specific questions requiring children to answer how much/how many/how far a distance/how long a time, etc. Teachers can also help children via prompting to relate stories to their own real-life experiences. In a thematic approach, teachers can select several books on the same theme, like rain forests or undersea life. This affords richer extended conversations about the theme. It also allows teachers to "recycle" vocabulary by modeling and encouraging use of thematically related words, which enhances memory and in-depth comprehension of meanings. Teachers can plan activities based on book themes, like painting pictures/murals, sculpting, making collages, or constructing models, which gives children additional motivation to use the new language they learn from shared readings of books.

READING ALOUD

Just before reading a story aloud to young students, the teacher should identify vocabulary words in the story that s/he will need to go over with the children. The teacher can write these words on the board or on strips of paper. Discussing these words before the reading will give the children definitions for new/unfamiliar words, and help them understand word meanings within the story's context. Teachers can also give young children some open-ended questions to consider when listening to the story. They will then repeat these questions during and after the reading. Questions should NOT be ones children can answer with yes/no. When discussing vocabulary words, the teacher can also ask the children to relate words to personal life experiences. For example, with the word fish, some children may want to talk about going fishing with parents. Teachers can encourage children to tell brief personal stories,

Copyright © Mometrix Media. You have been licensed one copy of this document for personal use only. Any other reproduction or redistribution is strictly prohibited. All rights reserved.

which will help them relate the story they are about to hear to their own real-life experience, making the story more meaningful.

Before reading a story aloud, adults should tell young children its title and the author's name. Then they can ask the children what an author does (children should respond "write stories" or something similar). Giving the illustrator's name, the adult also can then ask the children what illustrators do (children should respond "draw pictures" or something similar). Holding up the book, an adult can identify the front, spine, and back and ask the children if we start reading at the front or back (children should respond "at the front"). Adults can show young children the illustration on the front cover of the book and ask them, "From this picture, what do you think is going to happen in this story?" and remind them to answer this question in complete sentences. These exchanges before reading a story aloud activate children's fundamental knowledge regarding print and books, as well as the last example's exercising their imagination and language use.

When a teacher is reading a story aloud to young children, after reading each page aloud, s/he should have the children briefly discuss the picture illustrations on each page and how they relate to what the teacher just read aloud. After they read aloud each plot point, action, event, or page, they should ask the children open-ended (non yes/no) questions about what they just heard. This monitors and supports listening comprehension and memory retention/recall and stimulates expressive language use. When children associate something in the story with their own life experiences, teachers should have them explain the connection. As they read, teachers should stop periodically and ask the children to predict or guess what will happen next before continuing. This promotes abstract thinking, understanding of logical sequences, and also exercises the imagination. After reading the story, teachers should ask children whether they liked it and why/why not, prompting them to answer using complete sentences. This helps children to organize their thoughts and opinions and to develop clear, grammatical, complete verbal expression.

ENVIRONMENTAL PRINT

Street signs, traffic signs, store and restaurant names, candy wrappers, food labels, product logos, etc.— all the print we see in everyday life—are environmental print. Just as parents often play alphabetic games with children in the car ("Find something starting with A...with B..." etc.), adults can use environmental print to enhance print awareness and develop reading skills. They can ask children to find letters from their names on colorful cereal boxes. They can select one sign type, e.g. stop, one-way, or pedestrian crossing, and ask children to count how many they see during a car trip. They can have children practice reading each sign and talk about the phonemes (speech sounds) each letter represents. Adults can take photos of different signs and compile them into a little book for children to "read." By cutting familiar words from food labels, they can teach capitalized and lowercase letters; associate letters with phonemes; have children read the words; and sort words by their initial letters and by categories (signs, foods, etc.).

ALPHABETIC PRINCIPLE

The alphabetic principle is the concept that letters and letter combinations represent speech sounds. Children's eventual reading fluency requires knowing these predictable relationships of letters to sounds, which they can then apply to both familiar and unfamiliar words. Young children's knowing the shapes and names of letters predicts their later reading success: knowing letter names is highly correlated with the ability to view words as letter sequences and to remember written/printed words' forms. Children must first be able to recognize and name letters to understand and apply the alphabetic principle. Young children learn letter names first, via singing the alphabet song and reciting rhymes and alphabetical jump-rope chants ("A my name is Alice, I come from Alabama, and I sell Apples; B my name is Betty..." etc.). They learn letter shapes after names, through playing with lettered blocks, plastic/wood/cardboard letters, and alphabet books. Once they can recognize and name letters, children learn letter sounds after names and shapes and spellings after sounds.

Copyright © Mometrix Media. You have been licensed one copy of this document for personal use only. Any other reproduction or redistribution is strictly prohibited. All rights reserved.

To help young children understand that written or printed letters represent corresponding speech sounds, teachers should teach relationships between letters and sounds separately, in isolation, and should teach these directly and explicitly. They should give young children daily opportunities during lessons to practice with letter-sound relationships. These opportunities for practice should include cumulative reviews of sound-letter relationships they have already learned and new letter-sound relationships as well. Adults should begin early in providing frequent opportunities to young children for applying their increasing knowledge and understanding of sound-letter relationships to early experiences with reading. They can do this by providing English words that are spelled phonetically (i.e. spelled the same way that they sound) and have meanings that are already familiar to the young learners.

Print Awareness

Even before they have learned how to read, young children develop print awareness, which constitutes children's first preparation for literacy. Children with print awareness realize that spoken language is represented by the markings on paper (or computer screens). They understand that the information in printed books adults read comes from the words, not the pictures. Children who have print awareness furthermore realize that print serves different functions within different contexts. They know that restaurant menus give information about the foods available; books tell stories or provide information; some signs show the names of stores, hotels, or restaurants, and other signs give traffic directions or danger warnings. Moreover, print awareness includes knowledge of how print is organized, e.g. that words are combinations of letters and have spaces in between them. Children with print awareness also know that [English] print is read from left to right and top to bottom; book pages are numbered; words convey ideas and meaning; and reading's purpose is to understand those ideas and acquire that meaning.

One way in which a teacher can get an idea of whether or to what extent a young child has developed print awareness is to provide the child with a storybook. Then the teacher can ask the child the following: "Show me the front of the book. Show me the back of the book. Show me the spine of the book. Where is the book's title? Where in the book are you supposed to start reading it? Show me a letter in the book. Now show me a word. Show me the first word of a sentence. Can you show me the last word of a sentence? Now will you show me the first word on a page? Please show me the last word on a page. Can you show me a punctuation mark? Can you show me a capital letter? Can you find a small letter/lowercase letter?" The teacher should also praise each correct response, supply the correct answers for incorrect responses, and review corrected answers.

Teachers should show young children the organization of books and the purpose of reading. When they read to them, they should use books with large print, which are more accessible for young children to view and begin to learn reading. Storybook text should use words familiar/predictable to young children. While reading together, teachers should point out high-frequency words like the, a, is, was, you; and specific letters, words, and punctuation marks in a story. Teachers can use index cards to label objects, areas, and centers in the classroom, pairing pictorial labels with word labels, and direct children's attention to them. They can invite preschoolers to play with printed words by making greeting cards, signs, or "writing" shopping lists and personal letters. They should point out print in calendars, posters, and signs. Also, teachers can have children narrate a story using a wordless picture book; write down their narrative on a poster; and reinforce the activity with a reward related to the story (e.g. eating pancakes after narrating the book Pancakes).

Self-Concept

Self-concept development begins during early childhood. Children come to identify characteristics, abilities, values, and attitudes that they feel define them. From 18–36 months, children develop the Categorical Self. This is a concrete view of oneself, usually related to observably opposite characteristics, e.g. child versus adult, girl versus boy, short versus tall, and good versus bad. A four-year-old might say,

Copyright © Mometrix Media. You have been licensed one copy of this document for personal use only. Any other reproduction or redistribution is strictly prohibited. All rights reserved.

"I'm shorter than Daddy. I have blue eyes. I can help Mommy clean house!" Young children can also describe emotional and attitudinal aspects of self-concept, e.g. "I like playing with Joshua. I'm happy today." Preschoolers do not usually integrate these aspects into a unified self-portrait, however. Also, many preschoolers do not yet realize one person can incorporate opposite qualities; a person is either good or bad to them, rather than having both good and bad qualities. The Remembered Self develops with long-term memory, including autobiographical memories and things adults have told them, to comprise one's life story. The Inner Self is the child's private feelings, desires, and thoughts.

PHONICS INSTRUCTION

Because children display individual differences in their speeds of learning sound-to-letter relationships, instruction should consider this; there is no set rate. Generally, a reasonable pace ranges from two to four sound-letter relationship per week. Relationships vary in utility: many words contain the sounds/letters m, a, t, s, p, and h, which are high-utility; but x as in box, gh as in through, ey as in they, and the sound of a as in want are lower-utility. High-utility sound-letter relationships should be taught first. Teachers should first introduce consonant relationships using f, m, n, r, and s, which are continuous sounds children can produce in isolation with less distortion than word-initial or word-medial stops like p, b, t, d, k, and g. Teachers should also introduce similar-sounding letters like b and v or i and e, and similar-looking letters like b and d or p and g, separately to prevent confusion. Single consonants versus clusters/blends should be introduced in separate lessons. Blends should incorporate sound-letter relationships children already know.

LANGUAGE EXPERIENCE APPROACH (LEA)

The LEA teaches beginning reading by connecting students' personal life experiences with written/printed words. A unique benefit is students using their own language and words, enabling them to interact with texts on multiple levels simultaneously. They thus realize they acquire knowledge and understanding through not just instruction, but also their own experiences. Four steps for implementing the LEA with EC groups: (1) Children and teacher choose a topic, like an exciting trip, game, or recent TV show, to discuss with teacher guidance. (2) Each child takes a turn saying a sentence using his/her own words that advances the discussion/story. The teacher writes the children's words verbatim without corrections, visibly and clearly. (3) Every few sentences or several words, the teacher stops and reads the record aloud for children to confirm accuracy. (4) Record review: the teacher points to each word, they read aloud together, or children repeat after the teacher. The teacher gives children copies of the record for independent review and possible compilation into books of LEA stories.

WHOLE LANGUAGE APPROACH

The whole language approach concentrates on children's seeking, finding, and constructing meaning in language. As such, young children's early technical correctness is not the priority. Whole language teachers do not ignore children's errors. However, they do not make correction more important than overall engagement, understanding, and appreciation of reading, writing, and literature. Instead, teachers make formative assessments taking into account the errors each child makes. Then they design learning experiences for children that give them opportunities and assistance in acquiring mechanically correct linguistic forms and structures. While this holistic approach finds analytical techniques that break language down into components like phonemes and alphabet letters less useful, children with language processing/reading problems need to learn phonemic awareness, phonics, and other decoding skills to develop reading fluency. The National Reading Panel conducted a study (1997–2000) to resolve controversy over phonics vs. whole language as the best teaching method, finding that any effective reading instruction program must teach phonemic awareness, phonics, reading fluency, vocabulary development, and reading comprehension.

The whole language approach is based on constructivist philosophy and psychology: children construct their own knowledge through their interactions with their environments. In contrast to analytical approaches like phonics and alphabetic learning, constructivism views learning as an individual's

Copyright © Mometrix Media. You have been licensed one copy of this document for personal use only. Any other reproduction or redistribution is strictly prohibited. All rights reserved.

unique cognitive experience of acquiring new knowledge, shaped by the individual's existing knowledge and personal perspective. Whole language instruction emphasizes helping children create meaning from their reading and express meaning in their writing. The whole-language philosophy emphasizes cultural diversity, integrating literacy instruction across subject domains, reading high-quality literature, and giving children many opportunities for independent reading, small-group guided reading, and being read to aloud by teachers. Whole language believes children learn to read by writing and vice versa. Realistically purposeful reading and writing are encouraged, as is using texts that motivate children to develop a love for literature. Early grammatical/spelling/technical correctness is not stressed, which can be problematic for children with reading/language processing disorders, who need explicit instruction in decoding skills and strategies.

ADDRESSING EARLY MECHANICAL ERRORS IN LEARNING READING AND WRITING

The basal reader is America's commonest approach, used in an estimated 75–85 percent of K–8th-grade classrooms. The number of publishers offering basal reading series has decreased to about one-fourth of that in the 20th century, decreasing teacher responsibility for investigating/piloting readers for district approval. Using basal readers is a skills-based/bottom-up approach. Teaching smaller-to-larger reading subskills in systematic, rigid sequence assists students' transition from part to whole. Texts graded by reading level contain narration and exposition organized thematically by unit, including children's literature and diverse other genres. Phonics and other specific instructional strands with practice assignments develop skills, which are assessed with end-of-unit tests. For young children, text decoding is enabled through exact control of vocabulary items and word analysis skills, "big [enlarged] books," and word and picture cards. 20th-century and older series sacrificed comprehension and enjoyment for vocabulary control and skill acquisition, but 21st-century series vary methods more (like multiple story versions or book excerpts enabling selection sharing), affording children more motivation to read.

DIRECTED READING ACTIVITY (DRA) AND THE DIRECTED READING-THINKING ACTIVITY (DR-TA)

Using basal readers, the DRA comprises:

1. The teacher prepares children for reading by stimulating their motivation and introducing new concepts and/or vocabulary.
2. Students read silently, guided by teacher questions and statements.
3. The teacher develops student comprehension and students discuss characters, plots, or concepts to further comprehension.
4. After silent reading, students read aloud and read answers to teacher questions, known as "purposeful rereading."
5. Students' follow-up workbook activities/practice review comprehension and vocabulary.

Some selections may include enrichment activities relating them to writing, art, drama, or music. The DR-TA approach is designed to develop critical readers through instruction in group comprehension. It requires children's active engagement in reading by processing information, asking questions, and receiving feedback as they read. The first phase of DR-TA is the teacher's direction of student thought processes throughout reading. The second phase involves developing student skills according to their needs as identified in phase 1, and additional extension or follow-up activities.

Copyright © Mometrix Media. You have been licensed one copy of this document for personal use only. Any other reproduction or redistribution is strictly prohibited. All rights reserved.

DIFFERENCES BETWEEN DRA AND DR-TA APPROACHES

- One main difference is that the DR-TA approach gives teachers all the responsibility and greater flexibility for developing lessons. As such it contains fewer directions than the DRA approach, which contains specific materials and questions to use, specific guidelines, and is more teacher-manual-oriented and materials-oriented. Therefore DR-TA can be used for not only basal readers, but also planning lessons in other curriculum areas involving reading; the DRA approach applies more directly to basal reader programs.
- DRA manuals use mostly literal, factual questions, requiring only convergent thinking for student responses. However, in DR-TA, questions also demand divergent (creative) thinking of students, stimulating higher-level reading comprehension and interpretation.
- New vocabulary is pretaught in the DRA approach before children read. The DR-TA approach excludes preteaching, realistically requiring student decoding of new vocabulary words during reading.
- DRA manuals specify when to teach which skills for reading comprehension. DR-TA approaches do not, requiring more questioning expertise and acceptance of some alternative student responses by teachers.

Copyright © Mometrix Media. You have been licensed one copy of this document for personal use only. Any other reproduction or redistribution is strictly prohibited. All rights reserved.

Factors Influencing Development

EFFECT OF MATURATIONAL FACTORS ON THE DEVELOPMENT AND LEARNING

Many physiological factors affect the development of babies and young children. These dictate which kinds of learning activities are appropriate or ineffective for certain ages. For example, providing a newborn with visual stimuli from several feet away is wasted, as newborns cannot yet focus on distant objects. Adults cannot expect infants younger than about 5 months to sit up unsupported, as they have not yet developed the strength for it. Adults cannot expect toddlers who have not yet attained stable walking gaits to hop or balance upon one foot successfully. It is not coincidental that first grade begins at around 6 years: younger children cannot physically sit still for long periods and have not developed long enough attention spans to prevent distraction. This is also why kindergarten classes feature varieties of shorter term activities and more physical movement. Younger children also have not yet developed the self-regulation to keep from shouting out on impulse, getting up and running around, etc.—behaviors disruptive to formal schooling but developmentally normal.

NUTRITIONAL FACTORS IN DIET AFFECTING EARLY CHILDHOOD DEVELOPMENT

Babies are typically nourished via mother's milk or infant formula, and then with baby food; however, young children mostly eat the same foods as adults by the age of 2 years. Though they eat smaller quantities, young children have similar nutritional needs to those of adults. Calcium can be more important in early childhood to support the rapid bone growth occurring during this period; young children should receive 2–3 servings of dairy products and/or other calcium-rich foods. For all ages, whole-grain foods are nutritionally superior for their fiber and nutrients than refined flours, which have had these removed. Refined flours provide "empty calories" causing wider blood-sugar fluctuations and insulin resistance—Type 2 diabetes risks—than whole grains, which stabilize blood sugar and offer more naturally occurring vitamins and minerals. Darkly and brightly colored produce are most nutritious. Adults should cut foods into small, bite-sized pieces to prevent choking in young children, who have not yet perfected their biting, chewing, and swallowing skills.

CONSIDERATIONS FOR EARLY CHILDHOOD NUTRITION

Raw or lightly steamed vegetables are best because excess heat destroys nutrients and frying adds fat calories. Fresh, in-season and flash-frozen fruits are more nutritious/less processed than canned. Adults should monitor young children's diets to limit highly processed produce, which can have excessive sugar, salt, or preservatives. Good protein sources include legumes, nuts, lean poultry, and fish. Adults should take care with young children to avoid choking hazards by cutting foods into bite-sized pieces. Serving nut butters instead of whole nuts is safer, but spread thinly on whole-grain breads/crackers or vegetable pieces, because young children can choke on large globs of nut butter as well. Omega-3 fatty acids from salmon, mackerel, herring, flaxseeds, and walnuts control inflammation, prevent heart arrhythmias, and lower blood pressure. Monounsaturated fats from avocados, olives, peanuts, their oils, and canola oil prevent heart disease, lower bad cholesterol, and raise good cholesterol. Polyunsaturated fats from nuts, seeds, and corn, soy, sesame, sunflower, and safflower oils lower cholesterol. These fats/oils should be served in moderation, avoiding saturated fats.

CONSIDERATIONS FOR FEEDING YOUNG CHILDREN

Saturated fats from meats and full-fat dairy should be limited; they can cause health problems like high cholesterol, cardiovascular disease, obesity, and diabetes. Trans fats are produced chemically by hydrogenating normally liquid unsaturated fats and converting them to solid, saturated fats as in margarine and shortening used in many baked goods. These are considered even unhealthier than regular saturated fats and should be avoided. (The words "partially hydrogenated" in the ingredients signal trans fats.) Infants derive enough water from mother's milk/formula, but young children should be given plenty of water and/or milk in "sippy cups" to stay hydrated. The common practice of giving young children fruit juice should be avoided. Even without added sugars, fruit juices crowd out room in

43

Copyright © Mometrix Media. You have been licensed one copy of this document for personal use only. Any other reproduction or redistribution is strictly prohibited. All rights reserved.

small stomachs for food nutrients and cause dental cavities and weaken permanent teeth before they erupt. Children can also gain weight, as juice calories do not replace food calories the way actual fruit does with its fiber and solids. Young children should eat two-thirds of adult-sized portions.

CHARACTERISTICS OF YOUNG CHILDREN'S NUTRITIONAL NEEDS

Young children have smaller stomachs than adults and cannot eat as much at one time as teens or adults. However, it is common practice for today's restaurants to provide oversized portions. The historical tradition of encouraging young children to "clean their plates" is ill-advised considering these excessive portions and the abundance of food in America today. Adults can help young children by teaching them instead to respond to their own bodies' signals and eat only until they are satisfied. Adults can also place smaller portions of food on young children's plates and request to-go containers at restaurants to take leftovers home. Because young children cannot eat a lot at once, they must maintain their blood sugar and energy throughout the day by snacking between meals. However, "snack foods" need not be high in sugar, salt, and unhealthy fats. Cut pieces of fresh fruits and vegetables, whole-grain crackers and low-fat cheeses, and portable yogurt tubes make good snacks for young children.

FEEDING STRATEGIES SUPPORTING DEVELOPMENT OF NUTRITIOUS EATING HABITS AND ATTITUDES

Early childhood is an age range often associated with "finicky" eaters. Adults can experiment by substituting different foods that are similar sources of protein or other nutrients to foods young children dislike. Preparing meals to look like happy faces, animals, or have appealing designs can entice young children to eat varied foods. Engaging children age-appropriately in selecting and preparing meals with supervision can also motivate them to consume foods when they have participated in their preparation. Adults should model healthy eating habits for young children, who imitate admired adults' behaviors. Early childhood is when children form basic food-related attitudes and habits and so is an important time for influencing these. Children are exposed to unhealthy foods in advertising, at school, in restaurants, and with friends, so adult modeling and guidance regarding healthy choices are important to counteract these influences. However, adults should also impart the message early that no foods are "bad"/forbidden, allowing some occasional indulgences in small amounts, to prevent the development of eating disorders.

RELATIONSHIP OF SLEEP QUALITY TO BLOOD SUGAR CONTROL IN CHILDREN WITH TYPE 1 DIABETES

Researchers find blood sugar stability problematic for many children with Type 1 (juvenile) diabetes, despite all efforts by parents and children to follow diabetic health care rules, because of sleep differences. Diabetic children spend more time in lighter than deeper stages of sleep compared to nondiabetic children. This results in higher levels of blood sugar and poorer school performance. Lighter sleep and resulting daytime sleepiness tend to increase blood sugar levels. Sleep apnea is a sleep disorder that causes a person's breathing to be interrupted often during sleeping. These breathing interruptions result in poorer sleep quality, fatigue, and daytime sleepiness. Sleep apnea has previously been associated with Type 2 diabetes—historically adult-onset, though now children are developing it, too. It is now known that apnea is also associated with Type 1 diabetes in children: roughly one-third of diabetic children studied have sleep apnea, regardless of their weight (being overweight can contribute to apnea). Sleep apnea is additionally associated with much higher blood sugars in diabetic children.

GENERAL SLEEP NEEDS AND BEHAVIORS OF YOUNG CHILDREN

Sleep allows the body to become repaired and recharged for the day and is vital for young children's growth and development. Children aged 2–5 years generally need 10–12 hours of sleep daily. Children 5–7 years old typically need 9–11 hours of sleep. Their sleep schedules should be fairly regular. While occasionally staying up later or missing naps for special events is not serious, overall inconsistent/disorganized schedules cause lost sleep and lethargic and/or cranky children. Some young children sleep fewer hours at night but need long daytime naps, while others need longer, uninterrupted

Copyright © Mometrix Media. You have been licensed one copy of this document for personal use only. Any other reproduction or redistribution is strictly prohibited. All rights reserved.

nighttime sleep but seldom nap. Young children are busy exploring and discovering new things; they have a lot of energy and are often excited even when tired. Because they have not developed much self-regulation, they need adult guidance to calm down enough to go to sleep and will often resist bedtimes. Adults should plan bedtime routines. These can vary, but their most important aspect is consistency. Children then expect routines' familiar steps, and anticipating these comfort them.

Components and Characteristics of Good Bedtime Routines

Bedtime routines serve as transitions from young children's exciting, adventurous daytime activities to the tranquility needed for healthful rest. Adults should begin routines by establishing and enforcing a rule that daytime activities like rough-and-tumble physical play or TV watching stop at a specific time. While preschoolers may be less interested in computer/video games than older children, establishing limits early will help parents enforce stopping these activities at bedtime when they are older, too. Bath time is one good way to begin bedtime routines. Toys and games make baths fun, and bath washes with lavender and other soothing ingredients are now available to relax young children. Also, since young children eat smaller meals, healthy bedtime snacks are important. Too much/too little food will disrupt sleep, and too much liquid can cause bedwetting. Adults should plan nighttime snacks appropriately for the individual child. Bedtime reading promotes interest in books and learning, adult-child/family bonding, and calms children. Singing lullabies, hugging, and cuddling also support bonding, relax children, and make them feel safe and secure.

Helping Young Children Transition from Cribs to Regular Beds

One of young children's significant transitions from infancy is moving from a crib to a "big bed." Some become very motivated to escape cribs. For example, some bright, adventurous toddlers and even babies have untied padded crib bumpers, stacked them, and climbed out of the crib. For such children, injury is a greater danger from a crib than a bed. Others, whose cognitive and verbal skills are more developed than motor skills, may stand/jump up and down, repeatedly calling, "Hey, I'm up!" until a parent comes. These children should be moved to regular beds, with guardrails and/or body pillows to prevent rolling/falling-out accidents. If a child is moved to a bed to free the crib for a new baby, this should be done weeks ahead of the infant's arrival if possible, to separate these two significant life events. Most young children are excited about "grown-up" beds. Some, if hesitant, can sleep in the crib and nap in the bed for a gradual transition until ready for the bed full-time.

Considerations in Children's Bedrooms and Family Beds

The majority of early childhood experts think young children should not have adults in their rooms every night while they fall asleep. They believe this can interfere with young children's capacity for "self-soothing" and falling asleep on their own, making them dependent on an adult presence to fall asleep. Parents/caregivers are advised to help children relax until sleepy, and then leave, saying "Good night" and "I love you." Young children frequently feel more comfortable going to bed with a favorite blanket or stuffed animal and/or a night light. Regardless, fears and nightmares are still fairly common in early childhood. "Family beds," i.e. children sleeping in the same bed or adjacent beds with parents, are subject to controversy. However, this is traditional in many developing countries and was historically so in America. Whatever the individual family choice, it should be consistent as young children will be frustrated by inconsistent practices and less likely to develop good sleeping habits.

Hygiene in Early Childhood
Importance of Hand-Washing

A major change during early childhood is that hygiene transforms from something adults do for children to something children learn to do themselves. Toddlers are typically learning toilet-training, getting many germs on their hands. Preschoolers today are also often exposed to germs in daycare or school settings. Adults must explain to young children using concrete, easily understood terms how germs spread; how hand-washing removes germs; and when and how to wash their hands. Adults also need to

Copyright © Mometrix Media. You have been licensed one copy of this document for personal use only. Any other reproduction or redistribution is strictly prohibited. All rights reserved.

remind children frequently to wash their hands until it becomes a habit. Remind them hand-washing is required before eating, after toileting, after being outdoors, after sneezing/coughing, and after playing with pets. Because young children have short attention spans and can be impatient, they are unlikely to wash long or thoroughly enough. Adults can encourage this by teaching children to sing "Happy Birthday" or other 15- to 20-second songs/verses while washing, both assuring optimal hand-washing duration and making the process more fun.

BATHING

While infants are bathed by adults, by the time they are toddlers or preschoolers, they generally have learned to sit in a bathtub and wash themselves. However, regardless of their ability to bathe, young children should never be left unsupervised by adults in the bath. Young children can drown very quickly, even in an inch of water; an adult should always be in the bathroom. Also, adults should not let young children run bathwater: they are likely to make it too cold or hot. Adults can prevent scalding accidents by turning down the water heater temperature. The adult should adjust water temperature and test it on his/her own inner arm (an area with more sensitive skin). Parents/caregivers should choose baby shampoos, soaps, and washes that do not irritate young eyes or skin, and keep adult bath products out of children's reach and sight. Very active children may need to bathe daily; others suffering dry, itchy skin should bathe every other day and/or have parents/caregivers apply mild moisturizing lotion.

PROMOTING AND TEACHING DENTAL HYGIENE

Even while young children still have their deciduous/"baby" teeth, dental hygiene practices can affect their permanent/adult teeth before they erupt. For example, excessive sugar can weaken adult teeth before they even appear above the gumline. Adults should not only teach young children how important it is to brush their teeth twice and floss once daily at a minimum; moreover, they should model these behaviors. Children are far more likely to imitate parents' dental hygiene practices than do what parents only tell them but do not do themselves. Integrating tooth brushing into morning and bedtime routines promotes the habit. Adults can help motivate resistant children with entertaining toothbrushes that play music, spin, light up, and/or have cartoon illustrations. Young children have not developed the fine motor skills sufficient for flossing independently and will need adult supervision until they are older. Individual flossers are easier for them to use with help than traditional string dental floss.

EXERCISE BENEFITS FOR YOUNG CHILDREN

Young children need daily physical exercise to strengthen their bones, lungs, hearts, and other muscles. Throwing, catching, running, jumping, kicking, and swinging actions develop young children's gross motor skills. Children sleep better with regular physical activity and are at less risk for obesity. Playing actively with other children also develops social skills, including empathy, sharing, cooperation, and communication. Family playtimes strengthen bonding and let parents model positive exercise habits. Outdoor play is fun for youngsters; running and laughing lift children's moods. Pride at physical attainments moreover boosts children's self-images and self-esteem. At least 60 minutes of physical activity most days is recommended for children. This includes jungle gyms, slides, swings, and other playground equipment; family walks, bike-riding, playing backyard catch, baseball, football, or basketball; adult-supervised races or obstacle courses; and age-appropriate community sports activities/leagues. Adults should plan and supervise activities to prevent injuries. They should also provide repeated sunscreen applications for outdoor activities to prevent sunburn and long-term skin damage.

EXPOSURE TO TV/OTHER MEDIA AND OPTIMAL ENVIRONMENTAL CONDITIONS FOR LEISURE ACTIVITIES

Preschool-aged children are not yet cognitively able to distinguish between reality and fantasy. Therefore, overly violent or intense content in TV or other media can frighten them. Additionally, exposure to video violence has been proven to increase aggressive behaviors in young children. Moreover, using TV as a babysitter for long times excludes more cognitively stimulating and interactive

Copyright © Mometrix Media. You have been licensed one copy of this document for personal use only. Any other reproduction or redistribution is strictly prohibited. All rights reserved.

pursuits. Parents/caregivers can provide young children with paints, crayons, and modeling clay. They can play board games and simple card games, do puzzles, sing songs, and read stories with young children. Pretend/make-believe play develops during early childhood, so adults can encourage their playing "house," "dress-up," or "auto shop." Park/playground trips afford outdoor play and physical activity/exercise. Visiting local museums, zoos, or planetariums combine education and entertainment with outings. In multiple-child families, it is important for each child to get some one on one time with parents regularly, even in unstructured activities like going to the hardware store with Daddy or keeping Mommy company while she washes dishes.

DISADVANTAGES/ADVANTAGES AND RISK/PROTECTIVE FACTORS IN ECONOMICALLY DEPRIVED AND CULTURALLY DIVERSE ENVIRONMENTS

Historically, disadvantages of poverty have been the focus of research; e.g. lack of toys, inadequate verbal interactions limiting visual discrimination and linguistic development or risk factors like less education, poorer nutrition, family stressors, medical illness, inadequate social stimulation, and insufficient social-service support leading to school dropouts, delinquency, unemployment, and perpetuated poverty. However, more recent research also identifies poverty's advantages, including opportunities for young children to play with peers and older children with little adult intervention, promoting empathy, cooperation, self-control, self-reliance, and sense of belonging; experience with multiple teaching styles, especially modeling, observation, and imitation; and language acquisition within a culturally-specific context through rich cultural traditions of stories, songs, games, and toys. These findings illuminate the resiliency or stress resistance of some children. Recent research also identifies protective factors against risk factors. These protections contribute to child resiliency, including the child's personality traits; having stable, supportive, cohesive family units; and having external support systems promoting positive values and coping skills.

INFLUENCE OF CULTURES AND CULTURAL VALUES ON EARLY CHILDHOOD DEVELOPMENT

The culture in a society influences, even determines, our individual values, as do both historical and current social and political occurrences. Our values then influence the ways in which children are valued and raised. As American educators, we can understand the "American" perspective on early childhood better through understanding cultural diversity. We tend to fixate on our own culture's beliefs of truth as the only existing reality, but depending on our personal histories and values and current conditions, there can actually be multiple right ways of doing things. For example, Western cultures value children's early attainment of independence and individuality, but Eastern cultures value interdependence and group harmony more than individualism. In affluent societies, letting children explore the environment early and freely is valued, but in poor and/or developing societies, parents protect children, keeping them close and even carrying them while working, and thus do not value early freedom and exploration.

EFFECT OF AGE, ETHNICITY, AND INCOME ON HEALTH AND SCHOOL OUTCOMES

Research traces many variations in well-being and health to early childhood. These differences come from inequities in service access and treatment, congenital health problems, and early exposure to greater familial and community risk factors. Child groups at risk that are overrepresented in our population include young children, low-income children, and minority children. More young children than older children are likely to live in economically disadvantaged families. As of 2005, more than 10 million children aged 0–5 years lived in the U.S. 20 percent of these were in families classified as poor, i.e. with income below the federal poverty level (FPL), and 42 percent were in families designated low-income, i.e. with income below double the FPL. Of more than 2 million American children aged 0–5 living in families identified as extremely poor, i.e. with income less than half the FPL, minority groups were also overrepresented. The younger the children are, the greater the adverse effects of poverty are on their developmental outcomes.

Copyright © Mometrix Media. You have been licensed one copy of this document for personal use only. Any other reproduction or redistribution is strictly prohibited. All rights reserved.

ENVIRONMENT, SOCIAL AND EMOTIONAL SUPPORT, SELF-IMAGE, AND SUCCESS

Researchers have recently found that a child's sense of self is significant in predicting success in life. Even when a child's family environment involves multiple stressors, having a good relationship with one parent mitigates a child's psychosocial risks. As a child grows older, a close, supportive, lasting relationship with an adult outside the family can confer similar protection. Such relationships promote self-esteem in a child. Children with positive self-esteem are more able to develop feelings of control, mastery, and self-efficacy to achieve tasks, and they are more able to manage stressful life experiences. Such children demonstrate more initiative in forming relationships and accomplishing tasks. They reciprocally derive more positive experiences from their environments. Children with positive self-concepts pursue, develop, and sustain experiences and relationships that support success. Their positive self-images are further enhanced by these successes, generating additional supportive relationships and experiences. While we often hear about negative cycles of poverty, abuse, or failure, positive cycles of success can be equally as self-perpetuating.

INDIVIDUALISTIC VERSUS COLLECTIVISTIC CULTURES

Anthropologists have classified various world cultures along a continuum of how individualistic or interdependent their structures and values are. Investigating these differences is found to afford much insight and application for early childhood education. The predominant culture in America is considered very individualistic. Children are encouraged to assert themselves and make their own choices to realize their highest potentials, with the ultimate goal of individual self-fulfillment. Collectivistic/sociocentric cultures, however, place the highest importance on group well-being; if collective harmony is disrupted by individual assertiveness, such self-assertion is devalued. Some educators characterize this contrast as the difference between standing out (individualist) and fitting in (collectivist). Researchers note that when asked to finish "I am..." statements, members of interdependent cultures tend to supply a family role, religion, or organization (e.g. "a father/a Buddhist"); whereas members of individualistic cultures cite personal qualities (e.g. "intelligent/hardworking"). Research finds American culture most individualistic, Latin American and Asian cultures most interdependent, and European cultures in the middle.

HEALTH RISKS AND RESULTS RELATED TO RACIAL AND ETHNIC ORIGINS

Children are at higher risk for inadequate development when they are born prematurely or with low birth weights. Recent research found racial and ethnic disparities in these birth conditions. For example, rates of low birth weights in 2004 were almost double for African-Americans as for whites (13.4 percent versus 7.1 percent). Latinos had similar but slightly lower risk than whites for low birth weight (6.9 percent versus 7.1 percent). Native American/Alaska Natives had slightly higher risk than white (7.5 percent versus 7.1 percent), as did Asian/Pacific Islanders (7.9 percent versus 7.1 percent). In oral health, 28 percent of preschoolers have had tooth decay. Moreover, data show that in children aged 2–5 years, oral disease increased 15.2 percent from 1994–2002, equaling 600,000 more children. It was found 13.9 percent of children aged 2–5 years were overweight or obese. Risk for overweight/obesity is higher for low-income and minority children. These groups are also at higher risk for poorer quality and continuity in asthma treatment. Asthma's prevalence as well as asthma-related morbidity and deaths are higher in African-American children than white children.

48

Copyright © Mometrix Media. You have been licensed one copy of this document for personal use only. Any other reproduction or redistribution is strictly prohibited. All rights reserved.

Behavior Management

AGGRESSION

Preschoolers typically demonstrate some aggressive behavior, which tends to peak around age 4. Instrumental Aggression is one basic type: younger preschoolers frequently shout, hit, or kick others to get concrete objects they want. Middle preschoolers are more likely to exhibit Hostile Aggression, i.e. getting even for wrongs or injuries they feel others have done to them. Hostile Aggression occurs in two subtypes: Overt and Relational. Overt Aggression involves physically harming others or threatening to do so, while Relational Aggression involves emotional/social harm, e.g. rejecting/excluding another from a group of friends or spreading malicious rumors about another. Young boys are more likely to engage in Overt Aggression, while young girls are more likely to engage in Relational Aggression. These gender preferences in aggressive behaviors tend to remain the same at all ages if aggression exists. While most young children eventually phase out aggression as they learn other ways of resolving social conflicts, some persist in verbally and/or physically aggressive behavior, causing problems.

MINIMIZING AGGRESSIVE BEHAVIOR

While it is normal for preschoolers to exhibit some physical and verbal aggression until they have learned more mature ways of expressing feelings, getting what they want, and settling disputes, there are things adults can do to influence them such that aggressive behavior does not develop into a predominant method of social interaction. Adults set examples for children, and children learn by observing and imitating those examples. Therefore, parents, caregivers, and teachers should not model verbally and/or physically aggressive behaviors such as calling others names, yelling at others, or punishing others' undesirable behaviors using physical force. Not only should adults avoid disciplining children physically, they should also avoid physically and/or verbally violent interactions with other adults. Social learning theorist Albert Bandura proved that children who viewed violent videos imitated what they observed and engaged in more aggressive behavior, so adults should also prevent young children's exposure to violent TV programming and video games.

PREJUDICE AND DISCRIMINATION

Prejudice literally means prejudging, i.e. judging someone/something negatively before/without knowing anything about who/what one is judging. Prejudice gives rise to discrimination in that prejudiced ideas motivate unfair, i.e. discriminatory, behaviors toward others. Psychologist Albert Bandura, who developed social learning theory, identified the process whereby children acquire attitudes and behaviors they observe in others, which he named vicarious learning. Children commonly pick up beliefs, attitudes, and behaviors from adults around them, without applying any critical thinking to these. They are often not even aware of the attitudes and beliefs they assume in this way. Thus, they will engage in prejudicial attitudes and discriminatory behaviors without thinking through what they are doing. Though such behavior is not justified, children simply assume it is because of adults' examples. Thus, adults must carefully inspect their own beliefs and attitudes, as well as what they do and say, because these are what children will imitate.

PREJUDICIAL THINKING

Prejudicial thinking about certain groups of people is uninformed and/or misinformed thinking. It is typically based on fear of the unknown due to lack of knowledge and/or fear due to erroneous beliefs about people. Thus, the best way to dispel prejudice is to provide information where there was none and/or to correct wrong information. When unfamiliar groups become more familiar and when wrong assumptions are corrected, people's misconceptions are replaced by reality and they become less afraid. For example, children having no experience with people from other racial, ethnic, or socioeconomic groups are likely to fear these people (as are many adults). Adults can help young children by furnishing them with many opportunities—not just isolated ones—to interact with people from diverse cultural and socioeconomic milieus. For children to experience true learning, which will supersede negative,

49

Copyright © Mometrix Media. You have been licensed one copy of this document for personal use only. Any other reproduction or redistribution is strictly prohibited. All rights reserved.

uninformed first impressions, they must have multiple such social opportunities. School, outside classes, sports, and camp are activities affording such opportunities.

BULLYING

Children who are bullied by others are victims of prejudicial thinking and discriminatory actions. Common negative effects of bullying include rage, feelings of hopelessness, anxiety, and depression. Left untreated, children with these feelings can develop suicidal ideations and actions as they grow older if bullying persists. When young, children have the additional problem of not yet knowing how to manage their negative feelings caused by others' aggression or even how to express them. Adults can give them much-needed help by assisting them in articulating their emotions openly but nonviolently. Adults must realize that young children, especially those who have experienced others' violent treatment, may not recognize that anger can be expressed in any ways other than violent ones. Based on their experience, children may internalize assumptions that they can only act out their anger through self-destructive behaviors. When adults consistently model positive, proactive ways of discussing negative emotions, children observe that more constructive behaviors are possible and learn to adopt these as more effective coping strategies.

SEX/GENDER-ROLE DEVELOPMENT

Various theories of development, such as psychoanalytic, behaviorist, cognitive, and social learning, have differing views of why and how children develop sexual/gender identities. To address these differences, psychologists have endeavored to produce some general conclusions about young children's self-concepts of gender. They find that during preschool ages, children gradually develop concepts of what being a girl or a boy in their culture means. These concepts become clearly articulated and shape their behaviors. Between the ages of 2 and 6, children are in the process of putting together the pieces of these gender concepts. Developing sex-appropriate behaviors and developing categories of gender roles both appear to be influenced by a combination and interaction of biological and sociological variables. Psychologists additionally conclude that children perform some mental matching process enabling them to isolate features they share in common with others, and that young children's abilities to observe, imitate, and categorize influence their later concepts of sex-appropriate behaviors. By ages 5–6, most children clearly identify with one sex or the other.

COMBATING CULTURAL STEREOTYPES AND DISCRIMINATION

When children experience stereotyping of and discrimination against their cultural group, adults can counter these negative reflections on the group by correcting erroneous opinions they have heard. By giving children plenty of examples of positive accomplishments by members of their group, they convey cultural pride, affording children a sense of empowerment. Adults should consistently model positive, constructive, and no-violent methods of addressing prejudice for children. If prejudice proves ongoing, caregivers and teachers must assertively advocate on behalf of children and their cultures to shut down prejudicial sources. If they hear young children furthering cultural stereotypes they have absorbed, adults should immediately correct their statements and behaviors, explaining why certain words and actions harm others and are unacceptable. Extended discussions with young children are important for putting prejudice into perspective and context to help them understand it. Adults can also apply behavioral methods, such as associating prejudicial behaviors with consequences (e.g. losing a privilege or gaining work) and providing related learning activities to prevent repeated instances.

USING HISTORICAL CONTEXTS, CORRECTION, AND REAL-LIFE EXAMPLES TO ADDRESS PREJUDICIAL ATTITUDES

Because many prejudicial attitudes exist in our society on both individualized and institutionalized levels, it is all too easy for children to absorb and emulate them. When children who have been victims of prejudice learn they were attacked not as individuals, but members of a group, this does not eliminate negative effects, but can help them see it in a different perspective. Adults can place prejudice and discrimination in their historical contexts so children realize they are not lone victims but part of a

Copyright © Mometrix Media. You have been licensed one copy of this document for personal use only. Any other reproduction or redistribution is strictly prohibited. All rights reserved.

larger group. Correcting false beliefs, as in Albert Ellis's Rational-Emotive Behavior Therapy and other forms of cognitive-behavioral therapy, can be applied by adults' pointing out the irrational, flawed thinking involved and supplying examples contradicting that thinking. For example, if children have been influenced to think certain groups are less intelligent or lazier than others, adults can show them examples of many members of those groups with outstanding achievements in society. They can do this through book/video biographies, personal anecdotes, and introductions to living people.

GENETIC AND ENVIRONMENTAL INFLUENCES ON BEHAVIOR

Genetic and environmental influence a young child's risk of displaying antisocial behaviors. Research into factors influencing early childhood behavior identifies both genetic variables and environmental ones, like corporal punishment, affecting young children's propensities toward antisocial behavior. Children experiencing more corporal punishment display greater behavior problems; children at greater genetic risk also do. However, boys at higher genetic risk for behavior problems who also experience more corporal punishment exhibit the most antisocial behavior. Therefore, both genetic risk factors and corporal punishment significantly predict preschoolers' antisocial behavior. Additionally, the nature-nurture interaction of genetic risk factors and environmental punishment is statistically significant for young boys but not young girls. Such evidence shows that environmental learning is not wholly responsible for antisocial behavior: genetic variables predispose some young children to antisocial behaviors more than others.

BEHAVIORIST LEARNING THEORIES

Ivan Pavlov's experiments with dogs proved that when a stimulus evoking a reflexive response—drooling at the taste of meat—was repeatedly paired with an unrelated/"neutral" stimulus—a bell ringing—dogs came to associate the unrelated stimulus with the original response and drooled on hearing the bell without tasting meat. This proved generalizable to humans. Edward L. Thorndike's experiments with cats also applied to humans. Thorndike introduced the Law of Effect: we are more likely to repeat behaviors receiving desirable consequences. This set the stage for B. F. Skinner's later work. John B. Watson maintained that because inner states cannot be observed or measured, only observable outer behaviors should be used in psychology and learning. Skinner experimented with operant conditioning, wherein behaviors are trained and shaped through manipulating their antecedents/preceding stimuli and consequences/following stimuli. He expanded behaviorism into a comprehensive theory, including detailed rules for teaching new behaviors and modifying behavior (behavior modification).

POSITIVE AND NEGATIVE REINFORCEMENT AND POSITIVE AND NEGATIVE PUNISHMENT

In behaviorism, reinforcement means strengthening the probability a behavior will be repeated. Skinner used the terms positive vs. negative to mean introducing vs. removing, not good vs. bad. Therefore, positive reinforcement is introducing something rewarding immediately after a behavior. When a child's behavior is rewarded, s/he will repeat it to obtain repeated rewards: Johnny gets a treat or praise for putting away his toys; he will do it again. Negative reinforcement is rewarding by removing something unwanted: Johnny dislikes noisy crowds at preschool. One day he wakes up earlier, is taken to preschool earlier, finds it quieter and less crowded; he will want to get up and arrive earlier again. Positive punishment is introducing an aversive consequence for a behavior: Johnny refuses to put toys away; his parents then make him clean up the entire room; he is less likely to repeat the refusal. Negative punishment is removing a desirable stimulus: Johnny refuses to put away toys; his parents prohibit watching TV; he is less likely to keep refusing.

Behavioral techniques include positive reinforcement, introducing rewarding stimuli for emitting desired behaviors; negative reinforcement, removing unwanted stimuli for emitting desired behaviors; positive punishment, introducing aversive stimuli for unwanted behaviors; and negative punishment, removing desired stimuli for unwanted behaviors. Research has found positive reinforcement the most powerful of all these. One reason is that people are highly motivated by rewards. Another is that all

51

Copyright © Mometrix Media. You have been licensed one copy of this document for personal use only. Any other reproduction or redistribution is strictly prohibited. All rights reserved.

behaviors meet needs; punishment suppresses certain behaviors, but then other behaviors must emerge to fill the same need. If a child misbehaves to get attention, even scolding/other punishment can constitute attention. But if rewarded for more appropriate behavior to get attention, like asking an available adult or peer for interaction, the child meets the attention need while replacing a maladaptive behavior with an adaptive one. Another reason is punishment's limitations: preschoolers may stop misbehaving after one teacher's punishment, but not with another teacher; punishment not applied consistently loses its effect. Also, punishment can cause resentment, anger, defiance, or fearfulness in young children.

Copyright © Mometrix Media. You have been licensed one copy of this document for personal use only. Any other reproduction or redistribution is strictly prohibited. All rights reserved.

Developmentally Appropriate Learning Environment

LEV VYGOTSKY AND THE ZONE OF PROXIMAL DEVELOPMENT

Vygotsky identified an area or range of skills wherein a learner can complete a task s/he could not yet complete independently, given some help. He termed this area the Zone of Proximal Development. Vygotsky found if a child is given assistance, guidance, or support from someone who knows more—especially another child just slightly more advanced in knowledge and/or skills—the first child can not only succeed at a task s/he is still unable to do alone; but that child also learns best through accomplishing something just slightly beyond his/her limits of expertise to do alone. Jerome Bruner coined the term "scaffolding" to describe temporary support that others give learners for achieving tasks. Scaffolding is closely related to the ZPD in that only the amount of support needed is given, and it allows the learner to accomplish things s/he could not complete autonomously. Scaffolding is gradually withdrawn as the child's skills develop, until the child reaches the level of expertise needed to complete the task on his/her own.

MONTESSORI METHOD

SECTIONS OF THE MONTESSORI METHOD OF EARLY CHILDHOOD INSTRUCTION

The Practical Life area of Montessori classes helps children develop care for self, others, and the environment. Children learn many daily skills, including buttoning, pouring liquids, preparing meals, and cleaning up after meals and activities. The Sensorial area gives young children experience with learning through all five senses. They participate in activities like ordering colors from lightest to darkest; sorting objects from roughest to smoothest texture; and sorting items from biggest to smallest/longest to shortest. They learn to match similar tastes, textures, and sounds. The Language Arts area encourages young children to express themselves in words, and they learn to identify letters, match them with corresponding phonemes (speech sounds), and manually trace their shapes as preparation for learning reading, spelling, grammar, and writing. In the Mathematics and Geometry area, children learn to recognize numbers, count, add, subtract, multiply, divide, and use the decimal system via hands-on learning with concrete materials. In the Cultural Subjects area, children learn science, art, music, movement, time, history, geography, and zoology.

ASPECTS OF THE PHILOSOPHY OF THE MONTESSORI METHOD AS A CURRICULUM APPROACH

Maria Montessori's method emphasizes children's engagement in self-directed activities, with teachers using clinical observations to act as children's guides. In introducing and teaching concepts, the Montessori Method also employs self-correcting ("autodidactic") equipment. This method focuses on the significance and interrelatedness of all life forms, and the need for every individual to find his/her place in the world and to find meaningful work. Children in Montessori schools learn complex math skills and gain knowledge about diverse cultures and languages. Montessori philosophy puts emphasis on adapting learning environments to individual children's developmental levels. The Montessori Method also believes in teaching both practical skills and abstract concepts through the medium of physical activities. Montessori teachers observe and identify children's movements into sensitive periods when they are best prepared to receive individual lessons in subjects of interest to them that they can grasp readily. Children's senses of autonomy and self-esteem are encouraged in Montessori programs. Montessori instructors also strive to engage parents in their children's education.

GENERAL PRACTICES IN THE MONTESSORI METHOD

What Montessori calls "work" refers to developmentally appropriate learning materials. These are set out so each student can see the choices available. Children can select items from each of Montessori's five sections: Practical Life, Sensorial, Language Arts, Mathematics and Geometry, and Cultural Subjects. When a child is done with a work, s/he replaces it for another child to use and selects another work. Teachers work one on one with children and in groups; however, the majority of interactions are among children, as Montessori stresses self-directed activity. Not only teachers but also older children help

Copyright © Mometrix Media. You have been licensed one copy of this document for personal use only. Any other reproduction or redistribution is strictly prohibited. All rights reserved.

younger ones in learning new skills, so Montessori classes usually incorporate 2- or 3-year age ranges. Depending on students' ages and the individual school, Montessori schooldays are generally half-days, e.g. 9 a.m.–noon or 12:30 p.m. Most Montessori schools also offer afternoon and/or early evening options. Children wanting to "do it myself" benefit from Montessori, as do special-needs children. Individualized attention, independence, and hands-on learning are emphasized. Montessori schools prefer culturally diverse students and teach about diverse cultures.

SCHEDULES OF REINFORCEMENT IN BEHAVIORISM

Continuous schedules of presenting rewards or punishments are fixed. Fixed ratio schedules involve introducing reinforcement after a set number of instances of the targeted behavior. For example, when asking a preschooler to put away materials, a teacher might present punishment for noncompliance only after making three consecutive requests. The disadvantage is, even young children know they can get away with ignoring the first two requests, only complying just before the third. Fixed interval schedules introduce reinforcement after set time periods. Again, the disadvantages are, even multiply disabled infants quickly learn when to expect reinforcement, rather than associating it with how long they have engaged in a desired behavior; young children only change their behavior immediately before the teacher will observe and reward it. Variable ratio and variable interval schedules apply reinforcement following irregular numbers of responses or irregular time periods, respectively. The advantage of variable schedules is, since children cannot predict when they will receive reinforcements, they are more likely to repeat/continue desired behaviors more and for longer times.

BANK STREET CURRICULUM APPROACH TO EARLY CHILDHOOD EDUCATION

Lucy Sprague Mitchell founded the Bank Street Curriculum, applying theoretical concepts from Jean Piaget, Erik Erikson, John Dewey, and others. Bank Street is called a Developmental Interaction Approach. It emphasizes children's rich, direct interactions with wide varieties of ideas, materials, and people in their environments. The Bank Street method gives young children opportunities for physical, cognitive, emotional, and social development through engagement in various types of child care programs. Typically, multiple subjects are included and taught to groups. Children can learn through a variety of methods and at different developmental levels. By interacting directly with their geographical, social, and political environments, children are prepared for lifelong learning through this curriculum. Using blocks, solving puzzles, going on field trips, and doing practical lab work are among the numerous learning experiences Bank Street offers. Its philosophy is that school can simultaneously be stimulating, satisfying, and sensible. School is a significant part of children's lives, where they inquire about and experiment with the environment and share ideas with other children as they mature.

CLASSROOM CHARACTERISTICS FOR 5- TO 6-YEAR-OLDS

The Bank Street Developmental Interaction Approach to teaching recommends that children at the oldest early childhood ages of 5–6 years should have classrooms that are efficient, organized, conducive to working, and designed to afford them sensory and motor learning experiences. Classrooms should include rich varieties of appealing colors, which tend to energize children's imaginations and activity and encourage them to interact with the surroundings and participate in the environment. "Interest corners" in classrooms are advocated by the Bank Street approach. These are places where children can display their art works, use language, and depict social life experiences. This approach also recommends having multipurpose tables in the classroom that children can use for writing, drawing, and other classroom activities. The Bank Street Developmental Interaction Approach also points out the importance of libraries in schools, not just for supporting classroom content, but for providing materials for children's extracurricular reading.

REQUIREMENTS AND ROLES OF CLASSROOMS AND TEACHERS

The Bank Street Developmental Interaction Approach requires educators to create well-designed classrooms: this curriculum approach finds children are enabled to develop discipline by growing up in such controlled environments. Teachers are considered to be extremely significant figures in their

Copyright © Mometrix Media. You have been licensed one copy of this document for personal use only. Any other reproduction or redistribution is strictly prohibited. All rights reserved.

young students' lives. The Bank Street Approach requires that teachers always treat children with respect, to enable children to develop strong senses of self-respect. Teachers' having faith in their students and believing in their ability to succeed are found to have great impacts on young children's performance and their motivation to excel in school and in life. The Bank Street Curriculum emphasizes the importance of providing transitions from one type of activity to another. It also stresses changing the learning subjects at regular time intervals. This facilitates children's gaining a sense of direction and taking responsibility for what they do. Bank Street views these practices as helping children develop internal self-control, affording them discipline for dealing with the external world.

FROEBEL'S EDUCATIONAL THEORY REGARDING LEARNING AND TEACHING

Froebel, 19th-century inventor of Kindergarten, developed an influential educational theory. He found that observation, discovery, play, and free, self-directed activity facilitated children's learning. He observed that drawing/art activities develop higher level cognitive skills and that virtues are taught through children's games. He also found nature, songs, fables, stories, poems, and crafts effective learning media. He attributed reading and writing development to children's self-expression needs. Froebel recommended activities to develop children's motor skills and stimulate their imaginations. He believed in equal rather than authoritarian teacher-student relationships, and advocated family involvement/collaboration. He pointed out the critical nature of sensory experiences, and the value of life experiences for self-expression. He believed teachers should support students' discovery learning rather than prescribing what to learn. Like Piaget, Dewey, and Montessori, Froebel embraced constructivist learning, i.e. children construct meaning and reality through their interactions with the environment. He stressed the role of parents, particularly mothers, in children's educational processes.

FROEBEL'S FAMOUS ACHIEVEMENT

Friedrich Froebel (1782–1852) invented the original concept and practice of Kindergarten. His theory of education had widespread influences, including using play-based instruction with young children. Froebel's educational theory emphasized the unity of humanity, nature, and God. Froebel believed the success of the individual dictates the success of the race, and that school's role is to direct students' will. He believed nature is the heart of all learning. He felt unity, individuality, and diversity were important values achieved through education. Froebel said education's goals include developing self-control and spirituality. He recommended curricula include math, language, design, art, health, hygiene, and physical education. He noted school's role in social development. According to Froebel, schools should impart meaning to life experiences; show students relationships among external, previously unrelated knowledge; and associate facts with principles. Froebel felt human potential is defined through individual accomplishments. He believed humans generally are productive and creative, attaining completeness and harmony via maturation.

SALIENT ASPECTS REGARDING SOCIETY, EDUCATIONAL OPPORTUNITY, AND CONSENSUS

Friedrich Froebel originated the concept and practice of Kindergarten (German for "child's garden") in 1837. His educational theory had great influence on early childhood education. Froebel's theory addressed society's role in education. He saw education as defined by the "law of divine unity," which stated that everything is connected and humanity, nature, and God are unified. Froebel believed all developments are by God's plan; he found the social institution of religion an important part of children's education. He emphasized parental and sibling involvement in child education. He theorized that culture is changed not by acquiring ideas, but by the productivity, work, and actions of the individual. Froebel believed all children deserve respect and individual attention; should develop their individual potentials; and can learn, irrespective of social class or religion, providing they are developmentally ready for given specific content. Regarding consensus, Froebel's view was religious: he believed God's supreme plan determined social and moral order. He felt people should share common experiences and learn unity, while also respecting diversity and individuality.

Copyright © Mometrix Media. You have been licensed one copy of this document for personal use only. Any other reproduction or redistribution is strictly prohibited. All rights reserved.

SIEGFRIED ENGELMANN'S CONTRIBUTIONS TO EARLY CHILDHOOD EDUCATION

Engelmann (b. 1931) cofounded the Bereiter-Engelmann Program with Carl Bereiter with funding from the U.S. Office of Education. This project demonstrated the ability of intensive instruction to enhance cognitive skills in disadvantaged preschool-aged children, establishing the Bereiter-Engelmann Preschool Program. Bereiter and Engelmann also conducted experiments reexamining Piaget's theory of cognitive development, specifically concerning the ability to conserve liquid volume. They showed, contrary to Piaget's contention that this ability depended solely on a child's cognitive-developmental stage, it could be taught. Engelmann researched curriculum and instruction, including preschoolers with Down syndrome and children from impoverished backgrounds, establishing the philosophy and methodology of Direct Instruction. He designed numerous reading, math, spelling, language, and writing instruction programs, and also achievement tests, videos, and games. Engelmann worked with Project Head Start and Project Follow Through. The former included his and Wesley Becker's comparison of their Engelmann-Becker model of early childhood instruction with other models in teaching disadvantaged children. The latter is often considered the biggest controlled study ever comparing teaching models and methods.

ENGELMANN'S METHODS AND FEATURES OF HIS CURRICULA

In the 1960s, Siegfried Engelmann noted a lack of research into how young children learn. Wanting to find out what kinds of teaching effected retention, and what the extent was of individual differences among young learners, Engelmann conducted research, as Piaget had done, using his own children and those of colleagues and neighbors. With a previous advertising background, Engelmann formed focus groups of preschool children to test-market teaching methods. Main features of the curricula Engelmann developed included emphasizing phonics and computation early in young children's instruction; using a precise logical sequence to teach new skills; teaching new skills in small, separate, "child-sized" pieces; correcting learners' errors immediately; adhering strictly to designated teaching schedules; constantly reviewing to integrate new learning with previously attained knowledge; and scrupulous measurement techniques for assessing skills mastery. To demonstrate the results of his methods for teaching math, Engelmann sent movies he made of these to educational institutions. They showed that with his methods, toddlers could master upper-elementary-grade-level computations, and even simple linear equations.

DIRECT INSTRUCTION METHOD OF TEACHING CHILDREN

Direct Instruction (DI) is a behavioral method of teaching. Therefore, learner errors receive immediate corrective feedback, and correct responses receive immediate, obvious positive reinforcement. DI has a fast pace—10–14 learner responses per minute overall—affording more attention and less boredom; reciprocal teacher-student feedback; immediate indications of learner problems to teachers; and natural reinforcement of teacher activities. DI thus promotes more mutual student and teacher learning than traditional "one-way" methods. Children are instructed in small groups according to ability levels. Their attention is teacher-focused. Teacher presentations follow scripts designed to give instruction the proper sequence, including prewritten prompts and questions developed through field-testing with real students. These optimized prepared lessons allow teachers to attend to extra instructional and motivational aspects of learning. Cued by teachers, who control the pace and give all learners with varying response rates chances for practice, children respond actively in groups and individually. Small groups are typically seated in semicircles close to teachers, who use visual aids like blackboards and overhead projectors.

PROJECT FOLLOW THROUGH

In 1967, President Lyndon B. Johnson declared his War on Poverty. This initiative included Project Follow Through, funded by the U.S. Office of Education and Office of Economic Opportunity. Research had previously found that Project Head Start, which offered early educational interventions to disadvantaged preschoolers, had definite positive impacts; but these were often short-lived. Project Follow Through was intended to discover how to maintain Head Start's benefits. Siegfried Engelmann

Copyright © Mometrix Media. You have been licensed one copy of this document for personal use only. Any other reproduction or redistribution is strictly prohibited. All rights reserved.

and Wesley Becker, who had developed the Engelmann-Becker instructional model, invited others to propose various other teaching models in communities selected to participate in Project Follow Through. The researchers asked parents in each community to choose from among the models provided. The proponents of each model were given funds to train teachers and furnish curriculum. Models found to enhance disadvantaged children's school achievement were to be promoted nationally. Engelmann's Direct Instruction model showed positive results surpassing all other models. However, the U.S. Office of Education did not adopt this or other models found best.

APPROACHES TO REMEDIAL OR COMPENSATORY EDUCATION

A huge comparative study of curriculum and instruction methods, Project Follow Through incorporated three main approaches: Affective, Basic Skills, and Cognitive. Affective approaches used in Project Follow Through included the Bank Street, Responsive Education, and Open Education models. These teaching models aim to enhance school achievement by emphasizing experiences that raise children's self-esteem, which is believed to facilitate their acquisition of basic skills and higher-order problem-solving skills. Basic Skills approaches included the Southwest Labs, Behavior Analysis, and Direct Instruction models. These models find that mastering basic skills facilitates higher-order cognitive and problem-solving skills, and higher self-esteem. Cognitive approaches included the Parent Education, TEEM, and Cognitively Oriented Curriculum models. These models focus on teaching higher-order problem-solving and thinking skills as the optimal avenue to enhancing school achievement, and to improving lower-order basic skills and self-esteem. Affective and Cognitive models have become popular in most schools of education. Basic Skills approaches are less popular, but are congruent with other, very effective methods of specialized instruction.

CONTRIBUTIONS OF CONSTANCE KAMII TO EARLY CHILDHOOD EDUCATION

Professor of early childhood education Constance Kamii, of Japanese ancestry, was born in Geneva, Switzerland. She attended elementary school in both Switzerland and Japan, completing secondary school and higher education degrees in the United States. She studied extensively with Jean Piaget, also of Geneva. She worked with the Perry Preschool Project in the 1960s, fueling her subsequent interest in theoretically grounded instruction. Kamii believes in basing early childhood educational goals and objectives upon scientific theory of children's cognitive, social, and moral development; and moreover that Piaget's theory of cognitive development is the sole explanation for child development from birth to adolescence. She has done much curriculum research in the U.S., and published a number of books, on how to apply Piaget's theory practically in early childhood classrooms. Kamii agrees with Piaget that education's overall, long-term goal is developing children's intellectual, social, and moral autonomy. Kamii has said, "A classroom cannot foster the development of autonomy in the intellectual realm while suppressing it in the social and moral realms."

THEORETICAL ORIENTATION, PHILOSOPHY, AND APPROACH OF THE KAMII-DEVRIES APPROACH

Constance Kamii and Rhetta DeVries formulated the Kamii-DeVries Constructivist Perspective model of preschool education. It is closely based upon Piaget's theory of child cognitive development and on the Constructivist theory to which Piaget and others subscribed, which dictates that children construct their own realities through their interactions with the environment. Piaget's particular constructivism included the principle that through their interacting with the world within a logical-mathematical structure, children's intelligence, knowledge, personalities, and morality develop. The Kamii-DeVries approach finds that children learn via performing mental actions, which Piaget called operations, through the vehicle of physical activities. This model favors using teachers experienced in traditional preschool education, who employ a child-centered approach, and establish active learning settings, are in touch with children's thoughts, respond to children from children's perspectives, and facilitate children's extension of their ideas. The Kamii-DeVries model has recently been applied to learning assessments using technology (2003) and to using constructivism in teaching physics to preschoolers (2011).

57

Copyright © Mometrix Media. You have been licensed one copy of this document for personal use only. Any other reproduction or redistribution is strictly prohibited. All rights reserved.

HIGH/SCOPE CURRICULUM

David Weikart and colleagues developed the High/Scope Curriculum in the 1960s and 1970s, testing it in the Perry Preschool and Head Start Projects, among others. The High/Scope philosophy is based on Piaget's Constructivist principles that active learning is optimal for young children; that they need to become involved actively with materials, ideas, people, and events; and that children and teachers learn together in the instructional environment. Weikart and colleagues' early research focused on economically disadvantaged children, but the High/Scope approach has since been extended to all young children and all kinds of preschool settings. This model recommends dividing classrooms into well-furnished, separate "interest areas," and regular daily class routines affording children time to plan, implement, and reflect upon what they learn, and to participate in large and small group activities. Teachers establish socially supportive atmospheres; plan group learning activities; organize settings and set daily routines; encourage purposeful child activities, problem-solving, and verbal reflection; and interpret child behaviors according to High/Scope's key child development experiences.

HIGH/SCOPE CURRICULUM'S KEY EXPERIENCES FOR PRESCHOOLERS

The High/Scope Curriculum, developed by David P. Weikart and colleagues, takes a constructivist approach influenced by Piaget's theory, advocating active learning. The High/Scope curriculum model identified a total of 58 "key experiences" it finds critical for preschool child development and learning. These key experiences are subdivided into ten main categories: (1) Creative representation, which includes recognizing symbolic use, imitating, and playing roles; (2) Language and literacy, which include speaking, describing, scribbling, and narrating/dictating stories; (3) Initiative and social relations, including solving problems, making decisions and choices, and building relationships; (4) Movement, including activities like running, bending, stretching, and dancing; (5) Music, which includes singing, listening to music, and playing musical instruments; (6) Classification, which includes sorting objects, matching objects or pictures, and describing object shapes; (7) Seriation, or arranging things in prescribed orders (e.g. by size or number); (8) Numbers, which for preschoolers focuses on counting; (9) Space, which involves activities like filling and emptying containers; and (10) Time, including concepts of starting, sequencing, and stopping actions.

TECHNOLOGY USE, SCHOOL DAY DURATIONS AND SETTINGS, AND TARGETS FOR ITS APPLICATION

The High/Scope Curriculum frequently incorporates computers as regular program components, including developmentally appropriate software, for children to access when they choose. School days may be full-day or part-day, determined by each individual program. Flexible hours accommodate individual family needs and situations. High/Scope programs work in both child care and preschool settings. High/Scope was originally designed to enhance educational outcomes for young children considered at-risk due to socioeconomically disadvantaged, urban backgrounds, and was compatible with Project Head Start. This model of early childhood curriculum and instruction advocates individualizing teaching to each child's developmental level and pace of learning. As such, the High/Scope approach is found to be effective for children who have learning disabilities, and also for children with developmental delays. It works well with all children needing individual attention. High/Scope is less amenable to highly structured settings that use more adult-directed instruction.

HEAD START PROGRAM

Head Start was begun in 1964, extended by the Head Start Act of 1981, and revised in its 2007 reauthorization. It is a program of the U.S. Department of Health and Human Services designed to give low-income families and their young children comprehensive services of health, nutrition, education, and parental involvement. While Head Start was initially intended to "catch up" low-income children over the summer to reach kindergarten readiness, it soon became obvious that a six-week preschool program was inadequate to compensate for having lived in poverty for one's first five years. Hence the Head Start Program was expanded and modified over the years with the aim of remediating the effects of system-wide poverty upon child educational outcomes. Currently, Head Start gives local public, private, nonprofit, and for-profit agencies grants for delivering comprehensive child development

Copyright © Mometrix Media. You have been licensed one copy of this document for personal use only. Any other reproduction or redistribution is strictly prohibited. All rights reserved.

services to promote disadvantaged children's school readiness by improving their cognitive and social development. It particularly emphasizes developing early reading and math abilities preschoolers will need for school success.

GENESIS AND RATIONALE OF THE HEAD START PROGRAM

The Early Head Start program developed as an outgrowth of the original Head Start Program. Head Start initially aimed to remediate the deprivation of poor preschool-aged children by providing educational services over the summer to help them attain school readiness by kindergarten. Because educators and researchers soon discovered the summer program was insufficient to make up for poor children's lack of preparation, Head Start was expanded to become more comprehensive. Head Start was established in 1964 and expanded by the Head Start Act in 1981. After research had accumulated considerable evidence of how important children's earliest years are to their ensuing growth and development, the U.S. Department of Health and Human Services Administration for Children and Families' Office of Head Start established the Early Head Start Program in 1995. Early Head Start works to improve prenatal health; improve infant and toddler development; and enhance healthy family functioning. It serves children from 0–3 years. Like the original program, Early Head Start stresses parental engagement in children's growth, development, and learning.

EMERGENT LITERACY THEORY

EMERGENT LITERACY VERSUS READING READINESS

Historically, early childhood educators viewed "reading readiness" as a time during young children's literacy development when they were ready to start learning to read and write, and taught literacy accordingly. However, in the late 20th and early 20th centuries, research has found that children have innate learning capacities and that skills emerge under the proper conditions. Educational researchers came to view language as developing gradually within a child rather than a child's being ready to read at a certain time. Thus, the term "emergent" came to replace "readiness," while "literacy" replaced "reading" as referring to all of language's interrelated aspects of listening, speaking, writing, and viewing, as well as reading. Traditional views of literacy were based only on children's reading and writing in ways similar to those of adults. However, more recently, the theory of emergent literacy has evolved through the findings of research into the early preschool reading of young children and their and their families' associated characteristics.

EMERGENT LITERACY THEORY'S PRINCIPLES ABOUT HOW YOUNG CHILDREN LEARN TO READ AND WRITE

Through extensive research, emergent literacy theorists have found that: (1) Young children develop literacy through being actively involved in reading and rereading their favorite storybooks. When preschoolers "reread" storybooks, they have not memorized them; rather, theorists find this activity to exemplify young children's reconstruction of a book's meaning. Similarly, young children's invented spellings are examples of their efforts to reconstruct what they know of written language; they can inform us about a child's familiarity with specific phonetic components. (2) Adults' reading to children, no matter how young, is crucial to literacy development. It helps children gain a "feel" for the character, flow, and patterns of written/printed language, and an overall sense of what reading feels like and entails. It fosters positive attitudes toward reading in children, strongly motivating them to read when they begin school. Being read to also helps children develop print awareness and formulate concepts of books and reading. (3) Influenced by Piaget and Vygotsky, emergent literacy theory views reading and writing as developmental processes having successive stages.

PERSPECTIVE REGARDING INSTRUCTIONAL MODELS

The emergent literacy theoretical perspective yields an instructional model for the learning and teaching of reading and writing in young children that is founded on building instruction from the child's knowledge. Emergent literacy theory's assumption is that young children already know a lot about language and literacy by the time they enter school. This theory furthermore regards even 2- and 3-

Copyright © Mometrix Media. You have been licensed one copy of this document for personal use only. Any other reproduction or redistribution is strictly prohibited. All rights reserved.

year-olds as having information about how the reading and writing processes function, and as having already formed particular ideas about what written/printed language is. From this perspective, emergent literacy theory then dictates that teaching should build upon what a child already knows and should support the child's further literacy development. Researchers conclude that teachers should furnish open-ended activities allowing children to show what they already know about literacy; to apply that knowledge; and to build upon it. From the emergent literacy perspective, teachers take the role of creating a learning environment with conditions that are conducive to children's learning in ways that are ideally self-motivated, self-generated, and self-regulated.

HOW BABIES AND YOUNG CHILDREN LEARN TO READ AND WRITE

(1) According to the theory of emergent literacy, even infants encounter written language. Two- and three-year-old's commonly can identify logos, labels, and signs in their homes and communities. Also, young children's scribbles show features/appearances of their language's specific writing system even before they can write. For example, Egyptian children's scribbles look more like Egyptian writing; American children's scribbles look more like English writing. (2) Young children learn to read and write concurrently, not sequentially; the two abilities are closely interrelated. Moreover, though with speech, receptive language comprehension seems easier/sooner to develop than expressive language production, this does not apply to reading and writing: first learning activities involving writing are found easier for preschoolers than those involving reading. (3) Research finds that form follows function, not the opposite: young children's literacy learning is mostly through meaningful, functional, purposeful/goal-directed real-life activities. Literacy comprises not isolated, abstract skills learned for their own sake, but rather authentic skills applied to accomplish real-life purposes, the way children observe adults using literacy.

DEVELOPMENTALLY INAPPROPRIATE KINDERGARTEN AND PRESCHOOL LITERACY PRACTICES

Research finds some preschools are like play centers, but not optimal for literacy because their curricula exclude natural reading and writing activities. Researchers have also identified a trend in many kindergartens to ensure children's "reading readiness" by providing highly academic programs, influencing preschool curricula to get children "ready" for such kindergartens. Influenced and even pressured by kindergarten programs' academic expectations, parents have also come to expect preschools to prepare their children for kindergarten. However, experts find applying elementary-school programs to kindergartens and preschools developmentally inappropriate. Formal instruction in reading and writing and worksheets are not suitable for younger children. Instead, research finds print-rich preschool environments both developmentally appropriate and more effective. For example, when researchers changed classrooms from having a "book corner" to having a centrally located table with books plus paper, pencils, envelopes, and stamps, children spent 3 to 10 times more time on direct reading and writing activities. Children are found to take naturally to these activities without prior formal reading and writing lessons.

PLANNING A PLAY-BASED CURRICULUM

To plan a curriculum based on children's natural play with building blocks (Hoisington, 2008), a teacher can first arrange the environment to stimulate further such play. Then s/he can furnish materials for children to make plans/blueprints for and records and models of buildings they construct. The teacher can make time during the day for children to reflect upon and discuss their individual and group building efforts. Teachers can also utilize teaching strategies that encourage children to reflect on and consider in more depth the scientific principles related to their results. A teacher can provide building materials of varied sizes, shapes, textures, and weights, and props to add realism, triggering more complex structures and creative, dramatic, emotional, and social development. Teachers can take photos of children's structures as documents for discussions, stimulating language and vocabulary development. Supplying additional materials to support and stick together blocks extends play-based learning. Active teacher participation by offering observations and asking open-ended questions

Copyright © Mometrix Media. You have been licensed one copy of this document for personal use only. Any other reproduction or redistribution is strictly prohibited. All rights reserved.

promotes children's standards-based learning of scientific, mathematical, and linguistic concepts, processes, and patterns.

SUPPORTING AND INTEGRATING STANDARDS-BASED LEARNING IN SCIENTIFIC, MATHEMATICAL, AND LINGUISTIC DOMAINS

When children play at building with blocks, for example, they investigate material properties such as various block shapes, sizes, and weights and the stability of carpet vs. hard floor as bases. They explore cause-and-effect relationships; make conclusions regarding the results of their trial-and-error experiments; draw generalizations about observed patterns; and form theories about what does and does not work to build high towers. Ultimately, they construct their knowledge of how reality functions. Teachers support this by introducing relevant learning standards in the play context meaningful to children. For example, math standards including spatial awareness, geometry, number, operations, patterns, and measurement can be supported through planning play. By encouraging and guiding children's discussion and documentation of their play constructions, and supplying nonfictional and fictional books about building, a teacher also integrates learning goals and objectives for language and literacy development. Teachers can plan activities specifically to extend learning in these domains, like counting blocks; comparison/contrast; matching; sorting; sequencing; phonological awareness; alphabetic awareness; print awareness; book appreciation; listening, comprehension, speech, and communication.

USING THEMATIC TEACHING UNITS

To develop a thematic teaching unit, a teacher designs a collection of related activities around certain themes or topics that crosses several curriculum areas or domains. Thematic units create learning environments for young children that promote all children's active engagement, as well as their process learning. By studying topics children find relevant to their own lives, thematic units build upon children's preexisting knowledge and current interests, and also help them relate information to their own life experiences. Varied curriculum content can be more easily integrated through thematic units, in ways that young children can understand and apply meaningfully. Children's diverse individual learning styles are also accommodated through thematic units. Such units involve children physically in learning; teach them factual information in greater depth; teach them learning process-related skills, i.e. "learning how to learn"; holistically integrate learning; encourage cohesion in groups; meet children's individual needs; and provide motivation to both children and their teachers.

PROJECT APPROACH

The Project Approach (Katz and Chard, 1989) entails having young children choose a topic interesting to them, studying this topic, researching it, and solving problems and questions as they emerge. This gives children greater practice with creative thinking and problem-solving skills, which supports greater success in all academic and social areas. For example, if a class of preschoolers shows interest in the field of medicine, their teacher can plan a field trip to a local hospital to introduce a project studying medicine in depth. During the trip, the teacher can write down/record children's considerations and questions, and then use these as guidelines to plan and conduct relevant activities that will further stimulate the children's curiosity and imagination. Throughout this or any other in-depth project, the teacher can integrate specific skills for reading, writing, math, science, social studies, and creative thinking. This affords dual benefits: enabling both children's skills advancement, and their gaining knowledge they recognize is required and applies in their own lives. Children become life-long learners with this recognition.

INTEGRATED CURRICULUM AND EARLY CHILDHOOD EDUCATION

An integrated curriculum organizes early childhood education to transcend the boundaries between the various domains and subject content areas. It unites different curriculum elements through meaningful connections to allow study of wider areas of knowledge. It treats learning holistically and mirrors the interactive nature of reality. The principle that learning consists of series of interconnections is the

Copyright © Mometrix Media. You have been licensed one copy of this document for personal use only. Any other reproduction or redistribution is strictly prohibited. All rights reserved.

foundation for teaching through use of an integrated curriculum. Benefits of integrated curricula include an organized planning mechanism; greater flexibility; and the ability to teach many skills and concepts effectively, include more varied content, and enable children to learn most naturally. By identifying themes children find most interesting, teachers can construct webs of assorted themes, which can provide the majority of their curriculum. Research has proven the effectiveness of integrated teaching units for both children and their teachers. Teachers can also integrate new content into existing teaching units they have identified as effective. Integrated units enable teachers to ensure children are learning pertinent knowledge and applying it to real-life situations.

SKILLS, TOPICS, STRATEGIES, AND BENEFITS RELATED TO CREATING THEMATICALLY-BASED TEACHING UNITS

EC teachers can incorporate many skills into units organized by theme. This includes state governments' educational standards/benchmarks for various skills. Teachers can base units on topics of interest to young children, e.g. building construction, space travel, movie-making, dinosaurs, vacations, nursery rhymes, fairy tales, pets, wildlife, camping, the ocean, and studies of particular authors and book themes. Beginning with a topic that motivates the children is best; related activities and skills will naturally follow. In planning units, teachers should establish connections among content areas like literacy, physical activity, dramatic play, art, music, math, science, and social studies. Making these connections permits children's learning through their strongest/favored modalities and supports learning through meaningful experiences, which is how they learn best. Theme-based approaches effectively address individual differences and modality-related strengths, as represented in Gardner's theory of Multiple Intelligences. Thematic approaches facilitate creating motivational learning centers and hands-on learning activities, and are also compatible with creating portfolio assessments and performance-based assessments. Teachers can encompass skill and conceptual benchmarks for specific age/developmental levels within engaging themes.

GUIDELINES FOR INDOOR AND OUTDOOR SPACE USE

Indoor and outdoor EC learning environments should be safe, clean, and attractive. They should include at least 35' square indoors and 75' square outdoors of usable play space per child. Staff must have access to prepare spaces before children's arrival. Gyms/other larger indoor spaces can substitute if outdoor spaces are smaller. The youngest children should be given separate outdoor times/places. Outdoor scheduling should ensure enough room, plus prevent altercations/competition among different age groups. Teachers can assess if enough space exists by observing children's interactions and engagement in activities. Children's products and other visuals should be displayed at child's-eye level. Spaces should be arranged to allow individual, small-group, and large-group activity. Space organization should create clear pathways enabling children to move easily among activities without overly disturbing others, should promote positive social interactions and behaviors; and activities in each area should not distract children in other areas.

ARRANGEMENT OF LEARNING ENVIRONMENTS
ARRANGING INDOOR LEARNING ENVIRONMENTS ACCORDING TO CURRICULAR ACTIVITIES

EC experts indicate that rooms should be organized to enable various activities, but not necessarily to limit activities to certain areas. For example, mathematical and scientific preschool activities may occur in multiple parts of a classroom, though the room should still be laid out to facilitate their occurrence. Sufficient space for infants to crawl and toddlers to toddle are necessary, as are both hard and carpeted floors. Bolted-down/heavy, sturdy furniture is needed for infants and toddlers to use for pulling up, balancing, and cruising. Art and cooking activities should be positioned near sinks/water sources for cleanup. Designating separate areas for activities like block-building, book-reading, musical activities, and dramatic play facilitates engaging in each of these. To allow ongoing project work and other age-appropriate activities, school-aged children should have separate areas. Materials should be appropriate for each age group and varied. Equipment/materials for sensory stimulation, manipulation,

Copyright © Mometrix Media. You have been licensed one copy of this document for personal use only. Any other reproduction or redistribution is strictly prohibited. All rights reserved.

construction, active play, dramatic play, and books, recordings, and art supplies, all arranged for easy, independent child access and rotated for variety, are needed.

ARRANGING LEARNING ENVIRONMENTS TO CHILDREN'S PERSONAL, PRIVACY, AND SENSORY NEEDS

In any EC learning environment, the indoor space should include easily identifiable places where children and adults can store their personal belongings. Since EC involves children in groups for long time periods, they should be given indoor and outdoor areas allowing solitude and privacy while still easily permitting adult supervision. Playhouses and tunnels can be used outdoors, small interior rooms and partitions indoors. Environments should include softness in various forms like grass outdoors; carpet, pillows, and soft chairs indoors; adult laps to sit in and be cuddled; and soft play materials like clay, Play-Doh, finger paints, water, and sand. While noise is predictable, even desirable in EC environments, undue noise causing fatigue and stress should be controlled by noise-absorbing elements like rugs/carpets, drapes, acoustical ceilings and other building materials. Outdoor play areas supplied/arranged by school/community playgrounds should be separated from roadways and other hazards by fencing and/or natural barriers. Awnings can substitute for hills, and inclines/ramps for shade, when these are not naturally available. Surfaces and equipment should be varied.

PRINCIPLES RELATED TO EARLY CHILDHOOD BEHAVIOR MANAGEMENT

Repetition and consistency are two major elements for managing young children's behavior. Adults must always follow and enforce whichever rules they designate. They must also remember that they will need to repeat their rules over and over to make them effective. Behaviorism has shown it is more powerful to reward good behaviors than punish bad behaviors. Consistently rewarding desired behaviors enables young children to make the association between behavior and reward. Functional behavior analysis can inform adults: knowing the function of a behavior is necessary to changing it. For example, if a toddler throws a tantrum out of frustration, providing support/scaffolding for a difficult task, breaking it down to more manageable increments via task analysis, and giving encouragement would be appropriate strategies; but if the tantrum was a bid for attention, adults would only reinforce/strengthen tantrum recurrence by paying attention. Feeling valued and loved within a positive relationship greatly supports young children's compliance with rules. The "10:1 Rule" prescribes at least 10 positive comments per 1 negative comment/correction.

INCLUDING FAMILIES IN CHILDREN'S EDUCATION

First, ECE personnel can make sure that communication between the school/program and family is reciprocal and regular. EC educators should promote and support the enhancement and application of parenting skills. They should also acknowledge that parents have an integral part in supporting children's learning. All school personnel should make parents feel welcome in school, and moreover should seek parents' help and support. When school administrators, teachers, and other staff make educational decisions that affect the children and their families, they should always be sure that the children's parents are involved in these decisions. In addition, educational personnel should not just work on children's educational goals, learning objectives, and curricular and instructional planning and design on their own, keeping the school or program isolated; they should make use of all available community resources. Instead of trying to educate young children within a school bubble, educators who collaborate with their communities realize benefits of stronger families, schools, and child learning.

MANAGING THE NORMAL BEHAVIOR OF YOUNG CHILDREN

Before reacting to young children's behaviors, adults should make sure children understand the situation. They should state rules simply and clearly; repeat them frequently for a long time for young children to remember and follow them; and state and enforce rules very consistently to avoid confusion. Adults should tell children clearly what they expect of them. They should never assume they need do nothing when children follow rules; they should consistently give rewards for compliance. Adults should also explain to young children why they are/are not receiving rewards by citing the rule they did/did not follow. Adults can arrange the environment to promote success. For example, if a child throws things

Copyright © Mometrix Media. You have been licensed one copy of this document for personal use only. Any other reproduction or redistribution is strictly prohibited. All rights reserved.

that break windows, adults can remove such objects and substitute softer/more lightweight items. Organization is also important. Adults should begin with a simple, easy-to-implement plan and adhere to it. They should record children's progress; analyzing the records shows what does/does not work and why, enabling new/revised plans.

Copyright © Mometrix Media. You have been licensed one copy of this document for personal use only. Any other reproduction or redistribution is strictly prohibited. All rights reserved.

Diversity and Early Childhood Education

EFFECT OF RACIAL/ETHNIC, ECONOMIC, EDUCATIONAL, AND MENTAL HEALTH FACTORS ON THE EMOTIONAL, MENTAL HEALTH, AND SOCIAL OUTCOMES

Proportionately more mothers in minority and low-income groups—up to 40 percent—suffer maternal depression than in other parts of the population. Maternal depression is associated with poor mother-child bonding; lower child scores in language and reading; and higher prevalence of depression and other mental health problems later in children. Low-income and minority families are at higher risk for developmental difficulties and mental health issues. According to U.S. surveys, about one-third or over 3 million of young children have two or more health and developmental risk factors. These risk factors include maternal mental health, maternal education, family poverty, and race/ethnicity. Each added risk factor increases the probability of either greater developmental risk or worse health status. Risk increases exponentially with multiple factors. One risk factor doubles risk; two factors more than triple it; three causes almost five times the risk; and four risk factors represent 14 times the risk of developmental delay or poor health.

EFFECTS OF RACIAL, ETHNIC, AND ECONOMIC DISPARITIES UPON PARENTING, HOME SAFETY, AND SCHOOL READINESS

According to the National Survey on Early Childhood Health, significant differences are reported in Latino and African-Americans' parenting practices, home routines, and home safety measures. These differences are associated with differing degrees of positive early childhood development. Research studies have also revealed that American children in minority groups, on the average, demonstrate lower school readiness levels when they begin formal education than white American children do. The research furthermore shows that most of these differences in school readiness levels are associated with differences in family income. Researchers also comment that disparities among racial and ethnic groups in their school readiness and subsequent academic achievement in school may be additional contributors to discrimination against minority racial and ethnic groups by teachers and other educational personnel.

EFFECTS OF INCOME AND RACE/ETHNICITY UPON HEALTH CARE ASPECTS

Although the disparity in childhood immunizations between white and minority infants and toddlers has decreased, still, fewer minority children are receiving standard immunizations than white children in America. For example, the preschool rates for receiving each major vaccination from 2003–2004 in America were the lowest among non-Latino black, Native American, and Alaskan Native children. One sign of health service quality and continuity is having a regular health care provider. Recent national surveys have found that while more than 80 percent of children under the age of 5 in economically affluent families are seen at physicians' offices or HMOs for care when sick, not much more than 54 percent of children under age 5 in economically poor families are seen for sick care. The National Survey of Early Childhood Health has found African-American and Latino parents report more dissatisfaction with pediatricians and more unmet needs for early childhood development services than white parents. Twice as many Latino as white parents felt providers never or only occasionally understood their individual child's needs.

SOCIOECONOMIC AND RACIAL EFFECTS ON MENTAL, EMOTIONAL, AND SOCIAL HEALTH

According to the National Survey of Child and Adolescent Well-Being, in recent years over 40 percent of toddlers and over 68 percent of preschoolers who were in contact with the child welfare system had high levels of need, developmentally and behaviorally. But overall, fewer than 23 percent of these children were getting services to address these needs. Thus, young children of socioeconomically disadvantaged families were found to have more developmental and behavioral problems than children in other socioeconomic groups, yet were also less likely to receive help with such problems. Another social and emotional difference related to racial group membership has been reflected by levels of

65

Copyright © Mometrix Media. You have been licensed one copy of this document for personal use only. Any other reproduction or redistribution is strictly prohibited. All rights reserved.

violence in the family. 2003 data found that over 15 percent of African-American families experienced violent conflicts, compared to below 9 percent of white families and over 11 percent of Latino families. Racial groups classified as "other" constituted over 12 percent. Experts concede that styles of disagreeing can be influenced by cultural and demographic variables. However, they find the strongest influence on conflicts becoming violent to be parental stress.

INEQUITY IN HEALTH INSURANCE COVERAGE FOR CHILDREN OF MINORITY GROUPS

Research has demonstrated that after taking health insurance status into account, there are no significant socioeconomic differences in how family organization and doctor/health care practitioner visits are related. Furthermore, research has shown that having health insurance coverage decreases differences in developmental and health outcomes for young children. However, despite these findings, children of minority groups are less likely than their nonminority peers to have either private or public health care coverage. Regarding access to health care services, it has been found that parents whose first language was not English were only half as likely to get preventive health care for their infants as native English-speaking families. This inequity in service delivery was found to be constant across white, African-American, and Latino families that had infants, but not in Asian-American families having infants.

According to data collected by the National Survey of Early Childhood Health, minority families have less communication and guidance from pediatric health care providers than white families. For example, African-American parents were found to make significantly fewer phone calls than white parents to pediatric health care practices. Latino parents made fewer than half the calls that white parents did; African-American parents made fewer than three-fourths of the calls white parents did. This survey also found that pediatricians and other pediatric health care service providers were more likely to emphasize topics of household alcohol and drug use and community violence when they talked with minority patient families than they did in discussions with white patient families. African-American children are found far more likely to have special health care needs than white children; yet researchers find that even after controlling for health status, insurance, and other pertinent variables, health care providers are still nearly twice as likely not to refer minority children to specialists and consultants.

EARLY CHILDHOOD COMPREHENSIVE SYSTEMS
DECREASING SOCIOECONOMICALLY AND RACIALLY INFLUENCED HEALTH CARE INEQUITIES

According to the National Center for Children in Poverty, Early Childhood Comprehensive Systems (ECCS) initiatives in each U.S. state have the ability to further methods that can decrease socioeconomically related health care inequities in early childhood, which generates positive impacts for the rest of children's lives. To raise and shape consciousness of health care issues affected by income and race, experts recommend that ECCS establish connections between projects/programs designed to eradicate poverty and racism and efforts in developing early childhood systems. Another consciousness-raising strategy recommended for ECCS is to work at increasing the general public's awareness of racial, ethnic, and economic disparities in early childhood health care and to work at increasing such awareness in health professionals, educators, early care providers, and other significant stakeholders who regularly provide services to young children. ECCS can also include racial/ethnic data in performance monitoring; encourage state SCHIP and Medicaid agencies to do the same; analyze state data for disparities in risk, access, and outcomes, including small-area analyses, geocoding, etc.; and identify and measure unequal treatment through data analysis.

IMPROVING AND EQUALIZING HEALTH CARE FOR ALL AMERICAN DEMOGRAPHIC GROUPS
ENHANCING COMMUNITY SUPPORT

Experts in early childhood development find that state ECCS should target their support toward communities with larger populations of minority and low-income families. Inasmuch as local systems have limited resources, some state ECCS might need to allocate more of these resources to communities having higher risks of adverse outcomes for children. ECCS can also provide assistance to communities

Copyright © Mometrix Media. You have been licensed one copy of this document for personal use only. Any other reproduction or redistribution is strictly prohibited. All rights reserved.

by helping them assess their local assets, strengths, needs, and risk factors. Early childhood development experts emphasize that state ECCS should focus their efforts on improving the quality of health care services that are available within communities where all or the majority of residents are members of minority groups and/or have low socioeconomic status. Another way in which state ECCS can strengthen the supports available in communities for citizens who are subject to unequal health care treatment according to their demographic groups is to offer and provide incentives for community development projects that are designed to decrease health care treatment disparities based on racial/ethnic and economic differences.

REDUCING UNEQUAL TREATMENT OF CULTURAL/LINGUISTIC MINORITIES

Early childhood experts advise that each U.S. state's ECCS should implement strategies designed to monitor health care providers and services for cultural and linguistic competency, and to improve these competencies. One example of such improvement is ensuring that specific training in cultural and linguistic competency and cross-cultural competency is integrated into the training of both health care providers and early childhood educators. ECCS can also be responsible for seeing that parent education materials and resources in health care are translated into the native languages of local families who are not native English speakers, and supporting interpreter and translator services for communities having families needing these. Experts find that ECCS can additionally improve child and family health services by supporting various early childhood service settings in employing nonprofessional/community health workers. Moreover, ECCS can help further equality and consistency of health care across varied demographic groups by applying research evidence-based guidelines regarding health care, family support, early learning, and related services and programs.

BENEFITS OF LEVELING INEQUALITIES IN CARE, HEALTH, AND EDUCATION

Eliminating unequal treatment in early childhood has significant benefits, including lowering overall national rates of poverty; improving overall health and education measures; saving long-term health care costs; decreasing disabilities; and lengthening lives by decreasing mortality rates. The effects of low income and racism on young children and their families are complex, and these influences interact with one another. Therefore, it is impossible or extremely difficult to solve problems generated by one of these social factors without including the other associated influencing factors. Because of the interrelationships of variables, strategies on a system level have the most potential for effectiveness. For example, job training and placement programs that could help parents economically are limited in effectiveness if quality child care is not also available to those parents. Enhancing educational programs could improve academic performance, but not if young students are too hungry to benefit from instruction. And the measurement and monitoring of developmental, health, and educational outcomes will not change their disparity unless treatment inequities are resolved.

INVOLVING FAMILIES IN THEIR CHILDREN'S EDUCATION

Flexibility and variety are key elements for involving diverse families, with changing situations and needs, in ECE. Adaptable approaches include these: Educators include families in designing children's Individual Family Service Plans (IFSPs) for preschoolers. They ask families to develop their own goals for educational participation. They create volunteer calendars, encouraging parents to collaborate when able. They communicate with families regularly, using speech if written/printed language presents barriers. They establish media libraries for parents/families to browse and check out resources. They facilitate parental meeting attendance and school visits by providing transportation and child care. They adapt to parental work schedules by convening meetings at alternative times of day. They often send families communications about both their children and class content, including information regarding important developmental milestones and methods for nurturing growth and development. They offer families individualized, specific strategies for home use. They recruit interested family members to help in preschool. They also function as clearinghouses to facilitate family access to community supports like local health care agencies, businesses, and universities.

Copyright © Mometrix Media. You have been licensed one copy of this document for personal use only. Any other reproduction or redistribution is strictly prohibited. All rights reserved.

Types of Disabilities and Exceptionalities and their Implications

CAUSES OF INTELLECTUAL DISABILITIES IN BABIES AND YOUNG CHILDREN

INFECTIONS

Congenital cytomegalovirus (CMV) is passed to fetuses from mothers, who may be asymptomatic. About 90% of newborns are also asymptomatic; 5% to 10% of these have later problems. Of the 10% born with symptoms, 90% will have later neurological abnormalities, including intellectual disabilities. Congenital rubella, or German measles, is also passed to fetuses from unvaccinated and exposed mothers, causing neurological damage including blindness or other eye disorders, deafness, heart defects, and intellectual disabilities. Congenital toxoplasmosis is passed to fetuses by infected mothers, who can be asymptomatic, with a parasite from raw or undercooked meat that causes intellectual disabilities, vision or hearing loss, and other conditions. Encephalitis is brain inflammation caused by infection, most often viral. Meningitis is inflammation of the meninges, or membranes, covering the brain and is caused by viral or bacterial infection; the bacterial form is more serious. Both encephalitis and meningitis can cause intellectual disabilities. Maternal human immunodeficiency virus (HIV) and acquired immunodeficiency syndrome (AIDS) can be passed to fetuses, destroying immunity to infections, which can cause intellectual disabilities. Maternal listeriosis, a bacterial infection from contaminated food, animals, soil, or water, can cause meningitis and intellectual disabilities in surviving fetuses and infants.

ENVIRONMENTAL, NUTRITIONAL, AND METABOLIC INFLUENCES

Environmental deprivation syndrome results when developing children are deprived of necessary environmental elements—physical, including adequate nourishment (malnutrition); climate or temperature control (extremes of heat or cold); hygiene, like changing and bathing; and so on. It also includes lack of adequate cognitive stimulation, which can stunt a child's intellectual development, and neglect in general. Malnutrition results from starvation; vitamin, mineral, or nutrient deficiency; deficiencies in digesting or absorbing foods; and some other medical conditions. Environmental radiation, depending on dosage and time of exposure, can cause intellectual disabilities. Congenital hypothyroidism (underactive thyroid) can cause intellectual disabilities, as can hypoglycemia (low blood sugar) from inadequately controlled diabetes or occurring independently and infant hyperbilirubinemia. Bilirubin, a waste product of old red blood cells, is found in bile made by the liver and is normally removed by the liver; excessive bilirubin buildup in babies can cause intellectual disabilities. Reye syndrome, caused by aspirin given children with flu or chicken pox, or following these viruses or other upper respiratory infections, or from unknown causes, produces sudden liver and brain damage and can result in intellectual disabilities.

GENETIC ABNORMALITIES AND SYNDROMES AFFECTING THE NERVOUS SYSTEM

Rett syndrome is a nervous system disorder causing developmental regression, particularly severe in expressive language and hand function. It is associated with a defective protein gene on an X chromosome. Having two X chromosomes, females with the defect on one of them can survive; with only one X chromosome, males are either miscarried, stillborn, or die early in infancy. Rett syndrome produces many symptoms, including intellectual disabilities. Tay-Sachs disease, an autosomal recessive disorder, is a nervous system disease caused by a defective gene on chromosome 15 resulting in a missing protein for breaking down gangliosides, chemicals in nerve tissues that build up in cells, particularly brain neurons, causing damage. Tay-Sachs is more prevalent in Ashkenazi Jews. The adult form is rare; the infantile form is commonest, with nerve damage starting in utero. Many symptoms, including intellectual disabilities, appear at 3 to 6 months and death occurs by 4 to 5 years. Tuberous sclerosis, caused by genetic mutations, produces tumors damaging the kidneys, heart, skin, brain, and central nervous system. Symptoms include intellectual disabilities, seizures, and developmental delays.

Copyright © Mometrix Media. You have been licensed one copy of this document for personal use only. Any other reproduction or redistribution is strictly prohibited. All rights reserved.

GENETIC OR INHERITED METABOLIC DISORDERS

Adrenoleukodystrophy is an X-linked genetic trait. Some female carriers have mild forms, but it affects more males more seriously. It impairs metabolism of very long-chain fatty acids, which build up in the nervous system (as well as adrenal glands and male testes). The childhood cerebral form, manifesting at ages 4 to 8, causes seizures, visual and hearing impairments, receptive aphasia, dysgraphia, dysphagia, intellectual disabilities, and other effects. Galactosemia is an inability to process galactose, a simple sugar in lactose, or milk sugar. By-product buildup damages the liver, kidneys, eyes, and brain. Hunter syndrome, Hurler syndrome, and Sanfilippo syndrome each cause the lack of different enzymes; all cause an inability to process mucopolysaccharides or glycosaminoglycans (long sugar-molecule chains). Hurler and Sanfilippo (but not Hunter) syndromes are autosomal recessive traits, meaning both parents must pass on the defect. All cause progressive intellectual disabilities. Lesch-Nyhan syndrome, affecting males, is a metabolic deficiency in processing purines. It causes hemiplegia, varying degrees of intellectual disabilities, and self-injurious behaviors. Phenylketonuria (PKU), an autosomal recessive trait, causes lack of the enzyme to process dietary phenylalanine, resulting in intellectual disabilities.

PRESCRIPTION DRUGS, SUBSTANCES OF ABUSE, SOCIAL DRUGS, AND DISEASES

Warfarin, a prescription anticoagulant drug to thin the blood and prevent excessive clotting, can cause microcephaly (undersized head) and intellectual disabilities in an infant when the mother has taken it during pregnancy. The prescription antiseizure drug Trimethadione can cause developmental delays in babies when it has been taken by pregnant mothers. Maternal abuse of solvent chemicals during pregnancy can also cause microcephaly and intellectual disabilities. Maternal crack cocaine abuse during pregnancy can cause severe and profound intellectual disabilities and many other developmental defects in fetuses, which become evident when they are newborns. Maternal alcohol abuse can cause fetal alcohol syndrome, which often includes intellectual disabilities, among many other symptoms. Maternal rubella (German measles) virus can cause intellectual disabilities as well as visual and hearing impairments and heart defects. Maternal herpes simplex virus can cause microcephaly, intellectual disabilities, and microophthalmia (small or no eyes). The varicella (chicken pox) virus in pregnant mothers can also cause intellectual disabilities as well as muscle atrophy in babies.

CHARACTERISTICS OF INFANTS AND YOUNG CHILDREN WITH INTELLECTUAL DISABILITIES

Newborns with intellectual disabilities, especially of greater severity, may not demonstrate normal reflexes, such as rooting and sucking reflexes, necessary for nursing. They may not show other temporary infant reflexes such as the Moro, Babinski, swimming, stepping, or labyrinthine reflexes, or they may demonstrate weaker versions of some of these. In some babies, these reflexes will exist but persist past the age when they normally disappear. Babies with intellectual disabilities are likely to display developmental milestones at later-than-typical ages. The ages when they do display milestones vary according to the severity of the disability and by individual. Young children with intellectual disabilities are likely to walk, self-feed, and speak later than normally developing children. Those who learn to read and write do so at later ages. Children with mild intellectual disabilities may lack curiosity and have quiet demeanors; those with profound intellectual disabilities are likely to remain infantile in abilities and behaviors throughout life. Intellectually disabled children will score below normal on standardized IQ tests and adaptive behavior rating scales.

POTENTIAL VARIABLES CAUSING LEARNING DISABILITIES

LDs are basically neurological disorders. Though they are more specific to particular areas of learning than global disorders like intellectual disabilities, scientific research has found correlations between LDs and many of the same factors that cause intellectual disabilities, including prenatal influences like excessive alcohol or other drug consumption, diseases, and so on. Once babies are born, glandular disorders, brain injuries, exposure to secondhand smoke or other toxins, infections of the central nervous system, physical trauma, or malnutrition can cause neurological damage resulting in LDs. Hypoxia and anoxia (oxygen loss) before, during, or after birth is a cause, as are radiation and chemotherapy. These same influences often cause behavioral disorders as well as LDs. Another factor is

Copyright © Mometrix Media. You have been licensed one copy of this document for personal use only. Any other reproduction or redistribution is strictly prohibited. All rights reserved.

genetic: Both LDs and behavior disorders have been observed to run in families. While research has not yet identified specific genetic factors, heritability does appear to be a component in influencing learning and behavioral disorders.

TYPES OF NEUROLOGICAL DAMAGE FOUND IN CHILDREN WITH LDS AND ADHD

Various neurological research studies have revealed that children diagnosed with LDs and ADHD have at least one of several kinds of structural damage to their brains. Scientists have found smaller numbers of cells in certain important regions of the brains of some children with learning and behavioral disorders. Some of these children are found to have brain cells of smaller than normal size. In some cases, dysplasia is discovered; that is, some brain cells migrate into the wrong area of the brain. In some children with learning and behavioral disorders, blood flow is found to be lower than normal to certain regions in the brain. Also, the brain cells of some children with learning and behavioral disabilities show lower levels of glucose metabolism; glucose (blood sugar) is the brain's main source of fuel, so inadequate utilization of glucose can affect the brain's ability to perform some functions related to cognitive processing, as in LDs, and to attention and impulse control, as in ADHD.

TYPES AND CHARACTERISTICS OF LEARNING DISABILITIES

Dyslexia, the most common LD, means deficiency or inability in reading. It primarily affects reading but can also interfere with writing and speaking. Characteristics include reversing letters and words, for example, confusing b and d in reading and writing; reading won as now, confusing similar speech sounds like /p/ and /b/, and perceiving spaces between words in the wrong places when reading. Dyscalculia is difficulty doing mathematical calculations; it can also affect using money and telling time. Dysgraphia means difficulties specifically with writing, including omitting words in writing sentences or leaving sentences unfinished, difficulty putting one's thoughts into writing, and poor handwriting. Central auditory processing disorder causes difficulty perceiving small differences in words despite normal hearing acuity; for example, couch and chair may be perceived as cow and hair. Background noise and information overloads exacerbate the effects. Visual processing disorders affect visual perception despite normal visual acuity, causing difficulty finding information in printed text or from maps, charts, pictures, graphs, and so on; synthesizing information from various sources into one place; and remembering directions to locations.

ATTACHMENT STYLES IDENTIFIED IN TODDLERS BY MARY AINSWORTH

Mary Ainsworth worked with John Bowlby, discovering the first empirical evidence supporting his attachment theory. From her Strange Situation experiments, she identified secure, insecure and avoidant, insecure and resistant, and insecure and disorganized attachment styles. Securely attached children show normal separation anxiety when mother leaves and happiness when she returns, avoid strangers when alone but are friendly with mother present, and use mother as a safe base for environmental exploring. Insecure and resistant children show exaggerated separation anxiety, ambivalence and resistance to mother upon reuniting, fear strangers, cry more, and explore less than secure or avoidant babies. Insecure and avoidant children show no separation anxiety or stranger anxiety and little interest on reunions with mother and are comforted equally by mother or strangers. Insecure and disorganized types seem dazed and confused, respond inconsistently, and may mix resistant and ambivalent and avoidant behaviors. Secure styles are associated with sensitive, responsive caregiving and children's positive self-images and other images, resistant and ambivalent styles with inconsistent caregiving, and avoidant with unresponsive caregivers. Avoidant, resistant, and disorganized styles, associated with negative self-images and low self-esteem, are most predictive of emotional disturbances.

EMOTIONAL DISTURBANCES IN YOUNG CHILDREN CLASSIFIED AS ANXIETY DISORDERS

Anxiety disorders include generalized anxiety disorder (GAD), obsessive-compulsive disorder (OCD), posttraumatic stress disorder (PTSD), panic disorder, social phobia, and specific phobias. All share a common characteristic of overwhelming, irrational, and unrealistic fears. GAD involves excessive

Copyright © Mometrix Media. You have been licensed one copy of this document for personal use only. Any other reproduction or redistribution is strictly prohibited. All rights reserved.

worrying about anything or everything and free-floating anxiety. Anxiety may be about real issues but is nonetheless exaggerated and spreads, overtaking the child's life. OCD involves obsessive and preoccupied thoughts and compulsive or irresistible actions, including often bizarre rituals. Germ phobia, constant hand washing, repeatedly checking whether tasks are done or undone, and collecting things excessively are common. PTSD follows traumatic experiences/events. Children have frequent, extreme nightmares, crying, flashbacks wherein they vividly perceive or believe they are experiencing the traumatic event again, insomnia, depression, anxiety, and social withdrawal. Symptoms of panic disorder are panic attacks involving extreme fear and physical symptoms like a racing heart, cold hands and feet, pallor, hyperventilation, and feeling unable to move. Children with social phobia develop fear and avoidance of day care, preschool, or other social settings. Specific phobias are associated with specific objects, animals, or persons and are often triggered by traumatic experiences involving these.

FACTORS CONTRIBUTING TO EMOTIONAL DISTURBANCES

Researchers have investigated emotional disturbances but have not yet established known causes for any. Some disturbances, for example the major mental illness schizophrenia, seem to run in families and hence include a genetic component; childhood schizophrenia exists as a specific diagnosis. Factors contributing to emotional disturbances can be biological or environmental but more often are likely a combination of both. Dysfunctional family dynamics can often contribute to child emotional disorders. Physical and psychological stressors on children can also contribute to the development of emotional problems. Some people have attributed emotional disturbances to diet, and scientists have also researched this but have not discovered proof of cause and effect. Bipolar disorder is often successfully treated with the chemical lithium, which affects sodium flow through nerve cells, so chemical imbalance may be implicated as an etiology. Pediatric bipolar disorder, which has different symptoms than adult bipolar disorder, correlates highly with histories of bipolar and other mood disorders or alcoholism in both parents.

SYMPTOMS OF PEDIATRIC BIPOLAR DISORDER

Bipolar, formerly called manic-depressive disorder, has similar depressive symptoms in children as adults. However, children's mood swings often occur much faster, and children show more symptoms of anger and irritability than other adult manic symptoms. Bipolar children's most common symptoms include frequent mood swings; extreme irritability; protracted (up to several hours) tantrums or rages; separation anxiety; oppositional behavior; hyperactivity, impulsivity, and distractibility; restlessness and fidgetiness; silly, giddy, or goofy behavior; aggression; racing thoughts; grandiose beliefs or behaviors; risk-taking; depressed moods; lethargy; low self-esteem; social anxiety; hypersensitivity to environmental or emotional triggers; carbohydrate (sugar or starch) cravings; and trouble getting up in the morning. Other common symptoms include bed-wetting (especially in boys), night terrors, pressured or fast speech, obsessive or compulsive behaviors, motor and vocal tics, excessive daydreaming, poor short-term memory, poor organization, learning disabilities, morbid fascinations, hypersexuality, bossiness and manipulative behavior, lying, property destruction, paranoia, hallucinations, delusions, and suicidal ideations. Less common symptoms include migraines, bingeing, self-injurious behaviors, and animal cruelty.

CONDUCT DISORDER IN CHILDREN

Factors contributing to conduct disorders in children include genetic predispositions, neurological damage, child abuse, and other traumatic experiences. Children with conduct disorders display characteristic emotional and behavioral patterns. These include aggression: They bully or intimidate others, often start physical fights, will use dangerous objects as weapons, exhibit physical cruelty to animals or humans, and assault and steal from others. Deliberate property destruction is another characteristic—breaking things or setting fires. Young children are limited in some of these activities by their smaller size, lesser strength, and lack of access; however, they show the same types of behaviors against smaller, younger, weaker, or more vulnerable children and animals, along with oppositional and defiant behaviors against adults. Also, while truancy is impossible or unlikely in preschoolers, and

Copyright © Mometrix Media. You have been licensed one copy of this document for personal use only. Any other reproduction or redistribution is strictly prohibited. All rights reserved.

running away from home is less likely, young children with conduct disorders are likely to demonstrate some forms of seriously violating rules, another symptom of this disorder.

SYMPTOMS OF CHILDHOOD-ONSET SCHIZOPHRENIA

The incidence of childhood-onset schizophrenia is rare, but it does exist. One example of differential diagnosis involves distinguishing qualitatively between true auditory hallucinations and young children's "hearing voices" otherwise: In the latter case, a child hears his or her own or a familiar adult's voice in his or her head and does not seem upset by it, while in the former, a child may hear other voices, seemingly in his or her ears, and is frightened and confused by them. Tantrums, defiance, aggression, and other acting-out, externalized behaviors are less frequent in childhood-onset schizophrenia than internalized developmental differences, for example, isolation, shyness, awkwardness, fickleness, strange facial expressions, mistrust, paranoia, anxiety, and depression. Children demonstrate nonpsychotic symptoms earlier than psychotic ones. However, it is difficult to use prepsychotic symptoms as predictors due to variance among developmental peculiarities. While psychiatrists find the course of childhood-onset schizophrenia somewhat more variable than in adults, child symptoms resemble adult symptoms. Childhood-onset schizophrenia is typically chronic and severe, responds less to medication, and has a more guarded prognosis than adolescent- or adult-onset schizophrenia.

DIAGNOSING THE EMOTIONAL DISTURBANCES IN CHILDREN CLASSIFIED AS PSYCHOTIC DISORDERS

Psychosis is a general psychiatric category referring to thought disturbances or disorders. The most common symptoms are delusions that is, believing things that are not true, and hallucinations, that is, seeing, hearing, feeling, tasting, or smelling things that are not there. While early childhood psychosis is rarer than at later ages, psychiatrists confirm it does occur. Moreover, prognosis is poorer for psychosis with onset in early childhood than in adolescence or adulthood. Causes can be from known metabolic or brain disorders or unknown. Younger children are more vulnerable to environmental stressors. Also, in young children, thoughts distorted by fantasy can be from normal cognitive immaturity, due to lack of experience and a larger range of normal functioning, or pathology; where they lie on this continuum must be determined by clinicians. Believing one is a superhero who can fly can be vivid imagination or delusional; having imaginary friends can be pretend play or hallucinatory. Other developmental disorders can also cloud differential diagnosis.

VISUAL IMPAIRMENTS

DEVELOPMENTAL CHARACTERISTICS OF INFANTS AND YOUNG CHILDREN WITH VISUAL IMPAIRMENTS

Historically, it was thought that VI children developed more slowly than normal; however, it is now known that ages for reaching developmental milestones are equally variable in VI babies as in others and that they acquire milestones within equal age ranges. One developmental difference is in sequence: VI children tend to utter their first words or subject-verb 2-word sentences earlier than other children. Some VI children also demonstrate higher levels of language development at younger-than-typical ages. For example, they may sing songs from memory or recall events from the past at earlier ages than other children. This is a logical development in children who must rely more on input to their hearing and other senses than to their vision when the latter is impaired. Totally blind babies reach for objects later, hence explore the environment later; hand use, eye-hand coordination, and gross and fine motor skills are delayed. Blind infants' posture control develops normally (rolling, sitting, all-fours, and standing), but mobility (raising on arms, pulling up, and walking) are delayed.

CAUSES OF VISUAL IMPAIRMENTS IN BABIES AND YOUNG CHILDREN

Syndrome-related and other malformations like cleft iris or lens dislocation causing VI can have prenatal origins. Cataracts clouding the eye's lens can be congenital, traumatic, or due to maternal rubella. Eyes can be normal, but impairment in the brain's visual cortex can cause VI. Infantile glaucoma, like adult

72

Copyright © Mometrix Media. You have been licensed one copy of this document for personal use only. Any other reproduction or redistribution is strictly prohibited. All rights reserved.

glaucoma, causes intraocular fluid buildup pressure and VI. Conjunctivitis and other infections cause VI. Strabismus and nystagmus are ocular-muscle conditions, respectively causing eye misalignments and involuntary eye movements. Trauma damaging the eyeball(s) is another VI cause. The optic nerve can suffer from atrophy (dysfunction) or hypoplasia, that is, developmental regression, usually prenatally due to neurological trauma; acuity cannot be corrected. Refractive errors like nearsightedness, farsightedness, and astigmatism are correctable. Retinoblastoma, or behind-the-eye tumors, can cause blindness and fatality; surgical or chemotherapeutic treatment is usually required before age 2. Premature infants can have retinopathy of prematurity or retrolental fibroplasia. Cryotherapeutic treatment seems to stop disease progression. Its effects range from none to severe VI (approximately 25% of children) to complete blindness.

IMPACTS OF BLINDNESS UPON COGNITIVE DEVELOPMENT

Blind children have more difficulty determining and confirming characteristics of things, hence defining concepts and organizing them into more abstract levels; their problem-solving is active but harder, and they construct different realities than sighted children. Blind babies typically acquire object permanence (the understanding that unseen objects still exists) a year later than normal; they learn to reach for objects only by hearing. Understanding cause-and-effect relationships is difficult without visual evidence. Blind babies and toddlers take longer to understand and object's constancy regardless of their orientation in space, affecting their ability to orient toys and their own hands. Blind children can identify object size differences and similarities, but classifying object differences and similarities in other attributes requires longer times and more exposures to various similar objects. Blind children's development of the abilities to conserve object properties like material or substance, weight, amount and volume, length, and liquid volume is later than normal.

EFFECTS OF BLINDNESS ON EMOTIONAL AND SOCIAL DEVELOPMENT

Blind babies and children are more dependent than others on adults, affecting development. With control of their inner realities but not of their outer environments, blind children may withdraw, seeking and responding less to social interaction. They may not readily develop concepts of the external world or self-concepts as beings separate from the world and the understanding that they can be both agents and recipients of actions relative to the environment. Mother-infant smiling initiates recognition, attachment, and communication in sighted babies; blind infants smile on hearing mother's voice at 2 months. Only tactile stimuli like tickling and nuzzling evoke regular smiling in blind babies. Missing facial expressions and other visual cues, blind children have more complicated social interactions. They often do not understand the basics of playing with others and seem emotionally ambivalent or uninterested and uncommunicative. Peers may reject or avoid them; adults often overprotect them. Self-help skills like chewing, scooping, self-feeding, teeth brushing, grooming, and toilet training are delayed in blind children.

HEARING IMPAIRMENTS
PREVALENCE AND ETIOLOGIES OF HEARING IMPAIRMENTS

Half or more (50% to 60%) of infant hearing losses have genetic origins—Down and other genetically based syndromes or the existence of parental hearing loss. About 25% or more of infant hearing losses are caused by maternal infections during pregnancy, such as cytomegalovirus (CMV), postnatal complications like blood transfusions or infection with meningitis, or traumatic head injuries. Included in this 25% or more are babies having nongenetic neurological disorders or conditions that affect their hearing. Malformations of the ears, head, or face can cause hearing loss in babies. Babies spending 5 days or longer in neonatal intensive care units (NICUs) or having complications while in the NICU are also more likely to suffer hearing loss. Around 25% of babies are diagnosed with hearing loss whose etiology is unknown.

Copyright © Mometrix Media. You have been licensed one copy of this document for personal use only. Any other reproduction or redistribution is strictly prohibited. All rights reserved.

SIGNS OF HEARING IMPAIRMENTS

If an infant does not display a startle response at loud noises, this is a potential sign of hearing loss. This can also indicate other developmental disabilities, but because hearing loss is the most prevalent disability among newborns, hearing screening is a priority. Between birth and 3 or 4 months old, babies should turn toward the source of a sound; if they do not, it could indicate hearing loss. A child who does not utter first words like mama or dada by age 1 could have hearing impairment. When babies or young children do not turn their heads when their names are called, adults may mistake this for inattention or ignoring; however, children turning upon seeing adults, but not upon hearing their names, can indicate hearing loss. Babies and children who seem to hear certain sounds but not others may have partial hearing losses. Delayed speech-language development or unclear speech, not following directions, saying "Huh?" often, and wanting higher TV or music volumes can indicate hearing loss in children.

SPEECH AND LANGUAGE IMPAIRMENTS
FACTORS CONTRIBUTING TO SPEECH AND LANGUAGE IMPAIRMENTS

Some speech and language disorders in children have unknown causes. Others have known causes such as hearing loss: Speech and language are normally acquired primarily through the auditory sense, so children with impaired hearing have delayed and impaired development of speech and language. Brain injuries, neurological disorders, viral diseases, and some medications can also cause problems with developing language or speech. Children with intellectual disabilities are more likely to have delayed language development, and their speech is also more likely to develop more slowly and to be distorted. Cerebral palsy causes neuromuscular weakness and incoordination of speech. When severe, it can cause inability to produce recognizable speech sounds; some children without speech can still vocalize, and some cannot. A cleft palate or lip and other physical impairments affect speech. Inadequate speech-language modeling at home inhibits speech-language development. Vocal abuse in children (screaming, coughing, throat clearing, or excessive talking) can cause vocal nodules or polyps, causing voice disorders. Stuttering can be related to maturation, anxiety or stress, auditory feedback defects, or unknown causes.

CHARACTERISTICS

In speech, most phonological disorders are articulatory; that is, children fail to pronounce specific speech sounds or phonemes correctly beyond the normal developmental age for achieving accuracy. Stuttering, disfluency, and rate and rhythm disorders cause children to repeat phonemes, especially initial word sounds; to repeat words; to prolong vowels or consonants; or to block, that is, straining so hard to produce a sound that, pressure builds, but no sound issues. Their speech rates may also speed and slow irregularly. Children with voice disorders can have voices that sound hoarse, raspy, overly nasal, higher- or lower-pitched than normal, overly weak or strident, and whispery or harsh. Hoarseness is common with vocal nodules and polyps. Cleft palate commonly causes hypernasality. In language, one of the most common impairments is delayed language development due to environmental deprivation, intellectual disabilities, neurological damage or defects, hearing loss, visual impairment, and so on. Children with neurological damage or disorders may exhibit aphasias, language disorders characterized by receptive difficulty with understanding spoken or written language, or expressive difficulty constructing spoken or written language.

PHYSICAL AND HEALTH IMPAIRMENTS
EXAMPLES OF PHYSICAL AND HEALTH IMPAIRMENTS

In the special education field of early childhood education, other health impairment is a term referring to health and physical conditions that rob a child of strength, vitality, or alertness or that cause excessive alertness to environmental stimuli, all having the end result of impeding the child's ability to attend or respond to the educational environment. Health problems can be acute, that is short-term or temporary but serious, or chronic, that is, long-term, persistent, or recurrent. Some examples of such health and physical impairments include: cerebral palsy, spina bifida, amputations or missing limbs, muscular

74

Copyright © Mometrix Media. You have been licensed one copy of this document for personal use only. Any other reproduction or redistribution is strictly prohibited. All rights reserved.

dystrophy, cystic fibrosis, asthma, rheumatic fever, sickle-cell anemia, nephritis or kidney disease, leukemia, Tourette syndrome, hemophilia, diabetes, heart disease, AIDS, and lead poisoning. All these conditions and others can interfere with a child's development and ability to attend and learn. In addition to seizure disorders, which often cause neurological damage, seizure-controlling medications also frequently cause drowsiness, interfering with attention and cognition. Attention deficit and attention deficit hyperactivity disorders (ADD and ADHD) limit attention span, focus, and concentration and thus are sometimes classified as health impairments requiring special education services.

CHARACTERISTICS OF BABIES AND CHILDREN WITH PHYSICAL AND HEALTH IMPAIRMENTS

The characteristics of children having various physical or health impairments can range from having no limitations to severe limitations in their activities. Children with cerebral palsy, for example, usually have deficiencies in gross and fine motor development and deficits in speech-language development. Physical and health conditions causing severe debilitation in some children not only seriously limit their daily activities but also cause multiple primary disabilities and impair their intellectual functioning. Other children with physical or health impairments function at average, above-average, or gifted intellectual and academic levels. An important consideration when working with babies and young children having physical or health impairments is handling and positioning them physically. Correctly picking up, holding, carrying, giving assistance, and physically supporting younger children and arranging play materials for them based on their impairment is not only important for preventing injury, pain, and discomfort; it also enables them to receive instruction better and to manipulate materials and perform most efficiently. Preschoolers with physical impairments also tend to have difficulty with communication skills, so educators should give particular attention to facilitating and developing these.

DEVELOPMENTAL DELAYS
FACTORS LEADING TO DEVELOPMENTAL DELAYS

Developmental delays can come from genetic or environmental causes or both. Infants and young children with intellectual disabilities are most likely to exhibit developmental delays. Their development generally proceeds similarly to that of normal children but at slower rates; milestones are manifested at later-than-typical ages. Sensory impairments such as with hearing and vision can also delay many aspects of children's development. Children with physical and health impairments are likely to exhibit delays in their motor development and performance of physical activities. Another factor is environmental: Children deprived of adequate environmental stimulation commonly show delays in cognitive, speech-language, and emotional and social development. Children with autism spectrum disorders often have markedly delayed language and speech development; many are nonverbal. Autistic children also typically have impaired social development, caused by and inability or difficulty with understanding others' emotional and social nonverbal communications. When they cannot interpret these, they do not know how to respond and also cannot imitate them; however, they can often learn these skills with special instruction.

CHARACTERISTICS INDICATING DEVELOPMENTAL DELAYS

Developmental delays mean that a child does not reach developmental milestones at the expected ages. For example, if most babies normally learn to walk between 12 and 15 months of age, a 20-month-old who is not beginning to walk is considered as having a developmental delay. Delays can occur in cognitive, speech-language, social-emotional, gross motor skill, or fine motor skill development. Signs of delayed motor development include stiff or rigid limbs, floppy or limp body posture for the child's age, using one side of the body more than the other, and clumsiness unusual for the child's age. Behavioral signs of children's developmental delays include inattention, or shorter than normal attention span for the age; avoiding or infrequent eye contact; focusing on unusual objects for long times or preferring objects over social interaction; excessive frustration when attempting tasks normally simple for children their age; unusual stubbornness; aggressive and acting-out behaviors; daily violent behaviors; rocking; excessive talking to oneself; and not soliciting love or approval from parents.

Copyright © Mometrix Media. You have been licensed one copy of this document for personal use only. Any other reproduction or redistribution is strictly prohibited. All rights reserved.

Traumatic Brain Injury (TBI)

IDEA's Legal Definition of Traumatic Brain Injury

TBI is defined by the IDEA law (the Individuals with Disabilities Education Act) as "an acquired injury to the brain from external physical force, resulting in total or partial functional disability or psychosocial impairment, or both, that adversely affect a child's educational performance." This definition excludes injuries from birth trauma, congenital injuries, and degenerative conditions. TBI is the foremost cause of death and disability in children (and teens) in the USA. The most common causes of TBI in children include falls, motor vehicle accidents, and physical abuse. In spite of the IDEA's definition, aneurysms and strokes are three examples of internal traumas that can also cause TBI in babies and young children. External head injuries that can result in TBI include both open and closed head injuries. Shaken baby syndrome is caused by forcibly shaking an infant. This causes the brain literally to bounce against the insides of the skull, causing rebound injuries, resulting in TBI and even death.

Characteristics

TBI can impair a child's cognitive development and processing. It can impede the language development of children, which is dependent upon cognitive development. Children who have sustained TBI often have difficulties with attention, retention and memory; reasoning, judgment, understanding abstract concepts and thinking abstractly, and problem-solving abilities. TBIs can also impair a child's motor functions and physical abilities. The sensory and perceptual functions of children with TBI can be abnormal. Their ability to process information is often compromised. Their speech can also be affected. In addition, TBIs can impair a child's psychosocial behaviors. Memory deficits are commonest, tend to be more long lasting, and are often area specific; for example, a child may recall personal experiences but not factual information. Other common characteristics of TBI include cognitive inflexibility or rigidity, damaged conceptualization and reasoning, language loss or poor verbal fluency, problems with paying attention and concentrating, inadequate problem solving, and problems with reading and writing.

Etiologies and Characteristics of Multiple Disabilities

The term multiple disabilities refers to any combination of more than one disabling condition. For example, a child may be both blind and deaf due to causes such as having rheumatic fever in infancy or early childhood. Anything causing neurological damage before, during, or shortly after birth can result in multiple disabilities, particularly if it is widespread rather than localized. For example, infants deprived of oxygen or suffering traumatic brain injuries in utero, during labor or delivery, or postnatally can sustain severe brain damage. So can babies having encephalitis or meningitis and those whose mothers abused drugs prenatally. Infants with this type of extensive damage can often present with multiple disabilities, including intellectual disabilities, cerebral palsy, physical paralysis, mobility impairment, visual impairment, hearing impairment, and speech-language disorders. They may have any combination of or all of these disabilities as well as others. In addition to a difficulty or inability with normal physical performance, multiply disabled children often have difficulty acquiring and retaining cognitive skills and transferring or generalizing skills among settings and situations.

Prematurity or Preterm Birth

Babies born before 37 weeks' gestation are classified as premature or preterm. Premature infants can have difficulty with breathing, as their lungs are not fully developed, and with regulating their body temperatures. Premature infants may be born with pneumonia, respiratory distress, extra air or bleeding in the lungs, jaundice, sepsis or infection, hypoglycemia (low blood sugar), severe intestinal inflammation, bleeding into the brain or white-matter brain damage, or anemia. They have lower-than-normal birth weights, body fat, muscle tone, and activity. Additional typical characteristics of premature infants include apnea (interrupted breathing); lanugo (a coating of body hair that full-term infants no longer have); thin, smooth, shiny, translucent skin through which veins are visible; soft, flexible ear cartilage; cryptorchidism (undescended testicles) and small, non-ridged scrotums in males; enlarged

76

Copyright © Mometrix Media. You have been licensed one copy of this document for personal use only. Any other reproduction or redistribution is strictly prohibited. All rights reserved.

clitorises in females; and feeding difficulties caused by weak or defective sucking reflexes or incoordination of swallowing with breathing.

DISABLING CONDITIONS RESULTING FROM PREMATURE BIRTHS

Physicians find it impossible to predict the long-term results of prematurity for any individual baby based on an infant's gestational age and birth weight. However, some related immediate and long-term effects can be identified. Generally, the lower the birth weight and the more prematurely a child is born, the greater the risk is for complications. Infants born at less than 34 weeks of gestation typically cannot coordinate their sucking and swallowing and may temporarily need feeding or breathing tubes or oxygen. They also need special nursery care until able to maintain their body temperatures and weights. Long-term complications of prematurity can include bronchopulmonary dysplasia, a chronic lung condition; delayed physical growth and development; delayed cognitive development; mental or physical delays or disabilities; and blindness, vision loss, or retinopathy of prematurity (formerly called retrolental fibroplasia). While some premature infants sustain long-term disabilities, some severe, other babies born prematurely grow up to show no effects at all; and any results within this range can also occur.

Copyright © Mometrix Media. You have been licensed one copy of this document for personal use only. Any other reproduction or redistribution is strictly prohibited. All rights reserved.

Screening, Assessment, Evaluation, and Referral

REQUIRED AND RECOMMENDED INFORMATION IN SCREENING FOR DEVELOPMENTAL DISORDERS

If a young child has been screened for developmental disorders or delays within the past 6 months and no changes have been observed or reported, repeat screening may be waived. Initial screenings are required. Hearing and vision screenings are mandatory in screening young children. Formal developmental measures are also required, which may include screening tests of motor skills development, cognitive development, social-emotional development, and self-help skills development. Formal screening tests of speech-language development are also required. Additional tests recommended during screening include informal measures. For example, checklists, rating scales, and inventories may be used to screen a child's behavior, mood, and performance of motor skills, cognitive skills, self-help skills, and social and emotional skills. On checklists, parents or caregivers check whether the child does or does not demonstrate listed behaviors, or assessors may complete them via parent or caregiver interviews or interviewing and observing the child. Rating scales ask parents, caregivers, and assessors to rate a child's behaviors, affect, mood, and so on, within a range of numbered and labeled descriptions. Inventories list demonstrated skills and needs. Behavioral observations and existing records and information are also used.

FEATURES OF DEVELOPMENTAL SCREENINGS AND EVALUATIONS

If a child's development is suspected of being delayed—for example, the child is not reaching developmental milestones during expected age ranges—a developmental screening may be administered. Screening tests are quickly performed and yield more general results. The hospital or doctor's office may give a questionnaire to the parent or caregiver to complete for a screening. Alternatively, a health or education professional may administer a screening test to the child. Screening tests are not intended to diagnose specific conditions or give details; they are meant to identify children who may have some problem. Screenings can overidentify or under-identify developmental delays in children. Hence, if the screening identifies a child as having developmental delay(s), the child is then referred for a developmental evaluation—a much longer, more thorough, comprehensive, in-depth assessment using multiple tests, administered by a psychologist or other highly-trained professional. Evaluation provides a profile of a child's strengths and weaknesses in all developmental domains. Determination of needs for early intervention services or treatment plans is based on evaluation results.

DEVELOPMENTAL EVALUATION DATA TYPES

The child's social history should be obtained. This is typically done by a social worker. Details of the child's developmental progress heretofore; the family's composition, socioeconomic status, and situation; and the child's and family's health and medical histories and status should be emphasized. A physician's or nurse's medical assessment is required, including a physical examination, and if indicated, a specialist's examination. A psychologist typically assesses intellectual and cognitive development; at least one such test is generally required. At least one test of adaptive behavior is also required to assess emotional-social development. Self-help skills are evaluated; this may be included within cognitive, adaptive behavior, or programming assessments. Communication skills are typically evaluated by a speech-language pathologist. Both receptive and expressive language must be tested and comprehensively rather than simply by single-word vocabulary tests. As indicated, speech articulation is also tested. At least one test of motor skills, typically administered by a physical or occupational therapist, is required. Programming evaluation requires at least one criterion-referenced or curriculum-based measure, typically administered by an educator.

BEHAVIORAL VARIATIONS AND CHARACTERISTICS OF ADHD

While the chief symptoms associated with ADHD are inattentiveness, impulsive behavior, distractibility, and excessive physical activity, there is considerable variation among individual children having ADHD.

Copyright © Mometrix Media. You have been licensed one copy of this document for personal use only. Any other reproduction or redistribution is strictly prohibited. All rights reserved.

For example, the degree of severity of this condition can vary widely from one child to the next. In addition, each child can vary in how much he or she exhibits each of these primary characteristics. Some children might not appear to behave very impulsively but show severe deficits in attention. Some may focus better, but only for short periods, and are very easily distracted. Some display very disruptive behavior, while others do not but may daydream excessively, not attending to programming. In general, children who have ADHD can show deficits in following rules and directions. Also, when their developmental skills are evaluated or observed, they are likely to demonstrate inconsistencies in performance over time. To identify or select specific intervention methods and strategies, professionals should use a comprehensive evaluation to obtain information about the child's specific behaviors in his or her natural environment that need remediation.

CHILD FIND

Child Find is an ongoing process with the aim of locating, identifying, and referring young children with disabilities and their families as early as possible for service programs. This process consists of activities designed to raise public awareness and screenings and evaluations to identify and diagnose disabilities. The federal IDEA law mandates under Part B that disabled children are guaranteed early childhood special education services and under Part C that infants and toddlers at risk for developmental delays are guaranteed early intervention programs. (Eligibility guidelines vary by U.S. states.) The IDEA requires school districts to find, identify, and evaluate children with disabilities in their attendance areas. School districts have facilitated this Child Find process by establishing community informed referral networks whose members refer children who may have exceptional educational needs (EENs). Network members typically include parents, doctors, birth-to-3 programs, child care programs, Head Start programs, public health agencies, social service agencies, and any other community members with whom the young children come into contact.

CURRENT COLLABORATIVE APPROACHES AND MODELS OF SCREENING

Historically, the tradition was to conduct kindergarten screenings of children entering schools around age 5. However, in recent years, school districts have developed community referral networks to assist in the processes of Child Find, screening, evaluation, and referral for early intervention and early childhood special education and related services. Current models are more informal, proactive, and collaborative. Cooperative educational interagency service efforts give parents information about normal early childhood development and available community resources and offer opportunities for developmental screenings of their young children. Specific procedures are governed by individual U.S. state laws. Generally, district networks implementing current models send developmental review forms to parents to complete in advance, and then they attend a developmental screening at a community site. Parents discuss normal early childhood growth and development with program staff, while in the same room, trained professionals observe their children as they play. Children's vision and hearing are also screened. Parents can discuss their children's current development with psychologists, early childhood educators, or counselors. Thereafter, they can learn about community resources.

DEFINING DEVELOPMENTAL DELAYS IN INFANTS AND TODDLERS

The IDEA Part C specifies the areas of development that states must include in defining developmental delays. However, individual states must identify the criteria they use to determine eligibility, including pertinent diagnostic instruments, procedures, and functional levels. States currently use quantitative and qualitative measures. Quantitative criteria for developmental delay include: difference between chronological age and performance level, expressed as a percentage of chronological age; performance at a given number of months below chronological age; or number of standard deviations (SDs) below mean of performance on a norm-referenced test. Qualitative criteria include: development considered atypical or delayed for established norms or observed behaviors considered atypical. At least one state differentially defines delay according to a child's age in months, with the rationale that a 25% delay, for example, is very different for a 1-year-old than a 3-year-old. Quantitative criteria for defining delay and

Copyright © Mometrix Media. You have been licensed one copy of this document for personal use only. Any other reproduction or redistribution is strictly prohibited. All rights reserved.

determining eligibility vary widely among states. A 25% or 20% delay; 2 SDs below mean in 1+ areas or 1.5 SD below mean in 2+ areas are some common state criteria.

SINGLE AND MULTIPLE RISK FACTORS IN INFANTS AND TODDLERS FOR DEVELOPMENTAL DELAYS

Scientists find that developmental outcomes for children are not reliably predicted by any one risk factor or event. Developmental risk increases with increased biological, medical, or environmental risk factors. However, researchers have found some variables that afford resiliency in children to offset risk factors. These can include the child's basic temperament, the child having high self-esteem, the child having a good emotional relationship with at least one parent; and the child having experiences of successful learning. These findings indicate that assessments should include criteria for multiple biological and environmental risk factors, for cumulative biological and environmental risk factors, and for protective or resilience factors, considering all of these in the context of change occurring over time. Under the IDEA (the Individuals with Disabilities Education Act), U.S. states have the option to provide early intervention services to children considered at risk for adverse developmental outcomes as well as those already identified with them. Some states apply multiple-risk models, requiring three to five risk factors for service eligibility. Some states also determine eligibility with less DD when biological, medical, or environmental risk factors also exist.

INFORMATION SOURCES ON EARLY INTERVENTION AND PRESCHOOL SPECIAL EDUCATION SERVICES

Military families stationed both in the United States and overseas who have young special needs children can seek information and assistance from the federally funded organization Specialized Training of Military Families (STOMP). The staff of STOMP is composed of parents having special needs children themselves, who also have been trained to work with other parents of special needs children. STOMP staff members are spouses of military personnel who thus understand the unique, specialized circumstances and needs of military families. Another government agency, the U.S. Department of Defense, includes the office of the Department of Defense Education Activity (DoDEA) and provides comprehensive guidance to military families with special needs children who are eligible to receive, or are receiving, free appropriate public education (FAPE) as mandated by the IDEA law (the Individuals with Disabilities Education Act), whether that education is located in the United States or in other countries.

PROVIDING SPECIAL EDUCATION SERVICES FOR PRESCHOOLERS

If parents observe that their preschooler is not attaining developmental milestones within the expected age ranges or does not seem to be developing in the same way as most other children, they should seek evaluation for possible developmental delay or disability. Although 3- to-5-year-olds are likely not in elementary school yet, the elementary school in a family's school district is still the best first contact because the IDEA law (the Individuals with Disabilities Education Act) specifies that school districts must provide special education services at no family cost to eligible children, including preschoolers. Another excellent source of more information about special education is the National Dissemination Center for Children with Disabilities (NICHCY) of the U.S. Department of Education's Office of Special Education Programs. They partner with nonprofit organizations like the Academy for Educational Development (AED) to produce useful documents for families with special needs children. NICHCY supplies state resource sheets listing main contacts regarding special education services in each U.S. state. Families can obtain these sheets at NICHCY's website or by telephone.

INFORMATION SOURCES FOR EVALUATION TO DETERMINE DEVELOPMENTAL DISABILITY

Under the IDEA (the Individuals with Disabilities Education Act), evaluation information sources include: physicians' reports, the child's medical history, developmental test results, current classroom observations and assessments (when applicable), completed developmental and behavioral checklists, feedback and observations from parents and all other members of the evaluation team, and any other

Copyright © Mometrix Media. You have been licensed one copy of this document for personal use only. Any other reproduction or redistribution is strictly prohibited. All rights reserved.

significant records, reports, and observations regarding the child. Under the IDEA, involved in the evaluation are parents, at least one regular education teacher and special education teacher if the child has these, and any special education service provider working with the child—for children receiving early intervention services from birth through age 2 and transitioning to preschool special education, it may be an early intervention service provider; a school administrator knowledgeable about children with disabilities, special education policies, regular education curriculum, and resources available; a psychologist or educator who can interpret evaluation results and discuss indicated instruction; individuals with special expertise or knowledge regarding the child (recruited by school or parents); when appropriate, the child; and other professionals, for example, physical or occupational therapists, speech therapists, medical specialists, and so on.

SPECIAL EDUCATION SERVICES FOR PRESCHOOL CHILDREN

Special education for preschoolers is education specifically designed to meet the individual needs of a child aged 3 to 5 years with a disability or developmental delay. The specialized design of this instruction can include adaptations to the content, to the teaching methods, and the way instruction is delivered to meet a disabled child's unique needs. Special education for preschoolers includes various settings, such as in the home, in classrooms, hospitals, institutions, and others. It also includes a range of related services, such as speech-language pathology services, specialized physical education instruction, early vocational training, and training in travel skills. The school district's special education system provides evaluation and services to eligible preschoolers free of charge. Evaluation's purposes are to determine whether a child has a disability under the IDEA's (the Individuals with Disabilities Education Act) definitions and determine that child's present educational needs.

POST-EVALUATION AND THE INDIVIDUALIZED EDUCATION PROGRAM

After a preschool child is evaluated, the parents and involved school personnel meet to discuss the evaluation results. Parents are included in the group that decides whether the child is eligible for special education services based on those results. For eligible children, the parents and school personnel will develop an IEP. Every child who will receive special education services must have an IEP. The main purposes of the IEP are (1) to establish reasonable educational goals for the individual child and (2) to indicate what services the school district will provide to the child. The IEP includes a statement of the child's present levels of functioning and performance. It also includes a list of more general instructional goals for the child to achieve through school and parental support along with more specific learning objectives reflecting those goals and specifying exactly what the child will be able to demonstrate, under what circumstances, how much of the time—for example, a percentage of recorded instances—and within what time period (e.g., 1 year).

INDIVIDUALIZED EDUCATION PROGRAM GOALS AND OBJECTIVES

In an IEP, the goals are more global, describing a skill for the child to acquire or a task to master. The objectives are more specific articulations of achievements that will demonstrate the child's mastery of the goal. For example, if a goal is for the child to increase his or her functional communicative vocabulary, a related objective might be for the child to acquire X number of new words in X length of time; another related objective could be for the child to use the words acquired in 90% of recorded relevant situations. If the goal is for the child to demonstrate knowledge and discrimination of colors, one objective might be for the child to identify correctly a red, yellow, and blue block 95% of the time when asked to point out each color within a group of blocks. Progress toward or achievement of some objectives may be measured via formal tests; with preschoolers, many others are measured via observational data collection.

PROGRESS MONITORING, UPDATING, AND REVISING IEPS

Once a child has been identified with a disability, determined eligible for special education and related services under the IDEA (the Individuals with Disabilities Education Act), and had an IEP developed and implemented, the child's progress must be monitored. Monitoring methods may be related to evaluation

Copyright © Mometrix Media. You have been licensed one copy of this document for personal use only. Any other reproduction or redistribution is strictly prohibited. All rights reserved.

methods. For example, if a child identified with problem behaviors was initially evaluated using a behavioral checklist, school personnel can use the same checklist periodically, comparing its results to the baseline levels of frequency and severity originally obtained. If an affective disorder or disturbance was identified and instruments like the Beck Depression Inventory or Anxiety Inventory were used, these can be used again periodically; reduced symptoms would indicate progress. If progress with IEP goals and objectives is less or greater than expected, the IEP team meets and may revise the program. This can include specifying shorter or longer times to achieve some goals and objectives; lowering or raising requirements proving too difficult or easy; resetting successive objective criteria in smaller or larger increments; changing teaching methods, content, or materials used, and so on.

INFORMAL ASSESSMENT INSTRUMENTS

EC teachers assess pre-K children's performance in individual, small-group, and whole-class activities throughout the day using informal tools that are teacher-made, school/program/district-furnished, or procured by school systems from commercial educational resources. For classroom observations, teachers might complete a form based on their observations during class story or circle time, organized using three themes per day, each targeting different skills—social-emotional, math, alphabet knowledge, oral language, or emergent writing. They note the names of children demonstrating the specified skill and those who might need follow-up, and provide needed one on one interventions daily. For individual observations, teachers might fill out a chart divided into domains like physical development; oral language development; math; emergent reading; emergent writing; science and health; fine arts; technology and media; social studies; social-emotional development; and approaches to learning, noting one child's strengths and needs in each area per chart. In addition to guided observation records, teachers complete checklists; keep anecdotal and running records; and assemble portfolio assessments of children's work. Tracking children's progress informs responsive instructional planning.

SCREENING VERSUS ASSESSMENT INSTRUMENTS

A variety of screening and assessment instruments exist for EC measurement. Some key areas where they differ include which developmental domains are measured by an instrument; for which applications an instrument is meant to be used; to which age ranges an instrument applies; the methods by which a test or tool is administered; the requirements for scoring and interpreting a test, scale, or checklist; whether an instrument is appropriate for use with ethnically diverse populations; and whether a tool is statistically found to have good validity and reliability. EC program administrators should choose instruments that can measure the developmental areas pertinent to their program; support their program's established goals; and include all EC ages served in their program. Instruments' administration, scoring, and interpretation methods should be congruent with program personnel's skills. Test/measure administration should involve realistic time durations. Instruments/tools should be appropriate to use with ethnically diverse and non-English-speaking children and families. Tests should also be proven psychometrically accurate and dependable enough.

TYPICAL APPLICATIONS OF SCREENING AND ASSESSMENT INSTRUMENTS

The ways in which screening and assessment instruments applicable to ECE are used include a wide range of variations. For example, ECE programs typically need to identify children who might have developmental disorders or delays. Screening instruments are used to identify those children showing signs of possible problems who need assessments, not to diagnose problems. Assessment instruments are used to develop and/or confirm diagnoses of developmental disorders or delays. Assessment tools are also used to help educators and therapists plan curricular and treatment programs. Another important function of assessment instruments is to determine a child's eligibility for a given program. In addition, once children are placed in ECE programs, assessment tools can be used to monitor their progress and other changes occurring through time. Moreover, program administrators can use assessment instruments to evaluate children's achievement of the learning outcomes that define their program goals—and by extension, the teachers' effectiveness in furthering children's achievement of those outcomes.

Copyright © Mometrix Media. You have been licensed one copy of this document for personal use only. Any other reproduction or redistribution is strictly prohibited. All rights reserved.

FORMAL ASSESSMENT INSTRUMENTS

Formal assessment instruments are typically standardized tests, administered to groups. They give norms for age groups/developmental levels for comparison. They are designed to avoid administrator bias and capture children's responses only. Their data can be scaled and be reported in aggregate to school/program administrators and policymakers. The Scholastic Early Childhood Inventory (SECI) is a formal one on one instrument to assess children's progress in four domains found to predict kindergarten readiness: phonological awareness, oral language development, alphabet knowledge, and mathematics. Other instruments measuring multiple developmental domains include the Assessment, Evaluation and Programming System (0–6 years) for planning intervention; the Bayley Scale for Infant Development (1–42 months) for assessing developmental delays; the Brigance Diagnostic Inventory of Early Development (0–7 years) for planning instruction; the Developmental Profile II (0–6 years) to assess special needs and support IEP development; the Early Coping Inventory (4–36 months) and Early Learning Accomplishment Profile (0–36 months), both for planning interventions; and the Infant-Toddler Developmental Assessment (0–42 months) to screen for developmental delays.

SCREENING AND ASSESSMENT INSTRUMENTS MEASURING DEVELOPMENT

The available screening and assessment instruments for EC development cover a wide range in scope and areas of focus. Some measures are comprehensive, assessing young children's progress in many developmental domains including sensory, motor, physical, cognitive, linguistic, emotional, and social. Some other instruments focus exclusively on only one domain, such as language development or emotional-social development. Some instruments even focus within a domain upon only one of its facets, e.g. upon attachment or temperament within the domain of emotional-social development. In addition, some tools measure risk and resiliency factors influencing developmental delays and disorders. Programs like Head Start that promote general EC development should select comprehensive assessment instruments. Outreach programs targeting better identification of children having untreated and/or undetected mental health problems should choose instruments assessing social-emotional development. Clinics treating children with regulatory disorders might select an instrument measuring temperament. Prevention programs helping multiple-needs families access supports and services could use a measure for risk and resiliency factors. Multifaceted EC programs often benefit most from using several instruments in combination.

AGE RANGES INCLUDED IN VARIOUS SCREENING AND ASSESSMENT INSTRUMENTS

An important consideration for screening and assessment in early childhood is that EC development is very dynamic and occurs rapidly. Hence screening and assessment instruments must be sensitive to such frequent and pronounced developmental changes. Some instruments target specific age ranges like 0–36 months. Others cover wider ranges, e.g. children aged 2–16 years. The latter may have internal means of application to smaller age ranges; for example, sections respectively for 3–6-month-old babies, 7–12-month-olds, and 12–18-month-olds. Or they indicate different scoring and interpretation criteria by age; for example, some screening tools specify different numbers of test items depending on the child's age to indicate a need for assessment. Choosing screening and assessment instruments covering the entire age range served in an ECE program is advantageous—not only because they can be used with all child ages in the program, but also because they can be administered and readministered at the beginning and end of programs and/or in between, to compare and monitor changes, which is difficult with separate, age-specific tests.

FEATURES OF PAPER-AND-PENCIL REPORTS

The most common form of paper-and-pencil report about infants and young children are questionnaires. Parents, caregivers, and teachers read printed questions or statements and respond by selecting Yes or No to a question or a number/level on a Likert-type scale showing the degree to which they agree with a statement. For self-administration, instruments must contain questions/statements written on reading levels accessible to the respondents and in their native languages. Alternatively, some questionnaires or surveys can be read to the respondent by an interviewer trained in or familiar with administration of

Copyright © Mometrix Media. You have been licensed one copy of this document for personal use only. Any other reproduction or redistribution is strictly prohibited. All rights reserved.

the chosen instrument. Such self-reporting instruments usually take fewer than 20 minutes to finish, and ECE program personnel need comparatively little training to administer them. However, employees may need further training to score and/or interpret responses, or already-trained specialists may score and interpret them in some cases. ECE schools/programs/agencies can obtain some self-reporting instruments free of charge; other tools' publishers charge for response forms; and others charge only for initially obtaining their materials, allowing purchasers to reproduce them thereafter.

FEATURES OF FORMAL AND INFORMAL OBSERVATIONS

Some instruments require EC staff to watch a child's behavior and/or interactions with parents/caregivers and/or peers. Formal observations involve watching activities structured for the screening/assessment instrument. Informal observations involve watching a child's activities in natural settings like at home or in preschool during play times. Formal observation tools typically require staff to be trained to administer them. The trained observers' findings can include records of which developmentally normal behaviors a child has attained, incidences of problem behaviors noted, descriptions and evaluations of the quality of a child's social interactions with other people, and other observations of the child's behaviors that can inform screening and assessment. Observational screening and assessment instruments usually take more than 20 minutes for administration. Publishers of observational tests typically charge EC programs to order single-use recording forms; some allow them to purchase templates and then reproduce the forms.

SCORING AND INTERPRETATION OF VARIOUS SCREENING AND ASSESSMENT INSTRUMENTS

Some instruments are fairly simple to score and interpret, needing little training of EC personnel. For example, paper-and-pencil questionnaires/surveys often only need the numbers/points for each item response added up for a total score; or a group of scores is obtained by summing values within sections. Interpreting some screening scores can be as simple as noting whether a child's score surpasses a designated cut-off value that signals assessment is needed. Such screenings can be scored and interpreted right after administration, and readily shared with parents and other stakeholders. Assessment instruments using more complicated scoring and interpretation include such procedures as weighting item values; reversing point values for certain items; converting raw scores into standardized scores or percentages; and referring to tables giving national norms for comparison. Standardized tests, including preschool IQ scales, commonly involve such methods. Assessors often need considerable training; advanced psychometric education and experience; thorough knowledge of EC development; and additional time to score and interpret these tests. Results may be discussed in separately scheduled meetings.

INTERVIEW FEATURES

In EC programs conducting assessments, personnel usually conduct interviews with a child's parents, teachers, and/or caregivers. Interviews can be made in structured formats, i.e. the administrator reads prescribed questions as written to the interviewee, or semi-structured formats, wherein the administrator uses his/her judgment to add more questions to the written ones until s/he determines that the information provided is complete enough. Interview questions vary, covering subjects of parental concern, the child's identified areas of strengths and accomplishments, the child's identified areas of deficits or needs, the interactions between parents and child, and the child's behavior. Interviews can be brief, but usually they are longer than paper-and-pencil self-reporting questionnaires, surveys, or checklists. EC personnel frequently need to be trained to administer published interview-based instruments. Publishers typically charge schools/programs/agencies for ordering multiple, single-use response forms, or they may require a one-time order and allow them to reproduce the forms from their initial purchase to use for multiple administrations.

FEATURES OF SCREENING AND ASSESSMENT TOOLS USING STRUCTURED TASKS

Screening and assessment instruments that use structured tasks involve a list of behaviors and/or skills that a child is expected to attain by a certain age range or developmental level. The administrators must

Copyright © Mometrix Media. You have been licensed one copy of this document for personal use only. Any other reproduction or redistribution is strictly prohibited. All rights reserved.

present various activities or tasks to a child, and then record the details of the child's performance of each activity or task. Instruments using structured tasks require EC staff training for administration. They take over 20 minutes to complete. EC programs/schools/agencies must buy testing equipment/materials and single-use recording forms. Because paper-and-pencil questionnaires/surveys are easy to administer; apply across various settings, e.g. preschools, pediatricians' waiting rooms, homes, etc.; cost comparatively little; require minimal administrator training; and are frequently short, they are appropriate for screening use. While formal/informal observational tools, structured/semistructured interview tools, and structured-task tools take more training, time, and expense, they also provide more detailed information, making them useful for determining diagnoses and/or developing individualized care/instruction plans. Instruments using multiple methods, e.g. collecting data from various settings and respondents, yield the most comprehensive information.

TEST-RETEST RELIABILITY

Test-retest reliability is how consistent/stable an instrument's results are across administrations. An instrument with good test-retest reliability yields the same results when administered twice or more to the same child within a short time. For example, the same assessor gives a child the same test twice within a few days or weeks, comparing the results. The more similar the results between/among administrations, the higher the test-retest reliability. This implies the instrument measures an attribute/construct that is stable over a short time. Due to the inherent rapidity and dynamism of EC development, we expect significant developmental changes over years and months; but over only weeks or days, we expect little or no substantial change. Therefore, instruments whose results are not stable over a short time are less utile for EC screening/assessment. For example, a child's scoring with "typical development" on one administration but "possible delay/disorder" a week later means the instrument does not define the child's developmental needs, and thus is not reliable.

INTER-RATER RELIABILITY OF SCREENING AND ASSESSMENT INSTRUMENTS

Inter-rater reliability is how consistent/stable an instrument's results are across different individual administrators/raters. Good inter-rater reliability means the instrument will give the same/similar results for the same child, at the same time, in the same setting, when administered by different people. This shows that the instrument measures a quality/construct that remains stable regardless of who administers the test. Significant differences among different raters' results present problems, especially with instruments using unstructured interviews, observations, or structured tasks. For example, if one rater scores a child as possibly having a developmental delay or disorder while another rater using the same test scores the same child as within the range of normal development, the instrument does not identify the child's true developmental needs and is unreliable. When different assessors (like parent vs. teacher) observe a child in different settings, though, like home vs. preschool, and/or at different times, varying results are expected and not necessarily indicative of inter-rater unreliability because children's behaviors can vary by setting.

INTERNAL CONSISTENCY REGARDING TEST INSTRUMENTS

A testing instrument is said to have internal consistency when its individual items correlate strongly with each other and with the total test score. This means that all of the individual items (questions, stimuli, tasks, etc.) measure parts of the same construct that the test is intended to measure. A test with low internal consistency could be measuring additional attributes that the authors did not define or mean for the test to measure. Children with disparate developmental needs could thus receive similar scores, based on different test items. With comprehensive screening and assessment instruments that cover multiple domains of development, EC educators should look for internal consistency within each subscale of the test or within each domain tested. However, they should not necessarily expect internal consistency among the different domains or at the level of the test's full-scale/overall score. For example, they should not expect high correlation between a test's subscale measuring a child's language skills development and its subscale measuring a child's gross motor skills development.

Copyright © Mometrix Media. You have been licensed one copy of this document for personal use only. Any other reproduction or redistribution is strictly prohibited. All rights reserved.

INTERNAL CONSISTENCY AND SCREENING AND ASSESSMENT INSTRUMENTS

Whether a test's individual items contribute to measuring the construct the test is supposed to measure is internal consistency. It is determined by how much the test's individual items correlate with one another and with the overall score. A test with high internal consistency more accurately measures the specific content area/developmental domain/construct it means to measure. A test with low internal consistency poses problems when children who might have very different needs get the same score. For example, if a test meant to measure aggression has low internal consistency, its individual items are not correlated with one another or the overall score, implying it tests more than one construct. Two children given this test could score beyond the cutoff level indicating diagnosis or assessment need, but their scores could be due to completely different individual test items. Since individual test items do not correlate, the two children might have markedly different needs. Furthermore, those needs may not be related to aggression, since the test probably unintentionally measures additional constructs.

CONCURRENT VALIDITY REGARDING SCREENING AND ASSESSMENT INSTRUMENTS

When a screening or assessment instrument yields results comparable to those of another instrument whose validity has been previously established, it has good concurrent validity. Since the test used for comparison was already found valid, users have confidence in its results. Therefore, their confidence is warranted in another test showing high concurrent validity with the established test. For example, the Stanford-Binet Intelligence Scales and the Wechsler Preschool and Primary Scales of Intelligence (WPPSI) are both well-established IQ tests with demonstrated statistical validity and reliability. So if EC educators have found or been given a new instrument for measuring intelligence, they are likely to find that its authors have compared the test's results to the results obtained by the Stanford-Binet and/or WPPSI. Educators who have confidence in the Stanford-Binet and/or the WPPSI are then justified in having comparable confidence in the new test if its results were found similar to those of the established tests, indicating its high concurrent validity.

CONTENT VALIDITY REGARDING SCREENING AND ASSESSMENT INSTRUMENTS

Whether a test instrument measures the entire content area it purports to measure is known as content validity. It determines whether a test can yield accurate and fair measures of the totality of the construct that the assessor wants to test. For example, if a screening instrument is intended to measure social-emotional development in a young child, it should include individual test items covering the range of this domain's important components. A screening test that covers a child's interactions with caregivers but not with peers; screens attention but not initiation of play; or screens for social skills but not communication skills would not address all elements of social-emotional development and thus not have good content validity. EC educators can use instruments with high content validity to generalize with more confidence about how a child's test performance predicts his/her levels of functioning in real life. By contrast, if a test has low content validity, generalizations about the tested child's development can exceed the test's scope and be inaccurate and/or unrealistic.

PREDICTIVE VALIDITY IN SCREENING AND ASSESSMENT INSTRUMENTS

A screening/assessment instrument's prediction of a child's behavior in real life is predictive validity. For example, an instrument screening for social-emotional disorders in preschool children might predict tantrum and/or oppositional behaviors in kindergarten. In another example, you would expect a screening instrument for social-emotional disorders to differentiate between children with normal/typical social-emotional development and those with mental health disorders. If a screening tool identifies a child with a potential mental health disorder and has high predictive validity, a complete clinical diagnostic evaluation of the screened child would diagnose a mental health disorder. Sensitivity is the instrument's accuracy—here, in identifying developmental disorders/delays, if it correctly identifies 9 of 10 children really having disorders/delays, it has 90 percent sensitivity. Specificity conversely would be accuracy in identifying children without disorders/delays. Despite high sensitivity and specificity, screeners yield some errors. False-positives over-identify delays/disorders where none exist; false-negatives under-identify existing delays/disorders. Unnecessary concern is a consequence of

86

Copyright © Mometrix Media. You have been licensed one copy of this document for personal use only. Any other reproduction or redistribution is strictly prohibited. All rights reserved.

false-positives; lack of prevention/early intervention/treatment is a more serious consequence of false-negatives.

NORM-REFERENCED VERSUS CRITERION-REFERENCED TESTS

Norm-referenced tests compare a child's test results to those of a comparison group of other children in the same age group, grade, or developmental level. This comparison group is called a normative or standardization sample. Norm-referenced tests show how an individual child's performance compares to that of the general population of children. Criterion-referenced tests compare a child's test results to a predetermined standard of performance for the child's age group/grade/level. They show how an individual child's performance compares to standards established by educational experts. Norm-referenced tests are useful for determining whether a child is similar to the "average" child and identifying children performing significantly above or below average. Criterion-referenced tests are good for measuring the extent to which an individual child has mastered areas or domains of development and for monitoring changes over time in the child's levels of mastery.

APPLYING ASSESSMENT RESULTS TO PLANNING INSTRUCTION FOR INDIVIDUALS AND GROUPS

ECE settings should provide organized outlines of developmentally appropriate guidelines for their children, including when and how to introduce and reinforce guidelines at each learning stage. These outlines are foundations for anecdotal observations and authentic assessments tracking developmental progress. ECE programs supply opportunities and activities to develop each discrete skill, including copious review and practice young children require for retention. Teachers should plan learning experiences meaningfully promoting developing identified guidelines and addressing children's interests. ECE settings should have organized progress-tracking systems following developmental sequences. These help teachers determine whether a child can move to the next level or prior skills that need additional reinforcement. Tracking systems should be easy to maintain and immediately give teachers basic information regarding each child's level of functioning for planning activities and discussions. Teachers should then create "ready reference" charts/graphs of assessment and monitoring results, giving an idea of the class/group's general functioning level, to inform activity/lesson planning and additional support needed for individual children—one on one for those below class/group level, enriched for those above it.

ESTABLISHING AND MAINTAINING GOOD COMMUNICATION WITH PARENTS

When teachers send home a letter to parents explaining classroom practices and giving contact information at the beginning of the school year, parents perceive them as approachable and available. When a teacher calls each parent/guardian during school's first two weeks, parents appreciate and enjoy conversations. Calls also make it easier for teachers to contact parents later in the year regarding child issues if needed. Experts find it effective to mail postcards home, addressed to children or parents. Establishing simple class websites including teacher contact information facilitates parental access. Teachers' printing business cards and attaching them to their first parent letters conveys professionalism. Teachers using Internet/e-mail/print to publish weekly/monthly class newsletters informally keep parents apprised of children's instruction and teach parents to expect communication. Teachers can send parents invitations to visit prior to school/program Open Houses: teachers are perceived as more approachable when more parents are comfortable in classrooms. Having children write appreciation letters to parents for Open Houses encourages children to invite parents; parents also perceive teacher appreciation by association.

Copyright © Mometrix Media. You have been licensed one copy of this document for personal use only. Any other reproduction or redistribution is strictly prohibited. All rights reserved.

Professionalism, Ethics, and Legal Responsibilities

IDEA LAW

Public Law 94-142, the Education for All Handicapped Children Act/Education for the Handicapped Act (EHA), passed in 1975; and Public Law 99-457, the EHA Amendments, passed in 1986, provided foundations that were expanded by new 1990 legislation. As a result, EHA was renamed the Individuals with Disabilities Education Act (IDEA). The IDEA's six main principles follow:

1. Publicly funded education cannot exclude any student because of the student's disability.
2. The rights of students with disabilities and of their parents are assured by the protection of due process procedures.
3. The parents of students with disabilities are encouraged to participate in their children's educations.
4. The assessment of all students must be fair and unbiased.
5. All students must be given a free, appropriate public education (FAPE), and it must be provided in the least restrictive environment (LRE) where the student and other students can learn and succeed.
6. Information related to students with disabilities and their families must be kept confidential.

SECTION 504, EHA, EHA AMENDMENTS, AND ADA

In 1973, Section 504 of the Rehabilitation Act, also called Public Law 93-112, was enacted to ensure individuals with disabilities equal access to federally financed programs and to promote their participation in them. A child must have a physical or mental impairment that substantially limits a major life activity to be eligible for a free, appropriate public education (FAPE) under Section 504. This law stimulated motivation to educate students with disabilities, contributing to the passage of the Education for All Handicapped Children Act, also called Public Law 94-142, in 1975. This law provides that all children with disabilities must receive a FAPE provided in the least restrictive environment possible and individualized. Its procedural safeguards mandate due process. The 1986's EHA amendments, or Public Law 99-457 extended special education to disabled preschoolers aged 3 to 5 years; services to infants and toddlers are at each U.S. state's discretion. And 1990's Americans with Disabilities Act (ADA) requires access for disabled people to public buildings and facilities, transportation, and communication but does not cover educational services.

U.S. FEDERAL LEGISLATION PASSED IN 1997, 2001, AND 2004

The 1990 Individuals with Disabilities Education Act (IDEA) was reauthorized in 1997 and numbered Public Law 108-446. It provided more access for children with disabilities to the general education curriculum and extended collaborative opportunities for teachers, other professionals, and families of children with disabilities. No Child Left Behind (NCLB, 2001, now the Every Student Succeeds Act, ESSA 2015), the reauthorization of the Elementary and Secondary Education Act (ESEA), stressed accountability for outcomes by identifying schools and districts needing improvement and assuring teacher quality. It required school performance data to include disabled students' standardized test scores. NCLB emphasized giving teachers and administrators better research information and schools more resources, parents more information about their children's progress and the school's performance, and more local flexibility and control in utilizing federal education funds and in improving teacher qualifications, for example, through alternative certifications. And, 2004's IDEA reauthorization, Individuals with Disabilities Education Improvement Act (IDEIA), covers better alignment of NCLB with IDEA, appropriately identifying students needing special education, ensuring reasonable discipline while protecting special needs students defining highly qualified teachers, reducing paperwork, and increasing cooperation to decrease litigation.

Copyright © Mometrix Media. You have been licensed one copy of this document for personal use only. Any other reproduction or redistribution is strictly prohibited. All rights reserved.

RECENT LEGAL CHANGES TO THE AMERICANS WITH DISABILITIES ACT

The ADA Amendments Act (ADAAA, 2009) overrules prior Supreme Court decisions narrowly interpreting the ADA. This qualifies many more conditions as disabilities.

- Physical or mental impairments substantially limiting one or more life activities now include immune system functioning; normal cell growth; brain, and neurological, respiratory, circulatory, endocrine, reproductive, digestive, bowel, and bladder functions, added to the existing activities of eating, sleeping, thinking, communicating, concentrating, lifting, and bending.
- Impairments include physical (deaf, blind, or wheelchair-bound); conditions (AIDS, diabetes, or epilepsy); mental illnesses and ADHD; record of impairment, for example, cancer in remission and regarded as impaired.
- Reasonable accommodations mean adaptations or modifications enabling persons with disabilities to have equal opportunities. The ADA describes this regarding equal employment opportunities, but it could also be interpreted relative to equal educational opportunities.
- Reasonable accommodations that would cause undue hardship, for example, financial, are not required.

LEGAL RESPONSIBILITIES OF EC PROFESSIONALS

Historically, special education was introduced with the purpose of separating special-needs children from their normally developing peers. However, since 1991, the IDEA legislation has established the necessity of inclusion in normal care and educational environments, including EC settings, for children with disabilities. EC professionals know excluding any child is illegal. Another example of legal responsibilities is the "mandated reporter" status of caregivers/teachers/other adults working with children and families. They are legally required to report suspected child abuse and neglect; the law penalizes them for not reporting. For example, an EC teacher sees injuries to a child. S/he knows the mother has a new boyfriend, displays a fearful attitude, and responds evasively to teacher questions. Later, the child tells the teacher the boyfriend hurt him/her. The teacher pities the mother, realizing she needs the boyfriend financially and emotionally, and reporting suspected abuse could make the mother lose her children or their home. Regardless, the teacher must report suspicions by law, which was enacted for stopping violence against children.

REGULATIONS REGARDING THE CONFIDENTIALITY OF RECORDS

In EC settings, records kept about children and their families must be treated with strict confidentiality. EC centers/programs/preschools/agencies should limit access to student records to children's immediate family members; only those employees authorized; and agencies having legal authority to access records. Confidentiality of records and restricted access to them in all centers/programs/preschools/agencies that receive federal funding are mandated by the Family Educational Rights and Privacy Act (FERPA). Moreover, with the ongoing trend toward educational inclusion, many EC settings serve children with disabilities, whose student records are additionally subject to regulations under the federal Individuals with Disabilities Education Act (IDEA), and also to the special education laws of their respective U.S. states. An exception to the laws regarding records confidentiality is mandated reporting by EC personnel of suspected child abuse and neglect. Laws applying to child abuse and neglect supersede FERPA regulations. Legally, EC employees are both required to report suspected abuse and neglect of children, and immune from liability for releasing child records information relevant to their reporting.

QUALITY CARE AND ECONOMIC CONSIDERATIONS

To furnish and sustain quality care in EC settings is always challenging to care providers. It is even more so during difficult economic times. Many EC centers must face decisions whether to downsize the services they offer or to go out of business. When administrators choose to remain in operation, they encounter equally difficult decisions regarding how to reduce services, but not at the expense of quality.

Copyright © Mometrix Media. You have been licensed one copy of this document for personal use only. Any other reproduction or redistribution is strictly prohibited. All rights reserved.

A legal issue related to such economic considerations is that EC personnel are often placed at legal risk when service quality is compromised. While EC employers, employees, young children's parents, and educational researchers are all interested in and pursue a definition of quality care, no single operational definition has been attained. However, EC professionals with ample work experience in EC centers have contributed various definitions. The consensus of their contributions includes the following common elements: a nurturing environment; employees trained in EC development and methods; age-appropriate curricula; sufficient space, equipment, and materials; safety and good maintenance of physical environments; and good parent-teacher communication.

MEDICAL CARE AND TREATMENT EMPHASIZED IN LEGAL REGULATIONS

The child care licensing regulations of each U.S. state government mostly govern children's medical care and treatment in EC settings. Overall, state regulations emphasize four areas of medical care and treatment: (1) Health requirements for all employees, such as having no communicable diseases; passing a TB test; having no health conditions preventing active child care; and maintaining accurate employee as well as child health records; (2) Administration by staff of medication to children being served in EC settings; (3) Management by EC staff of emergencies due to illness, injury, and accidents; and (4) Treatment of nonemergency minor illnesses, injuries, and accidents occurring to children in EC settings. To protect children's health and safety, EC programs/schools/centers must maintain written policies and procedures for emergency and nonemergency care. To protect personnel from litigation, they must adhere scrupulously to written policies and procedures. Litigation for damages/injury is likely when not following procedures. Not reporting suspected/observed child abuse/neglect and not completing accident reports also invite lawsuits.

ADMINISTRATION OF MEDICATION GUIDELINES

The administration of medication to children in EC settings has been subject to much controversy due to obvious issues of dangers and liability. EC centers/programs must write their policies and procedures to include their state government's licensing requirements for medical care and treatment, which they must follow closely. Experts recommend that parent and doctor permission be required for administering any prescription and nonprescription medications to children. EC settings should keep on file written parental consent for each medication, and review these records regularly for changes. They should also post separate charts, easily accessible to staff, with each child's name, medication, dosage, administration time, and teacher initials. These provide documentation of teachers following parent directions and can prevent mistakes. Staff should label all medications with the drug name, child's name, doctor's name and contact information, and administration instructions. EC centers seasonally and frequently contain many children simultaneously recovering from a variety of illnesses; labeling prevents giving children the wrong medication. Empty drug containers should be returned to parents.

TRANSPORTATION FROM EC LOCATIONS AND EMERGENCY MEDICAL TREATMENT BY EC EMPLOYEES

For a child's non-life-threatening medical emergencies, EC personnel should request transportation by the child's parents. However, if parents cannot transport the child, or in a more severe emergency, EC administrators should call an ambulance. In life-threatening emergencies that preclude waiting for an ambulance, EC administrators must designate the vehicle and responsible employee for transporting the child to the hospital; this information should be posted in the facility's emergency procedures. Administrators should keep the number of staff involved in emergency medical treatment to a minimum. Those employees they designate for involvement should be willing to take on the responsibility and should have current first aid training. The administrators can include a clause in these employees' job descriptions providing for their transporting children in the event of an emergency. The EC facility may also pay for additional or separate liability insurance coverage of the employees they designate as responsible for providing necessary emergency medical treatment.

Copyright © Mometrix Media. You have been licensed one copy of this document for personal use only. Any other reproduction or redistribution is strictly prohibited. All rights reserved.

CHILD CUSTODY ISSUES INVOLVING EC FACILITIES

EC facilities are affected by two types of issues involving child custody: (1) Parents are pursuing legal and/or physical custody of the child but they are not living together; and (2) State authorities have removed a child from the parents' legal and physical custody. Parents frequently demand the right to visit with and/or take the child home on occasion. Two types of custody are: legal custody, defined as an individual's or agency's right to make decisions on a child's behalf regarding the child's place of residence, medical treatment, and education; and physical custody, defined as an individual's or agency's right and responsibility to provide a child with immediate care, and a household or care facility for the present and immediate future. Physical custody does not include all of the rights of full legal custody. It is serious for a child to be in the middle of a custody battle between divorcing parents or between parents and foster parents; therefore, EC facilities need the most concise, clear-cut guidelines possible.

EMERGENCY MEDICAL TREATMENT AND FIRST AID RECOMMENDATIONS

EC programs and preschools must write specific, detailed procedures regarding emergency treatment and keep these on file. Children's parents, EC administrators, and EC staff need to be informed regarding what will occur in the event of a child's serious illness or injury. EC settings must also keep written, signed parental consent forms on file, as well as parent contact information, parental physician and hospital preferences, and health insurance information. EC staff should have current, regularly updated first aid training. First aid equipment should be stored in locations accessible to personnel, who should be frequently reminded of these locations. Lists of each staff member's first aid responsibilities and training should be posted, also accessibly. Licensing regulations require EC facilities to notify parents of emergencies; not doing so is subject to legal action. In non-life-threatening emergencies, staff should ask parents to furnish transportation and medical treatment. For grave emergencies, parental consent forms should be filed and updated semi-annually, including physician and hospital names, ambulance service, and other transportation procedures.

NON-EMERGENCY MEDICAL ILLNESSES

EC programs must keep procedures for, and reports on, non-emergency medical treatment of children on file just as they do for emergency procedures and reporting. Staff must contact and notify a sick child's parents, who decide if the child should leave the center/preschool. If so, parents should transport their child. Parental consent forms should authorize a doctor or nurse to provide routine medical treatment. EC centers/preschools should have sick children wait to be picked up in a location that is separate from other children and activities, but closely supervised by staff. For children with allergies, diabetes, and other chronic medical conditions, EC centers/preschools should not only keep this information on file in records, but also post it accessibly at all times for staff reference. Instructions for any special treatment should be included. For any health impairment(s) a child has that could potentially involve emergency treatment, directions for staff should be visibly posted, including specific employees designated to administer treatment. This protects children from harm and caregivers/educators from legal liability.

CUSTODY STATUS

It is recommended that during a child's enrollment, EC programs procure a signed, dated document clarifying the child's custody status, including names, contact information, and relationships of all individuals authorized to pick up the child. Copies of any separation agreement/court decree should also be filed. Any time EC staff do not recognize an individual coming to pick up a child, they should ask the person to produce photo identification, which they should closely inspect. EC program administrators cannot make decisions regarding who has legal or physical custody of a child they serve. When a parent or other adult enrolls a child in an EC program, that adult is asked to list other persons to be contacted in the event of an emergency. EC administrators are advised to present all parents/guardians with a statement that the EC center will only release their child to someone the enrolling parent/adult listed on the emergency form as authorized to pick up the child.

Copyright © Mometrix Media. You have been licensed one copy of this document for personal use only. Any other reproduction or redistribution is strictly prohibited. All rights reserved.

PICKING UP CHILDREN
NON-CUSTODIAL OR NON-AUTHORIZED ADULTS ATTEMPTING TO PICK UP CHILDREN

EC centers should always have up-to-date documentation on file of a child's custodial arrangements, signed and dated by the enrolling adult. If an adult not authorized to pick up the child attempts to do so, an EC administrator should inform that adult of the center's policies and procedures regarding custody. They may even show the unauthorized adult their copy of the custodial court order if needed. If the unauthorized adult then departs, the administrator must notify the enrolling adult of the incident; file a written report of it; meet with the custodial adult to clarify custody arrangements anew; document this meeting, including its date and signatures; and file the document in the child's record. If the unauthorized adult refuses to leave and makes a scene or threatens/displays violence, the EC administrator should call the police if needed. The EC center's having a procedure in place for protecting children against emotionally upsetting scenes and/or violent adult behavior is crucial to the children's safety and well-being.

LEGAL RESPONSIBILITIES WHEN CHILDREN ARE NOT PICKED UP TIMELY

If a child is not picked up on time from an EC center at the end of its defined day, the EC center has the legal responsibility for the child's welfare as long as the child is on the premises. In the event that a child is left at the EC center for a long time and the parent/authorized adult has not notified the center why and/or when the child will be picked up, EC personnel are advised that keeping the child at the center is less likely to incur legal liability than for the child to stay at an EC staff member's home, for example. If the child has to be removed, it is important for EC staff to inform the police of this and where they are taking the child. If parents are chronically tardy picking up children, EC staff should review the child's information and/or inquire further of parents to ascertain reasons and possible solutions because they are legally responsible for reporting suspected child neglect.

ATTRIBUTES INDICATING EC EDUCATORS' PROFESSIONALISM AND PROFESSIONAL RESPONSIBILITY

While care and instruction of young children are delivered through a variety of program types, EC educators share common general goals. They appreciate EC as a unique period in life. They work to educate holistically, considering the mind, feelings, and body of the whole child. The educational goals they develop are designed to support each child's fulfilling his/her individual potential within relationship contexts. EC professionals realize children are inseparable from their social milieus of family, society, and culture; they work to relate to and understand children in these contexts, while also appreciating and supporting family ties. They apply their knowledge of child development, teaching according to how children learn and what they need, and apply research in the field to differentiating common assumptions and myths from valid scientific findings. They have appropriate behavioral expectations for children at each developmental stage. EC professionals realize the significance of confidentiality: they never gossip or tell families personal information about other families. Lifelong learners, they set their own professional goals, pursuing ongoing professional development.

INTERACTIONS WITH ADULTS IN THE LEARNING ENVIRONMENT

Regarding teachers' roles, much of the focus is on observing children and their behaviors, helping children manage peer interactions, and giving children opportunities for developing peer-group social skills. Too often a similar emphasis is not accorded to teachers' reflecting on their interactions and behaviors with other adults; learning to collaborate with other adults; and developing skills for conflict resolution and managing disagreements with other adults. Some experts say teachers should work diligently and deliberately to make adult interactions integral parts of daily classroom activity. For group ECE settings to attain their goals, adults must make and implement plans collaboratively. However, mandatory staff meetings are commonly occupied with curricular and administrative requirements; beyond these, little or no attention or time is applied to nurturing adult-adult relationships. Adults interact during in-service trainings and professional development experiences, but

92

Copyright © Mometrix Media. You have been licensed one copy of this document for personal use only. Any other reproduction or redistribution is strictly prohibited. All rights reserved.

rarely outside of daily classroom settings. Nevertheless, these experiences can be used as foundations for better adult-adult communication within ECE contexts. Conscious efforts to develop adult-adult relationships benefiting children's growth, development, and learning are necessary.

CONDITIONS ENABLING AND SUPPORTING POSITIVE INTERACTIONS AMONG ADULTS WITHIN THE ECE SETTING

Adults engage in positive interactions with each other within ECE programs when they make time to share their anecdotal records and observations of their young students, and collaboratively plan instruction based on their collective contributions. When adults share information and communicate with one another about the children and their families with whom they work, they interact positively together. When EC educators engage in problem-solving activities and dialogues, these help them identify which learning goals and experiences they can make more effective for the children and how they can do this. Adults within ECE settings should engage in reciprocal exchanging of ideas about the EC learning environment and about how to share responsibilities for performing instructional tasks, rearranging classrooms as needed, setting up class projects, taking care of class pets and plants, and other such daily duties.

ADULT-ADULT INTERACTIONS NOT ADDRESSED IN RESEARCH, THEORETICAL LITERATURE, AND PROFESSIONAL DEVELOPMENT

ECE research contains little work addressing adults' cooperation and collaborative expertise with each other and the influences of these on children. However, the High/Scope curriculum model, The Creative Curriculum, and similar curriculum models and approaches do address adult-adult interactions by stressing how important teamwork is in planning lessons and sharing responsibilities and information. In addition, some educational experts have written about power struggles and other interactional dynamics in adult-adult relationships that can impede employee performance in a variety of settings. Professional development and training programs rarely include adult conflict-resolution techniques, instruction in working collaboratively, or adult learning principles. Hence educators must consider how their adult-adult interactions can support children's development of competence, capability, and confidence. Sharing instructional goals, planning learning experiences that support goals, and sharing responsibilities as a team for implementing projects establishes climates of safety and trust for children.

APPLYING QUALITY TIME TO EC EDUCATORS' INTERACTIONS WITH ADULTS

Educators have noted that attitudes and things we commonly say to children, e.g. "Your actions speak louder than your words" would equally benefit us addressing our own behaviors as adults. Applying the same principles we teach children to interactions among adults in the learning community can positively influence those interactions, which in turn affects adult-child/teacher-student interactions and overall classroom atmospheres. Without such atmospheres conducive to trust and honesty in adult relationships, educators can fall prey to misunderstandings and internalizing negative attitudes, which influence not only coworker interactions but moreover classroom climates. One solution is for adults in ECE to establish occasions affording "quality adult time." Psychotherapist and psychological theorist Virginia Satir, pioneer of family therapy, found interpersonal dynamics influenced by positive adult-adult communication. Trust-building, mutual colleague support, and sharing experiences/feelings—related or unrelated to classrooms—promote adult relationships that benefit teacher-learner relationships and thus enhance young children's development and learning.

Copyright © Mometrix Media. You have been licensed one copy of this document for personal use only. Any other reproduction or redistribution is strictly prohibited. All rights reserved.

Knowing and Integrating Subject Matter: Language and Literacy, Technology, Resources

Activities Promoting Development

USING INTEGRATED CURRICULA

Integrating subject/domain content across the curriculum has been used for years at every educational level, from higher education to early childhood education. However, recent demands for accountability, as exemplified and escalated by No Child Left Behind, can distract educators from holistic and overall learning toward preoccupation with developing isolated skills and using test scores to measure achievement. But rather than discarding teaching methods proven effective, early childhood educators need to integrate newer, mandate-related practices into existing plans and methods. Teaching integrated curricula in early childhood classrooms has proven effective for both children and teachers. Integrating learning domains and subject content in turn integrates the child's developing skills with the whole child. When teachers use topics children find interesting and exciting, in-depth projects focusing on particular themes, and good children's literature, they give children motivation to learn the important concepts and skills they need for school and life success. Children should bring home from preschool not only further developed skills, but also knowledge useful and meaningful in life.

USING MANIPULATIVES FOR PRESCHOOL MATH LEARNING

Young children learn primarily through visually inspecting, touching, holding, and manipulating concrete objects. While they are less likely to understand abstract concepts presented abstractly, such concepts are likelier accessible to preschoolers through the medium of real things they can see, feel, and manipulate. Manipulatives are proven as effective learning devices; some early math curricula (e.g. Horizons) even require them. They are also particularly useful for children with tactile or visual learning styles. Many math manipulatives are available for sale, e.g. linking cubes; 3-dimensional geometric shapes and "geoboards"; large magnetized numbers for whiteboards; weights, scales, and balances for measurements; math blocks; math games; number boards and color tiles; flash cards; play money, toy cash registers, and activities; objects for sorting and patterning; or tangrams for recognizing shapes, reproducing and designing patterns, and spatial problem-solving. Teachers can create homemade math manipulatives using bottle caps/lids; seashells, pebbles/stones; buttons; keys; variously sized, shaped, and colored balls; coffee stirrers; or cardboard tubes from paper products.

HELPING YOUNG CHILDREN USE INQUIRY AND DISCOVERY IN SCIENCE

EC teachers are advised to "teach what they know," i.e. use materials with which they are familiar. For example, teachers who like plants can have young children plant beans, water and watch them grow, moreover incorporating this activity with the story "Jack and the Beanstalk." Teachers can bring in plants, leaves, and flowers for children to observe and measure their sizes, shapes, or textures. Experts recommend teachers utilize their everyday environments to procure learning materials, such as pine needles and cones; loose feathers and leaves found outdoors; animal fur from pets or groomers; and/or snakeskins or turtle shells from local pet stores. Experts advise teachers to use their observational skills during inquiry and discovery activities: if children apply nonstandard and/or unusual uses of some materials, teachers should observe what could be a new discovery, wherein students teach adults new learning, too. Teachers should let children play with and explore new materials to understand their purposes, uses, and care before using them in structured activities.

Copyright © Mometrix Media. You have been licensed one copy of this document for personal use only. Any other reproduction or redistribution is strictly prohibited. All rights reserved.

PROCESS SKILLS DEVELOPED BY PRESCHOOL SCIENCE PROGRAMS

Experts find three process skills that good EC science programs help develop are observation, classification, and communication. Young children are inherently curious about the world and hence enjoy many activities involving inquiry and discovery. Teachers can uncover science in many existing preschool activities. For example, since young children relate to activities focusing on themselves, teachers can have them construct skeletons of dry pasta, using their pictures as heads. Cooking activities involve science, as do art activities. Teachers can have children explore various substances' solubility in water, which colors are produced by mixing which other colors, etc. They can have them compare/contrast similarities/differences among objects. They can create inexpensive science centers using animal puppets; models; thematically-related games, puzzles, books, and writing materials; mirrors, prisms, magnifiers; scales, magnets; and various observable, measurable objects. Teachers should regularly vary materials to sustain children's interest.

PRESCHOOL ACTIVITIES FOR DEVELOPING PHYSICAL COORDINATION, FINE MOTOR SKILLS, AND LARGE MUSCLE SKILLS

Preschoolers are more likely to fall because their lower bodies are not yet developed equally to their upper bodies, giving them higher centers of gravity. Therefore, seeing how long they can balance on one foot and hopping exercises help improve balance and coordination. Hopping races let preschoolers participate in groups and observe peer outcomes, which can also enhance self-confidence and supporting others. "Freeze dancing" (like Musical Chairs without the chair-sitting), without eliminations, provides physical activity and improves coordination. Using writing implements, tying shoes, and playing with small items develop fine motor skills. With preschoolers, it is more effective and developmentally appropriate to incorporate fine motor activities into playtime than to separate quiet activity from play. For example, on nature walks, teachers can have children collect pebbles and twigs and throw them into a stream, developing coordination and various muscles. Running, skipping, and playing tag develop large muscle skills. Kicking, throwing, and catching balls give good unstructured exercise without game rules preschoolers cannot understand. Preschoolers' short attention spans preclude long activity durations.

BENEFITS OF AESTHETIC EXPERIENCES

To help children learn color names and develop sensory discrimination and classification abilities, some art museums offer preschool lessons, which teachers can also use as models. For example, a teacher can read a children's story or sing a song about color, then present a painting/artwork for children to examine, and then a separate display with circles/squares/ovals of colors used by the artist, asking children to name these and any other colors they know, and identify any other colors the artist used not represented in the second display. The teacher then demonstrates how mixing produces other colors. After this demonstration with children's discussion, the teacher gives each child a piece of heavy-duty paper and a brush. The teacher pours about an inch-sized puddle of each of the three primary colors— red, blue, and yellow—in the middle of each child's paper. The teacher then tells the children to use their brushes to explore mixing colors and see the variety of other colors they can create.

BENEFITS OF THE LINE IN VISUAL ARTS

Activities focusing on line in art help young children expand their symbol recognition, develop their comparison-making ability, and facilitate shape recognition. Teachers can begin by singing a song or reading a children's story about lines. Then they can present one painting/drawing/artwork and help children point at various kinds of lines that the artist used. The teacher can draw various line types on a separate piece of paper, e.g. wavy, pointy, spiral, and ask children to find similar lines in the artwork. Then the teacher can ask children to try drawing these different lines themselves. Teachers should also inform children of various tools for drawing lines and let them experiment with these, e.g. crayons, pencils, markers, chalk, paint. An EC teacher can also supply butcher paper or other roll paper for each child to lie down on in whatever creative body positions they can make. The teacher outlines their body

95

Copyright © Mometrix Media. You have been licensed one copy of this document for personal use only. Any other reproduction or redistribution is strictly prohibited. All rights reserved.

shapes with a marker. Then the teacher has the children explore drawing different kinds of lines, using various kinds of drawing tools, to enhance and personalize their individual body outlines.

AESTHETIC EXPERIENCES INVOLVING SHAPE

Giving young children learning activities that focus on shape used in art helps them develop their abilities to form concepts and identify discrepancies. Manipulating basic geometric shapes also stimulates their creative thinking skills and imaginations, as well as developing early geometric math skills. For example, an EC teacher can first read aloud a children's book about shapes, of which many are available. After reading it through, the teacher can go back through the story asking children to point to and name shapes they recognize. Then the teacher can show children an artwork. Using line drawings and/or solid geometric shapes, they discuss what shapes the artist used. The teacher can help children arrange solid shapes to form different images (people, flowers, houses). The teacher can then give children paper pulp trays/heavy paper/board, assorted wooden/cardboard/plastic shapes, and instructions to think and arrange shapes they can make with them, and then give them glue to affix the shapes to their trays/paper/board. They can paint their creations after the glue dries.

EXPLORING TEXTURE IN ART

Preschoolers learn much through looking at and touching concrete materials. Activities involving visual and tactile examination and manipulation plus verbal discussion enhance young children's representational/symbolic thinking abilities. Such activities also enable children to explore various ways of representing different textures visually. Teachers can provide "feely bags/boxes"—bags/boxes with variously textured items inside, e.g. sandpaper, fleece, clay, wool, or tree bark—for children to feel and describe textures before seeing them, and identify objects based on feel. A teacher can then show children a selected artwork; they discuss together which textures are included, e.g. smooth, rough, jagged, bumpy, sharp, prickly, soft, or slippery. The teacher can then demonstrate using plaster/thickened paste/clay how to create various textures using assorted tools (e.g. tongue depressors, plastic tableware, chopsticks, small toys, or child-safe pottery tools) and have children experiment with discovering and producing as many different textures as they can. After children's products dry, they can paint them the next day.

PROVIDING AFFECTIVE LEARNING EXPERIENCES

Providing affective experiences supports young children's emotional development, including understanding and expressing their emotions. These enable development of emotional self-regulation/self-control. Emotional development is also prerequisite to and supportive of social interactions and development. Affective activities also help teachers understand how children feel, which activities they find most fascinating, and/or why they are not participating. "Feelings and Faces" activities are useful. For example, a teacher can have each child draw four different "feeling" faces on paper plates—e.g. happy, sad, angry, confused, excited—and discuss each. A teacher can offer various scenarios, like learning a new song, painting a picture, getting a new pet, or feeling sick, and ask children how they feel about each. Then the teacher can give them new paper plates, having them draw faces showing feelings they often have. Gluing Popsicle sticks to the plates turns them into "masks." The teacher can prompt the children on later days to hold up their masks to illustrate how they feel on a given day and about specific activities/experiences.

MOST IMPORTANT SOCIAL SKILLS

Experts find it crucial for young children's later success in school and life to have experiences that develop understanding of their own and others' emotions; constructive management of their strong feelings; and skills in forming and maintaining relationships. Young children use earlier developed motor skills like pushing/shoving, biting, hitting, or kicking, to get what they want rather than later developing verbal skills. Since physical aggression is antisocial, social development includes learning more acceptable, verbal emotional expressions. "Punch and Judy"–type puppet-shows depicting aggression's failures entertain preschoolers; discussing puppet behavior develops social skills. Teachers

Copyright © Mometrix Media. You have been licensed one copy of this document for personal use only. Any other reproduction or redistribution is strictly prohibited. All rights reserved.

have children say which puppets they liked/disliked and considered good/bad; what happened; what might happen next; and how puppets could act differently. Teachers can reinforce children's discussion of meeting needs using words, not violence. Many read-aloud stories explain why people behave certain ways in social contexts; discussion/question-and-answer groups promote empathy, understanding, and listening skills. Assigning collaborative projects, like scrapbooking in small groups, helps young children learn cooperation, turn taking, listening, and verbally expressing what they want.

PROVIDING AFFECTIVE EXPERIENCES AND PROMOTING EMOTIONAL DEVELOPMENT, PHYSICAL ACTIVITY, AND CREATIVITY

Early childhood teachers can help children understand their feelings and others' feelings, express their emotions, engage in physical exercise, use creative thinking, and have fun by using emotional movement activities. For example, the teacher can begin with prompting the children to demonstrate various types of body movements and postures, like crawling, walking, tiptoeing, skipping, hopping, crouching, slouching, limping, or dancing. Then the teacher can ask the children which feelings they associate with each type of movement and body position. The teacher can play some music for children to move to, and give them instructions such as "Move like you are happy... like you are sad... like you are scared... like you are surprised... like you are angry..." Teachers can also use "freeze"/"statue" dances or games, wherein children move to music and must freeze in position like statues when the music stops; for affective practice, teachers instruct children to depict a certain emotion each time they freeze in place.

Copyright © Mometrix Media. You have been licensed one copy of this document for personal use only. Any other reproduction or redistribution is strictly prohibited. All rights reserved.

English Language Arts Foundations

PHONOLOGICAL AWARENESS, PHONEMIC AWARENESS, AND PHONICS

Phonological awareness refers to the awareness of the sounds that make up a spoken language. This includes being aware of the fact that certain speech sounds rhyme with one another, and that it is possible to break down spoken sentences into individual words, words into individual syllables, and syllables into individual phonemes or speech sounds. Phonological awareness also includes the abilities to talk about speech sounds; to think about them; and to manipulate them into various combinations, sequences, and patterns. The latter includes changing one word into another by inserting, deleting, or exchanging an individual phoneme. Moreover, phonological awareness is an understanding of the relationship between spoken and written language. Typically, children's phonological awareness skills develop continuously and gradually throughout the later preschool years. Children develop phonological awareness through their exposure to language and through direct training, both of which are provided by the adults around them and in their lives.

Phonological awareness focuses on the awareness of speech sounds, which young children typically develop and learn before they learn to read. Phonemic awareness refers to awareness of the individual phonemes or speech sounds used in the child's native language, which the child hears in the language spoken by the adults and older children around them in their environment. Phonological awareness instruction teaches children to recognize the speech sounds they hear, to identify and differentiate these sounds, to produce them accurately, and to manipulate them. Good phonological awareness facilitates children's ability to make connections between sounds and alphabet letters, hence facilitating phonics. Phonics is the instructional method used to establish the Alphabetic Principle (i.e. the concept of sound-to-letter correspondence) and teach skills for decoding (breaking words down to their component sounds/letters) and encoding (blending/combining individual sounds/letters to form words).

IMPORTANCE OF DEVELOPING PHONOLOGICAL AND PHONEMIC AWARENESS SKILLS

By developing phonological and phonemic awareness skills, young children develop awareness of the sounds used in their native language. Significantly, they also learn to make the association between the speech sounds (phonemes) they hear and the written/printed letter symbols that represent them. Understanding this connection gives young children the foundation they need for the development of future skills, including word recognition skills and the decoding skills needed to read printed/written language. When young children develop phonological and phonemic awareness, they are less likely to experience deficits or delays in learning to read, and are more likely to achieve success in reading and spelling. The consensus of a great deal of educational research is that strong phonological and phonemic awareness in children is often a predictor of future long-term success in spelling, reading, and overall literacy performance. Research has also found that this awareness is a more accurate predictor of future success than vocabulary knowledge, intelligence, socioeconomic status, and other related factors.

EXAMPLES OF PHONOLOGICAL AWARENESS SKILLS

Young children who have developed phonological awareness can typically recognize the sounds of alliteration in spoken language, which is the repeated use of the same or similar consonants (e.g., "She sells seashells by the seashore"); the sounds of rhyming words; the sounds of words with the same initial sounds (e.g., "Wee Willie Winkie"); and final sounds. They can typically divide words into smaller parts, such as syllables and phonemes (speech sounds). They can usually also count these smaller parts. When given isolated speech sounds, they are typically able to blend these separate phonemes together to form familiar words. Children with good phonemic awareness realize that words are composed of phonemes, and that these individual sounds are symbolically represented by written/printed letters. Hence, they understand the relationship between speech and writing/print. Phonologically aware preschool children can typically also manipulate spoken language by adding, removing, or substituting specific speech sounds to create different words.

Copyright © Mometrix Media. You have been licensed one copy of this document for personal use only. Any other reproduction or redistribution is strictly prohibited. All rights reserved.

BENEFITS OF PHONOLOGICAL AND PHONEMIC AWARENESS INSTRUCTION

Phonological and phonemic awareness (PPA) instruction benefits all children learning to read, which includes preschoolers, kindergarteners, and first-graders. In addition, PPA instruction is important for children who are at risk for reading problems. Such children typically have fewer alphabetic skills due to less exposure to and less experience with using the alphabet. This can be because their families have less access to books and/or libraries; their parents have different expectations of reading, or they prioritize reading differently; or their parents do not realize the importance of reading aloud to children to literacy development. Preschoolers with delayed language development, who are more likely to be diagnosed with reading disorders by the time they reach school age, also benefit from PPA instruction. Enhanced PPA enables enhanced awareness of correct speech, so children with articulation disorders also benefit. According to research, children with spelling disorders perform poorly when given PPA tasks. Phonemic instruction improves their understanding of sound-to-letter relationships and their ability to recognize common spelling units found in words, thereby strengthening their spelling skills.

ORAL LANGUAGE DEVELOPMENT

Because of the amount of variation among individual children in the process of normal oral language development, it is neither easy nor accurate to pin down any linguistic developmental milestone to a specific age. Therefore, ranges rather than ages are identified. For example, most normally developing children will utter their first recognizable words sometime between the ages of 12 months and 18 months. However, the progress of normal language acquisition is unpredictable in the individual child, a statement which holds true for other areas of normal growth and development. For example, one child may say his/her first word at the age of 10 months, while another child may begin using words at 20 months. The majority of typically developing children tend to begin speaking in complex sentences around the ages of four to four-and-a-half years. But again, because the pace of normal language development can vary, some children might use complex sentences by three years old, while others only develop this ability by five-and-a-half years old.

CONSIDERATIONS FOR ADULTS

The vast majority of children's oral language develops with great natural efficiency. Adults need not try to force it, but can nurture it by providing language-rich environments. Practices that may help include talking to children regularly starting at birth; reading regularly to babies, toddlers, and preschoolers; naming objects, actions, and events children encounter for them; and playing games with speech sounds, words, rhymes, etc. Adults need not be concerned when younger children distort or substitute more difficult phonemes like /r/ and /s/ with easier ones; this is normal. However, if a child still mispronounces such sounds beyond the age of about eight or nine, hearing and speech testing and therapy are indicated. Newborn hearing screenings are vital, as hearing loss is the most common disability in infants. If a child seems not to hear others' speech, a child's closest family/friends have trouble understanding the child's speech, or a child's communication is obviously different from that of same-age peers, adults should consult hearing and speech language specialists.

GENETIC AND ENVIRONMENTAL INFLUENCES

As with so many other aspects of human growth and development, oral language development is a product of the combined influences of nature and nurture, and of the interactions between the two. Humans have inborn inclinations to seek out social interaction with other people. Babies communicate their needs and wants through crying and gesturing before acquiring spoken language, and they frequently understand adult communication. Researchers have pointed out that social interactions and oral language development do not take place for the purpose of learning rules, but for connecting with others and making sense of the reality we experience. Children have inherent abilities to decipher linguistic rules through their environmental exposure to spoken language. They can do this without formal instruction. This is evidence of the influence of nature on oral language development, as is over-regularization. An example of the latter includes applying regular verb rules to irregular exceptions (e.g., "tooths," "freezed," "goed," etc.) until exceptions are learned. Adults' constant corrections during this

99

Copyright © Mometrix Media. You have been licensed one copy of this document for personal use only. Any other reproduction or redistribution is strictly prohibited. All rights reserved.

learning stage are typically futile. In addition to natural and environmental influences, children's language development is also influenced by their own cognitive abilities.

PHONOLOGY, MORPHOLOGY, SEMANTICS, SYNTAX, AND PRAGMATICS

Phonology is concerned with the rules for the combinations of speech sounds within a given language. For example, while some African languages include words beginning with the –ng/[ŋ] phoneme, in English this sound is only word-medial or word-final, never word-initial. Most speakers follow such rules unconsciously. Morphology focuses on the smallest structural/grammatical units that convey or affect meaning. For example, in books, the noun book and the plural –s ending are each morphemes. Semantics focuses on the meanings of morphemes, words, and sentences. Syntax refers to sentence structure and word order, and is related to a language's rules for correctly combining morphemes and words into suffixes/inflections, sentences, questions, imperatives, etc. For example, features like participial modifiers and the verbs they modify are placed in a different order in German and English. The verb-containing phrase "I walked" would follow modifiers like "happily," "down the street," and "on a sunny day" in German, but would precede most if not all modifiers in English. Pragmatics focuses on rules for using language appropriately in various situations. An example of pragmatics would be how to speak at home versus how to speak at school or work.

SUPPORTING NATURAL DEVELOPMENT

Teachers should realize that whatever language and/or dialect a child speaks is a reflection of that child's family's and community's values, identity, and experiences. As such, it is a valid communication system that deserves respect. Adults should treat babies and young children as conversationalists even before they begin talking, because they learn conversational rules very early (e.g., attentive gazing, facial expressions, and turn-taking). A significant component of language development is peer learning, particularly in mixed-age child groups. Adults should encourage child interaction by providing activities conducive to talking and using a broad range of materials. Individual and collaborative activities should be balanced. Sharing books, building with blocks, engaging in dramatic play, and taking part in "shop"/carpentry-related activities all stimulate interaction and discussion. While peer learning is important, adults are children's main resources for initiating conversations, questioning, listening, responding, and maintaining language development. Adults should always keep this in mind. Continued interaction into the elementary grades and written language comprehension also support oral language development in children. Language informs all curriculum areas, so active learners in classrooms are always communicating.

APPROACHES TO COMMUNICATING WITH YOUNG CHILDREN

Researchers have found that a common practice among teachers when they are using language in their classrooms is to use linear or one-way questions requiring linear/one-way responses. However, experts recommend using reciprocal instructional approaches (e.g., asking open-ended questions that enable two-way/three-way responses). Studies also reveal that teachers are likely to dominate the classroom verbally. Experts believe a better approach would be to encourage and elicit children's conversational language and higher order cognitive skills by deliberately incorporating these into children's play activities. Experts state that teachers should have someone record a video of them during children's play time so they can monitor their own verbal behavior. Teachers should note how many times they verbally describe what the children do, how many times they repeat what a child says and then add some further information to it, how often they comment on and describe the properties of objects, and how often they ask open-ended questions. They should reflect not only on the number and duration of verbal interactions, but also on the quality of each conversation.

"FOLLOWING THE CAR" TEACHING STRATEGY

Some researchers recommend using a teaching strategy called "Following the CAR" to engage in conversations with two- to five-year-old children. The C in CAR stands for Comment. In this step, the adult should comment on what a child is looking at, handling, or talking about. The adult should then

100

Copyright © Mometrix Media. You have been licensed one copy of this document for personal use only. Any other reproduction or redistribution is strictly prohibited. All rights reserved.

wait five seconds. Experts find that this interval is important because it gives the young child time to hear and cognitively process the adult's comment, experience a response, formulate that response into verbal form, and then express it orally. The A stands for Ask. To continue the conversation the adult has begun and/or to start a new one, the adult should then ask the child questions about something the child is looking at, handling, or talking about. The adult should again wait five seconds to give the child time to respond. The R stands for Respond. Once the child gives an oral response, the adult should respond to what the child says by repeating the child's response and then adding a bit more information to extend the child's knowledge.

"REAL" CONVERSATIONS

Experts define "real" conversations as those that interest the child and consist of three to four exchanges/"turns" between the child and the adult. Having at least one real conversation with each child on a daily basis is a highly effective way to improve vocabulary development and develop listening comprehension beyond the level of individual words. Teaching strategies that support children's active participation in real conversations include the following: attentively listening to what the children say; inviting the children to join extended conversations with adults and peers; demonstrating genuine interest in and affection for the children; sending verbal and nonverbal messages that are consistent; avoiding making judgmental comments about children or anybody else to or in front of the children; addressing the children with courtesy; availing oneself of spontaneously occurring opportunities for informal conversations with each child, and/or even planning some opportunities; basing conversations on children's specific interests; and using children's experiences, as well as songs, stories, and books, as topics for conversation.

USING STAGE-APPROPRIATE PROMPTS WITH CHILDREN LEARNING ENGLISH AS A SECOND LANGUAGE

Children in the preproduction stage of ESL acquisition comprehend little English. They do not speak English, but can nod, point, and draw. Teachers can give prompts like "Where is...?" "Who has...?" "Show me the..." or "Circle the...." In the early production stage, children's comprehension is limited. They can give one- or two-word answers, use some important words and familiar phrases, and use verbs in present tense. Teachers can ask "Yes/No" and "Either/Or" questions and questions requiring short answers consisting of one or two words. They can also use lists and labels to access and expand vocabulary knowledge. In the speech emergence stage, comprehension improves and simple sentences emerge, albeit with grammatical and pronunciation errors. Teachers can now ask children "Why...?" "How...?" and "Explain..." questions, and can expect answers in the form of phrases or short sentences. In the intermediate fluency stage, when students have excellent comprehension and can use correct grammar more often, teachers can ask children more abstract questions like "What would happen if...?" or "Why do you think...?" During the advanced fluency stage, when students approach native proficiency, teachers can instruct students to retell stories and make decisions.

STAGES OF SECOND LANGUAGE ACQUISITION

For ESL children, the first stage of second language acquisition is preproduction, which takes place during roughly the first six months of learning. Listening comprehension is minimal. The child does not speak in English, but can nod/shake the head "yes/no," draw pictures, and point at things. In the second, early production stage, which lasts from roughly six months to one year into learning, children have limited English comprehension. They can utter one- to two-word answers, essential words, familiar phrases, and present tense verbs. In the third, speech emergence stage, which lasts from about one to three years into learning, children comprehend English well. They can speak in simple sentences, but still make mistakes in pronunciation and grammar. They often misunderstand jokes in English. The fourth stage is intermediate fluency, which begins about three years into the language acquisition process and extends to about the fifth year. By this stage, children have attained excellent English listening comprehension, and do not make many grammatical errors. In the fifth, final stage of advanced

Copyright © Mometrix Media. You have been licensed one copy of this document for personal use only. Any other reproduction or redistribution is strictly prohibited. All rights reserved.

fluency, children's English language proficiency is similar to that of a native English speaker. Children typically reach this stage between five and seven years after they start learning English.

IMPROVING (ESL) INSTRUCTION

Research in the early 1990s found that regardless of the type of bilingual education language programs used (e.g., early-exit, late-exit transitional, or immersion), teachers tended to ask ESL students questions requiring low levels of English language proficiency and lower-order cognitive skills. Teacher knowledge of what stages of second language acquisition students are in, as well as an awareness of the kinds of prompts and questions that are appropriate for each stage both enable teachers to approach children using suitable levels of discourse. Another advantage of knowing the stages is that teachers can assess students' content knowledge as well as their English language proficiency. A third benefit is that knowing language acquisition levels enables teachers to use what Vygotsky termed the zone of proximal development (ZPD), the gap between a learner's current capability and the next level of ability. Vygotsky found that the ZPD can be utilized by providing necessary temporary support—which Bruner called scaffolding—that is gradually withdrawn as students progress.

USING SCAFFOLDING AND THE ZONE OF PROXIMAL DEVELOPMENT (ZPD)

Scaffolding, a term coined by Jerome Bruner, involves temporarily providing the support a learner needs to accomplish tasks just above his/her current performance level (i.e. things s/he cannot do independently, but can achieve with assistance). Lev Vygotsky identified the ZPD as the gap between a learner's current ability and the next level. He found that providing scaffolding enables teachers to exploit the ZPD to enhance learning. Teachers can apply this concept to ESL language development through direct instruction, by asking challenging questions, and/or by modeling correct English pronunciation and grammar. For example, a student in the first, preproduction stage of second language acquisition is able to find things, point at objects, and circle pictures, and such tasks are stage appropriate. However, a teacher can promote higher development by providing scaffolding to support students in answering Yes/No questions and/or giving one-word answers. These are tasks associated with the second, early production stage. With teacher support, the student can move to a higher stage of ESL acquisition.

CONVERSATIONAL VERSUS ACADEMIC ENGLISH FOR ESL LEARNERS

Conversational English requires basic skills that are used in interpersonal communication in everyday life, including basic vocabulary, grammar, and pronunciation. Conversational English enables ESL students to comprehend and participate in informal conversations with adults and peers. ESL children generally develop it after living in English-speaking locations for about two years. Conversational English is not particularly difficult cognitively. Children with conversational English skills sound fluent to most people. They converse in English, understand teacher questions, and may even translate for parents. However, their conversational fluency is often not reflected in school homework and tests. Teachers and parents may wrongly assume a child is unmotivated/learning disabled/lazy, when the true reason for the child's academic underachievement is that he or she lacks a knowledge of more cognitively demanding academic English (such as content specific vocabulary in math, science, etc.) and complex-compound sentence syntax. ESL students take at least five to seven years to become fluent in academic English, and take even longer when they lack native language literacy at the time they enroll in an English language school. To understand textbooks, solve word problems, write reports/papers, and develop the problem solving and critical thinking skills needed to comprehend and communicate abstract and novel concepts, students must master academic English.

USING WORD WALLS TO ENHANCE VOCABULARY BUILDING FOR ESL CHILDREN

Young ESL children learn English vocabulary words by repeatedly singing the same familiar songs and chants, and by hearing the same stories many times. Such repetition is also favored by young children. While ESL children are involved in activities featuring repeated story readings, rhyme recitations, and/or singing, teachers can supplement these activities to enhance further vocabulary building by

Copyright © Mometrix Media. You have been licensed one copy of this document for personal use only. Any other reproduction or redistribution is strictly prohibited. All rights reserved.

providing word walls. A word wall uses visuals to illustrate concepts represented by vocabulary words, as well as by related words. Key characteristics of vocabulary words and related words may also be shown. A word wall can also illustrate concepts like synonyms and subcategories. For example, a word wall for "Chicken Little," "The Little Red Hen," or another poultry-related story could have a picture of a chicken at the top labeled Chicken. Below it on the left might be several related pictures labeled with their names: Rooster, Hen, and Chick. Under the main chicken picture on the right could be several labeled pictures showing chicken characteristics (e.g., Feathers, Beak, and the Eggs that hens lay).

INPUT HYPOTHESIS

Krashen and Terrell, who identified the stages of second language acquisition, posited the input hypothesis. This states that when an ESL learner in one stage of acquisition is given instructional input that includes some structures characteristic of the next stage of acquisition, and is also encouraged to use language reflective of that next, higher stage, the learner will advance to that next stage in listening and speaking. The input hypothesis is expressed as i + 1, where i represents the speaker's actual or current level (or stage) of second language acquisition, and i + 1 represents the speaker's potential second language development level. Teachers who know the stages of second language acquisition and the appropriate types of prompts to use for each stage can adapt their prompting so that students respond commensurately with their current stage of English language development and with the next higher stage at the same time.

APPLICATION OF THE WORD-MES FORMULA TO ESL INSTRUCTION

Jane Hill's "Word-MES" stands for "Word selection," "Modeling," "Expanding," and "Sounding like a book," respectively. Include examples in your response. "Word-MES" is a mnemonic for the key steps in applying the stages of second language development to ESL instruction. Students in the preproduction stage need to learn English vocabulary Words. Teachers should focus on helping students learn and correctly apply basic vocabulary. For example, using the story of "Goldilocks and the Three Bears," teachers can teach words like house, bed, cereal, oatmeal, too, hot, cold, hard, and soft. When working with students in the early production stage, teachers should Model correct English usage. For example, if a child says "Goldie runned," the teacher can respond, "Yes, Goldilocks ran and ran." Teachers should not make explicit corrections. When working with children in the speech emergence stage, teachers can focus on Expanding spoken/written sentences. For example, if a child says, "Bed was too soft," the teacher can expand on this by saying, "Yes, the second bed was too soft," adding the correct article and specifying adjective. Teachers can help students in intermediate and advanced fluency stages to Sound like books by exposing them to words outside their repertoires, repeatedly reading familiar books and singing songs, and using supplementary word walls.

CAUSES AND SIGNS OF ARTICULATION DISORDERS

Articulation refers to the pronunciation of specific speech sounds and phonemes. Some phonemes are harder to produce than others. Therefore, it is normal for young children not to produce some sounds correctly until they reach a certain level of maturity. For example, children are around seven or eight on average before they can pronounce difficult phonemes like /r/ and /s/. Some children continue to distort, omit, or substitute a certain sound beyond the age norm. Speech therapy can help address these types of issues. If a child mispronounces multiple phonemes beyond the typical age ranges, testing is needed to determine the cause. Multiple factors can affect articulation, including hearing loss, misaligned teeth/jaws, missing teeth, a tongue that is shorter or longer than normal, velopharyngeal insufficiency interfering with complete vocal tract closure, breathing problems, mild cerebral palsy causing neuromuscular weakness and incoordination of the speech mechanisms, mild to moderate intellectual disabilities, and others. Some children's speech is difficult to understand due to multiple misarticulations, which may also be caused by any combination of the factors outlined above.

Copyright © Mometrix Media. You have been licensed one copy of this document for personal use only. Any other reproduction or redistribution is strictly prohibited. All rights reserved.

CAUSES AND SIGNS OF DELAYED LANGUAGE DEVELOPMENT

Some children develop skills for understanding and using spoken and written language significantly later than normal, even when individual variations are taken into account. This can be due to a number of causes. Children with mild or moderate intellectual disabilities are likely to show delayed language development as well as delayed cognitive development, as these are closely related. Some children do not test with obvious cognitive deficits, but may have minimal neurological damage, which can delay language development. Other children may have no organic basis for the delay, but have been born into environments where they are deprived of adequate environmental stimulation. For example, if a child's parents and/or caregivers/teachers do not routinely talk to them, have limited daily interactions with them, and never read to them, young children are likely to exhibit delayed language development. Some parents who do interact with and talk to their children may still be linguistically, educationally, and culturally deprived themselves. Their children may feel loved and have good self-esteem, but may have a level of language development that is below average for their age.

ALPHABETIC PRINCIPLE AND ITS PREDICTIVE VALUE FOR FUTURE LITERACY

The concept that written/printed letters and their patterns correspond to speech sounds is called the alphabetic principle. Children's future success with reading is strongly predicted by their early knowledge of the shapes and names of written/printed letters. Children's development of the abilities to view words as series of letters and to remember printed/written word forms is closely associated with their knowledge of letter names. Children cannot learn letter sounds or recognize words without knowing letter names. Being able to recognize and name multiple letters is a prerequisite for comprehending the alphabetic principle, which explains that spoken sounds and printed letters have predictable, systematic relationships. Children follow a sequence of first learning letter names, then learning letter shapes, and finally learning letter sounds. Singing the "ABC" song and reciting rhymes help children learn letter names. Playing with lettered blocks, large 3-D letters, and alphabet books helps them learn letter shapes. Teachers can plan informal instruction so that children are given multiple, varied opportunities to view, compare, and manipulate letters. Relevant activities may include identifying, naming, and writing upper-case and lower-case letters.

INSTRUCTION PRINCIPLES IN TEACHING THE ALPHABETIC PRINCIPLE

Not all children begin preschool or school with good alphabetic knowledge, which refers to an awareness that written letters represent spoken sounds. For those who have not developed this prerequisite skill, educators must provide well-organized instruction to enable students to identify, name, and write the letters of the alphabet. Once they master these skills, they will have the foundation necessary to learn letter sounds and word spellings. A general instructional plan revolving around the alphabetic principle includes several elements. First, teachers should give children explicit instruction in isolated letter-sound correspondences. Second, during each day's lessons and activities, teachers should give children opportunities to practice their developing knowledge of letter-sound relationships. Teachers should both review children's cumulative learning of letter-sound correspondences already taught and create opportunities for children to practice new letter-sound relationships they are just learning. Finally, to give students opportunities to apply their expanding knowledge of the alphabetic principle early and frequently, teachers can supply phonetic spellings of words with meanings familiar to children for them to read.

PACE AND ORDER OF LESSONS IN TEACHING THE ALPHABETIC PRINCIPLE

There is no expert consensus regarding the speed or sequence that should be used to teach young children letter-to-sound relationships. However, educators generally agree that phonemes and letters with the highest utility—those used most often—should be taught earliest. These include m, a, t, s, p, and h. Conversely, x as in "box," gh as in "through," ey as in "they," and a as in "want" are letter-phoneme relationships that are used less frequently. The letter-sound relationships of consonants least subject to distorted articulation when pronounced in isolation should be taught first. These include f, m, and n. Word-initial or word-medial stops (p, b, t, d, k, and g) are more difficult for young children to combine

104

Copyright © Mometrix Media. You have been licensed one copy of this document for personal use only. Any other reproduction or redistribution is strictly prohibited. All rights reserved.

with other sounds than continuous (fricative/affricate) phonemes are. Sounds that are easily confused (like /b/ and /v/) or letters that look similar (like b and d, or p and g) should be introduced to young children in separate lessons.

SOUND-TO-ALPHABET LETTER RELATIONSHIPS INSTRUCTION

When a teacher is instructing preschoolers on the relationships between spoken sounds and written letters (known as the alphabetic principle), s/he might begin by introducing a few (e.g., two, three, or four) single consonant sounds and one or two short vowel sounds. Once the children have mastered these, the teacher can present some additional new single consonant sounds, present some additional new short vowel sounds, and introduce one long vowel sound in a subsequent lesson. Then, the teacher could introduce consonant blends like st-, cl-, etc. in a separate lesson. Another lesson after the one on consonant blends could focus on digraphs (e.g., ch, sh, and th), which would enable children to read frequently used words like "chair," "she," and "the." A later lesson could introduce consonant clusters such as str-, spl-, etc. Teachers should always teach young children single consonants and consonant blends/clusters in separate lessons to avoid confusion.

PACING AND ORDER OF LESSONS ON SOUND-LETTER CORRESPONDENCES

Early childhood alphabetic principle instruction should be logical and consistent with the rates at which young children are able to learn. Teachers should introduce sound-to-letter relationships that will enable children to work with words as early as possible. According to research findings, direct and explicit instruction controlled by the teacher is more effective for teaching children the alphabetic principle than indirect and implicit methods are. Many teachers also use eclectic approaches, combining multiple teaching methods. Educators should remember that individual children normally learn sound-letter relationships at varying rates. A reasonable rate for introducing sound-letter relationships ranges from two to four relationships weekly. The earliest relationships teachers should introduce are high-utility ones. When introducing consonants and vowels, teachers should present them in an order that facilitates children's reading words readily. Teachers should avoid presenting similar-sounding phonemes and/or similar-looking letters together. They should use separate sessions/lessons to introduce single consonant sounds and consonant blends/clusters. Instruction in blending letters/sounds should use words with letter-sound relationships children have already learned.

ENGLISH LITERACY DEVELOPMENT IN ESL STUDENTS

To teach ESL students to read English, teachers must know the essential elements of literacy development, the principles of second language acquisition, and the differing conventions of both the students' first (L1) and second (L2) languages. Second language acquisition is an ongoing, lifelong process. In many ways, the process of second language acquisition parallels that of first language acquisition. Regardless of their L1 or their formal L2 instruction, students demonstrate predictable error patterns in learning. Acquiring language is not a linear process. While formal instruction can expand knowledge and inform and ease the process of language acquisition, it cannot accelerate it. Therefore, it is also detrimental to require sequential mastery of each curriculum element before proceeding onto the next element. Activities using language that are meaningful to students within a relevant context and teacher guidance help develop L2 acquisition. Varying language conventions must be kept in mind during instruction. For example, letter-sound correspondences are more consistent in Spanish than in English. Spanish letters are pronounced the same way they are spelled, so Spanish-speaking children can find the multiple pronunciations of the same phoneme in English confusing.

PHONOLOGICAL DIFFERENCES BETWEEN SPANISH AND ENGLISH AFFECTING THE ELL PROCESS

Because letter-sound correspondences are more consistent in Spanish than in English, Spanish vowels have fewer possible pronunciations than English vowels. Spanish has fewer total vowel sounds than English, regardless of spelling. This makes learning English more complicated for Spanish-speaking children. In modern Spanish, the pronunciation for the consonants v and b is the same, but these letters

Copyright © Mometrix Media. You have been licensed one copy of this document for personal use only. Any other reproduction or redistribution is strictly prohibited. All rights reserved.

have different pronunciations in English. Spanish and English both contain the phoneme /ð/. In Spanish, it is represented by the letter d; in English, it is represented by the letters th. In English, the consonant clusters /sk/, /sp/, and /st/ are word-initial, as in school, special, and star. In Spanish, they are always preceded by /e/, as in escuela (school), especial (special), and estrella (star). Spanish speakers thus have difficulty pronouncing such initial clusters, and often end up using Spanish conventions, saying "estart" for start, "espeak" for speak, etc. Some sounds exist in L2 but not in L1; some L1 sounds transfer to L2; and letter-sound correspondences may differ between languages. Therefore, phonological and phonemic awareness and oral language development are crucial for ELLs.

ENGLISH LITERACY DEVELOPMENT VERSUS SPANISH LITERACY DEVELOPMENT

In English literacy instruction with native English-speaking children, educators teach individual phonemes/speech sounds and their corresponding alphabetic letters (phonics instruction). Spanish, however, is a syllabic language, and Spanish reading is taught using syllables rather than single phonemes. Spanish instruction uses syllables to teach word spellings, word divisions, stressed/accented parts of a word, word reading, and simple sentence construction. English-speaking children are taught to "sound out" a new word they encounter while reading by separating it into individual letters representing individual sounds. Spanish-speaking children are taught to "sound out" words by separating them into their component syllables. For example, in English, children sound out "man" as /m/, /æ/, and /n/. In Spanish, children sound out manzana (apple) as man, za, and na. Teachers must realize that ELLs encounter many phonological, syntactic, and semantic differences between their first and second languages, and that children with less English proficiency depend more on L1 cues. ELLs also expend double the cognitive effort of native English speakers through their attention to new language sounds, meanings, and structures, as well as their attempts to learn new literacy concepts and skills.

WRITING SYSTEMS OF DIFFERENT LANGUAGES

Not only do different languages have phonological and orthographic differences, but they also use different writing systems. For example, although Spanish is syllabic in phonology and Spanish literacy instruction is syllabic, the Spanish writing system and letter-sound correspondences are (like English) alphabetic. The Chinese writing system is logographic. Rather than using alphabet letters to symbolize speech sounds, Chinese uses ideographs, or characters depicting concepts, to symbolize words. The Japanese language has a combined logographic and syllabic writing system. Directionality can differ, too. In English, Spanish, and other European-based languages, lines of writing/print go from left to right. In Hebrew, they go from right to left; in Chinese, they go from top to bottom. Therefore, children's ESL progress relies on their phonological awareness, their oral language knowledge, their grasp of the alphabetic principle, and their print awareness and book knowledge. These are best developed in purposeful contexts that are relevant to children.

HELPING ELL STUDENTS DEVELOP ENGLISH LANGUAGE LITERACY

When teaching children learning English as a second language, teachers should make their instruction understandable to them. They can do this by providing visual aids, graphic organizers, and concrete examples of what they are teaching. They should consistently monitor children's language for development levels and use. They can paraphrase to clarify unfamiliar words and the concepts they describe. Teachers should take advantage of every opportunity to establish connections between children's L1 and English. They must repeat things frequently. They can also help ELLs by establishing a safe atmosphere where children receive ongoing support and feel comfortable taking risks. Teachers should adopt and communicate high learning expectations. They should enable children to develop necessary language and literacy skills that are consistent with their current levels of oral English proficiency. Literacy instruction should build upon children's comprehension, the alphabetic principle, and print concepts. Teachers should use language that children understand and find meaningful.

Teachers should assess their students' specific needs, and then design instructional programs that address those needs. They should also design instructional plans expressly for new students. They

Copyright © Mometrix Media. You have been licensed one copy of this document for personal use only. Any other reproduction or redistribution is strictly prohibited. All rights reserved.

should design instruction so children can understand it. They should assess student progress often. Based on data they collect through assessment and monitoring, teachers should make instructional decisions, including adjusting schedules accordingly. They should create plenty of opportunities for children to participate in extended conversations in English. Teachers should also seek out others in their preschool's community who have expertise in one or more areas, and should use these assets when creating their curriculum. ESL teaching strategies should be integrated into instruction in all content areas. Teachers should activate and access children's background knowledge and connect instructional content to children's real lives. They should give children opportunities to discuss learning materials, topics, and early texts. Teachers must also acknowledge and value diverse cultural patterns of speech and discourse.

PRINT AWARENESS

Print awareness, also called print literacy, emerges gradually during the preschool years in normally developing children. Print awareness is the understanding that print conveys meaning, and the understanding of print's form and function. Research has found that children typically tend to develop print awareness between three and five years of age. Some researchers have observed that at this age, children go through a significant metamorphosis, wherein they demonstrate exponential increases in self-motivated, independent interactions with print. Such interactions include reciting the alphabet, identifying printed letters, recognizing printed words, and using print as a communicative mechanism. Many studies have concluded that the development of these print literacy skills by preschool-aged children is a strong predictor of their future achievement in reading. Studies have also shown that while four-year-olds have not mastered either word concepts or print concepts, they may acquire many print concepts sooner than word concepts.

INSTRUCTIONAL STRATEGIES FOR PROMOTING LITERACY DEVELOPMENT AND READING COMPREHENSION

Instructional strategies designed to promote early literacy development and reading comprehension that are used in many ECE programs (like the EC component of the Partners for Literacy [PfL] Curriculum) include interactive book reading, the 3N strategy, extended teaching, problem solving, and curriculum-embedded assessments. These are also suitable for teaching ESL children. Interactive book reading is a teaching method that should be used at least once per day with each child. Children participate either individually or in pairs. This interactive reading is done in addition to (not instead of) reading in large and small groups. The purpose of interactive book reading is to stimulate responsive, reciprocal instructional conversations between each child and the teacher. Interactive book reading employs three main component strategies: the 3S strategy (3S stands for see, show, and say), wh-questions, and expanded book reading.

USING 3S STRATEGY AND WH- QUESTIONS IN INTERACTIVE BOOK READING

Interactive book reading is a strategy aimed at generating responsive instructional conversations between the child and teacher. In the 3S strategy, the 3 S's are see, show, and say. First, the teacher asks the child to see/look at a specific feature in a book, such as the main character. If the child succeeds, the teacher then asks him/her to locate an image or a word on a page. If the child does this correctly, the teacher then asks the child to say a word/answer a question. This requires multiple responses, promoting children's attending behavior and building upon each student's abilities. During the say part of 3S, the teacher asks the child questions beginning with who, what, where, when, and why. These wh-questions help teachers assess children's listening and/or reading comprehension levels, and also encourage ongoing conversations between each child and the teacher.

USING INTERACTIVE ACTIVITIES IN EXPANDED BOOK READING

Expanded book reading is an instructional strategy that is part of the interactive book reading teaching format, which is used to promote early childhood literacy development. In expanded book reading, teachers can ask children to predict the possible subject matter of a book. They can give children an

Copyright © Mometrix Media. You have been licensed one copy of this document for personal use only. Any other reproduction or redistribution is strictly prohibited. All rights reserved.

overview of a book. They can discuss setting, characters, and events in a book with children. They can help children relate the story in a book to their own lives, thereby making the book meaningful and relevant to children and helping them establish connections between literature and real life. Teachers can enhance the meaning of stories in books by acting them out using puppets and other props. To integrate literacy into all content areas across the curriculum, teachers can design math, science, art, and/or music activities that are related to a book students read. Teachers can ask children to retell the story they read together, which is an excellent way to informally assess their comprehension. This activity also assesses children's receptive and expressive language processing and speech-language production abilities.

PROMOTING EARLY CHILDHOOD LITERACY DEVELOPMENT WITH THE 3N STRATEGY

In the 3N strategy, the 3 Ns are notice, nudge, and narrate. This teaching strategy involves providing scaffolding. Scaffolding is temporary support that helps a child advance from his or her current skill, knowledge, or competency level to a higher level. Scaffolding permits advancement that the child could not achieve on his or her own. The 3N teaching strategy can be employed to make any activity a learning experience for a young child, because it provides a structure for how teachers should interact with children. First, the teacher notices the level of an individual child's literacy skill(s). Second, the teacher verbally nudges the child to do things that are a step above his or her current skill level. Third, the teacher narrates what the child does, verbally describing and reflecting the child's activities. A number of literacy games designed for young children, including the Partners for Literacy curriculum's Literacy Games, utilize a 3N instructional strategy.

INCORPORATING PROBLEM-SOLVING STRATEGIES AND SKILLS INTO CURRICULUM AND DAILY INSTRUCTION

During each preschool day, teachers can help young children recognize their emotions, identify their own needs and wants, develop empathy for and identify with the emotions of others, recognize situations involving problems, come up with simple solutions to problems, and think about the potential consequences of problem solutions. These activities help children develop age appropriate and developmentally appropriate competencies for solving problems and making decisions. Periods of both formal and informal instruction afford opportunities for children to develop these skills. Developing problem-solving and decision-making skills at an early age has a number of benefits. Young children learn to self-regulate their emotions and behaviors through this development. They develop social skills for interacting with others. Moreover, developing early problem-solving and decision-making skills prepares children for the further development of the higher order cognitive skills they will need to succeed in formal primary, secondary, and higher education settings, as well as in everyday life.

STRATEGIES TO HELP READ NEW AND/OR DIFFICULT WORDS

Phonics helps children read unknown/difficult words by teaching them how to sound out the phonemes represented by each printed letter. Teachers can help when children mispronounce words that have irregular spellings. They can also confirm children's correct pronunciations of words they have not heard or seen before. Context helps children deduce which of several possible words is most likely to be found in a particular sentence, paragraph, or book by examining its meaning in relation to the overall subject matter. Looking at a word's part of speech and how it fits into the sentence in question is also an example of using context. For example, reed and read have different spellings and meanings, but sound the same (homonyms). After reading the sentence "Reeds grow in marshes," a child knowing the meaning of "reads" can rule this word out even without knowing how it is spelled because it makes no sense in the context of the sentence. Children could also use their knowledge of language structure to analyze the sentence above. Children can ascertain whether a new word is a noun (person/place/thing) or a verb (action/state of being) by looking at its syntactic placement and its relation to the other words in the sentence that they are familiar with.

Copyright © Mometrix Media. You have been licensed one copy of this document for personal use only. Any other reproduction or redistribution is strictly prohibited. All rights reserved.

CHILDREN'S LITERATURE
FORMATS AND GENRES IN CHILDREN'S LITERATURE

The picture book is both a genre and a format that encompasses various other genres. It includes wordless storybooks, which contain only pictures. Picture books integrate pictures and text to create a multimodal experience. Text is the most important feature of illustrated story books. Illustrations are secondary but complementary to the text. Poetry books contain poems rather than prose. Poems can use concrete verse, free verse, and rhymed and metered verse. Poetry emphasizes the sounds and meanings of words, and appeals to both readers' emotions and thoughts. Traditional literature is an adapted form of oral storytelling. It includes fairy tales, fables, folklore, epics, and proverbs. "Once upon a time…" introductions and happy endings are common features. Modern fantasy is based on traditional literature, but it is original. It includes modern fairy tales, such as those written by Lewis Carroll and Hans Christian Andersen. White's Charlotte's Web and Milne's Winnie the Pooh are also examples. Fantasy stories are imaginary, and often focus on good vs. evil conflicts, magic, and/or quests. Non-fiction informational books include narrative, how-to, question and answer, activity, life cycle, and concept texts.

FEATURES PROMOTING LITERACY DEVELOPMENT

Books that some EC educational experts refer to as "predictable books" contain repetitive text throughout. A salient characteristic of young children is their behavior of repeating familiar rhymes/songs/chants/phrases and stories over and over. Children find such repetition enjoyable. They also ask adults to read them the same books repeatedly. In addition to being enjoyable, repetition provides young children with opportunities to practice words and language patterns, and also encourages retention. Children also like repetitive books because they can immediately participate in the reading of the story. Some examples of good "predictable" children's books include the traditional stories "The Three Little Pigs" and "The Little Red Hen." Other examples are Dr. Seuss's "Green Eggs and Ham" and his story "What Was I Scared Of?" found in the compilation Yertle the Turtle. Another feature of children's books promoting early literacy development is pictures. Picture books with equal, interrelated/interdependent pictures and text help young children learn to recognize and begin to read letters and words by relating them to familiar visual images. The pictures in illustrated storybooks inform text, supporting beginning readers' continuing literacy development.

CHARACTERISTICS OF GOOD CHILDREN'S LITERATURE

To select good children's literature, adults should determine whether a book tells an interesting story. The story should be age appropriate. It should also be appealing to a teacher's students. Books should be well-written, and should have original, believable, and well-constructed plots. Story characters should be credible and convincing, and they should grow and change as a result of their experiences. Dialogue should suit the characters, and should sound natural. Stories should have themes that are important to children. Adults should consider whether a book's theme is obviously moralistic. They should consider what the reader can expect based on a book's title and format. Illustrations should contribute to text, and vice versa. Good children's books avoid stereotypes based on race, gender, etc. They should afford pleasant reading/listening experiences. Adults can also read book reviews for guidance. Children's book authors should be knowledgeable about their subject matter, and they should write in a style suitable for the subject being discussed. Informational books should be accurate and well-organized.

ABILITIES DEMONSTRATING PHONOLOGICAL AND PHONEMIC AWARENESS

Young children with phonological awareness recognize rhymes they hear, can rhyme words, can "count" the number of syllables in a word by clapping, and can identify words with matching initial sounds (e.g., "mother" and "milk"). Children with phonemic awareness can manipulate individual phonemes in words. For example, they can separate the word "cat" into the sounds /k/, /æ/, and /t/. Children who have problems with phonemic awareness frequently experience reading problems without early intervention. There are several issues teachers may observe in the classroom that can indicate

Copyright © Mometrix Media. You have been licensed one copy of this document for personal use only. Any other reproduction or redistribution is strictly prohibited. All rights reserved.

phonological and/or phonemic awareness deficits. Children may not correctly combine individual phonemes to make a word. For example, they may not be able to select and blend the phonemes /k/, /æ/, and /t/ to make "cat." A child may not correctly perform phoneme substitution tasks to make different words. For example, a child may not be able to change the /k/ in "cat" to /m/ to make "mat." A child may have difficulty determining how many syllables are in a word like "paper." A child may also have problems rhyming, syllabicating, or spelling new words based on how they sound.

WORD DECODING AND PHONICS

Word decoding ability consists of being aware of letter-sound correspondences and letter patterns, and applying them to correctly pronounce the words we read. Phonics is a reading instruction approach that focuses on letter-sound correspondences, exceptions to general rules, and strategies for sounding out new words. In the classroom, if a teacher observes a child is having trouble matching up letters with sounds (or vice versa), this can signal decoding and phonics problems that can interfere with a child's ability to read and spell. Children who can decode words, but must use a great deal of effort to do so, may have decoding and phonics problems. Difficulties with spelling words phonetically and reading are also signs of possible problems. Children who struggle greatly with phonics activities and patterns may have decoding deficits. Children who try to guess words based on the first one or two letters may have problems with decoding and phonics. If after teaching several letter sounds/patterns to a class, a teacher finds that certain children cannot recognize them while reading words and do not include these sounds and patterns in their writing, the teacher should suspect that these children are having problems with decoding and phonics.

TYPES OF VOCABULARY

Educators frequently divide vocabulary into listening, speaking, reading, and writing vocabulary. These are not necessarily the same. Listening vocabulary refers to the words we must know to understand what we hear others say. Speaking vocabulary refers to the words we use when we talk. Reading vocabulary refers to the words we must know to comprehend what we read. Writing vocabulary refers to the words we use when we write. To read print, children must understand the majority of the words they encounter in a text. Children learn the majority of word meanings indirectly through daily life experiences. Well-designed instruction teaches them additional vocabulary. If a teacher observes that a child has more questions than usual about what words mean in age appropriate/developmentally appropriate texts, the child may have vocabulary issues. A teacher may observe that a child does not use or recognize many words compared to his or her peers, which could also indicate vocabulary issues. A child who cannot see connections/relationships among words in different texts may have vocabulary deficits. If a child frequently cannot find the correct word to express a thought, idea, etc., this could also indicate vocabulary difficulties.

READING FLUENCY

Reading fluency is the ability to read quickly, accurately, and smoothly both silently and aloud, and to read aloud with appropriate vocal intonations and expression. Children who do not read fluently sound awkward and choppy when they read aloud. Some students who read dysfluently have word decoding problems. Others simply need more reading practice to read quickly and smoothly. Reading fluency is important to children's reading motivation. When children find reading laborious or view it as a chore rather than an enjoyable experience, they dislike reading and avoid it. This exacerbates reading problems. Reading fluency becomes more important in upper elementary grades, when the volume of required reading increases exponentially for students. Therefore, younger children with poor reading fluency will also have difficulty meeting academic reading demands in the future. When teachers conduct correct words per minute assessments, children who do not meet the criteria for their grade level may have fluency issues. Struggling and becoming frustrated with speed and/or accuracy while reading aloud may indicate fluency problems. Reading aloud without expression is another sign of fluency issues, as are failing to pause at meaningful breaks in a sentence or a paragraph and failing to "chunk" words into meaningful units.

Copyright © Mometrix Media. You have been licensed one copy of this document for personal use only. Any other reproduction or redistribution is strictly prohibited. All rights reserved.

ABILITIES NECESSARY TO HAVE GOOD READING COMPREHENSION

To have good reading comprehension, children must be able to (1) decode the words they read, (2) connect what they read to things they already know, and (3) think about what they have read in depth. Knowing enough word meanings (i.e. having enough vocabulary) plays a major role in reading comprehension. Children with good comprehension can make conclusions about what they read, including identifying factual elements, determining the causes of specific events, and identifying comedic characters. Therefore, comprehension involves a combination of reading, thinking, and reasoning. Teachers may observe a number of signs of reading comprehension problems. A child may focus on details/"trees" to the exclusion of the main point/"forest." This child can report how stories end, but cannot explain why. A child may not speculate about characters' motivations or upcoming events when reading a book. When trying to relate reading to his/her life, a child may choose irrelevant information. A child may not be able to recount logical event sequences in stories or isolate main facts in informational texts. A child may appear to have inadequate vocabulary to understand a text. Finally, a child may be unable to relate details of a story, such as the setting, what the characters look like, etc.

BASIC READING COMPONENTS OF PHONOLOGICAL AND PHONEMIC AWARENESS

The five basic reading components of phonological and phonemic awareness are word decoding, phonics, fluency, vocabulary, and comprehension. A deficit in any of these components can lead to reading problems. In addition to deficits in one or more of these areas, about two to three percent of children have central auditory processing disorders (CAPDs). Our ears receive environmental sound waves and convert them to acoustic impulses that are carried by nerves to the brain, which interprets these signals as various sounds, including speech. This is auditory processing. Children with CAPD have problems attending to, listening to, and remembering spoken information, and often take longer to process auditory input. They frequently cannot differentiate among sounds in words that sound similar to other phonemes, despite being able to hear them clearly. This causes decoding difficulties, which interferes with reading. Some children with strong auditory (and language) processing skills have deficits in phonological processing (i.e. processing phonemes/speech sounds specifically). This also typically causes decoding and hence reading difficulties. Language processing problems are broader, including deficiencies in linguistic experiences, vocabulary, comprehension (despite being able to correctly decode words), reading, and writing.

ROLE OF MEMORY IN CHILDREN'S READING DEVELOPMENT

For children to read, understand what they read, and switch efficiently between the printed language they see and the information they have stored in their memories, children must be able to store information and retrieve it as it is needed. There are three main types of memory. Short-term memory holds small pieces of information for short periods of time. For example, when we hold a phone number in our mind only long enough to dial it, but do not retain it after it is dialed, we use our short-term memory. Working memory holds interim information in the mind for use during calculations. For example, we use our working memory when mentally multiplying double digit numerals or doing long division. Processing new information so that it can be stored for a long period of time, searching for stored information, and retrieving information as it is needed are also functions of working memory. Phonological working memory is a component of phonological processing that is important in reading comprehension, spelling, written expression, and retention. We store enormous amounts of information for many years in our long-term memory. This information influences our differential attention to various environmental factors and our perceptions of the world.

DYSLEXIA

DIFFICULTIES DISPLAYED WHEN SPEAKING THAT MAY BE SIGNS OF DYSLEXIA

Preschoolers and kindergarteners who have trouble learning alphabet letters are more likely to have trouble identifying sound-letter correspondences in first grade, and are more likely to have subsequent life-long difficulties with reading. Issues related to children's speech that can indicate dyslexia include

111

Copyright © Mometrix Media. You have been licensed one copy of this document for personal use only. Any other reproduction or redistribution is strictly prohibited. All rights reserved.

mispronouncing unfamiliar, long, or complex words. This may include omitting word parts and/or arranging syllables or word parts in the wrong sequence. Other signs of dyslexia include speech that is not fluent (e.g., speech that is marked by frequent hesitations, "um's," and pauses); speech that uses vague or non-specific wording, such as "things" or "stuff," instead of correct nouns and names of specific objects; speech that suggests the child is having difficulty finding words while speaking, which is indicated when students confuse words that sound similar (e.g., substituting "volcano" for "tornado," substituting "humidity" for "humility," etc.); and speech that shows an inability to generate verbal responses to questions quickly and on demand. Students with dyslexia may also require more time than normal to respond orally to language stimuli; and may also have difficulties with rote memory (e.g., retaining and/or retrieving names, dates, phone numbers, random lists, and other isolated items contained in information presented verbally).

OBSERVABLE READING PROBLEMS

Children with dyslexia typically show abnormally slow progress in their acquisition of reading skills. They often lack systematic strategies for reading new words (decoding, sounding out, etc.), and make wild guesses instead. Being unable to read short function words (e.g., "an," "on," and "that") is common, as is stumbling over multisyllabic words. They will often miss parts of words when reading and/or fail to decode word parts, and may, for example, read a word aloud with its middle syllable missing (e.g., "imation" for "imagination"). Children with dyslexia tend to fear and hence avoid oral reading because they have made errors in the past and have an expectation that they will make additional errors if they attempt to read aloud again. When they do read aloud, they may omit appropriate inflections; sound like they are reading a foreign language; sound laborious and choppy, rather than fluent and smooth; mispronounce numerous words; and make numerous omissions and substitutions. While reading, they depend on the context to comprehend meaning, and have more difficulty understanding single/isolated words. Their performance on objective (e.g., multiple choice) tests is typically much poorer than their intelligence and knowledge would predict.

Children who consistently cannot complete written tests in the time allowed may have dyslexia. Children who cannot pronounce more difficult printed words and substitute easier ones for them instead (e.g., "car" for "automobile") may have dyslexia. In math, dyslexia causes difficulty reading word problems. Children with dyslexia will often misspell words. The spellings are not phonetic, but are often bizarre and wildly different from actual spellings and from native language conventions. Children with dyslexia read very slowly, finding it laborious and exhausting. Reading is such a chore to them that they do not enjoy it, do not read for pleasure, and will avoid reading whenever possible. Such children have a lot of trouble learning foreign languages. Despite good fine motor skills and word processing abilities, they often have poor handwriting. Homework seems to take forever for these children. Some students ask parents to read so they don't have to. Their reading becomes more accurate with time and practice, but still remains labored and dysfluent. They often have family histories of problems with reading, spelling, and learning foreign languages. Dyslexia can cause low self-esteem. This is not always obvious, but can be detected by sensitive, skilled professionals.

LEARNING TO SPELL

Children must understand the alphabetic principle—the concept that words are comprised of individual phonemes/speech sounds, and that the letters of our alphabet represent those sounds in writing/print—in order to learn how to spell. They must also develop a knowledge of specific letter-to-sound correspondences. As children gain more experience hearing, understanding, and using words, they start to observe patterns in the ways in which letters are combined. They also notice repeated series of letters that create syllables, common roots for many related words, prefixes, suffixes, word endings, and other word features. When children know these basic patterns and have also learned their language's basic spelling principles and rules, they can usually figure out how to spell new words they hear. Moreover, children can usually read words that they can spell. Therefore, children's development of good spelling skills promotes the development of good reading and writing skills as well.

Copyright © Mometrix Media. You have been licensed one copy of this document for personal use only. Any other reproduction or redistribution is strictly prohibited. All rights reserved.

SALIENT CHARACTERISTICS OF THE STAGES OF SPELLING DEVELOPMENT

(1) Precommunicative stage: Children use alphabet letters, but may not know the whole alphabet, may not differentiate between upper case and lower case letters, or may not know that English is written from left to right. They do not demonstrate knowledge of letter-to-sound correspondences. (2) Semiphonetic stage: Children begin to comprehend letter-to-sound correspondences. They frequently use simple logic to symbolize words with single letters. A good example is using "U" for "you" (early texting potential!). (3) Phonetic stage: Children use letters to represent all speech sounds they hear in words. These representations may not always be correct, but are systematic and understandable (e.g., writing "kom" instead of "come"). (4) Transitional stage: Children begin the transition from phonetically spelling words according to their sounds to visually and structurally learning conventional word spellings. They still make errors as they assimilate this new knowledge (e.g., writing "highked" instead of "hiked"). (5) Correct stage: Children know fundamental English orthographic rules, including silent letters, irregular and alternative spellings, prefixes, suffixes, and other word features. They have learned many word spellings, and recognize misspellings. Their knowledge of exceptions to spelling rules and the generalizations they make about spelling are usually correct.

INVENTED SPELLING AND WHAT IT REVEALS ABOUT PHONETIC AWARENESS

When young children have not yet learned how to spell many (or any) words, they commonly "invent" spellings for spoken words they hear. They do this by identifying letters that correspond to the separate phonemes (speech sounds) they hear and arranging them in a sequence that matches the word's sounds. Linguistic researchers (e.g., Read, 1975) studying preschoolers have found that different children choose the same phonetic spellings. These children have developed phonemic and phonetic awareness, enabling them to invent spellings before they have actually learned to spell. This skill is a prerequisite to learning how to read, spell, and write. Researchers observe that neither adult influence nor chance could explain diverse children's high incidence of selecting the same phonetic spellings. Therefore, even at young ages, children can identify the phonetic properties of English words that are symbolized by their real spellings. Experts conclude from these observations that spelling is a developmental process rather than merely a word memorization process, and that it results in comprehension that goes beyond understanding simple sound-to-letter correspondences.

WRITING

According to the National Institute for Literacy, writing is defined as "the ability to compose text effectively for various purposes and audiences." We use writing as a tool to help us collect detailed information, document it, and disseminate it to widespread audiences. We use writing to express our ideas, thoughts, and feelings, and to persuade our readers to believe or agree with what we write. Researchers have also found that the learning capacity of an individual increases when his or her writing skills improve. This aspect of writing skills mirrors that of reading skills in that the development of both improves learning ability. Students need instruction to learn to write well. Reading skills have been found both to be reinforced by and to reinforce important writing skills like spelling and grammar. Thus, when teachers help children improve their writing, they are contributing to the improvement of their reading abilities as well.

STAGES OF WRITING SKILLS DEVELOPMENT

(1) Scribbling and drawing: Young children grasp crayons/pencils with their fists, exploring form, space, and line. As their fine motor skills and cognitive understanding of symbolic representation develop concurrently, they progress to (2) letter-like forms and shapes. They comprehend that written symbols represent meanings. They start including shapes like circles and squares into their drawing and writing, but they are randomly located without much spatial orientation. Children in this stage commonly write figures and ask parents, "What does this say?" (3) Letters: Children can form letters, and start writing them randomly. They usually write consonants first. They do not initially possess a knowledge of symbol-to-sound correspondence; this develops gradually. Children tend to favor writing their own initials. (4) Letters and spaces: Children realize that printed/written words are separated by spaces,

Copyright © Mometrix Media. You have been licensed one copy of this document for personal use only. Any other reproduction or redistribution is strictly prohibited. All rights reserved.

develop an understanding of the concept of a word, use 1:1 word correspondence, and write correctly spaced words. They write initial and final word sounds and vowels, correct the spelling of some high frequency words, and experiment with sentence construction and punctuation. (5) <u>Conventional writing and spelling:</u> Children write, spell, and punctuate correctly most of the time. They view various forms of purposeful writing as more important.

POWER STRATEGY

One popular model of the writing process proposed by experts, the POWER strategy, has five steps. In (1) planning, student and teacher ask and select Yes/No on a checklist to decide whether the student selected a good topic, researched/read about the topic, considered what information readers would want to know, and wrote down all of his/her ideas. In (2) organization, the student and teacher ascertain if the student grouped similar ideas together, selected the best ideas for the composition, and arranged the ideas in a logical sequence. In (3) writing, the student and teacher decide whether the student wrote down his/her ideas in sentences. They also decide whether the student did his/her best to get help when it was required. To get the necessary information and assistance, the student may have consulted a text, asked a learning partner/classmate for assistance, and/or asked the teacher for help. In (4) editing, the student and teacher consider whether the student read his/her first draft to himself/herself, marked the parts s/he liked and those that might need changing, read the first draft to his/her partner/classmate, and listened to the other student's input. In (5) rewriting, the student and teacher look at whether the student made changes in his/her composition, edited it for correct mechanics, and wrote the final draft using his/her best handwriting.

RATING EARLY WRITING EFFORTS

One easy rating scale (Clay, 1993) focuses on three areas: language level, message quality, and directional principles. Each category has six progressive levels.

For <u>language level</u>, the categories are

1. alphabetical (writes letters),
2. word (writes any recognizable word),
3. word group (writes any two-word phrase),
4. sentence (writes any simple sentence),
5. punctuated story (writes two or more related sentences), and
6. paragraphed story (includes two themes).

The levels for <u>message quality</u> are as follows:

1. Student has a concept of signs/symbols.
2. Student has a concept that a message is communicated.
3. Student copies a message.
4. Student repeats sentence patterns like "This is a…"
5. Student tries to record his/her own ideas in writing.
6. Student writes a successful composition.

The levels for <u>directional principles</u> are as follows:

1. Student does not demonstrate knowledge of directionality.
2. Student exhibits partial directional knowledge (e.g., left to right or start at the top left or return from top right down to the left).
3. Student reverses the direction.
4. Student follows the correct directional pattern.
5. Student uses correct directionality and spacing between words.
6. The student writes extensively without problems related to arranging and spacing text.

Copyright © Mometrix Media. You have been licensed one copy of this document for personal use only. Any other reproduction or redistribution is strictly prohibited. All rights reserved.

WRITTEN ENGLISH

Written English should meet the standard conventions of correct spelling, capitalization, punctuation, grammar, and handwriting. Traditionally, teachers have paid more attention to a composition's appearance, length, word usage, and spelling than to how well-organized it is or how appropriate its content is. This habit can cause a superficial focus on imperfect form, while essentially ignoring the fact that the function is effective and meaningful. Other readers also form negative first impressions of writing when its appearance and/or format are less than acceptable, even if it otherwise effectively conveys its message. One type of common spelling error is vowel combination reversals (e.g., writing "siad" instead of "said," writing "freind" instead of "friend," etc.). Capitalization errors include failing to capitalize words at the start of sentences, months of the year, and proper nouns/names. Another type of capitalization error is incorrectly capitalizing words/letters within words. Punctuation errors include omitting commas in dates, omitting commas before conjunctions in compound sentences, omitting/substituting semicolons in complex sentences, and adding extraneous punctuation marks. Grammatical errors include incorrect/conflicting verb tenses, subject-verb disagreement, missing articles, misplaced modifiers, and dangling participles. Handwriting errors/problems include illegible writing, poor alignment, and incorrect/poor spacing.

TECHNIQUES AND ACTIVITIES TO MOTIVATE YOUNG CHILDREN TO WRITE

Experts note that like adults, children prefer participating in activities they find exciting rather than ones they find unexciting/uninteresting. To motivate students to write, teachers can share personal journals and other samples of their own writing, post e-mailed/handwritten letters/notes in classrooms, display favorite magazines and books, and show children fun greeting cards/invitations. They should also invite children to bring writing samples from home. Teachers can create classroom "writing corners" that contain varied writing examples contributed by children and teachers. Diverse writing activities help children stay enthusiastic about writing. Children can take turns contributing a sentence for a daily class newsletter/journal/newspaper, and teachers can have students practice sounding out and spelling words as they dictate their sentences. Teachers can deliberately make some transcribing errors and have children correct them. Daily pages can be compiled into monthly class books. Connecting writing subjects to people/things that are familiar and exciting to children, and guiding students in how to write and ask classmates "interview" questions using modeling and other techniques both help motivate students. Encouraging/guiding children to evaluate and record their comments about authors, illustrators, and books can also be a motivational tool. Ultimately, children will learn to write their own critiques.

Copyright © Mometrix Media. You have been licensed one copy of this document for personal use only. Any other reproduction or redistribution is strictly prohibited. All rights reserved.

Knowing and Integrating Subject Matter: Mathematics, Science, Social Studies, Arts, Health, Physical Education

Math Foundations

PROBLEM SOLVING SKILLS

Being able to solve problems is fundamental to all other components of mathematics. Children learn the concept that a question can have more than one answer and a problem can have more than one solution by participating in problem solving activities. To solve problems, a child must be able to explore a problem, a situation, or a subject; think through the problem, situation, or subject; and use logical reasoning. These abilities are needed to not only solve routine/everyday problems, but also novel/unusual ones. Using problem solving skills not only helps children think mathematically, but also promotes their language development and their social skills when they work together. Children are naturally curious about how to solve everyday problems. Adults can take advantage of this inherent curiosity by discussing everyday challenges, asking children to propose ways to solve them, and asking them to explain how they arrived at their solutions. Adults can also invite children to propose problems and ask questions about them. This helps them learn to analyze different types of problems and realize that many problems have multiple possible solutions.

COMMON STEPS THAT PREPARE CHILDREN TO LEARN MATH

The process of solving problems often involves the following steps: understanding the problem; coming up with a plan to solve the problem; putting that plan into action; and, finally, observing the outcome and reflecting on whether the solution was effective, and whether the answer arrived at makes sense. Solving problems not only involves learning this series of steps, but also requires children to develop the qualities needed to solve problems. Children who are able to solve problems have a number of characteristics. For example, children who are effective problem solvers are able to focus their attention on the problem and its individual component parts. They can formulate hypotheses about the problem/situation, and then test them for veracity. They are willing to take risks within reason. They are persistent if they do not solve a problem right away, and do not give up if their first attempt at solving a problem is unsuccessful. They maintain flexibility, and experiment with alternate methods. They also demonstrate self-regulation skills.

USING PROBLEM SOLVING SKILLS IN DAILY LIFE

Young children continually explore their environments to unravel mysteries about how things work. For example, preschoolers use math concepts to understand that they have three toys, to comprehend that three fingers equals three toys, or to understand that two cookies plus one more equals three cookies. To do abstract mathematics in the future, young children will need two major skills that are also used to solve problems: being able to visualize a scenario, and being able to apply common sense thinking. Thinking and planning to achieve goals within the constraints of the properties of the surrounding environment is a natural behavior for young children. They will persist in their efforts to get an older sibling to stop another activity to play with them, to repair broken toys with tape or chewing gum, to manipulate a puzzle or plastic building blocks to get one uncooperative piece to fit, etc. The great 20th century mathematician and teacher George Polya stated that problem solving is "the most characteristically human activity." He pointed out that problem solving is a skill learned by doing, and that developing this skill requires a great deal of practice.

Copyright © Mometrix Media. You have been licensed one copy of this document for personal use only. Any other reproduction or redistribution is strictly prohibited. All rights reserved.

GAMES/ACTIVITIES THAT ENCOURAGE THE USE OF PROBLEM SOLVING SKILLS

One method that has been found to enhance children's reasoning skills is using adult-child conversations to play mental mathematics games. For example, once children are able to count beyond five, adults can give them basic oral story problems to solve (e.g., "If you have two plums and I give you two more, how many will you have?"). Using children's favorite foods in story problems, which takes advantage of their ready ability to envision these foods, is a good place to start. Thereafter, adults can add story problems involving pets, toys, cars, shopping, and other familiar objects/animals/activities. Experts advise adults not to restrict the types of problems presented to a child based solely on the child's grade level. Children can work with any situation if they can form mental imagery. Adults can sometimes insert harder tasks (e.g., problems involving larger numbers, problems involving division with remainders, or problems with negative number answers). Even toddlers can solve problems such as how to divide three cookies between two people. The division may not be fair, but it will likely be efficient. Adults should use the Socratic method, asking guiding questions to allow children to arrive at a solution to a problem themselves, rather than telling them a "right" answer.

BENEFICIAL PRACTICES OF PLAYING MENTAL MATH GAMES

Adults can use children's favorite foods and toys to pose story problems to children that involve addition and subtraction. For example, they can ask them questions like "If I give you [this many] more, how many will you have?" or "If we take away [this many], how many are left?" It is better to ask children questions than to give them answers. It is important to use turn taking. In this method, the adult poses a story problem to the child, and then the child gets to pose one to the adult. Adults must try to solve the problem, even if the child makes up numbers like "bazillion" or "eleventy." Games should be fun, not strictly factual like math tests. Adults can introduce age-appropriate story topics as children grow older. At the end of early childhood/around school age, children can handle the abstract algebraic concept of variables/unknown numbers (which some experts call "mystery numbers") and use this concept in games. Adults can pose riddles where "x" or "n" is the unknown number, and children must use an operation (e.g., $x + 4 = 7$) to solve the riddle.

> **Review Video: Mathematical Operations**
> Visit mometrix.com/academy and enter code: 208095

REASONING SKILLS

COMMUNICATING WITH CHILDREN TO PROMOTE MATHEMATICAL REASONING SKILLS

Adults reciprocally talk to and listen to children during communication that is focused on using mathematical skills like problem solving, reasoning, making connections, etc. To promote young children's understanding, adults can express mathematical concepts using pictures, words, diagrams, and symbols. Encouraging children to talk with their peers and adults helps them clarify their own thoughts and think about what they are doing. Communicating with children about mathematical thinking problems also develops their vocabularies and promotes early literacy and reading skills. Adults should listen to what children want to say, and should have conversations with them. Communicating about math can also be accomplished through reading children's books that incorporate numbers and/or repetition or rhyme. In addition to talking, adults can communicate math concepts to children by drawing pictures or diagrams and using concrete objects (e.g., blocks, crayons, pieces of paper, fingers, etc.) to represent numbers and/or solve problems. Children also share their learning of math concepts through words, charts, drawings, tallies, etc. Even toddlers hold up fingers to tell others how old they are.

USING REASONING SKILLS TO UNDERSTAND AND APPLY EARLY MATHEMATICAL AND SCIENTIFIC CONCEPTS

A major component of problem solving is reasoning. Children reason when they think through questions and find usable answers. They use reasoning skills to make sense of mathematical and scientific subject

Copyright © Mometrix Media. You have been licensed one copy of this document for personal use only. Any other reproduction or redistribution is strictly prohibited. All rights reserved.

matter. Children use several abilities during the reasoning process. For example, they use logic to classify objects or concepts into groups. They follow logical sequences to arrive at conclusions that make sense. They use their analytical abilities to explain their own thought processes. They apply what they have learned about relationships and patterns to help them find solutions to problems. They also use reasoning to justify their mental processes and problem solutions. To support children's reasoning, adults can ask children questions, give them time to think about their answers, and listen to their answers. This simple tactic helps children learn how to reason. Adults can also ask children why something is as it is—letting them think for themselves rather than looking for a particular answer—and listen to the ideas they produce.

ROLE OF REPRESENTATION SKILLS IN CHILDREN'S LEARNING

Young children develop an understanding of symbolic representation—the idea that objects, written letters, words, and other symbols are used to represent other objects or concepts—at an early age. This is evident in their make-believe/pretend play, and in their ability to learn written language and connect it to spoken language. As children develop early math skills, representing their ideas and information they acquire helps them organize, document, and share these ideas and facts with others. Children may count on their fingers; create tallies using check marks/tick marks and/or words; draw pictures or maps; and, as they grow older, make graphs. Teachers must help children apply mathematical process skills as they use learning center materials. For example, when a child enjoys sorting rocks by color, the teacher can state that the child is classifying them, bridging informal math activities with math vocabulary. Asking the child how s/he is categorizing the rocks emphasizes math vocabulary. Asking the child after s/he finishes what other ways s/he could classify the rocks encourages problem solving.

MAKING CONNECTIONS AND HELPING CHILDREN TRANSITION FROM INTUITIVE TO FORMAL MATH THINKING

Children informally learn intuitive mathematical thinking through their everyday life experiences. They naturally apply mathematical concepts and reasoning to solve problems they face in their environment. However, one frequent problem among children when they begin formal education is that they can come to see academic mathematics as a collection of procedures and rules, instead of viewing it as a means of finding solutions to everyday, real-life problems. This view will interfere with children's ability to apply the formal mathematics they learn to their lives in a practical and useful way. Teachers can help prevent this outcome by establishing the connection between children's natural intuitive math and formal mathematics. They can do this by teaching math through the use of manipulative materials familiar to children. They can use mathematics vocabulary words when describing children's activities, which enables children to develop an awareness of the natural mathematical operations they use in their daily lives. When a teacher introduces a new mathematical concept to children, s/he can give illustrative examples that draw upon the children's actual life experiences.

RELATIONSHIP OF MATHEMATICS TO EVERYDAY LIFE AND OTHER ACADEMIC SUBJECTS

We use math throughout our lives during everyday activities. There are countless examples and combinations of various mathematical concepts in the real world. Additionally, math concepts inform other academic content areas, including music, art, and the sciences. Therefore, it is important for children not to view math as an isolated set of procedures and skills. Children comprehend math more easily when they can make connections, which involve applying common mathematical rules to multiple, varied functions, processes, and real-life activities. For example, adults can ask children to consider problems they encounter daily and solve them. When a parent asks a child to help put away groceries, the child practices sorting categories of foods and packages, and experiments with comparative package sizes and shapes. Parents need not be concerned with what specific mathematical processes are involved, but should simply look for examples of math in everyday life and expose children to these examples on a regular basis. For example, pouring liquid into containers of various sizes and speculating which one will hold the most is an easy, fun activity that incorporates a number of skills and concepts, including estimation, measurement, spatial sense, and conservation of liquid volume.

Copyright © Mometrix Media. You have been licensed one copy of this document for personal use only. Any other reproduction or redistribution is strictly prohibited. All rights reserved.

PATTERNS AND RELATIONSHIPS

Patterns are generally defined as things that recur or are repeated regularly. Patterns can be found in images, sounds, numbers, events, actions, movements, etc. Relationships are generally defined as connections or associations between things that are identified and/or described using logic or reasoning. Being aware of patterns and relationships among aspects of the environment helps us comprehend the fundamental structure of these aspects. This awareness enables us to predict what will occur next in a series of events, even before it actually happens. This gives us more confidence in our environment and in our ability to interact with it. We find patterns and relationships in such areas of life as art, music, and clothing. Math-specific activities like counting numbers and working with geometrical shapes, lines, arcs, and curves also involve patterns and relationships. When children understand patterns and relationships, they can understand repetition; rhythm; categorization; and how to order things from smallest to biggest, from shortest to longest, etc.

Adults can help young children develop their understanding of patterns and relationships in life by looking at pictures and designs with them, encouraging and guiding them to identify patterns within drawings, paintings, and abstract designs such as prints on fabrics and other decorative designs. When children participate in movement activities, including dancing to music, running, skipping, hopping, playing simple musical instruments, etc., adults can help them identify patterns in their own and others' movements. Adults can encourage young children to participate in hands-on activities, such as stringing wood, plastic beads, or penne and other hollow dry pasta tubes onto pieces of string to make necklaces with simple patterns (e.g., blue-yellow-blue-yellow). As children grow older, adults can encourage them to create more complicated patterns. They can alternate a larger number of colors, and they can vary the numbers of each color in more complex ways (e.g., three blue, two yellow, one red, etc.).

CONTRIBUTION OF NUMBER SENSE AND NUMBER OPERATIONS TO MATH COMPREHENSION

Counting is one of the earliest numeracy skills that young children develop. Even before they have learned the names of all the numbers, young children learn to count to three, then to five, etc. However, number sense involves a great deal more than just counting. Number sense includes understanding the various applications of numbers. For instance, we use numbers as tools for conveying and manipulating information, as tools for describing quantities, and as tools for characterizing relationships between or among things. Children who have developed number sense are able to count with accuracy and competence. Given a specific number, they can count upwards from that number. They can also count backwards. They are able to break down a number and then reassemble it. They are able to recognize relationships between or among different numbers. When children can count, are familiar with numbers, and have good number sense, they can also add and subtract numbers. Being familiar with numbers and being able to count easily helps young children understand all other areas of mathematics.

ACTIVITIES TO HELP DEVELOP NUMBER SENSE AND NUMERACY SKILLS

As children complete their daily activities, it is beneficial for adults to count real things with children and encourage them to count as well. This helps children understand numbers by using their own experiences with objects in the environment, and gives them practice counting and using numbers. To help children understand that we use numbers to describe quantities and relationships, adults can ask children to sort objects by size, shape, or color similarity. They can also ask children to sort objects according to their differences (e.g., which object is bigger/smaller). Adults can also discuss with children how numbers are used to find street addresses and apartment numbers, and to keep score during games. To help children count upwards and downwards with efficiency and accuracy, adults can point out that counting allows us to determine how many items are in a group. Adults should point to each object as they count it. They can count on their fingers and encourage young children to do the same. Adults should also help children count without repeating or skipping any numbers.

Copyright © Mometrix Media. You have been licensed one copy of this document for personal use only. Any other reproduction or redistribution is strictly prohibited. All rights reserved.

COUNTING

Counting is considered a math skill milestone for young children. Typical four-year-olds enjoy counting aloud. Experts identify three levels of counting. The first is counting from 1 to 12, which requires memorization. The second level is counting from 13 to 19, which requires not only memorization, but also an understanding of the more unusual rules for "teen" numbers. The third level is counting from 20 on. This process is very consistent, and the numbers are ordered according to regular rules. Experts in math education believe that at this level of counting, children are discovering a regular mathematical pattern for the first time, which is base ten (i.e. 20, 30, 40, 50, etc. are 2 tens, 3 tens, 4 tens, 5 tens, etc., and after the base a number between 1 and 9 is added). Researchers and educators in early childhood mathematics programs recommend encouraging children as young as four years old to learn to count up to 100. They find that doing this helps young children learn about and explore patterns in depth.

PERCEIVING AND IDENTIFYING SHAPES

The three levels of perceiving shapes that children typically move through sequentially are seeing, naming, and analyzing. Very young children recognize simple shapes like circles, squares, and triangles. As their cognitive and language skills develop, they learn the names for these shapes, and use these names to identify single shapes. The third level is analyzing each shape to understand its properties. Whereas identifying shapes visually is intuitive and based on association, analyzing their properties is more abstract, since a shape can have a number of different appearances. For example, three-year-olds can differentiate a triangle from other shapes. However, if you show them a very tall, skinny/short, wide/lopsided/crooked triangle, they will have trouble identifying it as a triangle. At the analysis level, children realize that a triangle has three sides, which are not necessarily equal in length. An activity that young children enjoy is closing their eyes, reaching into a bag of assorted shapes, finding a triangle by touch, and explaining why it is a triangle. This involves both the second and third levels of naming and analysis.

SPATIAL SENSE AND GEOMETRY

Spatial sense is an individual's awareness of one's own body in space and in relation to the objects and other people around the individual. Spatial sense allows young children to navigate environmental spaces without colliding with objects and other people; to see and hear adequately, and to be aware of whether others can see and hear them; and to develop and observe a socially and culturally appropriate sense of their own and others' personal space. Geometry is the area of mathematics involving space, sizes, shapes, positions, movements, and directions. Geometry gives descriptions and classifications of our physical environment. By observing commonplace objects and spaces in their physical world, young children can learn about solid objects and substances, shapes, and angles. Adults can help young children learn geometry by identifying various shapes, angles, and three-dimensional figures for them; asking them to name these shapes, angles, and figures when they encounter them in the future; and asking them to describe different shapes, draw them in the air with their fingers, trace drawings of the shapes with their fingers, and then draw the shapes themselves.

ACTIVITIES TO HELP DEVELOP SPATIAL SENSE AND GEOMETRY

Because it involves many physical properties like shape, line, and angle, as well as abstract concepts, young children learn geometry most effectively via hands-on activities. Learning experiences that allow them to touch and manipulate concrete objects, such as boxes, containers, puzzles, blocks, and shape sorters, usually work best. Everyday activities can also help children learn geometry concepts. For example, adults can cut children's sandwiches into various geometrical shapes and let children fit them together and/or rearrange them into new patterns. Children become better able to follow directions and navigate through space when they develop geometric knowledge and spatial sense. Adults can provide activities that promote the development of geometric knowledge and spatial sense. For example, they can let children get into and out of big appliance boxes; climb over furniture; and go into, on top of, out of, under, around, over, and through different objects and structures to allow children to experience the relationship between their bodies and space and solids. As they mature, children can play games in

Copyright © Mometrix Media. You have been licensed one copy of this document for personal use only. Any other reproduction or redistribution is strictly prohibited. All rights reserved.

which they search for "hidden" shapes. Such shapes may be irregular, may lack flat bases, or may be turned in various directions.

MEASUREMENT

Measurement is the process of determining how long, wide, and tall something is physically and how much it weighs by using measuring units such as inches, feet, yards, square feet, ounces, and pounds. Measurement is also used to quantify time using units like seconds, minutes, hours, days, weeks, months, years, centuries, millennia, etc. Measurement is not just a formal means of quantifying size, area, and time. It is also an important method for young children to seek and identify relationships between and among things they encounter outside of school in everyday life. When young children practice measuring things, they are able to understand not only the sizes of objects and beings, but also their comparative sizes (i.e. how large or small something is compared to another object used as a reference). Furthermore, they are able to figure out how big or little something is on their own.

While it is obviously important for children to eventually learn standardized measurement units like inches, feet, yards, etc., adults can facilitate early development of measurement skills by letting children choose their own measurement units. For example, they might use their favorite toy to describe a playmate or sibling as "three teddy bears tall"; or they might describe a room as "seven toy cars long." Similarly, when children are too young to know formal time measurements like minutes and hours, adults can support children's ability to quantify time using favorite TV shows. For example, four-year-olds can often relate to the idea of one episode of a show (whether it is 30 minutes or 60 minutes long) as a time measurement. Adults can apply this with statements like, "Daddy will be home in one episode." Numerous everyday activities, including grocery shopping, cooking, sewing, gardening, woodworking, and many others, involve measurement. Adults can ask children to help with these tasks, and then discuss measuring with children as they participate.

MEASUREMENT OF TIME

Younger children typically do not have an understanding of the abstract concept of time. However, adults can still help children understand that time elapses, and that we count/measure this process. For example, adults can ask younger children simple questions, such as "Who can stand on one foot longer?" This comparison strategy helps children figure out which of two or more actions/activities takes a longer/the longest period of time. Even when children do not yet understand what "five minutes" means, adults should still make such references (e.g., "You can play for five minutes longer, and then we must leave."). Repeating such references will eventually help children understand that time passes. Adults can time various everyday activities/events and tell children how long they took. They can also count the second hand's ticks on a watch/clock (e.g., "one second...two seconds...three seconds..."). This familiarizes children with counting, and with using counting to track the passage of time. Until children are old enough to understand abstractions like today/yesterday/tomorrow, adults can use concrete references like "after lunch" or "before bedtime."

FRACTIONS

Fractions are parts or pieces of a whole. While adults understand this and do not remember ever not understanding it, very young children think differently in this regard. As Piaget showed, children in the preoperational stage of cognitive development cannot perform logical or mathematical mental operations. They focus on one property of an object rather than all of its properties, a practice he called centration. Hence, if you cut an apple into pieces, very young children see that there are more pieces than there were before, and they believe that several apple pieces are more than one apple. They cannot yet comprehend the logical sequence of dividing an apple into fractions. To comprehend fractions, children must know what a whole unit consists of, how many pieces the unit is divided into, and whether the pieces are of equal size. Adults can help children understand fractions through informal sharing activities, such as slicing up a pizza or a pan of brownies, and/or equally dividing household/preschool chores and play materials.

Copyright © Mometrix Media. You have been licensed one copy of this document for personal use only. Any other reproduction or redistribution is strictly prohibited. All rights reserved.

ESTIMATION

Estimation is making an educated or informed guess about a measurement when no actual measurement is available. As adults, we often make estimates about the sizes of objects when we do not know their exact measurements, about the amounts of substances we have not actually measured, and about the numbers of small objects in large collections when we have not actually counted the objects. However, young children are in the process of learning the concepts of sizes and numbers. Children must comprehend concepts of comparison and relativity (e.g., larger, smaller, more, less, etc.) before they will be able to make accurate estimates. When children start to develop the ability to estimate amounts or sizes, this process helps them learn related math vocabulary words, such as "about" or "around," and "more than" and "less than" [something else]. Through estimating, they also learn how to make appropriate predictions and arrive at realistic answers. It is important for young children to learn how to make estimates, to recognize when it is appropriate to apply the estimation method, and to recognize when their estimates are reasonable.

ACTIVITIES TO HELP DEVELOP ESTIMATION

To accustom young children to the idea of estimating, adults should regularly use words related to estimation in their conversations with children (e.g., "around," "about," "approximately," "near," "more than [some other amount or number]," "less than [some other amount or number]," "between [two numbers or amounts]," etc.). During everyday activities like shopping or eating, adults can ask children to estimate amounts of foods, numbers of items, or lengths of time. Later, adults can help children compare the actual outcome with their original estimate. This process helps children learn to make realistic/reasonable estimates. Activities promoting estimation skills can be very simple. Adults can ask children, for example, to guess which of their friends is tallest, and then test the accuracy of the guess using real measurements. When children grow older, adults can write down estimates and real measurements, and can then repeat the exercise described above or present a similar one. With repetition, children will eventually begin making more accurate estimates. The goal is not for children to come up with exact measurements, but ones that are close to actual amounts/numbers. Giving children opportunities to practice improves their estimating skills.

PROBABILITIES AND STATISTICS

In general, when people work with statistics, they present them in graphs or charts to organize them, interpret them, and make it easier to see relationships among individual statistics. Graphs are a visual alternative that depict mathematical information and show relationships among individual statistics, especially changes over time. Graphs also allow for the comparison of different groups. Probabilities indicate the likelihood that something will happen. Adults use probabilities to predict things, such as people's risks of developing or dying from various diseases or medical conditions; the chances of accidents; children's risks of experiencing academic difficulties, dropping out, or developing emotional and behavioral disorders; and the chances that a certain area will receive rain or snow. Scientists use probabilities to predict the likelihood of various behaviors or outcomes they are studying. They use statistics to show the numbers and proportions of responses or results obtained in research studies. Calendars are one type of chart. Adults can help children use them to organize daily and weekly activities, and to understand how we organize information.

CHARTS AND GRAPHS

According to experts, almost every daily activity can be charted in some way. For example, adults can help children peel the little stickers off of plums, bananas, etc. and stick them to a piece of paper/poster board divided into columns. After a week, they can count each column to determine how many pieces of each kind of fruit they ate. Similarly, adults can show children how to use removable stickers or color forms to document the number of times they performed any daily activity. For example, children could place a color form near the telephone every time it rings and/or every time somebody picks it up to make a call. They could also place a color form near the front door every time somebody comes in, goes out, and/or rings the doorbell/knocks. This enables children to count the number of times given events

122

Copyright © Mometrix Media. You have been licensed one copy of this document for personal use only. Any other reproduction or redistribution is strictly prohibited. All rights reserved.

occur by recording them. Some children are better able to understand math by viewing and making graphs. This is because creating graphs involves representing quantities visually instead of just listing numbers.

RATIONAL NUMBERS AND IRRATIONAL NUMBERS

In mathematics, rational numbers are numbers that can be written as ratios or fractions. In other words, a rational number can be expressed as a fraction that has a whole number as the numerator (the number on top) and the denominator (the number on the bottom). Therefore, all whole numbers are automatically rational numbers, because all whole numbers can be written as fractions with a denominator of 1 (e.g., 5 = 5/1, 68 = 68/1, 237 = 237/1, etc.). Even very large, unwieldy fractions (e.g., 9,731,245/42,754,021) are rational numbers, because they can be written as fractions. Irrational numbers can be written as decimal numbers, but not as fractions, because the numbers to the right of the decimal point that are less than 1 continue indefinitely without repeating. For example, the value of pi (π) begins as 3.141592..., and continues without end. The square root of 2 ($\sqrt{2}$) = 1.414213.... There are an infinite number of irrational numbers between 0 and 1. However, irrational numbers are not used as commonly in everyday life as rational numbers.

> **Review Video: Rational and Irrational Numbers**
> Visit mometrix.com/academy and enter code: 280645

CARDINAL, ORDINAL, NOMINAL, AND REAL NUMBERS

Cardinal numbers are numbers that indicate quantity. For example, when we say "seven buttons" or "three kittens," we are using cardinal numbers. Ordinal numbers are numbers that indicate the order of items within a group or a set. For example, when we say "first, second, third, fourth, fifth, etc.," we are using ordinal numbers. Nominal numbers are numbers that name things. For example, we use area code numbers along with telephone numbers to identify geographical calling areas, and we use zip code numbers to identify geographical mailing areas. Nominal numbers, therefore, identify categories or serve as labels for things. However, they are not related to the actual mathematical values of numbers, and do not indicate numerical quantities or operations. Real numbers include all rational and irrational numbers. Rational numbers can always be written as fractions that have both numerators and denominators that are whole numbers. Irrational numbers cannot, as they contain non-repeating decimal digits. Real numbers may or may not be cardinal numbers.

INTEGRATING MATH INTO EVERYDAY ACTIVITIES AND USING EARLY CHILDHOOD MATH CURRICULA

Integrating math into the context of everyday activities has been the philosophy of early childhood math education until recently. For example, when teachers have children line up, they ask them who is first, second, third, etc. to practice counting. When children play with blocks, teachers ask them to identify their shapes and whether one block is larger/smaller than another. During snack times, teachers help children learn 1:1 correspondence by having them place one snack on each plate. These activities are quite valuable. However, some educators maintain that they are insufficient when used on their own, because in larger classes it is not always possible to take advantage of "teachable moments" with every child. Therefore, this educational approach cannot be applied systematically. These educators recommend that in addition to integration strategies, EC teachers should use a curriculum. The HighScope curriculum, the Creative Curriculum, and Big Math for Little Kids are just a few examples. Many teachers combine several curricula, selecting parts of different programs. Using a curriculum allows teachers to use a more planned approach to integrate math into all activities.

Copyright © Mometrix Media. You have been licensed one copy of this document for personal use only. Any other reproduction or redistribution is strictly prohibited. All rights reserved.

CLINICAL INTERVIEW
BACKGROUND, METHOD, AND ADVANTAGES

Clinical interviews have long been used by individual and family therapists, as well as by researchers. Piaget used them along with observations and case histories to understand young children's thinking as he formulated his cognitive developmental theory. Interviewers ask structured/semi-structured/open-ended questions and listen to the responses, often recording them for accuracy. This method gives the interviewer a way to find out what the respondent is thinking and feeling inside, which cannot be determined by observing outward behaviors alone. In educational settings, a teacher might ask a child questions like, "How did you do this?" "What is happening now?" "Can you tell me more about this?" "Why are you doing this?" "What are you thinking about now?" etc. Flexible questioning helps uncover the child's thought process, which is what is leading him/her to engage in specific behaviors. Just observing the behaviors alone does not allow the child to express his/her knowledge. While fully interviewing each child in a classroom is not practical, teachers can adapt this method by asking clinical interview-type questions as part of their instruction.

USING QUESTIONING

Teachers can gain a lot of information and insight about how children are learning math concepts by observing their behaviors. For children to actually express their knowledge and thinking processes, however, teachers must ask them questions. For example, when a teacher introduces new shapes to young children, s/he can ask them the shapes' names, how they differ from one another, and why they think the shapes differ. Teachers can then use children's various responses to elicit further responses from them. This technique requires children to use language in significant ways during math activities. Therefore, these activities not only teach math skills, but also promote literacy development. Asking clinical interview-type questions promotes children's development of math communication skills, one of the essential components of math education. Additionally, being able to put one's knowledge and thoughts into words is a skill that is very important in all areas of education, not just math education. Using clinical interview-type questions helps children learn to use language to explain their thinking, share ideas, and express themselves, promoting and strengthening children's awareness of the functions of mathematical language.

CHARACTERISTICS OF YOUNG CHILDREN'S THINKING AND LEARNING THAT INFORM EC MATH CURRICULA

Young children think in concrete ways and cannot understand abstract concepts, so effective EC math curricula typically use many concrete objects that children can see, feel, and manipulate to help them understand math concepts. Young children also naturally learn through exploring their environments, so good EC math curricula have many exploration and discovery activities that allow and encourage hands-on learning. In everyday life, young children start to observe relationships as they explore their surroundings. They match like objects, sort unlike objects, categorize objects, and arrange objects in simple patterns based on shared or contrasting properties. They start to understand words and phrases like "a little," "a lot," "more," "less," and "the same [as…]." Preschoolers use available materials such as sticks, pieces of string, their feet, their hands, their fingers, etc. as tools to measure objects. They also use rulers, measuring cups, and other conventional tools. They use their measurements to develop descriptions, sequences, and arrangements, and to compare various objects.

ACTIVITIES THAT HELP CHILDREN DEVELOP SPATIAL AWARENESS

When preschool children build structures with blocks and put together pieces of puzzles during play, they are not only having fun, but are also developing spatial awareness. The relationships of objects to each other and within space are important concepts for children to learn, and serve as a foundation for the principles of geometry and physics that children will learn later. When they are moving around, preschoolers begin to notice how other people and objects are positioned in space, and how their own bodies move through space in relationship to objects and other people. This type of spatial awareness

Copyright © Mometrix Media. You have been licensed one copy of this document for personal use only. Any other reproduction or redistribution is strictly prohibited. All rights reserved.

supports children's developing gross motor skills, coordination, and social skills. Young children can and should learn a number of math concepts and skills, such as the ones recommended by preschool math curricula like the High Scope program's "Numbers Plus" preschool mathematics curriculum. These concepts and skills include number symbols and names, counting, shapes, spatial awareness, relationships of parts to the whole, measurement, units, patterns, and analyzing data.

ACTIVITIES AND GAMES THAT MAKE LEARNING FUN

BUTTON BOARD

By gluing buttons of various sizes and colors to a piece of cardboard, teachers can initiate a number of activities that help preschoolers learn math concepts while having fun. Preschoolers are commonly learning shapes and how to draw them. Teachers can give children lengths of string/twine/yarn or long shoelaces and show them how to wrap them around different buttons to form shapes like rectangles, triangles, and squares. To practice counting and 1:1 correspondence, teachers can ask children to wrap their string around a given number of buttons. Preschoolers need to learn the concept that spoken number words like "five" can equate to a group of five concrete objects (such as buttons), and this activity promotes that learning. The button board is also useful for giving preschool children practice with sorting or classifying objects into groups based on a common characteristic. For example, the teacher can ask children to wrap their pieces of string around all the big buttons, all the little buttons, only the red buttons, only the blue buttons, etc.

BEANBAGS AND HOPSCOTCH

Teachers can encourage preschool children's counting and number development by creating a grid on the floor with the numbers 1 to 10 using masking tape, construction paper, and markers. Teachers could also draw the grid outdoors by drawing on pavement with chalk. The teacher arranges the numbers in ascending order within the grid of 10 squares/rectangles. S/he asks the children if they can name these numbers. The teacher provides beanbags. Each child gets a chance to throw a beanbag into any one of the numbered squares. Children can see how far they can throw and/or practice their aim. Each child names the number inside the square/rectangle where his/her beanbag lands. The children then play a version of hopscotch by hopping from numbered square to square, collecting their beanbags, and then hopping back. If desired, the teacher can write the number each child's beanbag lands on onto a "scoreboard" graph. Children will observe his/her writing the same numbers found on the floor/ground onto a "scoreboard." Teachers can review learning after the game to assess whether children can count using number words, name selected numbers, and throw accurately with consistency.

REUSING SECTIONED PLASTIC TRAYS

A teacher can wash and reuse the compartmentalized plastic trays from the grocery store that are used for vegetable and fruit to create a preschool counting activity. The teacher supplies beads, pennies, erasers, or other small objects, as well as about a dozen sticky notes. S/he writes a number on each note. For older preschoolers, the teacher can write the numeral and the word (e.g., "7" and "seven"). For younger children, the teacher can write the numeric symbol ("7," for example) plus seven dots or other marks as a clue to that number symbol. The teacher puts one numbered note in each compartment and the supply of small objects in the central dip compartment. Then, s/he guides each child to transfer the correct number of each small object to the correct compartment. The child should count aloud while transferring each small object, and should repeat this process until all compartments with a numbered sticky note have the correct number of objects. Children can then repeat the process to practice and perfect their counting, or the teacher can place notes with different numbers in the tray's compartments.

FISHING FOR NUMBERS

Teachers can help preschoolers practice identifying numbers and counting by creating a fun "fishing for numbers" game. Teachers cut 10 fish shapes that are about 6 inches long from pieces of construction paper that are different colors. Teachers then write a single number between 1 and 10 on each "fish." Near each fish "mouth," the teacher punches a hole and inserts a paper clip through it. The teacher

Copyright © Mometrix Media. You have been licensed one copy of this document for personal use only. Any other reproduction or redistribution is strictly prohibited. All rights reserved.

makes "fishing rods" by tying strings to dowels and gluing a magnet to each string. After spreading out the fish so the children can easily see the numbers, the teacher assigns each child a number and they "fish" for it, picking up the fish by bringing the magnet close to the paper clip. The children then "reel in" their catches. This gives children practice correctly identifying number names. The game can be adapted for more advanced math concepts as well. For example, the teacher can cut out fish shapes of various sizes and have children "fish" for larger/smaller fish. The activity can also be adapted to promote literacy development. The teacher can write letters instead of numbers on the fish to give students practice with alphabet recognition, or s/he can write a Dolch word/sight word on each fish to give students practice recognizing and identifying important vocabulary words.

COLLAGES

Fundamental math skills that prepare preschoolers for kindergarten include shape recognition. To introduce children to an activity they will view as fun rather than as work, teachers can show children how to make a collage of a familiar figure. This will also give children the opportunity to experiment with an artistic process. For example, they can create a Santa Claus or an Easter Bunny as a holiday art project. They can make collages of other imaginary/real people for various events/seasons/topics. Teachers cut out paper templates, including circles for heads, triangles for hats, squares for bodies, and narrow rectangular strips for limbs. First, they help children name each shape. They have each child trace the template shapes onto paper and cut them out with child-safe scissors. The teacher then instructs children to arrange their cutout shapes on a piece of cardboard/construction paper. Once they are in the correct positions, the children glue the shapes in place. Teachers can subsequently teach additional shapes (octagons, ovals, etc.), challenging children to make new, different collages.

GRAB BAG

Young children learn to name numbers in a way that is similar to how they learn to recite alphabet letters. However, learning to associate number symbols with concrete objects in the real world environment is a major advance in their cognitive development. The concept of 1:1 correspondence entails matching number symbols to the quantities they represent, an essential early math skill. Teachers can support the development of this math skill with a simple "grab bag" game youngsters enjoy. The teacher writes a number from 1 to 10 on each of ten cards, folding each card in half and putting them into a paper lunch bag. The teacher provides each child with a handful of pennies/play coins/buttons/little blocks to use as counting tokens. Each child takes a turn closing his/her eyes and pulling a card out of the bag. The child reads the number on the card, counts out the corresponding number of pennies/tokens, and puts them with the card. As children learn, teachers can place additional and/or different numbers (e.g., 11 to 20) in the grab bag. To promote the development of early literacy skills, teachers can also include the name of the number on each card.

PATTERN RESIST ART

A significant mark of progress in early math skills development is the ability to not only identify various shapes, but also to draw them. Once young children develop this ability, they typically want to practice it all the time. Teachers can encourage this by helping children make pattern resist paintings. The teacher tapes white paper to children's tables/trays, gives them crayons, and invites them to fill the paper with drawings of different shapes of various sizes and colors. Teachers can introduce young children to new shapes (e.g., ovals, stars, crescent moons, etc.) by drawing them on separate pieces of paper for children to look at and copy. Then, the teacher replaces the crayons with water, watercolor paints, and brushes; shows the children how to dip brushes into paint and water to dilute the colors; and allows them to paint over their crayoned shapes, covering all the white paper with color. The children see the shapes show through the paint, creating the pattern resist. Dipping brushes and diluting various colors also develop children's color recognition skills and their hand-eye coordination.

Copyright © Mometrix Media. You have been licensed one copy of this document for personal use only. Any other reproduction or redistribution is strictly prohibited. All rights reserved.

ICE CUBE NECKLACES

In hot weather, making ice cube necklaces is a fun activity that helps young children cool off while learning to sequence objects. The activity also helps children develop their manual motor skills and learn about liquid and solid states of matter. Regular ice cube trays are fine; those with "fun-shaped" compartments are even better. The teacher cuts plastic drinking straws so that they will fit into each ice cube compartment. The children participate, watching and/or helping pour water into trays and adding various food colorings/fruit juices. The teacher places one straw clipping into each compartment. While putting the trays into the freezer, the teacher tells children that 32° Fahrenheit/0° Celsius is the temperature at which water freezes. Children practice making scientific observations by noting how long the water takes to freeze. They empty the cubes into a big bowl. The children put on bathing suits or other clothing that can get wet, and the class goes outdoors. The teacher provides strings that are knotted at one end, and calls out a color pattern (e.g., one blue cube, then a yellow cube, etc.). Children follow the teacher's instructions to create color-patterned necklaces they can tie, wear, and watch melt.

RED ROVER

Red Rover is a good game for groups of children who are attending parties or playing outdoors at parks/playgrounds. Two teams take turns calling and roving. The child called runs to the other team and tries to fit into its line. If successful, s/he gets to call another player to bring back to his/her home team. If not, s/he joins the opposite team. The game continues until one team has no more members. Teachers can adapt this game to teach shape recognition by cutting out various shapes from construction paper of different colors and pinning a shape to each child's shirt. In large groups, more than one child can have the same shape or color. Instead of children's names, the teacher instructs players to use shapes and colors when calling (e.g., "Red Rover, Red Rover, blue circles come over!"). This supports the development of shape and color recognition skills. Teachers can vary action verbs (e.g., "....hop over/jump over/skip over") to support vocabulary development and comprehensive skills. When children perform such movements, they are also practicing and developing gross motor skills.

COUNTING ON FINGERS

A common practice among preschool children is counting on their fingers. Young children learn concretely before they develop abstract thought, so they must have concrete objects to work with to understand abstract mathematical concepts. They use their fingers to count because fingers are concrete. A simple activity that allows children to continue finger counting while removing additional visual support is "blind finger counting." Using eyesight to count objects we can see is relatively easy. However, when children cannot see objects, they must learn to count mentally instead. This allows them to take another step in their progress from concrete to abstract thinking. To count mentally without visual reinforcement takes practice. Teachers can tape a shoebox lid to the box and cut a small hole in it. Children can fit a hand through the hole, but cannot see inside. Children close their eyes; the teacher drops several small objects into the box; and each child reaches in, counting the objects using only touch. Varying objects and quantities maintains the fun of this activity.

SORTING AND CATEGORIZATION

One of the major learning accomplishments of young children is being able to identify similarities and differences among objects. Developing this ability enables children to sort like objects into groups, and to place objects into categories based on their differences. When preschoolers compare and contrast objects, they demonstrate an important early step in the development of critical thinking, analytical, and problem solving skills. For an easy, entertaining guessing game, adults can select assorted household items familiar to children and put them into a bag/pillowcase. They then give children various clues (e.g., "I stir lemonade with this...," "It's made of wood," "We keep it in the kitchen drawer...," etc.) and ask them to guess which items are in the bag. It is important to give young children one to two minutes to consider each clue before they make a guess. Adults repeat clues when children guess incorrectly. If children guess correctly, they are allowed to look inside the bag. Youngsters greatly enjoy seeing that

Copyright © Mometrix Media. You have been licensed one copy of this document for personal use only. Any other reproduction or redistribution is strictly prohibited. All rights reserved.

the object they guessed is actually inside the bag. Adults can gradually make the game more challenging by beginning with very common objects, and then eventually progressing to more unusual ones.

BAKING COOKIES

Young children are typically curious about adult activities like baking. They usually want to know more about the process, and often ask many questions. They also love to be included and to participate, frequently offering/asking to help. Letting them help builds their self-esteem and self-efficacy (i.e. their confidence in their competence to accomplish a task). Adults can allow children to help while also providing instruction and practice with shape recognition, measurement, sorting, and categorization. The adult prepares a favorite cookie recipe. Some children can help measure ingredients, which helps develop the math skill of measurement. With the dough rolled out, children use cookie cutters of various shapes. Recognizing, naming, and selecting the shapes promote the development of shape recognition skills. Adults "shuffle"/mix the baked cookie shapes and have children separate cookies with like shapes into groups, which promotes sorting skills. Having children identify similar/different shapes, sizes, and colors promotes categorization skills. Arranging cookie shapes into patterns for children to identify promotes pattern recognition skills, which are necessary to the development of math skills and many other skills. Giving each child a cookie to eat afterward is naturally reinforcing.

CREATIVE CRAFTS

Prerequisite abilities that young children need in order to develop early math skills include the ability to identify, copy, expand, and create patterns; as well as the ability to count. Adults can promote the development of these skills by giving children a craft project and introducing them to an interactive game they can play using their crafts. First, the children paint six ping pong balls red on one side to make red-and-white balls. Then, the children paint six ping pong balls blue on one side to make blue-and-white balls. Once the paint dries, the adult puts several balls into an egg carton so that one color is face up. The adult starts making a simple pattern (e.g., two white, then two red, then two blue), and asks each child to continue the pattern. Then, the adult allows each child to create his or her own original color patterns. Once a child masters creating patterns using solid colors, he or she can then use both the white and colored sides of the balls to create more complex patterns. Children can design an infinite number of patterns, which are often quite artistic.

SHAPE MATCHING GAMES

In one type of shape matching game, EC teachers help children make a game board out of construction paper that is shaped like a tree. Teachers first help the children cut a treetop and leaf shapes from green paper. They discuss children's preferences for tall/short and thick/thin trunks, giving them practice using descriptive vocabulary words, particularly ones related to size. This step builds both general and math concept vocabulary. Children cut trunks from brown paper and paste/glue them on the treetops. While out of the children's sight, the teacher cuts 5 to 10 (or more) pairs of shapes per child/tree from different colors of construction paper. Pairs should not match exactly (e.g., a blue square can be paired with a red square). The teacher glues one of each pair of shapes to each child's tree while the child is not looking. The teacher then gives each child the rest of the shapes, and invites children to see how quickly they can match each shape to its "partner" on the tree. The teacher can provide "warmer/cooler" distance clues, and should provide reinforcement each time a child correctly matches a pair of shapes. Teachers can make this activity more challenging by using more shapes and/or getting students to match shapes that are different sizes (e.g., children can be asked to match smaller diamonds to larger diamonds).

HOMEMADE BEANBAG GAME

Young children enjoy tossing objects and practicing their aim. Adults can make a beanbag game that helps children learn numbers and identify sets, while also allowing them to construct their own game rules. First, the adult should cover five big, equally-sized coffee (or similar) cans with paper that is adhesive on one side. The adult should then use markers to write a number from 1 to 5 and draw the

128

Copyright © Mometrix Media. You have been licensed one copy of this document for personal use only. Any other reproduction or redistribution is strictly prohibited. All rights reserved.

corresponding number of dots on each can. The next step is to fill 15 tube socks with beans and knot/tie/sew them shut. The following numerals and the corresponding number of dots should be written on each homemade beanbag using markers: the number 1 on five beanbags, the number 2 on four beanbags, the number 3 on three beanbags, the number 4 on two beanbags, and the number 5 on one beanbag. Next, the adult should attach the cans to the floor with tape or Velcro. Then, the adult should mark a line on the floor that children must stand behind, and should direct children ONLY to toss the beanbags into the cans. Children will devise various games/rules. First, they may simply toss the beanbags into the cans; then, some may try to toss beanbags into a can that has the same number as the one marked on the beanbag. Eventually, some may throw three beanbags into the "3" can. They may/may not keep score. Allowing children to determine the details and rules gives them an opportunity to develop their imagination and decision making skills, and to create their own games while learning number and set identification.

GUESSING GAME

Adults can adapt the format of "20 Questions," "I Spy," and other similar guessing games to focus on numbers and help children learn number concepts. For example, adults could say, "I'm thinking of a number from 1 to 10…." and then give children 10 guesses. Adults give children cues as they guess, such as "higher" and "lower," to help them narrow down the number of possible correct answers. As children improve, adults can increase the number range (e.g., from 0 to 50) or use larger numbers (e.g., from 20 to 40). As children's skills and self-confidence develop, adults can reverse roles, having children think of numbers and give clues while adults guess. Young children enjoy the fun of guessing, getting closer using clues, deducing correct answers, and fooling adults with their own clues. Concurrently, they learn to describe numbers, compare them, and sequence them. Adults can make the game more difficult by limiting the number of guesses allowed and/or setting time limits. They can make it easier by providing a written number line for children to reference. This game requires no materials (or just a basic number line), is a great way to pass time, and entertains children while helping to develop numeracy skills.

ARTS AND CRAFTS

According to the U.S. Department of Agriculture, preschoolers need three ½-cup servings of fruit and three ½-cup servings of vegetables daily. However, many young children are picky/resistant. Adults can motivate them to eat produce with a "food rainbow" project. Adults show children a picture of a rainbow, and discuss its colors and their sequence (teaching some earth science, optics, and color theory!). A fun art project is allowing students to color their own rainbows, which improves fine motor skills. Then, adults can have children cut out pictures from grocery circulars and name each food. The adult can help children find one healthy fruit/vegetable for each color, gluing each food to its corresponding stripe on the rainbow. Adults can then help children pull apart cotton balls and glue them to their rainbow pictures to represent clouds. Children can then post their food rainbows on refrigerators as artwork and as healthy eating reminders. At the bottom, children can draw and color one box (bottom-up) for each food they eat (e.g., blue = blueberries, orange = carrots, red = apples, etc.) to create a bar graph. Children should try to "eat" the entire rainbow every week. This activity gives children the opportunity to produce colorful art, eat better, track and document their diets, and develop graphing skills.

> **Review Video: Data Interpretation of Graphs**
> Visit mometrix.com/academy and enter code: 200439

TREASURE HUNT

A treasure hunt is an ideal outdoor activity for young children, and can also be adapted for indoor fun. The treasure can be anything (e.g., a small toy/play money/chocolate "coins"/rocks spray painted gold or silver, etc.). The adult should put the treasure in a paper bag marked with a large X. The adult should hide it somewhere where it is not visible, but will not be overly difficult for children to find. Then, the adult should make a treasure map, using few words and many pictures, sketching landmark objects in

Copyright © Mometrix Media. You have been licensed one copy of this document for personal use only. Any other reproduction or redistribution is strictly prohibited. All rights reserved.

the area (trees, houses, etc. if the activity will be done outdoors, and furniture, walls, etc. if the activity will be done indoors). The adult should ensure the map is developmentally appropriate for young children, and that they will be able to read it independently. Adults with time and motivation can make the map look authentic by soaking it in tea/coffee, drying it in a 200° oven, or even charring its edges. Adults should include a dotted line on the map that reinforces the simple directions and indicates the path to the treasure, which is indicated on the map by a large X. Children have fun, use their imaginations, make connections between symbols and images to corresponding real-world physical objects, and begin learning to read maps.

Pasta Necklace

Stringing beads/noodles is an activity that helps young children develop hand-eye coordination, which they will need for writing and other everyday activities that require fine motor coordination. Noodles are typically the perfect size for young children's hands. They are inexpensive, usually costing less than comparably-sized beads. Moreover, pasta is non-toxic, an advantage when working with little persons who put things in their mouths. Hollow, tubular noodles like penne, ziti, wagon wheels, etc. are ideal. Fishing line/craft beading string/other stiff string is best; soft, limp string/yarn is harder for young children to manipulate. Using multicolored vegetable pasta removes the need to use markers or dye to add color. If using white pasta, children can color the noodles with markers, but adults should keep in mind that the ink can bleed onto skin/clothes even when it is dry. Adults should cut pieces of string that are long enough to allow children to easily slip the necklaces on and off after they are tied. Adults should also use a knot to secure a noodle to one end of the string. By providing more than one noodle shape, adults can invite children to string the noodles to create patterns, which develops pattern recognition and pattern creation abilities. These abilities also inform repetition, rhythm, categorization, and sequencing skills, which are important in math, music, art, literature, clothing design, etc.

Number Dash

A game for young children that some educators call "Number Dash" (Miller, ed. Charner, 2009) builds foundational math concepts and skills, while providing physical activity. It can involve small or large groups (the referenced authors say "the more the merrier"). Help children write large numbers on a paved area with sidewalk chalk. Make sure numbers are spread far enough apart so children will not collide while running. There should be one of each number for each child (e.g., six "1s," "2s," "3s," etc. if there are six children). Use chalk colors that contrast with the pavement color to ensure the numbers will be highly visible. Tell children to run ("dash") to whichever number you call out and stand on it until you call another number. Call out numbers randomly. Encourage children who have located the number to help their classmates/playmates. This game develops gross motor skills, number writing skills, and number recognition skills. It also provides experience with playing organized games, following rules, following directions, and cooperating with and helping others. This game can also be played with letters, colors, and/or shapes.

Introducing Standard Measurement Using a Ruler

A teacher is introducing standard measures to her class as part of a unit on measurement, one of the early math skills. She shows the children a ruler, explaining that it is one foot long, and that we can use it to measure inches and parts of inches. She demonstrates placing the ruler on paper to measure a given length, explaining that the ruler can also be used as a straight edge for drawing lines. One child asks, "How come you started with zero? Why don't you start with one like when we count?" The teacher responds, "That's a very good question! Zero means none/nothing. When we count, we start with one because we already have at least one of something. When you were born, you were not one year old; your age began at zero. After a year, on your first birthday, you were one year old. We also begin measuring distances at zero/none/nothing. The first piece/unit of measurement is one, not two. The distance from zero to one is equal to one. To get to one inch, for example, we need to start at zero."

Copyright © Mometrix Media. You have been licensed one copy of this document for personal use only. Any other reproduction or redistribution is strictly prohibited. All rights reserved.

LEARNING ABOUT GEOMETRIC SHAPES AND THEIR PROPERTIES

A teacher has been working with students to help them develop their shape identification skills. They can recognize shapes by sight, and have also learned the defining properties of different shapes (number of sides, etc.). The teacher shows the class this figure:

She asks how many rectangles they can find in the figure. One student answers, "There is one rectangle," which is incorrect because a square is a rectangle; this figure has four rectangles that are squares. Moreover, the entire figure is itself a rectangle. Another student therefore says, "There are five rectangles." This response is also incorrect. Two adjacent squares also form a rectangle; this means there are three additional rectangles. Three adjacent squares also form a rectangle; this means there are two additional rectangles. Thus, the figure has a total of 10 rectangles. Solving this puzzle requires the use of many skills, including analyzing visual information, synthesizing visual information, recognizing patterns, recognizing shapes, and identifying the properties of shapes.

COLLECTING, ORGANIZING, AND DISPLAYING DATA USING STICKY NOTES AND A TEACHER-MADE CHART

A preschool teacher is teaching her group of ten children about basic data collection, data arrangement, and data display. She shows children yellow, blue, and green sticky notes, and has each child select his/her favorite color. Five children choose yellow notes, three select blue, and two choose green. By choosing one of three colors, each child has participated in data collection. The teacher draws lines to divide a sheet of paper into three columns, and labels each column with one of the colors. She helps the children place their chosen sticky notes in the correct columns. By arranging the colored sticky notes into columns, the teacher and children have organized the data they gathered. Once all notes are in their proper color columns, the completed chart is an example of how collected, organized data can be displayed.

	Yellow sticky note	
	Yellow sticky note	
Blue sticky note	Yellow sticky note	
Blue sticky note	Yellow sticky note	Green sticky note
Blue sticky note	Yellow sticky note	Green sticky note
BLUE	**YELLOW**	**GREEN**

SELECTING ONE OF THREE COLORS OF STICKY NOTES, ORGANIZING THEM BY COLOR, AND DISPLAYING THEM

The teacher had ten children each choose one of three colors of sticky notes, an example of basic data collection. She used a chart with three columns to organize the children's choices as follows:

	Yellow sticky note	
	Yellow sticky note	
Blue sticky note	Yellow sticky note	
Blue sticky note	Yellow sticky note	Green sticky note
Blue sticky note	Yellow sticky note	Green sticky note
BLUE	**YELLOW**	**GREEN**

The chart displays the collected and organized data. The teacher asks the children which color was chosen the most. Seeing five yellow notes, they answer, "yellow." She asks which color was chosen the least, and they say, "green." She asks them to use numbers to arrange the color choices from most popular to least popular. They arrive at, "five yellow, three blue, and two green." Together, the teacher

Copyright © Mometrix Media. You have been licensed one copy of this document for personal use only. Any other reproduction or redistribution is strictly prohibited. All rights reserved.

and the children point to and count ten children. She tells them five equals half of ten, and asks which color half of the children chose. Together, they figure out it was yellow. These are examples of analyzing and interpreting data.

Copyright © Mometrix Media. You have been licensed one copy of this document for personal use only. Any other reproduction or redistribution is strictly prohibited. All rights reserved.

Science Foundations

SCIENCE CONCEPTS YOUNG CHILDREN LEARN DURING EVERYDAY ACTIVITIES

Science entails asking questions, conducting investigations, collecting data, and seeking answers to the questions asked by analyzing the data collected. Natural events that can be examined over time and student-centered inquiry through hands-on activities that require the application of problem solving skills are most appropriate for helping young children learn basic science. In their everyday lives, young children develop concepts of 1:1 correspondence through activities like fitting pegs into matching holes or distributing one item to each child in a class. They also develop counting concepts by counting enough items for each child in the group or counting pennies in a piggy bank. They develop classification concepts when they sort objects into separate piles according to their shapes or some other type of category (e.g., toy cars vs. toy trucks). When children transfer water, sand, rice, or other substances from one container to another, they develop measurement concepts. As they progress, children will apply these early concepts to more abstract scientific ideas during grade school.

SCIENCE CONCEPTS INFANTS AND TODDLERS LEARN IN NORMAL DEVELOPMENTAL PROCESSES

Infants use their senses to explore the environment, and are motivated by innate curiosity. As they develop mobility, children gain more freedom, allowing them to make independent discoveries and think for themselves. Children learn size concepts by comparing the sizes of objects/persons in the environment to their own size, and by observing that some objects are too large to hold, while others are small enough to hold. They learn about weight when trying to lift various objects. They learn about shape when they see that some objects roll away, while others do not. Babies learn temporal sequences when they wake up wet and hungry, cry, and have parents change and feed them. They also learn this concept by playing, getting tired, and going to sleep. As soon as they look and move around, infants learn about space, including large/small spaces. Eventually, they develop spatial sense through experiences like being put in a playpen/crib in the middle of a large room. Toddlers naturally sort objects into groups according to their sizes/shapes/colors/uses. They experiment with transferring water/sand among containers of various sizes. They learn part-to-whole relationships by building block structures and then dismantling them.

NATURALISTIC, INFORMAL, AND STRUCTURED LEARNING EXPERIENCES

Children actively construct their knowledge of the environment through exploring it. Young children's learning experiences can be naturalistic (i.e. spontaneously initiated by the child during everyday activities). During naturalistic learning, the child controls his/her choices and actions. Informal learning experiences also allow the child to choose his or her actions and activities, but they include adult intervention at some point during the child's engagement in naturalistic pursuits. In structured learning experiences, the adult chooses the activities and supplies some direction as to how the child should perform the associated actions. One consideration related to EC learning that teachers should keep in mind is that within any class or group of children, there are individual differences in learning styles. Additionally, children from different cultural groups have varying learning styles and approaches. EC teachers can introduce science content in developmentally appropriate ways by keeping these variations in mind.

NATURALISTIC LEARNING EXPERIENCES

Motivated by novelty and curiosity, young children spontaneously initiate naturalistic experiences during their everyday activities. Infants and toddlers in Piaget's sensorimotor stage learn by exploring the environment through their senses, so adults should provide them with many objects and substances they can see, hear, touch, smell, and taste. Through manipulating and observing concrete objects/substances, preschoolers in Piaget's preoperational stage begin learning concepts that will enable them to perform mental operations later on. Adults should observe children's actions and

Copyright © Mometrix Media. You have been licensed one copy of this document for personal use only. Any other reproduction or redistribution is strictly prohibited. All rights reserved.

progress, and should give positive reinforcement in the form of looks, facial expressions, gestures, and/or words encouraging and praising the child's actions. Young children need adult feedback to learn when they are performing the appropriate actions. For example, a toddler/preschooler selects a tool from the toolbox, saying, "This is big!" and the mother responds, "Yes!" A four-year-old sorting toys of various colors into separate containers is another example of a naturalistic experience. A five-year-old who observes while painting that mixing two colors yields a third color is yet another example.

INFORMAL LEARNING EXPERIENCE

Informal learning experiences involve two main components. First, the child spontaneously initiates naturalistic learning experiences during everyday activities to explore and learn about the environment. Second, the adult takes advantage of opportunities during naturalistic experiences to insert informal learning experiences. Adults do not plan these in advance, but take advantage of opportunities that occur naturally. One way this happens is when a child is on the right track to solve a problem, but needs some encouragement or a hint from the adult. Another way is when the adult spots a "teachable moment" during the child's naturalistic activity, and uses it to reinforce a basic concept. For example, a three-year-old might hold up three fingers, declaring, "I'm six years old." The parent says, "Let's count fingers: one, two, three. You're three years old." Or, a teacher asks a child who has a box of treats if s/he has enough for the whole class, and the child answers, "I don't know." The teacher then responds, "Let's count them together," and helps the child count.

STRUCTURED LEARNING EXPERIENCES

Naturalistic learning experiences are spontaneously initiated and controlled by children. Informal learning experiences involve unplanned interventions by adults during children's naturalistic experiences, which is when adults offer suitable correction/assistance/support. Structured learning experiences differ in that the adult pre-plans and initiates the activity/lesson, and provides the child with some direction. For example, a teacher who observes a four-year-old's need to practice counting can give the child a pile of toys, and then ask him/her how many there are. To develop size concepts, a teacher can give a small group of children several toys of different sizes, and then ask the children to inspect them and talk about their characteristics. The teacher holds up one toy, instructing children to find one that is bigger/smaller. If a child needs to learn shape concepts, the teacher might introduce a game involving shapes, giving the child instructions on how to play the game. Or, a first grade teacher, recognizing the importance of the concept of classification to the ability to organize scientific information, might ask students to bring in bones to classify during a unit on skeletons.

KINDERGARTEN ACTIVITY FOR COLLECTING AND ORGANIZING DATA

Preschoolers and kindergarteners continue their earlier practices of exploration to learn new things, and they apply fundamental science concepts to collect and organize data in order to answer questions. To collect data, children must have observation, counting, recording, and organization skills. One activity kindergarteners and teachers enjoy is growing bean sprouts. For example, the teacher can show children two methods: one using glass jars and paper towels saturated with water, the other using cups of dirt. The children add water daily as needed, observe developments, and report to the teacher, who records their observations on a chart. The teacher gives each child a chart that they add information to each day. The children count how many days their beans took to sprout in the glass jars and in the cups of dirt. They then compare their own results for the two methods, and they compare their results to those of their classmates. The children apply concepts of counting, numbers, time, 1:1 correspondence, and comparison of numbers. They also witness the planting and growing process.

SCIENCE PROCESS SKILLS

Science process skills include observation (using the senses to identify properties of objects/situations), classification (grouping objects/situations according to their common properties), measurement (quantifying physical properties), communication (using observations, classifications, and measurements to report experimental results to others), inference (finding patterns and meaning in

Copyright © Mometrix Media. You have been licensed one copy of this document for personal use only. Any other reproduction or redistribution is strictly prohibited. All rights reserved.

experiment results), and prediction (using experimental experience to formulate new hypotheses). Inferences and predictions must be differentiated from objective observations. Classification, measurement, and comparison are basic math concepts which, when applied to science problems, are called process skills. The other science process skills named, as well as defining and controlling variables, are equally necessary to solve both science and math problems. For example, using ramps can help young children learn basic physics concepts. Teachers ask children what would happen if two balls were rolled down a ramp at the same time, if two balls were rolled down a ramp of a different height/length, if two ramps of different heights/lengths were used, etc. In this activity, children apply the scientific concepts of observation, communication, inference, and prediction, as well as the concepts of height, length, counting, speed, distance, and comparison.

SCIENTIFIC METHOD

Children are born curious, and naturally engage in problem solving to learn. Problem solving and inquiry are natural child behaviors. EC teachers can use these behaviors to promote children's scientific inquiry. Scientific inquiry employs the scientific method. The first step in the method is to ask a question, which is another natural child behavior. Just as adult scientists formulate research questions, the first step of the scientific method for children is asking questions they want to answer. Next, to address a question, both adults and children must form a hypothesis (i.e. an educated guess about what the answer will be). The hypothesis informs and directs the next steps: designing and conducting an experiment to test whether the hypothesis is true or false. With teacher instruction/help, children experiment. For example, they might drop objects of different weights from a height to see when each lands, as Galileo did. Teachers help record outcomes. The next steps are deciding whether the results prove/disprove the hypothesis and reporting the results and conclusions to others.

> **Review Video: The Scientific Method**
> Visit mometrix.com/academy and enter code: 191386

PHYSICAL SCIENCE AND MATTER

Physical science is the study/science of the physical universe surrounding us. Everything in the universe consists of matter (i.e. anything that has mass and takes up space) or energy (i.e. anything that does not have mass or occupy space, but affects matter and space). Three states of matter are solid, liquid, and gas. Solids preserve their shape even when they are not in a container. Solids have specific, three-dimensional/crystalline atomic structures and specific melting points. Liquids have no independent shape outside of containers, but have specific volumes. Liquid molecules are less cohesive than solid molecules, but more cohesive than gas molecules. Liquids have flow, viscosity (flow resistance), and buoyancy. Liquids can undergo diffusion, osmosis, evaporation, condensation, solution, freezing, and heat conduction and convection. Liquids and gases are both fluids, and share some of the same properties. Gases have no shape, expanding and spreading indefinitely outside of containers. Gases can become liquid/solid through cooling/compression/both. Liquids/solids can become gaseous through heating. Vapor is the gaseous form of a substance that is solid/liquid at lower temperatures. For example, when water is heated it becomes steam, a vapor.

> **Review Video: States of Matter**
> Visit mometrix.com/academy and enter code: 742449

LIQUIDS

Of the three states of matter—solid, liquid, and gas—liquids have properties that fall somewhere in between those of solids and gases. The molecules of solids are the most cohesive (i.e. they have the greatest mutual attraction). Gas molecules are the least cohesive, and liquid molecules are in between. Liquids have no definite shape, while solids do. Liquids have a definite volume, whereas gases do not. The cohesion of liquid molecules draws them together, and the molecules below the surface pull surface molecules down, creating surface tension. This property can be observed in containers of water. Liquid

135

Copyright © Mometrix Media. You have been licensed one copy of this document for personal use only. Any other reproduction or redistribution is strictly prohibited. All rights reserved.

molecules are also attracted to other substance's molecules (i.e. adhesion). Surface tension and adhesion combined cause liquids to rise in narrow containers, a property known as capillarity. Liquids are buoyant (i.e. they exert upward force so objects which have more buoyancy than weight float in liquids, while objects which have more weight than buoyancy sink in liquids). Liquids can be made solid by freezing, and can be made gaseous by heating/evaporation. Liquids can diffuse, which means they can mix with other molecules. Liquid diffusion across semi-permeable membranes is known as osmosis.

SOLIDS

Solids are one of the three forms of matter. The other two are liquids and gases. Solids maintain their shape when they are not inside of containers, whereas liquids and gases acquire the shapes of containers holding them. Containers also prevent liquids and gases from dispersing. Of the three forms of matter, solids have the most cohesive molecules. Solid molecules are most attracted to each other, and solid molecules are held together most strongly. Solid atoms are organized into defined, three-dimensional, lattice-shaped patterns (i.e. they are crystalline in structure). Solids also have specific temperatures at which they melt. Some substances that seem solid, such as plastic, gel, tar, and glass, are actually not true solids. They are amorphous solids because their atoms do not have a crystalline structure, but are amorphous (i.e. the positions of their atoms have no long-range organization). They also have a range of melting temperatures rather than specific melting points.

GASES

Gas, liquid, and solid are the three states of matter. Gases have the least cohesive (i.e. mutually attracted) molecules of the three states of matter, while solids have the most cohesive molecules. Gases do not maintain a defined shape, while solids do. If not contained within a receptacle, gases spread and expand indefinitely. Gases can be elementary or compound. An elementary gas is composed of only one kind of chemical element. At normal temperatures and pressures, 12 elementary gases are known: argon*, chlorine, fluorine, helium*, hydrogen, krypton*, neon*, nitrogen, oxygen, ozone, radon*, and xenon*. Compound gases have molecules containing atoms of more than one kind of chemical element. Carbon monoxide (which contains one carbon and one oxygen atom) and ammonia (which contains nitrogen and hydrogen atoms) are common compound gases. Heating gas molecules/atoms charges them electrically, making them ions. Plasma combines positive gas ions and electrons. Some gases are colorless and odorless, while others are not. Some burn with oxygen, while others do not. *Noble/inert gases have single atoms that do not normally form compounds with other elements.

LIGHT

REFLECTION AND SCATTERING

When a beam of light hits a smooth surface like a mirror, it bounces back off that surface. This rebounding is reflection. In physics, the law of reflection states that "the angle of incidence equals the angle of reflection." This means that when light is reflected, it always bounces off the surface at the same angle at which it hit that surface. When a beam of light hits a rough rather than a smooth surface, though, it is reflected back at many different angles, not just the angle at which it struck the surface. This reflection at multiple and various angles is scattering. Many objects we commonly use every day have rough surfaces. For example, paper may look smooth to the naked eye, but actually has a rough surface. This property can be observed by viewing paper through a microscope. Because light waves striking paper are reflected in every direction by its rough surface, scattering enables us to read words printed on paper from any viewing angle.

ABSORPTION

When light strikes a medium, the light wave's frequency is equal or close to the frequency at which the electrons in the medium's atoms can vibrate. These electrons receive the light's energy, making them vibrate. When a medium's atoms hang on tightly to their electrons, the electrons transmit their vibrations to the nucleus of each atom. This makes the atoms move faster and collide with the medium's

Copyright © Mometrix Media. You have been licensed one copy of this document for personal use only. Any other reproduction or redistribution is strictly prohibited. All rights reserved.

other atoms. The energy the atoms got from the vibrations is then released as heat. This process is known as absorption of light. Materials that absorb light, such as wood and metal, are opaque. Some materials absorb certain light frequencies but transmit others. For example, glass transmits visible light (and therefore appears transparent to the naked eye), but absorbs ultraviolet frequencies. The sky looks blue because the atmosphere absorbs all colors in the spectrum except blue, which it reflects. Only blue wavelengths/frequencies bounce back to our eyes. This is an example of subtractive color, which we see in paints/dyes and all colored objects/materials. Pigments absorb some frequencies and reflect others.

REFRACTION

When light moves from one transparent medium to another (e.g., between water and air/vice versa), the light's speed changes, bending the light wave. It bends either away from or toward the normal line, an imaginary straight line running at right angles to the medium's surface. We easily observe this bending when looking at a straw in a glass of water. The straw appears to break/bend at the waterline. The angle of refraction is the amount that the light wave bends. It is determined by how much the medium slows down the light's speed, which is the medium's refraction index. For example, diamonds are much denser and harder than water, and thus have a higher refraction index. They slow down and trap light more than water does. Consequently, diamonds sparkle more than water. Lenses, such as those in eyeglasses and telescopes, rely on the principle of refraction. Curved lenses disperse or concentrate light waves, refracting light as it both enters and exits, thus changing the light's direction. This is how lenses correct (eyeglasses) and enhance (telescopes) our vision.

MAGNETISM

Magnetism is the property some objects/substances have of attracting other materials. The form of magnetism most familiar to us is certain materials attracting iron. Magnets also attract steel, cobalt, and other materials. Generators supplying power include magnets, as do all electric motors. Loudspeakers and telephones contain magnets. Tape recorders use magnets. The tape they play is magnetized. Magnets are used in compasses to determine the location of north and various corresponding directions. In fact, the planet Earth is itself a giant magnet (which is why compasses point north). Hence, like the Earth, all magnets have two poles: a north/north-seeking pole and a south/south-seeking pole. Opposite poles attract, and like poles repel each other. Magnets do not need to touch to attract/repel each other. A magnet's effective area/range is its magnetic field. All materials have some response to magnetic fields. Magnets make nearby magnetic materials into magnets, a process known as magnetic induction. Materials that line up parallel to magnetic force field lines are paramagnetic, while materials that line up perpendicular to magnetic force field lines are diamagnetic.

MODERN THEORY OF MAGNETISM AND WHAT SCIENTISTS DO/DO NOT KNOW

Scientists have known about the effects of magnetism for hundreds of years. However, they do not know exactly what magnetism is, or what causes it. French physicist Pierre Weiss proposed a theory of magnetism in the early 20th century that is widely accepted. This theory posits that every magnetic material has groups of molecules—domains—that function as magnets. Until a material is magnetized, its domains have a random arrangement, so one domain's magnetism is cancelled out by another's. When the material comes into a magnetic field—the range/area wherein a magnet is effective—its domains align themselves parallel to the magnetic field's lines of force. As a result, all of their north-seeking/north poles point in the same direction. Removing the magnetic field causes like poles to repel one another as they normally do. In easily magnetized materials, domains revert to random order. In materials that are harder to magnetize, domains lack sufficient force to disassemble, leaving the material magnetized. Later versions of Weiss's theory attribute domain magnetism to spinning electrons.

> **Review Video: Magnets**
> Visit mometrix.com/academy and enter code: 570803

Copyright © Mometrix Media. You have been licensed one copy of this document for personal use only. Any other reproduction or redistribution is strictly prohibited. All rights reserved.

INSULATION, CONDUCTION, AND THE FLOW OF ELECTRICITY

The smallest units of all matter are atoms. The nuclei of atoms are orbited by negatively charged electrons. Some materials have electrons that are strongly bound to their atoms. These include air, glass, wood, cotton, plastic, and ceramic. Since their atoms rarely release electrons, these materials have little or no ability to conduct electricity, and are known as electrical insulators. Insulators resist/block conduction. Metals and other conductive materials have free electrons that can detach from the atoms and move around. Without the tight binding of insulators, materials with loose electrons enable electric current to flow easily through them. Such materials are called electrical conductors. The movements of their electrons transmit electrical energy. Electricity requires something to make it flow (i.e. a generator). A generator creates a steady flow of electrons by moving a magnet close to a wire, creating a magnetic field to propel electrons. Electricity also requires a conductor (i.e. a medium through which it can move from one place to another).

MOVEMENT OF ELECTRICAL CURRENTS BY A GENERATOR

Magnetism and electricity are related, and they interact with each other. Generators work by using magnets near conductive wires to produce moving streams of electrons. The agent of movement can range from a hand crank, to a steam engine, to the nuclear fission process. However, all agents of movements operate according to the same principle. A simple analogy is that a generator magnetically pushes electrical current the way a pump pushes water. Just as water pumps apply specific amounts of pressure to specific numbers of water molecules, generator magnets apply specific amounts of "pressure" to specific numbers of electrons. The number of moving electrons in an electrical circuit equals the current, or amperage. The unit of measurement for amperage is the ampere, or amp. The amount of force moving the electrons is the voltage. Its unit of measurement is the volt. One amp equals 6.24×10^{18} electrons passing through a wire each second. For example, a generator could produce 1 amp using 6 volts when rotating 1,000 times per minute. Today's power stations rely on generators.

POSITIONS AND MOTIONS OF OBJECTS AND NEWTON'S LAWS OF PHYSICS

Moving physical objects changes their positions. According to Newton's first law of motion, an object at rest tends to stay at rest and an object in motion tends to stay in motion, unless/until an opposing force changes the object's state of rest/motion. For example, an object at rest could be a small rock sitting on the ground. If you kick the rock into the air, it moves through the air. The rock will continue to move, but when a force like gravity acts on it, it falls/stops moving. The resulting motion from kicking the rock illustrates Newton's third law of motion: for every action there is an equal and opposite reaction. The acceleration or increase in velocity (a) of an object depends on its mass (m) and the amount of force (F) that is applied to the object. Newton's second law of motion states that F = ma (force equals mass times acceleration). Thus, moving objects maintain their speeds unless some force(s) cause acceleration or slowing/stopping, as frictional forces do.

HEAT

Heat is transmitted through conduction, radiation, and convection. Heat is transmitted in solids through conduction. When two objects at different temperatures touch each other, the hotter object's molecules are moving faster. They collide with the colder object's molecules, which are moving slower. As a result of the collision, the molecules that are moving more rapidly supply energy to the molecules that are moving more slowly. This speeds up the movement of the (previously) slower moving molecules, which heats up the colder object. This process of transferring heat through contact is called thermal conductivity. An example of thermal conductivity is the heat sink. Heat sinks are used in many devices. Today, they are commonly used in computers. A heat sink transfers the heat building up in the computer processor, moving it away before it can damage the processor. Computers contain fans, which blow air across their heat sinks and expel the heated air out of the computers.

Copyright © Mometrix Media. You have been licensed one copy of this document for personal use only. Any other reproduction or redistribution is strictly prohibited. All rights reserved.

ACOUSTICAL PRINCIPLES AND THE HUMAN HEARING PROCESS

When any physical object moves back and forth rapidly, this is known as vibration. The movements that occur during vibration disturb the surrounding medium, which may be solid, liquid, or gaseous. The most common sound conducting medium in our environment is gaseous: our atmosphere (i.e. the air). An object's vibratory movements represent a form of energy. As this acoustic energy moves through the air, it takes the form of waves, sound waves specifically. The outer ear receives and amplifies the sound and transmits it to the middle ear, where tiny bones vibrate in response to the sound energy and transmit it to the inner ear. The inner ear converts the acoustic energy into electrical energy. The electrical impulses are then carried by nerves to the brain. Structures in the brain associated with hearing receive these electrical signals and interpret them (i.e. make sense of them) as sounds. The ears' reception of sound waves is auditory sensation, and the brain's interpretation of them is auditory perception.

SOLAR SYSTEM

SOLAR SYSTEM'S LOCATION AND COMPONENTS

The universe is composed of an unknown (possibly infinite) number of galaxies or star systems, such as the Spiral Nebula, the Crab Nebula, and the Milky Way. Our sun, Sol, is one of billions of stars in the Milky Way. The solar system's planets are held in position at varying distances (according to their size and mass) from the Sun by its gravitational force. These planets orbit or revolve around the Sun. From the closest to the Sun to the farthest away, the solar system's planets are Mercury, Venus, Earth, Mars, Jupiter, Saturn, Uranus, and Neptune. Pluto was historically included as the ninth planet, but was demoted to a "dwarf planet" by the International Astronomical Union in 2006. Due to angular momentum, planets rotate on their axes, which are imaginary central lines between their north and south poles. One complete Earth rotation equals what we perceive as one 24-hour day. As the Earth turns, different portions face the Sun. These receive daylight, while the portions turned away from the Sun are in darkness. One complete revolution of the Earth around the Sun represents one calendar year.

PLUTO

Since more powerful observatories have enabled greater detection and measurement of celestial objects, the International Astronomical Union has defined three criteria for defining a planet. First, it must orbit the Sun. Pluto meets this criterion. Second, it must have enough gravitational force to shape itself into a sphere. Pluto also meets this criterion. Third, a planet must have "cleared the neighborhood" in its orbit. This expression refers to the fact that as planets form, they become the strongest gravitational bodies within their orbits. Therefore, when close to smaller bodies, planets either consume these smaller bodies or repel them because of their greater gravity, clearing their orbital area/"neighborhood." To do this, a planet's mass must sufficiently exceed the mass of other bodies in its orbit. Pluto does not meet this criterion, having only 0.07 times the mass of other objects within its orbit. Thus, astronomers reclassified Pluto as a "dwarf planet" in 2006 based on its lesser mass and the many other objects in its orbit with comparable masses and sizes.

EARTH

Earth is roughly spherical in shape. Its North and South Poles at the top and bottom are farthest away from and least exposed to the Sun, so they are always coldest. This accounts for the existence of the polar ice caps. The Equator, an imaginary line running around Earth at its middle exactly halfway between the North and South Poles, is at 0° latitude. Sunrises and sunsets at the Equator are the world's fastest. Days and nights are of virtually equal length at the Equator, and there is less seasonal variation than in other parts of the world. The equatorial climate is a tropical rainforest. Locations close to the North Pole, like Norway, are at such high latitudes that their nights are not dark in summertime, hence the expression "Land of the Midnight Sun." They also have very little light in wintertime. As Earth revolves around the Sun over the course of a year, the distance and angle of various locations relative to

Copyright © Mometrix Media. You have been licensed one copy of this document for personal use only. Any other reproduction or redistribution is strictly prohibited. All rights reserved.

the Sun change, so different areas receive varying amounts of heat and light. This is what accounts for the changing seasons.

ROCKS FOUND ON THE EARTH'S SURFACE

SEDIMENTARY ROCKS

Earth's rock types are sedimentary, igneous, and metamorphic. These categories are based on the respective processes that form each type of rock. Igneous rocks are formed from volcanoes. Metamorphic rocks are formed when igneous and sedimentary rocks deep inside the Earth's crust are subjected to intense heat and/or pressure. Sedimentary rocks are formed on Earth's surface, and characteristically accumulate in layers. Erosion and other natural processes deposit these layers. Some sedimentary rocks are held together by electrical attraction. Others are cemented together by chemicals and minerals that existed during their formation. Still others are not held together at all, but are loose and crumbly. There are three subcategories of sedimentary rock. Clastic sedimentary rocks are made of little rock bits—clasts—that are compacted and cemented together. Chemical sedimentary rocks are frequently formed through repeated flooding and subsequent evaporation. The evaporation of water leaves a layer of minerals that were dissolved in the water. Limestone and deposits of salt and gypsum are examples. Organic sedimentary rocks are formed from organic matter, such as the calcium left behind from animal bones and shells.

METAMORPHIC ROCKS

Sedimentary rocks are formed on the Earth's surface by layers of eroded material from mountains that were deposited by water, minerals like lime, salt and gypsum deposited by evaporated floodwater, and organic material like calcium from animal bones and shells. Igneous rocks are formed from liquid volcanic rock—either magma underground or lava on the surface—that cools and hardens. Metamorphic rocks are formed from sedimentary and igneous rocks. This happens when sedimentary and/or igneous rocks are deep inside the Earth's crust, where they are subjected to great pressure or heat. The process of metamorphism does not melt these rocks into liquid, which would happen inside a volcano. Rather, the pressure and/or heat change the rocks' molecular structure. Metamorphic rocks are thus more compact and denser than the sedimentary or igneous rocks from which they were formed. They also contain new minerals produced either by the reconfiguration of existing minerals' structures or by chemical reactions with liquids infiltrating the rock. Two examples of metamorphic rocks are marble and gneiss.

IGNEOUS ROCKS

Igneous or volcanic rocks are formed from the magma emitted when a volcano erupts. Magma under the Earth's surface is subject to heat and pressure, keeping it in liquid form. During a volcanic eruption, some magma reaches the surface, emerging as lava. Lava cools rapidly in the outside air, becoming a solid with small crystals. Some magma does not reach Earth's surface, but is trapped underground within pockets in other rocks. Magma cools more slowly underground than lava does on the surface. This slower cooling forms rocks with larger crystals and coarser grains. The chemical composition and individual cooling temperatures of magma produce different kinds of igneous rocks. Lava that cools rapidly on the Earth's surface can become obsidian, a smooth, shiny black glass without crystals. It can also become another type of extrusive rock, such as andesite, basalt, pumice, rhyolite, scoria, or tuff (formed from volcanic ash and cinders). Magma that cools slowly in underground pockets can become granite, which has a coarse texture and large, visible mineral grains. It can also become another type of intrusive rock, such as diorite, gabbro, pegmatite, or peridotite.

EROSION

Erosion is a natural process whereby Earth's landforms are broken down through weathering. Rain, wind, etc. wear away solid matter. Over time, rain reduces mountains to hills. Rocks break off from mountains, and in turn disintegrate into sand. Weathering and the resulting erosion always occur in downhill directions. Rain washes rocks off mountains and down streams. Rains, rivers, and streams

Copyright © Mometrix Media. You have been licensed one copy of this document for personal use only. Any other reproduction or redistribution is strictly prohibited. All rights reserved.

wash soils away, and ocean waves break down adjacent cliffs. Rocks, dirt, and sand change their form and location through erosion. They do not simply vanish. These transformations and movements are called mass wasting, which occurs chemically (as when rock is dissolved by chemicals in water) or mechanically (as when rock is broken into pieces). Because materials travel as a result of mass wasting, erosion can both break down some areas and build up others. For example, a river runs through and erodes a mountain, carrying the resulting sediment downstream. This sediment gradually builds up, creating wetlands at the river's mouth. A good example of this process is Louisiana's swamps, which were created by sediment transported by the Mississippi River.

WEATHER, CLIMATE, AND METEOROLOGY

Meteorology is the study of the atmosphere, particularly as it pertains to forecasting the weather and understanding its processes. **Weather** is the condition of the atmosphere at any given moment. Most weather occurs in the troposphere and includes changing events such as clouds, storms, and temperature, as well as more extreme events such as tornadoes, hurricanes, and blizzards. **Climate** refers to the average weather for a particular area over time, typically at least 30 years. Latitude is an indicator of climate. Changes in climate occur over long time periods.

> **Review Video: Climates**
> Visit mometrix.com/academy and enter code: 991320

WINDS AND GLOBAL WIND BELTS

Winds are the result of air moving by convection. Masses of warm air rise, and cold air sweeps into their place. The warm air also moves, cools, and sinks. The term "prevailing wind" refers to the wind that usually blows in an area in a single direction. *Dominant winds* are the winds with the highest speeds. Belts or bands that run latitudinally and blow in a specific direction are associated with *convection cells*. *Hadley cells* are formed directly north and south of the equator. The *Farrell cells* occur at about 30° to 60°. The jet stream runs between the Farrell cells and the polar cells. At the higher and lower latitudes, the direction is easterly. At mid latitudes, the direction is westerly. From the North Pole to the south, the surface winds are Polar High Easterlies, Subpolar Low Westerlies, Subtropical High or Horse Latitudes, North-East Trade winds, Equatorial Low or Doldrums, South-East Trades, Subtropical High or Horse Latitudes, Subpolar Low Easterlies, and Polar High.

RELATIVE HUMIDITY, ABSOLUTE HUMIDITY, AND DEW POINT TEMPERATURE

Humidity refers to water vapor contained in the air. The amount of moisture contained in air depends upon its temperature. The higher the air temperature, the more moisture it can hold. These higher levels of moisture are associated with higher humidity. **Absolute humidity** refers to the total amount of moisture air is capable of holding at a certain temperature. **Relative humidity** is the ratio of water vapor in the air compared to the amount the air is capable of holding at its current temperature. As temperature decreases, absolute humidity stays the same and relative humidity increases. A hygrometer is a device used to measure humidity. The **dew point** is the temperature at which water vapor condenses into water at a particular humidity.

PRECIPITATION

After clouds reach the dew point, **precipitation** occurs. Precipitation can take the form of a liquid or a solid. It is known by many names, including rain, snow, ice, dew, and frost. **Liquid** forms of precipitation include rain and drizzle. Rain or drizzle that freezes on contact is known as freezing rain or freezing drizzle. **Solid or frozen** forms of precipitation include snow, ice needles or diamond dust, sleet or ice pellets, hail, and graupel or snow pellets. Virga is a form of precipitation that evaporates before reaching the ground. It usually looks like sheets or shafts falling from a cloud. The amount of rainfall is measured with a rain gauge. Intensity can be measured according to how fast precipitation is falling or by how severely it limits visibility. Precipitation plays a major role in the water cycle since it is responsible for depositing much of the Earth's fresh water.

Copyright © Mometrix Media. You have been licensed one copy of this document for personal use only. Any other reproduction or redistribution is strictly prohibited. All rights reserved.

CLOUDS

Clouds form when air cools and warm air is forced to give up some of its water vapor because it can no longer hold it. This vapor condenses and forms tiny droplets of water or ice crystals called clouds. Particles, or aerosols, are needed for water vapor to form water droplets. These are called **condensation nuclei**. Clouds are created by surface heating, mountains and terrain, rising air masses, and weather fronts. Clouds precipitate, returning the water they contain to Earth. Clouds can also create atmospheric optics. They can scatter light, creating colorful phenomena such as rainbows, colorful sunsets, and the green flash phenomenon.

LIVING ORGANISMS

All living organisms have fundamental needs that must be met. For example, plants that grow on land need light, air, water, and nutrients in amounts that vary according to the individual plant. Undersea plants may need less/no light. They need gases present in the water, but not in the air above the water. Like land plants, they require nutrients. Like plants, animals (including humans) need air, water, and nutrients. They do not depend on light for photosynthesis like most plants, but some animals require more light than others, while others need less than others or none at all. Organisms cannot survive in environments that do not meet their basic needs. However, many organisms have evolved to adapt to various environments. For example, cacti are desert plants that thrive with only tiny amounts of water, and camels are desert animals that can also go for long periods of time with little water. Penguins and polar bears have adapted to very cold climates. Internal cues (e.g., hunger) and external cues (e.g., environmental change) motivate and shape the behaviors of individual organisms.

TYPES OF ANIMAL LIFE CYCLES

Most animals, including mammals, birds, fish, reptiles, and spiders, have simple life cycles. They are born live or hatch from eggs, and then grow to adulthood. Animals with simple life cycles include humans. Amphibians like frogs and newts have an additional stage involving a metamorphosis, or transformation. After birth, they breathe through gills and live underwater during youth (e.g., tadpoles). By adulthood, they breathe through lungs and move to land. Butterflies are examples of animals (insects) that undergo complete metamorphosis, meaning they change their overall form. After hatching from an embryo/egg, the juvenile form, or larva, resembles a worm and completes the majority of feeding required. In the next stage, the pupa does not feed, and is typically camouflaged in what is called an inactive stage. Mosquito pupae are called tumblers. The butterfly pupa is called a chrysalis, and is protected by a cocoon. In the final stage, the adult (imago) grows wings (typically) and breeds. Some insects like dragonflies, cockroaches, and grasshoppers undergo an incomplete metamorphosis. There are egg, larva, and adult stages, but no pupa stage.

ECOLOGY

Ecology is defined as the study of interactions between organisms and their environments. Abiotic factors are the parts of any ecosystem that are not alive, but which affect that ecosystem's living members. Abiotic factors also determine the locations of particular ecosystems that have certain characteristics. Abiotic factors include the sunlight; the atmosphere, including oxygen, hydrogen, and nitrogen; the water; the soil; the temperatures within a system; and the nutrient cycles of chemical elements and compounds that pass among living organisms and their physical environments. Biotic factors are the living organisms within any ecosystem, which include not only humans and animals, but also plants, microorganisms, etc. The definition of biotic factors also includes the interactions that occur between and among various organisms within an ecosystem. Sunlight determines plant growth and, hence, biome locations. Sunlight, in turn, is affected by water depth. Ocean depths where sunlight penetrates, called photic zones, are where the majority of the photosynthesis on Earth occurs.

> **Review Video: Photosynthesis**
> Visit mometrix.com/academy and enter code: 227035

Copyright © Mometrix Media. You have been licensed one copy of this document for personal use only. Any other reproduction or redistribution is strictly prohibited. All rights reserved.

ORGANISM REPRODUCTION

A few examples of the many ways in which organisms reproduce include binary fission, whereby the cells of prokaryotic bacteria reproduce; budding, which is how yeast cells reproduce; and asexual reproduction. The latter occurs in plants when they are grafted, when cuttings are taken from them and then rooted, or when they put out runners. Plants also reproduce sexually, as do humans and most other animals. Animals, including humans, produce gametes (i.e. sperm or eggs) in their gonads through the process of meiosis. Gametes are haploid, containing half the number of chromosomes found in the body's cells. During fertilization, the gametes combine to form a zygote, which is diploid. It has the full number of chromosomes (half from each gamete), which are arranged in a genetically unique combination. Zygotes undergo mitosis, reproducing their gene combination with identical DNA sequences in all new cells, which then migrate and differentiate into organizations of specialized organs and tissues. These specialized organs in biologically mature organisms, alerted by signals such as hormonal cues, undergo meiosis to create new haploid gametes, beginning the cycle again.

PLANT REPRODUCTION

Most plants can reproduce asexually. For example, cuttings can be rooted in water and planted. Some plants put out runners that root new growths. Many plants can be grafted to produce new ones. Plants also reproduce sexually. Plants' sexual life cycles are more complex than animals', since plants alternate between haploid form (i.e. having a single set of chromosomes) and diploid form (i.e. having two sets of chromosome) during their life cycles. Plants produce haploid cells called gametes* (equivalent to sperm and egg in animals) that combine during fertilization, producing zygotes (diploid cells with chromosomes from both gametes). Cells reproduce exact copies through mitosis (asexual reproduction), becoming differentiated/specialized to form organs. Mature diploid plants called sporophytes—the plant form we usually see—produce spores. In sporophytes' specialized organs, cells undergo meiosis. This is part of the process of sexual reproduction, during which cells with half the normal number of chromosomes are produced before fertilization occurs. The spores produced by the sporophyte generation undergo mitosis, growing into a haploid plant of the gametophyte generation that produces gametes*. The cycle then repeats.

ECOLOGICAL RELATIONSHIPS

Organisms interact, both with other organisms and their environments. Relationships wherein two differing organisms regularly interact so that one or both of them benefit are known as ecological relationships. In mutualistic relationships, both organisms benefit. For example, bacteria live in termites' digestive systems. Termites eat wood. However, they cannot digest the cellulose (the main part of plant cell walls) in wood. The bacteria in termites' guts break down the cellulose for them, releasing the wood's nutrients. Reciprocally, the termites as hosts give the bacteria a home and food. In commensalistic relationships, one organism benefits and the other one is unaffected. One example is barnacles attaching to whales. Barnacles, which are filter feeders, benefit from the whales' swimming, which creates currents in the water that bring the barnacles food. The whales are not disturbed by the barnacles. In parasitic relationships, the parasite benefits, but the host suffers. For example, tapeworms inside animals' digestive tracts get nutrients. The hosts lose the nutrients stolen by the worms, and can sustain tissue damage because of the presence of the tapeworms.

Copyright © Mometrix Media. You have been licensed one copy of this document for personal use only. Any other reproduction or redistribution is strictly prohibited. All rights reserved.

Social Studies Foundations

HUMAN SOCIALIZATION AND MAJOR SOCIALIZING AGENCIES

Socialization is the process by which individuals learn their society's norms, values, beliefs, and attitudes; and what behaviors society expects of them relative to those parameters. This learning is imparted by agencies of socialization. The family, peer groups, and leaders of opinion are considered primary socializing agencies. The family is probably the most important because it has the most significant influence on individual development. Families influence the self-concept, feelings, attitudes, and behaviors of each individual member. As children grow, they encounter peer groups throughout life, which also establish norms and values to which individual group members conform. Schools, workplaces, religions, and mass media are considered secondary socializing agencies. Schools dictate additional academic and behavioral norms, values, beliefs, and behaviors. Workplaces have their own cultures that continue, modify, and/or add to the values and behaviors expected of their members. Religions also regulate members' behavior through beliefs, values, goals, and norms that reflect moral principles within a society. Mass media communicate societal conventions (e.g., fashion/style), which enables individuals to learn and adopt new behaviors and/or lifestyles.

INFLUENCE OF INSTITUTIONS ON THE DEVELOPMENT OF INDIVIDUAL IDENTITY, RELATIONSHIPS, BELIEFS, AND BEHAVIORS

Family is the first and most important socializing agent. Infants learn behavioral patterns from mothers. Their primary socialization is enabled through such early behaviors as nursing, smiling, and toddling. Babies soon interact with other family members. All the infant's physiological and psychological needs are met within the family. Babies learn their sleeping, eating, and toileting habits within the family environment. Babies' personalities also develop based on their early experiences, especially the amounts and types of parental love and affection they receive. School is also a critical socializing agent. Children extend family relationships to society when they go to school. Cognitive and social school experiences develop children's knowledge, skills, beliefs, interests, attitudes, and customs, and help determine the roles children will play when they become adults. In addition to family relationships, receiving reinforcements at school and observing and imitating teachers influence personality development. Peer groups that are based on friendships, shared ideas, and common interests in music, sports, etc. teach children/teens about conforming to rules and being rejected for not complying with these rules. Mass media like TV profoundly influence children, both negatively and positively.

CULTURE

While no single definition of culture is universally embraced, one from the cultural anthropology perspective is "...a system of shared beliefs, values, customs, behaviors and artifacts that members of society use to cope with their worlds and with one another, and that are transmitted from generation to generation through learning." (Bates and Fratkin, 2002) Cultural groups are based on a wide range of factors, including geographic location, occupation, religion, sexual orientation, income, etc. Individuals may follow the beliefs and values of more than one culture concurrently. For instance, recent immigrants often espouse values and beliefs from both their original and adopted countries. Traditionally, social systems like education and healthcare have approached cultural diversity by focusing on race/ethnicity and common beliefs about various racial/ethnic group customs. These are frequently generalizations (e.g., lumping Mexican, Cuban, and Puerto Rican cultures together and describing them as "Latino" culture). This type of practice can lead to oversimplified stereotypes, and therefore to unrealistic behavioral expectations. Service professionals need more detailed knowledge of cultural complexities and subtleties to effectively engage and interact with families.

COLLECTIVISM AND INDIVIDUALISM

Certain world cultures are oriented more toward collectivism, while others are oriented more toward individualism. Native American, Latin American, Asian, and African cultures are more often collectivistic,

Copyright © Mometrix Media. You have been licensed one copy of this document for personal use only. Any other reproduction or redistribution is strictly prohibited. All rights reserved.

focusing on interdependence, social interactions, relationships, and connections among individuals. North American, Canadian, European, and Australian cultures are more commonly individualistic, focusing on independence, uniqueness, self-determination, and self-actualization (realizing one's full potential). Individualism favors competition and distinguishing oneself as an individual, while collectivism favors cooperation that promotes and contributes to the harmony and well-being of the group. Individualist cultures value teaching young children object manipulation and scientific thinking, while collectivist cultures value social and relational behaviors. For example, adults in collectivist cultures may interpret a child's first steps as walking toward the adult, while adults in individualist cultures interpret them as developing motor skills and autonomy. These interpretations signify what each culture values most, forming the child's cultural orientation early in life. The planning and design of educational and other programs should be informed by a knowledge of these and other cultural differences.

CULTURAL COMPETENCE

CULTURALLY COMPETENT PROFESSIONALS

A culturally competent professional demonstrates the ability to enable "...mutually rewarding interactions and meaningful relationships in the delivery of effective services for children and family whose cultural heritage differs from his or her own." (Shonkoff, National Research Council and Institute of Medicine, 2000) Providing interpreters and/or translators does not on its own constitute cultural competence. Hiring racially diverse educational staff in schools is also not enough. Culturally competent educators demonstrate highly developed self-awareness of their own cultural values and beliefs. They must also have and/or develop communication skills that allow them to elicit information from students and families regarding their own cultural beliefs. Further, they must be able to understand how diverse cultural views may affect a child's education, as well as how parents/families receive, comprehend, interpret, and respond to educators' communications. Therefore, educators must develop communication skills to meet educational goals.

ASPECTS OF CULTURAL COMPETENCE

It is important for educational professionals to acquire and demonstrate cultural competence at the individual level to effectively interact with individual children and their families. Moreover, cultural competence is also important at the program level, the school level, and the system level. According to the National Center for Cultural Competence (NCCC), system level cultural competence is a continuing process that includes "...valuing diversity, conducting self-assessments (including organizational assessments), managing the dynamics of differences, acquiring and institutionalizing cultural knowledge, and adapting to the diversity and cultural contexts of the individuals and communities served." (Goode, 2001) Individual educational interactions are informed by a knowledge of cultural diversity and of the importance of such diversity in educational settings, an ability to adapt to the population's cultural needs, and a willingness to engage in ongoing self-reflection. This same set of knowledge and skills is also applied at the system level. Family engagement is important in EC care and education. This includes understanding the developmental needs of families as well as their children, especially when families and/or children speak different languages.

ACCULTURATION VERSUS ASSIMILATION

Acculturation describes the process whereby people adapt or change their cultural traditions, values, and beliefs as a result of coming into contact with and being influenced by other cultures over time. Some cultures adopt certain characteristics from other cultures they are exposed to, and two or more separate cultures may sometimes virtually fuse. However, assimilation, wherein various ethnic groups unite to form a new culture, is different from acculturation. One dominant culture may assimilate others. A historical example is the Roman Empire, which forced many members of ancient Greek, Hebrew, and other cultures to abandon their own cultures and adopt Roman law, military allegiance, traditions, language, religion, practices, and customs (including dress). The extent of a diverse cultural group's acculturation influences how it interacts with social systems like education and healthcare. Groups that

145

Copyright © Mometrix Media. You have been licensed one copy of this document for personal use only. Any other reproduction or redistribution is strictly prohibited. All rights reserved.

are strongly motivated to maintain their cultural identity may interact less with mainstream systems that significantly conflict with or vary from their own cultural beliefs.

MEASURING THE ACCULTURATION OF IMMIGRANTS AND DIVERSE CULTURAL GROUPS IN AMERICA

Social scientists currently use indices such as people's country of birth, how long they have lived in America, their knowledge of the English language, and their level of English language use to study acculturation. However, these factors are measured not because they are the core elements of acculturation, but because they are easier to validly and reliably measure than the underlying cultural beliefs, attitudes, and behaviors they reflect, which are harder to quantify. The interactions between American educators and culturally diverse families can be problematic on both sides. Educators have difficulty interacting, communicating, and collaborating with families that come from a variety of other countries, speak various other languages, and differ in their degree of acculturation to American culture. On the other hand, immigrant and culturally diverse families encounter a foreign language, different cultural customs and practices, and an unfamiliar educational system with different methods of assessment, placement, curriculum planning and design, instruction, and evaluation—not to mention different special education laws and procedures. Thus, the acculturation challenges related to interactions between American educators and culturally diverse families are bilateral.

CULTURAL DIFFERENCES IN PARENTS' GOALS FOR RAISING THEIR CHILDREN

Depending on their cultural group, parents have varying goals for their children, and use different practices to achieve those goals. For example, research on four different cultural groups in Hawaii found the following differences related to what parents visualized when they pictured their children as successful adults: Native Hawaiians most wanted their children to have social connections, be happy in their social networks, and demonstrate self-reliance as adults. Caucasian American parents most valued self-reliance, happiness, spontaneity, and creativity as developmental outcomes for their children. Filipino American parents most valued the development of traits related to obedience, citizenship, respect for authority, and good conduct and manners in their children. Japanese American parents placed priority on their children's achievement, as well as their ability to live well-organized lives, stay in contact with family, and master the demands of life. Such distinct, significant differences imply that these parent groups would vary in how they would respond to young children's assertive behaviors, in their disciplinary styles (e.g., permissive, authoritative, authoritarian), and in the emphasis they would place on activities focusing on physical and cognitive skill mastery vs. social competence and connection.

EDUCATIONAL SERVICES ACCESSED BY DIFFERENT CULTURES

Parents in America have been found to show distinct preferences for the kinds of care and educational services they access for their children. For example, Caucasian parents in America are more likely to turn to preschool centers for help with their young children's care and instruction. This preference is influenced not only by custom, but also by scientific evidence that center-based preschool experience improves children's skills and prepares them for school. Hispanic parents in America are more likely to use home-based and/or family-based care settings. This preference probably reflects the more collectivist Hispanic perspective, which places more importance on social relationships than on structured learning in early childhood. Educators can take a culturally competent approach to such cultural diversity by looking for ways in which young children's school readiness skills can be promoted in family and home-based child care settings.

DIFFERENT VIEWS ON CARE, EDUCATION, AND THE NATURE OF THEIR COGNITIVE ABILITIES

Depending on their native culture, parents vary in terms of the early experiences they select for their young children. For example, Latino parents tend to prefer family-based/home-based care. White parents tend to prefer center-based daycare and education designed to promote school readiness. Another cultural difference is parental beliefs about children's learning capacities. For example, research in California found that the majority of Latino parents believed their children's learning capacity is set at birth; only a small minority of white parents held this belief. Parents subscribing to a transactional child

Copyright © Mometrix Media. You have been licensed one copy of this document for personal use only. Any other reproduction or redistribution is strictly prohibited. All rights reserved.

development model view the complex interaction between child and environment as creating a dynamic developmental process. These parents are more likely to value the stimulation of early childhood development, seek/implement activities that will provide such stimulation, and access early intervention services for children with developmental delays/difficulties. Parents subscribing to a view of fixed, innate cognitive capacity are less likely to believe their children's cognitive abilities can be influenced by educational experiences, and may not see the benefits of or seek out early learning stimulation and intervention.

CULTURAL AND OTHER INFLUENCES AND HOW MUCH PARENTS IN AMERICA READ TO THEIR CHILDREN

Researchers analyzing national early childhood surveys have identified significant variations in how often white, Asian, and Hispanic parents read to their young children. This variation is not solely due to varying cultural values. Additional factors include parents' financial limitations; time limitations; familiarity and comfort with accessing libraries and other government resources, websites, etc.; and literacy levels in both English and their native languages. Educators must realize that trying to encourage or even teach parents to read to their children earlier and/or more often is unlikely to be successful if parents do not place value or priority on the benefits of being read to, or do not view the outcomes of reading aloud to children as benefits. Reading to children is known to promote school readiness and academic success. Educators should also understand that some children, despite not being read to in early childhood, become successful adults. Additionally, some cultures, including African Americans, emphasize oral learning traditions more than written ones, developing different skills, such as the basic understanding of story flow.

FACTORS AFFECTING PARENTS WHO ARE IMMIGRANTS TO AMERICA

Parents educated in other countries may not know a great deal about the American educational system, and may not be aware of the educational demands made on their children, even in early childhood. Educators need to work with these parents to find common ground by identifying shared goals for children. While culturally diverse parents may disagree with some educators' goals, they can collaborate with educators to promote those on which they do agree. Immigrant parents may also be unaware of additional services available in America for children with developmental and/or learning problems. Educators can help parents by providing this information. Another consideration is that some other cultures have more paternalistic educational systems. Parents from such cultures, rather than vocally advocating for their children who need services, tend to wait for teachers/specialists to voice concerns before communicating any problems they have observed. Thus, they could miss out on the chance to obtain helpful services. Even worse, educators could misconstrue their behavior as a lack of interest in children's progress, or as resistance to confronting problems.

DEVELOPMENTAL MILESTONES VARYING BY CULTURE

Research has found that different cultures have different age expectations for many early childhood developmental milestones. For example, Filipinos expect children to eat using utensils at 32.4 months. Anglo families expect children to do this at 17.7 months, and Puerto Ricans expect children to reach this milestone at 26.5 months. Filipino cultures expect children to sleep all night by 32.4 months; Puerto Rican and Anglo cultures expect this at 14.5 and 14.4 months, respectively. Similarly, while Anglos expect children to sleep by themselves at around 13.8 months and Puerto Ricans at around 14.6 months, Filipinos do not expect this until 38.8 months. Filipinos expect children to eat solid food by 6.7 months; Anglos by 8.2 months; and Puerto Ricans by 10.1 months. In Anglo families, an 18-month-old not drinking from a cup could indicate developmental delay if parents introduced the cup when s/he was one year old and regularly continued encouraging cup use. But, Filipino parents of an 18-month-old have likely not even introduced the child to a cup yet, so the fact that the child is not using a cup would not be cause for concern from a development standpoint.

147

Copyright © Mometrix Media. You have been licensed one copy of this document for personal use only. Any other reproduction or redistribution is strictly prohibited. All rights reserved.

When EC researchers investigated the average expectations of different cultural groups of when children would reach various developmental milestones, some of the milestones they examined included: eating solid food, weaning from nursing, drinking from a cup, eating with the fingers, eating with utensils, sleeping alone, sleeping through the night, choosing one's own clothes, dressing oneself, and playing alone. They also looked at daytime and nighttime toilet training. Educators must become aware of different cultures' different socialization goals before assuming culturally diverse children have developmental delays. On the other hand, they must also avoid automatically attributing variations in milestone achievement to cultural child rearing differences when full developmental assessments might be indicated. Family expectations and values influence the complex process of developmental assessment. When families and assessors share common cultures, it is more likely that valid data will be collected and interpreted. When their cultures differ, however, it is more likely that the assessment information will be misinterpreted. Employing EC teachers/care providers who are familiar with the child, family, and assessment setting as mediators can make developmental assessments more culturally competent.

ESSENTIAL GEOGRAPHICAL CONCEPTS

Ten concepts considered essential to the study of geography are: location, distance, achievability, pattern, morphology, agglomeration, utility value, interaction, area differentiation, and spatial interrelatedness. (1) Location: This concept identifies "where" a place is and examines the positive and negative properties of any place on the surface of the Earth. Absolute location is based upon latitude and longitude. Relative location is based upon changing characteristics of a region, and is influenced by surrounding areas. For example, urban areas have higher land prices than rural ones. (2) Distance: This identifies "how far" a place is, and is often described in terms of location. It is also related to the effort required to meet basic life needs. For example, the distance of raw materials from factories affects transportation costs and hence product prices. In another example, land costs less the farther it is from highways. (3) Achievability: The conditions on the Earth's surface dictate how accessible a geographic area is. For example, villages on beaches are easier to reach. Villages surrounded by forests or swamps are harder to reach. As its economy, science, technology, and transportation develop, a region's level of dependency on other areas changes.

(4) Patterns These are found in geographical forms and in how geographical phenomena spread, which affect dependency on those phenomena. For example, in fold regions (areas where the folding of rocks forms mountains), the rivers typically form trellis patterns. Patterns are also seen in human activity that is based on geography. For example, in mountainous regions, settlements predominantly form spreading patterns. (5) Morphology This is the shape of our planet's surface resulting from inner and outer forces. For example, along the northern coast of Java, sugarcane plantations predominate on the lowlands. (6) Agglomeration This is defined as collecting into a mass, and refers to a geographic concentration of people, activities, and/or settlements within areas that are most profitable and relatively narrow in size. (7) Utility value This refers to the existence and relative usefulness of natural resources. For example, fishermen find more utility value in the ocean than farmers do, and naturalists perceive more utility value in forests than academics would.

(8) Interaction This is the reciprocal and interdependent relationship between two or more geographical areas, which can generate new geographical phenomena, configurations, and problems. For example, a rural village produces raw materials through activities like mining ores or growing and harvesting plant crops, while a city produces industrial goods. The village needs the city as a market for its raw materials, and may also need the city's industrial products. The city needs the village for its raw materials to use in industrial production. This interdependence causes interaction. (9) Area differentiation This informs the study of variations among regional geographical phenomena. For example, different plants are cultivated in highlands vs. lowlands due to their different altitudes and climates. Area differentiation also informs the study of regional variations in occupation (farming vs. fishing, etc.). (10) Spatial interrelatedness This shows the relationship between/among geographic and

Copyright © Mometrix Media. You have been licensed one copy of this document for personal use only. Any other reproduction or redistribution is strictly prohibited. All rights reserved.

non-physical phenomena, like rural and urban areas. The example above of village-city interaction also applies here.

GEOGRAPHICAL MAPS

GENERAL FEATURES AND PURPOSES

Maps can be drawn to show natural or man-made features. For example, some maps depict mountains, elevations (altitudes), average rainfall, average temperatures, and other natural features of an area. Other maps are made to depict countries, states, cities, roads, empires, wars, and other man-made features. Some maps include both natural and man-made features (e.g., a map showing a certain country and its elevations). Different types of maps are described according to their purposes. For example, political maps are made to depict countries, areas within a country, and/or cities. Physical maps are drawn to display natural features of the terrain in an area, such as rivers, lakes, and mountains. Thematic maps are drawn to focus on a more specific theme or topic, such as the locations and names of battles during a war or the average amounts of rainfall a country, state, or region receives in a given year or month. Some maps are made for more than one purpose, and indicate more than one of the types of information described above.

BASIC TOOLS SUPPLIED ON MAPS

On maps depicting local, national, and world geography, cartographers supply tools for navigating these maps. For example, the compass rose indicates the directions of north, south, east, and west. By looking at the compass, people can identify the locational relationships of places (e.g., in South America, Chile is west of Argentina). The scale of miles indicates how distances on a map correspond to actual geographical distances, enabling us to estimate real distances. For example, the scale might show that one inch is equal to 500 miles. By placing a piece of paper on the map, we can mark it to measure the distance between two cities (e.g., Washington, DC, in the USA and Ottawa in Canada) on the map, and then line the paper up with the scale of miles to estimate an actual distance of approximately 650 miles between the two cities. Map keys/legends identify what a map's symbols and colors represent.

GRIDS

Maps show absolute geographic location (i.e. the precise "address" of any place on the planet) using a grid of lines. The lines running from east to west are called parallels or latitudes, and they correspond to how many degrees away from the equator a place is located. The lines running from north to south are called meridians or longitudes, and they correspond to how many degrees away from the prime meridian a place is located. To determine the absolute location of a place, we find the spot on the map where its latitude and longitude intersect. This intersection is the place's absolute location. For example, if we look at Mexico City on a map, we will find that its latitude is 19° north and its longitude is 99° west, which is expressed in cartography as 19° N, 99° W. Numbers of latitudes and longitudes like these are also referred to as coordinates.

READING AND ANALYZING A SPECIAL PURPOSE MAP

(1) First, read a map's title and look at the overall map. This provides a general idea of what the map shows. For example, a map entitled "Battles of the Punic Wars" would not be a good choice if someone was looking for the political boundaries of modern day Greece, Italy, and Spain. (2) Next, read the map's legend/key to see what symbols and colors the map uses, and what each represents. For example, some lines represent divisions between countries/states; some, roads; some, rivers; etc. Different colors can indicate different countries/states, elevations, amounts of rainfall, population densities, etc. These are not uniform across all maps, so legends/keys are necessary references. (3) Use the legend/key to interpret what the map shows. For example, by looking at colors representing elevations, one can determine which area of a country has the highest/lowest altitude. (4) Draw conclusions about what the map displays. For example, if a country map mainly has one color that indicates a certain elevation range, it can be concluded that this is the country's most common elevation.

Copyright © Mometrix Media. You have been licensed one copy of this document for personal use only. Any other reproduction or redistribution is strictly prohibited. All rights reserved.

GRAPHS

Graphs display numerical information in pictorial forms, making it easier to view statistics quickly and draw conclusions about them. For example, it is easier to see patterns/trends like increases/decreases in quantities using visual graphs than columns of numbers. Line graphs, bar graphs, and pie charts are the most common types of graphs. Line graphs depict changes over time by plotting points for a quantity measured each day/week/month/year/decade/century etc. and connecting the points to make a line. For example, showing the population of a city/country each decade in a line graph reveals how the population has risen/fallen/both. Bar graphs compare quantities related to different times/places/people/things. Each quantity is depicted by a separate bar, and its height/length corresponds to a number. Bar graphs make it easy to see which amounts are largest/smallest within a group (e.g., which of several cities/countries has the largest population). Pie charts/circle graphs divide a circle/"pie" into segments/"slices" showing percentages/parts of a whole, which also facilitates making comparisons. For example, the city/country with the largest population is the largest segment on a pie chart or circle graph.

> **Review Video: Data Interpretation of Graphs**
> Visit mometrix.com/academy and enter code: 200439

IMPORTANCE OF CHRONOLOGICAL THINKING TO UNDERSTANDING HISTORY

To see cause-and-effect relationships in historical events and explore and understand relationships among those events, students must have a solid grasp of when things happened and in what time sequence (chronology). Teachers can help students develop chronological thinking by using and assigning well-constructed/well-written narratives. These include histories written in the same style as stories, works of historical literature, and biographies. These hold students' attention, allowing them to focus on authors' depictions of temporal relationships among antecedents, actions, and consequences; of historical motivations and deeds of individuals and groups; and of the time structure of sequential occurrences. By middle school, students should have the skills needed to measure time mathematically (e.g., in years/decades/centuries/millennia), interpret data displayed in timelines, and calculate time in BC and AD. High school students should be able to analyze patterns of historical duration (e.g., how long the U.S. Constitutional government has lasted) and patterns of historical succession (e.g., the development of expanding trade and communication systems, from Neolithic times through ancient empires and from early modern times to modern global interaction).

EDUCATIONAL STANDARDS THAT DEMONSTRATE SKILLS IN HISTORICAL AND CHRONOLOGICAL THINKING

Students should be able to differentiate among past, present, and future. They should be able to identify the beginning, middle, and end/outcome of historical narratives/stories. They also should be able to construct their own historical narratives, including working forward and backward in time from some event to explain causes and temporal development of various events, issues, etc. Students should be able to calculate and measure calendar time, including days/dates, weeks, months, years, centuries, and millennia. They should be able to describe time periods using BC and AD They should be skilled at comparing calendar systems (e.g., Roman, Gregorian, Julian, Hebrew, Muslim, Mayan, and others) and at relating the calendar years of major historical events. They should be able to look at timelines and interpret the information they contain, and make their own timelines using equidistant time intervals and recording events sequentially. Students should be able to explain change and continuity in history through reconstructing and applying patterns of historical duration and succession. They should be able to identify the structural principles that are the bases of alternative periodization models, and to compare these models.

Copyright © Mometrix Media. You have been licensed one copy of this document for personal use only. Any other reproduction or redistribution is strictly prohibited. All rights reserved.

REASONS/PURPOSES FOR OUR COUNTRY'S LAWS AND TEACHING CITIZENSHIP

Young children must understand the purposes of rules/laws: They identify acceptable/unacceptable citizen behaviors; make society and life predictable, secure, and orderly; designate responsibilities to citizens; and prevent persons in authority positions from abusing their roles by limiting their power. Understanding these functions of laws/rules enables children to realize that our government consists of individuals and groups authorized to create, implement, and enforce laws and manage legal disputes. Some creative EC teachers have used children's literature to illustrate these concepts. Children can relate personally to stories' characters, and story situations make the concepts real and concrete to children. Stories can be springboards for discussing rules and when they do/do not apply. One activity involves children in small groups making class rules (e.g., "No talking" and "Stay in your seat"), and then rewriting these to be more realistic (e.g., "Talk softly in class; listen when others talk" and "Sit down and get right to work"). Children consider issues of safety and fairness, and develop an understanding of judicial and legislative roles.

Copyright © Mometrix Media. You have been licensed one copy of this document for personal use only. Any other reproduction or redistribution is strictly prohibited. All rights reserved.

Health and Physical Education Foundations

HUMAN HEALTH AND WELLNESS AND DISEASE PREVENTION

Health and disease prevention begin before birth. Expecting mothers need to be/become informed about good nutrition for all humans and the supplemental nutrition required for prenatal support of developing embryos and fetuses. Mothers also need to get sufficient but not overly strenuous exercise; avoid undue stress; have/learn effective coping skills to deal with unavoidable life stressors; and avoid exposure to environmental toxins, such as radiation, pollution, and chemicals. They should avoid alcohol, tobacco, and exposure to secondhand smoke, as well as most drugs—street, over-the-counter, herbal, and prescription—unless they are prescribed by obstetricians/other physicians who are aware of the pregnancy. Babies initially need their mother's colostrum to provide immunity, and subsequently require breast milk or approved infant formula. Babies must also be held, cuddled, and given attention and affection to ensure survival, growth, and health. Young children need smaller amounts of food than adults that is equally as nutritious; sufficient exercise; adequate sleep; and cognitive, emotional, and social stimulation and interaction. Appropriate nutrition and exercise, avoidance of alcohol/tobacco/other drugs, and positive relationships and interactions are essential for wellness and disease prevention at all ages.

2009 AMERICAN RECOVERY AND REINVESTMENT ACT

The 2009 American Recovery and Reinvestment Act has allotted $650 million for preventing chronic disease. To apply these funds, the U.S. Department of Health and Human Services (HHS) has designed a comprehensive initiative entitled Communities Putting Prevention to Work. This initiative aims to create sustainable positive health changes in American communities, prevent or delay chronic disease, reduce disease risk factors, and promote child and adult wellness. Obesity and tobacco use, considered the foremost preventable sources of disability and death, are targeted by this initiative's evidence-based research programs and strategies, which are intended to reinforce state abilities and mobilize community resources. The initiative's central, $373-million community program includes support from the Centers for Disease Control and Prevention in selected communities for attaining the prevention outcomes of increasing physical activity levels, improving nutrition, reducing the incidence of obesity and higher than optimal body weights, decreasing tobacco use, and decreasing secondhand smoke exposure. Through this initiative, HHS hopes to produce effective models that can be reproduced in states and communities nationwide.

ENVIRONMENTAL HEALTH RISKS

Children's body systems, unlike those of mature adults, are still developing. They eat, drink, and breathe more in proportion to their body sizes than adults do. Typical child behaviors expose children to more potentially toxic chemicals and organisms. Therefore, children can be more vulnerable to environmental health risks. To protect children, adults can prohibit smoking in homes and cars; keep homes free of dust, mold, pet dander, and pests that can trigger allergies; avoid outdoor activities on high-pollution/"ozone alert" days; and carpool and/or use public transportation. Adults can prevent lead poisoning by only giving children cold water to drink and using cold water to prepare infant formula and cook food; washing bottles, pacifiers, and toys frequently; and protecting children from lead-based paints in older buildings. Adults must ensure children do not have access to toxic chemicals. Maintaining furnaces, chimneys, and appliances; using outdoor gas appliances and tools properly; refraining from using gas appliances and tools indoors; and installing approved CO alarms can all help prevent carbon monoxide poisoning. Choosing fish carefully can help prevent mercury toxicity. Keeping infants out of direct sunlight, using sun-protective clothing, and applying sunscreen on young children are also important.

Copyright © Mometrix Media. You have been licensed one copy of this document for personal use only. Any other reproduction or redistribution is strictly prohibited. All rights reserved.

FEDERAL EXECUTIVE ORDER 13045: PROTECTION OF CHILDREN FROM ENVIRONMENTAL HEALTH RISKS AND SAFETY RISKS (1997)

Passed by President Clinton, Executive Order 13045 declares a policy for identifying and assessing environmental health and safety risks that affect children disproportionately, and for addressing these risks through the policies, standards, programs, and activities of every independent federal regulatory agency. This order defines environmental health and safety risks as those that can be attributed to substances children ingest or contact (e.g., air they breathe; food they eat; water they drink, bathe in, and swim in; soil they live upon; and products they are exposed to or use). The order established a task force reporting to the president and consulting with the Domestic Policy Council, the National Science and Technology Council, the Council on Environmental Quality, and the Office of Management and Budget. The task force is co-chaired by the HHS secretary and the EPA administrator. The task force oversees a coordinated, integrated federal research agenda and reports relevant research/data biennially; issues principle, policy, and priority statements; recommends appropriate federal/state/local/tribal government, nonprofit, and private sector partnerships; makes public outreach/communication proposals; identifies related high-priority initiatives; and evaluates new legislation to determine whether it will meet the goals of Executive Order 13045.

CIRCULATORY SYSTEM

The circulatory system continuously supplies blood containing oxygen and nutrients to all body tissue cells, exchanges oxygenated blood for the waste products produced during the metabolism process, and transports waste for elimination. Central to the vascular (vessel) system is the heart, which is located in the mediastinum within the thoracic cavity. The heart is encased and protected by the pericardium, a double-walled, tough fibrous sac. The heart has four chambers: two atria and two ventricles. A system of valves regulates opening/closing among the chambers, the aorta, the pulmonary artery, and the great vessels. The aorta, originating at the heart, is the body's largest artery. The pulmonary artery branches to the left and to the right, and transports venous blood from the heart's lower right chamber to the lung for oxygenation. The pulmonary veins return oxygenated blood from the lung to the left atrium of the heart. The superior and inferior venae cavae are vessels that empty into the heart's right atrium.

INTEGUMENTARY AND MUSCULOSKELETAL SYSTEMS

In the human body, the integumentary system consists of skin, hair, nails, and oil and sweat glands. The skin has three layers: the epidermis, the dermis, and subcutaneous tissues. Skin protects tissues underneath it from bacterial infections, blocks most chemicals from entering, prevents fluid loss, and reduces the probability of mechanical injury to underlying body structures. Skin regulates body temperature and synthesizes needed chemicals. It is also a sense organ, as it has sensory receptors for touch, pressure, heat/cold, and pain. It also contains motor fibers that enable necessary reactions to these sensations and stimuli. The musculoskeletal system includes bones, joints, and connective tissues: tendons, ligaments, and cartilage. It is responsible for our body shape, and provides stability and support. It also protects our internal organs and enables locomotion. Bones store calcium and other minerals, and bone marrow produces required blood cells. Muscle fibers contract to enable movement. Depending on their innervation, muscles can have voluntary or involuntary (like the heart) movements. Muscles need blood supply and oxygen to work. Thus, the musculoskeletal system depends on other systems, including the circulatory, nervous, and respiratory systems.

> **Review Video: Integumentary System**
> Visit mometrix.com/academy and enter code: 655980
>
> **Review Video: Skeletal System**
> Visit mometrix.com/academy and enter code: 256447

Copyright © Mometrix Media. You have been licensed one copy of this document for personal use only. Any other reproduction or redistribution is strictly prohibited. All rights reserved.

LYMPHATIC SYSTEM

The lymphatic system includes lymph (a fluid), collection ducts, and tissues. Lymphatic tissues comprise the lymph nodes, the thymus gland, the tonsils, and the Peyer's patches of the intestinal tract. Lymphoid components are also present in the lungs, the mucosa in the stomach and the appendix, and the bone marrow. Microscopic capillaries merge to form lymph-collecting ducts. These ducts drain to specific centers of lymphatic tissue. The lymph system's functioning is supported by the spleen and thymus glands. While not all characteristics and functions of the lymphatic system are established, known functions include: return transportation of lymph, protein, and microorganisms to the cardiovascular system; production of lymphocytes by the lymph nodes; filtering of the blood by the lymph nodes; production of antibodies to enable immune response against infection; absorption of fats and fat soluble substances from the intestine; formation of blood cells in response to some illnesses/conditions; and phagocytosis (i.e. the surrounding/swallowing/"eating" of infectious particles by cells lining the sinuses of the lymph nodes, spleen, and liver). The lymph system defends the body against infection and supports the veins by helping to return fluids to the bloodstream.

RESPIRATORY SYSTEM

The respiratory system provides oxygen to the body and removes carbon dioxide, the waste product of respiration (breathing). In doing so, the respiratory system and many other body systems work together through complex interactions. Twelve thoracic vertebrae, twelve pairs of ribs, the sternum, the diaphragm, and the intercostal muscles comprise the thoracic cage containing the lungs. As one breathes in and out, the thoracic cage is always moving. The diaphragm, a muscular wall dividing the chest cavity and abdominal cavity, functions as a bellows for breathing. (It also plays a role in expelling feces and delivering babies.) There are air pathways between the nose/mouth, pharynx, trachea, bronchi, bronchioles, and lungs. Alveoli, tiny air sacs in the lungs, exchange oxygen and carbon dioxide. During inspiration/inhalation, the ribs and sternum rise, the diaphragm contracts and lowers, the intercostal muscles contract, air pressure in the lungs decreases, and air enters the lungs. During exhalation, the intercostal muscles and diaphragm relax, the ribs and sternum return to a resting position, air pressure in the lungs increases, and air exits the lungs.

> **Review Video: Respiratory System**
> Visit mometrix.com/academy and enter code: 783075

THE BRAIN

The brain is divided into five major parts: the cerebrum, the midbrain, the cerebellum, the pons, and the medulla oblongata. The cranial nerves are: I – olfactory, which controls the sense of smell; II – optic, which controls vision; III – oculomotor, which controls the movements of the eye muscles, the movements of the upper eyelids, and the pupillary reflexes (expanding and contracting to admit more/less light); IV – trochlear, which controls the movements of the superior oblique eye muscles; V – trigeminal, which controls facial sensation, the eye's corneal reflex, and chewing; VI – abducens, which controls the movements of the lateral rectus eye muscle; VII – facial, which controls movement of the facial muscles and the taste sensation in the front two-thirds of the tongue; VIII – vestibulocochlear, which controls equilibrium (balance) via the vestibular system in the inner ear, and hearing (the cochlea is in the inner ear); IX – glossopharyngeal, which controls the taste sensation in the rear one-third of the tongue; X – vagus, which controls pharyngeal contraction (gag reflex), vocal cord movements, and soft palate movements; XI – spinal accessory, which controls movement of the sternocleidomastoid and trapezius muscles; and XII – hypoglossal, which controls tongue movements.

> **Review Video: Brain Anatomy**
> Visit mometrix.com/academy and enter code: 222476

Copyright © Mometrix Media. You have been licensed one copy of this document for personal use only. Any other reproduction or redistribution is strictly prohibited. All rights reserved.

CENTRAL NERVOUS SYSTEM

Some main functions of the central nervous system (i.e. the brain and spinal cord) include controlling consciousness and all mental processes, regulating the functions and movements of the body, and sending and receiving nerve impulses to and from all parts of the body. For example, when we touch something hot, sensory nerve endings in our fingers send impulses to the brain, which interprets them as heat and sends a signal along motor nerves to pull our fingers away. The autonomic nervous system is automatic and involuntary. For example, it makes our heart beat. We cannot voluntarily start/stop our heartbeat. The voluntary nervous system is under our conscious control. For example, our brains use it to send impulses to our skeletal muscles when we want to sit/stand/walk, etc., which contract in response. The autonomic nervous system is divided into parasympathetic and sympathetic components. The parasympathetic portion stimulates muscular activity in the organs and gland secretion. The sympathetic portion stimulates heartbeat, vasoconstriction, and sweating. These two portions of the autonomic nervous system oppose/balance each other to regulate system

DIGESTIVE SYSTEM

The chief functions of the digestive system are to provide nutrition to the body's cells and eliminate waste products left after nourishment is extracted from foods. The process consists of three phases: ingestion (i.e. taking in foods and liquids), digestion (i.e. converting ingested nutrients through physical and chemical means into forms that the cells of the body tissues can absorb and distribute), and elimination (i.e. removing the byproducts of digestion—also known as waste—that cannot be utilized). Other body systems work with the digestive system to process nutrients. For example, the nervous system plays a role in appetite, which is a signal for us to eat. The central nervous system also stimulates the release and flow of digestive juices. The endocrine system supplies chemicals (e.g., juices from the pancreas) that aid in digestion. The circulatory system delivers digested and absorbed nutrients to the tissue cells, and also picks up waste products produced as a result of the metabolism process.

During chewing, our teeth and tongue physically break down food. Glands secrete saliva to provide lubrication during chewing and swallowing, and provide digestive enzymes to begin the process of chemically breaking down the foods we eat. The pharynx delivers food to the esophagus, where muscular contractions (peristalsis) move food downward. The epiglottis closes the trachea (windpipe) during swallowing to prevent food from being aspirated into the lungs. Glands in the stomach lining secrete gastric fluid comprised of hydrochloric acid and other chemicals, which dissolve food into semiliquid chyme. Chyme gradually passes into the small intestine, where most digestion and absorption occur. The small intestine is made up of the duodenum, the jejunum, and the ileum. The pancreas secretes digestive juices, the gallbladder secretes bile, and the intestinal mucosa secretes other juices into the duodenum to digest chyme. Digested nutrients are absorbed through the intestinal walls into capillaries and lymphatic vessels to be distributed to body cells. The large intestine consists of the cecum, the colon (ascending, transverse, descending, and sigmoid), the rectum, and the anus. The colon completes digestion and absorption, and delivers wastes to the rectum, which eliminates them through the anus.

> **Review Video: Gastrointestinal System**
> Visit mometrix.com/academy and enter code: 378740

URINARY SYSTEM

The function of the urinary system is to eliminate the liquid wastes produced through nutrient metabolism by excreting them from the body. The urinary system is made up of two kidneys, two ureters, the bladder, and the urethra. Behind the abdominal cavity at the thoraco-lumbar level are the kidneys, a pair of large bean-shaped glands. They continually remove water, salts, toxins, and nitrogenous wastes from the bloodstream, and convert these substances into urine. Urine droplets flow from the kidneys into the ureters. The ureters are long, narrow tubes carrying urine to the bladder, which is a hollow, muscular, elastic organ. When enough urine collects in the bladder, nerves stimulate

Copyright © Mometrix Media. You have been licensed one copy of this document for personal use only. Any other reproduction or redistribution is strictly prohibited. All rights reserved.

the body to empty it via urination. In human females, the urethra is about an inch and a half long, and is located in the upper vaginal wall. In males, the urethra is about eight inches long, and extends from the bladder through the prostate gland and the penis. Both urine and sperm pass through the male urethra, while the female urethra and vaginal canal are separate.

> **Review Video: Urinary System**
> Visit mometrix.com/academy and enter code: 601053

ENDOCRINE SYSTEM

The human endocrine system is one of the most complex body systems. Scientists understand many of its functions, but not all of them. It is a system of ductless, internally secreting glands (some necessary to life) that extract various substances from tissue fluids and the bloodstream to create completely new substances (i.e. hormones). Operating without ducts, endocrine glands secrete hormones directly into the blood and lymph circulatory systems for distribution to the organs. The endocrine system's main glands include the pituitary, thyroid, parathyroid, and adrenal glands; the Islets of Langerhans in the pancreas; and the gonads (male testes and female ovaries). Additionally, the pancreas is both an endocrine and an exocrine gland. Its endocrine (internal secretion) function is to secrete insulin to regulate sugar metabolism; its exocrine (external secretion) function is to secrete pancreatic juice into the duodenum to aid in digestion. If the pancreas produces insufficient insulin, type 1 diabetes results. If the body responds insufficiently to insulin, type 2 diabetes results.

> **Review Video: Endocrine System**
> Visit mometrix.com/academy and enter code: 678939

PITUITARY, THYROID, AND PARATHYROID GLANDS

The pituitary and thyroid glands are both components of the endocrine system. The pituitary gland functions directly by regulating physical growth, development, and sexual maturation in children and adolescents; regulating the retention and excretion of fluid; regulating the balance of electrolytes (sodium, potassium, and chloride) in blood and tissues; and regulating new mothers' lactation (milk production). The pituitary is termed the hypophyseal /"master gland" because it also regulates all other glands in the endocrine system. Therefore, it is involved in regulating food assimilation and metabolism through hydrating the thyroid gland; regulating body composition, adaptation, and resistance to stress through acting on the adrenal and parathyroid glands; regulating breathing, circulation, digestion, urine excretion, and muscular action through the collective activity of multiple hormones; and regulating sexual development, activity, and reproduction through acting on the gonads. The thyroid gland manufactures and secretes hormones that regulate child growth and development, as well as certain metabolic processes and their rates. It also stores iodine. The parathyroid glands secrete hormones that regulate blood calcium levels, phosphorus metabolism, and muscle and nervous system excitation.

REPRODUCTIVE SYSTEM

MALE

The scrotum and the penis are the external reproductive organs of the human male. The internal organs of the male reproductive system include two testes, two epididymides, two seminal ducts, two seminal vesicles, two ejaculatory ducts, two spermatic cords, the urethra, the prostate gland, and several other glands. The testes, which are glandular organs, hang on either side of the scrotum from spermatic cords. These cords contain the vas deferens, blood vessels, and supportive tissues. Male sperm cells and hormones are produced by the testes. Each testis has an epididymis connecting it to the vas deferens, an excretory seminal duct. The vas deferens travel upward inside the spermatic cords to the prostate gland, which is in front of the neck of the urinary bladder. There, the vas deferens join with the pouch-like glands called seminal vesicles to form ejaculatory ducts. The prostate gland and seminal vesicles secrete

Copyright © Mometrix Media. You have been licensed one copy of this document for personal use only. Any other reproduction or redistribution is strictly prohibited. All rights reserved.

substances into the semen that promote sperm motility. The ejaculatory ducts release semen into the urethra, and from here the semen is ejected through the penis during sexual intercourse.

FEMALE

The external female reproductive organs include the mons pubis, the labia majora, the labia minora, the clitoris, the vestibule, the hymen, the Bartholin's glands, and several other glands. The breasts/mammary glands can also be considered parts of the reproductive system, as they produce milk for infants following reproduction. Internal organs include the vagina, the two fallopian tubes, the uterus, and the two ovaries. Hormones stimulate either ovary to produce an ovum/egg roughly once a month. A follicle containing an egg cell forms. When the egg matures, the follicle ruptures, releasing the egg. This is known as ovulation. The ovum passes into a fallopian tube and travels toward the uterus. Hormones have meanwhile also stimulated the endometrium (uterine lining) to thicken and increase its blood supply. When the egg reaches the womb, it is implanted in the endometrium if it was fertilized in the fallopian tube by a male sperm. This is known as conception. If the egg was not fertilized, hormone signals subside, causing the endometrium to detach from the uterine wall. The sloughed off endometrial tissue, the resulting blood, and the unfertilized egg exit the body. This process is known as menstruation.

INFLUENCE OF PHYSICAL, EMOTIONAL, AND SOCIAL FACTORS ON PERSONAL PHYSICAL HEALTH

The parts of the body, including the brain, are connected, related, interactive, and interdependent. As humans also interact and are interdependent with their environment, both internal and external factors influence their health. For example, physical factors like exposure to air pollution or radiation can cause illnesses like asthma, other lung diseases, and various cancers. Too much or too little nutrition can cause obesity and diabetes* or malnutrition. Too much or too little exercise can cause exhaustion and injuries or weakness, diabetes*, and cardiovascular and pulmonary problems. Not exercising enough may also be a factor in being overweight or obese. *Diabetes itself causes many related health problems, including blindness, circulatory deficiencies, amputation, and cardiovascular disease. Water and/or sleep deprivation ultimately cause death. Emotional factors like depression, anxiety, and irritability can cause a host of health problems, including insomnia, overeating, anorexia, high blood pressure, and heart disease. Social factors include family influences. According to the family systems theory, dysfunctional family dynamics can cause a child to develop a physical illness. Whether the source is family, society outside the home, or both, stress is a social influence with multiple negative health impacts.

EFFECT OF NUTRITION ON DEVELOPMENT

Children must consume a full range of nutrients for their brains to work normally. They need protein for its amino acids, which enable the brain's neurotransmitters (chemical messengers) to fire and communicate with each other. They need fruit and vegetable sugars and other complex carbohydrates to supply fuel to power the brain's functioning. Children's nutrition begins before birth. Pregnant women who do not eat adequate nutrients, vitamins, and minerals have higher risks of delivering infants with low birth weights. Research has found that babies with low birth weights are more likely to experience hearing and vision problems, and to need special education services in school at some point. Children in school who consume insufficient amounts of protein have been found to score lower on achievement tests than their peers who are getting enough protein. Children with iron deficiencies display fatigue and ADHD-like symptoms, including impaired concentration, shortened attention spans, and irritability. Children who miss breakfast consistently perform slower on problem solving tests than those who do not. Their responses are also less accurate. Children who regularly miss meals have compromised immunity against illnesses and infections, and they miss more school.

MOTOR SKILLS

Motor skills are the large and small movements of the body. These movements include such things as pushing, pulling, lifting, and carrying larger objects using the legs, arms, and back; and picking up, grasping, and manipulating smaller objects using the hands and fingers. The former are gross motor

Copyright © Mometrix Media. You have been licensed one copy of this document for personal use only. Any other reproduction or redistribution is strictly prohibited. All rights reserved.

skills, and the latter are fine motor skills. To develop these, children must make effective use of their mind-body connection (i.e. getting the muscles and bones to perform the movements the mind intends). They must also have developed spatial awareness (i.e. an accurate sense of the relationship between their bodies and the surrounding space and other bodies/objects). Teaching children to move large and small muscles in time to rhythmic songs helps develop motor skills. Teaching directions like up, down, clockwise, counterclockwise, etc. helps with motor planning development. When children find motor skills challenging to master, educators must provide them with frequent instruction, adequate re-teaching, and ample modeling that allows them to observe and imitate problematic movements.

FINE MOTOR MOVEMENTS

Fine motor movements use small muscles in the eyes, lips, tongue, wrists, fingers, and toes. Fine/small motor movements work together with gross/large muscle movements to develop movement skills and patterns. Fine motor skills are often used for purposes of functional and expressive communication, like using tools, creating artworks, and writing and typing language. Eye-hand coordination, eye-foot coordination, and manual and finger dexterity are required for the fine motor movements used in drawing, writing, and typing. Fine motor practice also develops children's tactile (touch) awareness and spatial awareness. Rolling dough/putty/clay into balls and/or hiding things inside them promote fine motor skills. Tearing and cutting paper along dotted lines and creating patterns teach accurate size and shape perception and formation. Stringing, lacing, and creating structures using plastic building blocks develop hand-eye coordination and skills needed to create color patterns. Flip cards, pegs, and stickers promote object placement skills. Writing skills are developed by writing letters/numbers in shaving cream, sand, pudding, and/or on chalkboards using wet makeup sponges/cotton swabs; using toothbrushes on dry erase boards; and practicing placement on cardboard using rice, beans, wet/dry pasta, glitter, etc.

GROSS MOTOR SKILLS

The first motor movements of EC are gross motor skills (i.e. large body movements involving the torso, limbs, and feet). Sitting, standing, crawling, walking, running, galloping, jumping, catching, throwing, and kicking use these skills. Activities that help young children develop their gross motor skills include standing on dots/marks on the floor/ground; crawling under and climbing over things, including objects that are part of obstacle courses; and balancing on balance beams. These develop body control, coordination, laterality (using the left/right sides of the body separately), and synchronization of the body's left and right sides. Children develop body control and balance through hopping around objects. They develop coordination and overall gross motor skills through jumping over things like boxes, beanbags, lines/strings; and by kicking balls, balloons, etc. of various sizes. Walking and running around, through, and/or over obstacles like tires, hoops, etc. and/or participating in relays develop gross motor skills. Organized games involving skipping around things to music with various rhythms, and activities requiring twisting, turning, and bending all develop gross motor skills, preparing children for lifelong engagement in sports activities.

NEWBORN/INFANT MOTOR REFLEXES AND SKILLS

Newborns exhibit the tonic reflex, adopting the "fencing position." In this position, the head is turned to one side, the arm on that side is in front of the eyes, and the other arm is flexed. This normally disappears by the time an infant is around four months old. It may serve as preparation for reaching voluntarily for things/people. The stepping reflex disappears at around two months of age, and prepares babies for walking voluntarily. The palmar grasping reflex on an adult finger disappears by the time an infant is around three to four months old, and prepares babies for grasping voluntarily. When held upright, a baby can typically hold his/her head steady and erect by about six weeks of age on average. About 90 percent of infants will develop this skill between the ages of three weeks and four months. Babies lift up from the prone position using their arms by the time they are about two months old. About 90 percent of infants will develop this skill between the ages of three weeks and four months. Babies can also roll from side to back by the time they are about two months old. About 90 percent of infants will

Copyright © Mometrix Media. You have been licensed one copy of this document for personal use only. Any other reproduction or redistribution is strictly prohibited. All rights reserved.

develop this skill between the ages of three weeks and five months. An infant can grasp a cube by the age of three months and three weeks on average. About 90 percent of infants will develop this skill between the ages of two and seven months.

INFANT MOTOR SKILLS MILESTONES

By four and a half months on average, babies can roll from back to side. The range within which 90 percent of infants will be able to do this is two to seven months. Most babies can sit unsupported by seven months on average. The range within which 90 percent of infants will be able to do this is five to nine months. Most infants also crawl by seven months on average. The range within which 90 percent of infants will be able to do this is five to eleven months. Babies pull themselves up to a standing position by around eight months on average. The range within which 90 percent of infants will be able to do this is five to twelve months. Babies play "patty-cake" by nine months, three weeks on average. The range within which 90 percent of infants will be able to do this is seven to fifteen months. Babies/toddlers can stand alone by 11 months on average. The range within which 90 percent of infants will be able to do this is 9 to 16 months. Toddlers can walk unassisted by the age of 11 months, 3 weeks on average. The range within which 90 percent of infants will be able to do this is 9 to 17 months. Children can stack two cubes by the age of 13 months, 3 weeks on average. The range within which 90 percent of infants will be able to do this is 10 to 19 months. They scribble energetically by the age of 14 months on average. The range within which 90 percent of infants will be able to do this is 10 to 21 months. They can climb stairs with assistance by the age of 16 months on average. The range within which 90 percent of infants will be able to do this is 12 to 23 months. Normally developing children can typically can jump in place by the age of 23 months, 2 weeks on average. The range within which 90 percent of infants will be able to do this is 17 to 30 months.

CEPHALOCAUDAL AND PROXIMODISTAL DEVELOPMENT

Infant and child motor development follows the same developmental sequences as prenatal embryonic and fetal physical development. Cephalocaudal means head to tail. Just as the body develops from the head down before birth, babies and young children develop motor control of their heads before they develop control of their legs. Proximodistal means near to far (i.e. central to distant). Head, torso, and arm control develop before hand and finger control. Babies learn a lot about how things look, sound, and feel once they master gross motor skills for reaching and grasping. These then evolve toward fine motor skills. For example, at around three months of age an infant's voluntary reaching gradually becomes more accurate. The infant will not need arm guidance, because he or she has spatial awareness of location and motion. Babies reach less by five months when they can move things within reach. By nine months, babies can redirect reaching to grasp objects moving in different directions. By six to twelve months, development of the pincer grasp enhances babies' capacities for object manipulation.

MOTOR SKILLS DEVELOPING BETWEEN AGES 2 AND 6

Children develop motor skills most quickly between the ages of two and six years. They demonstrate basic locomotion skills, first walking and then running, skipping, hopping, galloping, and jumping. They also develop ball-handling skills, fine motor eye-hand coordination, and—as an extension of previously developed creeping skills—climbing skills. By two years of age, children develop balance for basic kicking, which evolves into the ability to execute full kicks (including backswings) by six years of age. They try throwing by two to three years of age. They develop related skills—including taking a forward step—by the age of six. They develop the ability to shuffle by three years of age, which develops into the ability to skip by six years of age. By the age of three, children walk automatically. They try running, but they are clumsy and lack adequate control. This ability improves by between four and five years of age. By this time, children are also more skilled at executing starts, stops, and turns. By the age of five or six, children can run like adults. They develop climbing skills (ladders, etc.) between the ages of three and six. The ability to jump longer distances and hopping and galloping skills develop by age six. Children can catch a large ball while holding their arm straight by the age of three. They can catch a ball while

Copyright © Mometrix Media. You have been licensed one copy of this document for personal use only. Any other reproduction or redistribution is strictly prohibited. All rights reserved.

holding their elbows out to the front by age four, and they can do this while holding their elbows at their sides by age six.

How Cooking and Self-Care Activities Help Develop Fine Motor Skills

Young children are often fascinated by adults' cooking activities, want to participate, and offer to help. Involving them is not only beneficial to their self-esteem, but also develops various skills. Measuring amounts of liquids and solids in different forms develops children's math skills. Mixing, stirring, and blending ingredients using different parts of their hands develop children's fine motor skills. Life skills include self-care skills, such as combing one's hair, brushing one's teeth, fastening and unfastening buttons and snaps on clothing, and lacing and unlacing shoes. Life skills also require being able to open and close drawers, doors, and jars; to clean a house; and to wash things. It is necessary to children's normal development that they learn to combine multiple fine motor skills. Children's development of fine motor skills also needs to be integrated with the development of various self-care and other life skills (such as those described above) that are required for normal activities of daily living.

Benefits of Physical Activity

When young children engage in physical activity, they learn new motor skills and reinforce, advance, and refine existing ones. They also learn important early math skills like spatial awareness. Whenever they attempt new activities, they encounter challenges, such as having to develop higher levels of coordination, control, precision, strength, speed, flexibility, and agility. They are also challenged to coordinate their mental and physical processes more closely and in a manner that is more complex. They learn to exert effort, and to persevere in the face of difficulty. When they succeed at meeting these challenges, their self-esteem and self-efficacy (sense of competence to perform tasks) are enhanced. Since motor skills generally develop ahead of language skills, physical activity is a valuable means of direct self-expression. Young children learn many social skills through interacting with peers and adults during physical games, sports activities, etc. In addition to all these benefits, young children normally seek out physical activity, deriving a great deal of fun and enjoyment through moving, playing games/sports, and interacting physically with others.

National Physical Education Standards

The National Association for Sport and Physical Education (NASPE) has developed six national physical education standards. These standards state that someone who is physically educated: (1) shows the motor skills and patterns of movement competencies s/he needs to conduct various physical activities; (2) shows comprehension of the basic concepts, main principles, methods, and techniques of movement as they relate to learning and executing physical activities; (3) regularly engages in physical activity; (4) reaches and sustains a level of physical fitness that enhances health; (5) demonstrates behaviors, personally and socially, that reflect self-respect and respect for others within contexts of physical activity; and (6) places value upon the benefits of physical activities and of being fit and active, such as the pleasure; the improvement and maintenance of health; the physical, personal, and social challenges; and the opportunities to interact socially and express oneself.

Physical, Emotional, and Social Factors

Young children who have already become overweight/obese because of an improper diet and lack of exercise are more likely than children who are within a healthy weight range to find physical activity uncomfortable and avoid it. Even those who enjoy activity are more at risk of injury if they are overweight or lack physical conditioning. Exercise is more challenging for children with illnesses. For example, asthma interferes with breathing. Therefore, asthmatic children must be supervised and monitored when exercising. So must diabetic children, whose blood sugar can fluctuate excessively due to exercising. Their food intake must be monitored and coordinated with exercise. Children with physical disabilities may require adaptive equipment and/or alternative methods of physical instruction and exercising. Emotionally, children experiencing depression are likely to be apathetic and uninterested in movement. Hyperactive children (e.g., those with ADHD) are often overactive physically

Copyright © Mometrix Media. You have been licensed one copy of this document for personal use only. Any other reproduction or redistribution is strictly prohibited. All rights reserved.

to the point of exhaustion. Children lacking adequate social skills, friends, and/or peer groups have fewer opportunities and are less likely to engage in physical games and sports with others, so their motor skills and physical fitness may suffer.

AMOUNTS AND PROPORTIONS OF ENGAGEMENT IN PHYSICAL ACTIVITY

The World Health Organization (WHO) advises that children between the ages of 5 and 17 should engage in a minimum of 1 hour (continuously or incrementally) of moderate to vigorous physical activity per day. According to the World Health Organization, exercising for more than one hour daily (within reason) will confer additional health benefits. The majority of children's physical activity should be aerobic in nature. Aerobic exercise uses large muscle groups, is rhythmic and continuous, and works the heart and lungs so that the pulmonary and cardiovascular systems become more efficient at absorbing and transporting oxygen. Children should take part in exercises and/or activities that strengthen the muscles and bones through weight bearing and other methods at least three times per week. Children's play activities that can fulfill bone-strengthening requirements include running, jumping, turning, and playing various games. Engaging in general play, playing games, playing sports, doing chores, using exercise as a means of transportation (e.g., walking, biking, etc.), participating in planned exercise sessions, and attending physical education classes are all activities available in family, community, and school settings that can allow children to meet physical activity and fitness requirements.

Copyright © Mometrix Media. You have been licensed one copy of this document for personal use only. Any other reproduction or redistribution is strictly prohibited. All rights reserved.

Fine Arts Foundations and Creativity

LEARNING OUTCOMES ACHIEVED THROUGH VISUAL ARTS

The arts are just as important to include in curricula as language, math, science, social studies, health, and physical education. Early learning standards in many states now reflect the goal to integrate the arts into the overall curriculum. Teachers need to provide young children with activities that promote development of fine motor skills, exploration of art materials and processes, and symbolic representation of concepts through artworks. EC educators should not merely assign isolated art activities. They can clarify many concepts and improve learning by providing art projects that fit into the overall curriculum and are relevant to individual learning units. Teachers should develop detailed, well-organized step lists for each activity. Clear directions not only maintain classroom order, but also provide children with a structure within which to experiment with art and enhance their sequencing skills. Teachers should use process-oriented activities, both on their own and within lessons that require products. For example, painting pictures of animals combines product (representing an animal) with process (exploring paint use). Teachers should supply and explain rules/steps for process activities that explore the use of art materials and processes.

PLANNING ART ACTIVITIES OR PROJECTS

EC teachers should first establish the concept they want to teach, the objectives they want to meet through planning and teaching the lesson/activity, and the learning objectives they want the children to meet through participating. Then, a teacher can construct a simple prototype for the project. This enables the teacher to estimate how long it will take the children to complete the activity, and to explore and discover the optimal sequencing of steps for the activity. The teacher should then write down the plan, step-by-step. Steps should include those that need to be completed before the activity. These might include preliminary discussion, book reading/sharing related to the project, viewing related artworks and/or photos, etc. Steps should also include those that need to be completed while setting up the activity, such as dispensing paints, clay, etc.; assembling paintbrushes/other instruments; and passing out paper and other materials. Teachers do not need to be artistically proficient. Young children are not art critics, and teachers can find a great deal of information about art materials and processes by reading books and searching online. Available professional development courses focusing on art can also give teachers more ideas for lesson plans.

FUNCTIONS OF ART

SOCIAL FUNCTIONS

Artworks can be created for physical, social, and personal purposes. When art focuses on the social lives of groups rather than on one individual's experiences or viewpoint, it serves social functions. Art carrying political stances/messages always performs social functions. Dadaist Oppenheim's hair-covered tea set did not perform any physical function, but served social functions by politically protesting World War I and many other social/political issues. During the Great Depression, photographers like Dorothea Lange, Gordon Parks, Walker Evans, and Arthur Rothstein commissioned by the Farm Security Administration produced stark records of people's suffering. These depictions of social conditions also served social functions. Fine artists like Francisco Goya and William Hogarth, as well as cartoonists like Thomas Nast and Charles Bragg, created satirical works of art lampooning various social and political customs and situations. Satire is intended not only to provide comic relief, insight, and perspective, but also to stimulate social change. Therefore, it serves social functions. Another social function is improving community status and pride through art treasures.

PHYSICAL FUNCTIONS

Ascertaining the function of a work of art requires considering its context. Half of the context involves the artist. Knowing the artist's country, the historical time period during which the artist lived, and the social and political culture of the time informs artwork and our ability to infer what the artist was

Copyright © Mometrix Media. You have been licensed one copy of this document for personal use only. Any other reproduction or redistribution is strictly prohibited. All rights reserved.

thinking and intending when he or she was creating it. The other half of the context involves the viewer. Knowing what the artwork means to you in your own place and time informs your perception of and response to it. Taken within context, art serves physical, personal, and social functions. For example, architecture, industrial design, and crafts have physical functions. A raku pottery bowl made in Japan serves a physical function during a tea ceremony. However, a teacup covered with hair (paired with a hair-covered saucer and spoon) by Dada artist Meret Oppenheim (1936) makes an artistic statement, but serves no physical function. When we view a tribal war club in a museum, regardless of the exquisite craftsmanship it may demonstrate, we realize it was made primarily for bludgeoning enemies.

PERSONAL FUNCTIONS

Works of art can have physical, social, and personal functions. Of these three, the personal functions of art are the most variable. Artists' motivations to create works include the desire to express their feelings and ideas, to obtain gratification through producing art, to communicate messages to viewers, to enable both themselves and their viewers to have an aesthetic experience, and to simply entertain viewers. Some artists also claim that they sometimes create art for no particular reason, and that the art produced has no meaning. Art can perform a personal function of control. For example, some artists use their work to give order to the world's apparent chaos. Others use art to create chaos in an overly orderly, boring environment. Art can be therapeutic for both artists and viewers. Much art has served the personal function of religion. Artworks with biological purposes, like cultural fertility symbols or bodily decorations designed to attract mates for procreation, are also examples of the personal functions of art.

LEARNING OBJECTIVES

When children participate in teacher-designed art activities, they can fulfill learning objectives such as exploring various art materials and processes; developing awareness of visual art and its basic elements (e.g., line, shape, color, and texture); using art forms to represent feelings, thoughts, and/or stories; developing the skills of color recognition and discrimination; and even building their vocabularies and language skills, depending on the activities. Teachers can integrate such objectives with an overall theme for each art activity/project that they integrate with the current theme for their lesson or curriculum unit. For example, if space travel is the class theme one week, constructing model rocket ships is more appropriate than painting self-portraits. Even open-ended activities to explore art materials and processes can be integrated with thematic units. For example, teachers can apply activities exploring cutting and gluing processes to a theme of one specific color by providing various materials and textures that are all the same color. In this way, teachers can connect a learning concept to experimentation with artistic processes.

CREATING, PERFORMING, AND RESPONDING

Three processes common to all branches of the arts—visual, musical, dance, dramatic, and performance art—are creating, performing, and responding. The first of these, creating, involves the genesis of the artistic product.

There are several steps in creating:

1. Imagining is the step during which the artist develops his/her ideas and considers the concepts and feelings which s/he wants to communicate and express through the work.
2. Planning is the step during which the artist researches, experiments with, and designs the means by which s/he will present her/his ideas and emotions (e.g., the materials that will be used and how they will be manipulated to produce the desired effects).
3. Making, evaluating, and refining is the step during which the artist applies her/his skills and various techniques to create an artistic product that will bring her/his ideas and feelings to life.

Copyright © Mometrix Media. You have been licensed one copy of this document for personal use only. Any other reproduction or redistribution is strictly prohibited. All rights reserved.

4. <u>Presenting</u> is the step during which the artist exhibits visual art in a gallery, private exhibit, or another type of showing. The artist might also perform music, dance, theater, or performance art for an audience so that others can participate in and respond to the artwork.

PROCESSES INVOLVED IN THE PRODUCTION AND RECEPTION OF WORKS OF ART

In all branches of the arts, artists and their audiences (who may also be participants in the case of performance art) complete three basic artistic processes that are closely related: creation, performance, and response.

The performance process includes five steps:

1. <u>Selecting</u> is the step during which the artist makes a choice about what to present. For example, musicians choose pieces to play. Dancers choose choreographic pieces to perform. Visual artists select which of their paintings, drawings, sculptures, mobiles/stabiles etc. to display. Theater producers, directors, and actors choose a play to perform.
2. <u>Analyzing</u> is the step during which the performer researches the background of the chosen work and analyzes its structure to understand it and its import.
3. <u>Interpreting</u> is the step during which the performer develops a personal idea about what their work should express or accomplish.
4. <u>Rehearsing, evaluating, and refining</u> is the step during which the performer applies her/his skills and techniques to develop a personal interpretation that will enable her/his performance to make the work come alive. The artist then evaluates the performance, and makes further refinements to subsequent presentations.
5. <u>Presenting</u> is the final step, during which the artist performs the work for others.

FUNDAMENTAL ARTISTIC PROCESSES COMMON TO ALL BRANCHES OF THE ARTS

Works of art, whether visual, musical, dramatic, literary, dance, or performance art, all involve three basic and interrelated processes: creation of the work, performance of the work for others, and the response of others (e.g., audiences, participants, viewers, or readers).

The artistic process of responding to artwork includes four steps:

1. <u>Selection</u> is the step during which the person(s) who will receive the artwork choose what they want to experience (possible choices include attending a gallery exhibit of paintings, drawings, or sculptures; going to see a theatrical play or a movie; attending a dance performance; attending/participating in a performance art show; or reading a book of poetry or prose).
2. <u>Analysis</u> is the step during which the viewers/audience/participants/readers see/hear and understand the components of the work, and mentally bring these components together to perceive the work as a whole.
3. <u>Interpretation</u> is the step during which those experiencing the work and/or its performance construct meaning from what they have witnessed, developing a personal response to the creator(s)' and performer(s)' expressions of concepts and emotions.
4. <u>Evaluation</u> is the final step, during which the respondent(s) assess the quality of the artwork and of its performance.

FACILITATING STUDENT LEARNING WITH CREATING, PERFORMING, AND RESPONDING

The artistic processes have many steps in common. This interrelatedness among the processes informs students' development of educated responses to artworks. For instance, when students learn the step of evaluating their own artworks, they learn to apply better critical approaches when interpreting the artworks created by others. They also use their experiences to direct their selection of works they want to witness and respond to in the future. When students learn how to evaluate and refine their own work, this facilitates their subsequent evaluation and selection of others' works to watch, to perform themselves, and/or to purchase. Teachers can promote this by encouraging students to transfer their

164

Copyright © Mometrix Media. You have been licensed one copy of this document for personal use only. Any other reproduction or redistribution is strictly prohibited. All rights reserved.

learning from one artistic process to another. For example, teachers can introduce students to others' work while they are creating their own so they can transfer what they learn about the creation process to the responding process. When students are solving specific creative/artistic problems, teachers can expose them to other artists' solutions and encourage students to consider these solutions.

LINES

In visual media, a line is the path of a moving point; the edge of a flat or two-dimensional shape; or the outline of a solid, three-dimensional object. Lines are longer than they are wide. The term measure refers to the width of a line. Lines can be straight, curved, wavy, angular, or zigzag. Lines can be horizontal (side to side), vertical (up and down), or diagonal (at an angle between vertical and horizontal). Lines can also be implied. In this case, they are not physically present, but the artist's arrangement of other elements suggests lines, which organize the picture and/or guide viewers' eyes. The movement a line follows/appears to show is called direction. Where and how a line is placed in a picture/design is called location. Lines define areas, and imply or create open or closed shapes like circles, rectangles, etc. Line combined with shape creates implied volume in paintings/drawings and actual volume in sculptures. Lines express various qualities by being jagged, loopy, bold, repetitive, etc., and evoke different emotional and mental viewer responses.

SHAPE, FORM, AND VALUE

Shape refers to two-dimensional areas created by connecting lines to outline the contours of objects depicted in art. Shapes can be positive or negative (i.e. defined not by their own outlines, but by the edges of surrounding shapes). Shapes may be biomorphic (i.e. shapes found in nature) or geometric. Variations in value, texture, or color can make shapes stand out in a piece. Form is the three-dimensional projection of shape. Form has dimension and volume. In paintings and drawings, form appears to have mass, while in sculptures it actually does have mass. The term "form" can also be used to describe an artwork's overall structure. Value refers to the appearance and range of lights and darks seen in a visual work of art. Regardless of color, value varies between black and white, with an indefinite range of various shades of gray between these two absolutes.

TEXTURE AND SPACE

Texture refers to how rough or smooth a surface appears and/or feels. Everyday materials have texture, as do works of art. An object or a work of art can look and/or feel spongy or glassy, wet or dry, soft or hard, etc. Texture can be real, as with sandpaper and other rough-textured materials used to create works of art. Or, it can be illusory, as when materials appear hard or soft, but are really not. Space is defined as the measurable distance between predetermined points. It can be shallow or limited, with a foreground and a background; or it can be deep or extended, with a middle ground as well as a foreground and a background. Two-dimensional space has height and width; three-dimensional space has height and width, plus volume and time. Like negative shape (shape that is not defined by its own outlines, but by the surrounding shapes and their outlines), negative space appears in art. It is the space around and between the positive objects or shapes depicted. This negative space forms its own shapes around positive subjects.

RHYTHM

In visual art, rhythm is achieved through repeating visual movement. Visual movement is created by arranging lines, shapes, and/or colors to give the viewer's eye a sense of motion and direction. Just as we hear rhythm in music through aural beats and varying note durations, we see rhythm in paintings through visual movement of lines, angles, shapes, and other elements. Just as Beethoven used repetition of musical phrases and themes to create mood, drama, and movement, artists use movement and repetition to create visual rhythm. For example, in "Nude Descending a Staircase, No. 2" (1912) by Marcel Duchamp, the artist depicts an abstracted human figure, repeating the figure using overlapping placements in a diagonal, downward pattern. The series of repeated shapes and angles gives the impression of viewing action in strobe lighting or via stop action photography. The figures are physically

Copyright © Mometrix Media. You have been licensed one copy of this document for personal use only. Any other reproduction or redistribution is strictly prohibited. All rights reserved.

still, but visually convey the effect of moving down a staircase. By directionally repeating the figure, Duchamp shows movement and rhythm within the static medium of a painting.

COLOR

Color refers to the wavelengths of light reflected by a surface. Some wavelengths are absorbed by paints and other visual art media/materials; we do not see these. Other wavelengths are reflected; these are the ones we see as colors. Primary colors are pure, individual colors that cannot be separated into other colors or produced by mixing colors. The three primary colors are red, blue, and yellow. Secondary colors are combinations of two primary colors (e.g., orange = red + yellow, green = blue + yellow, and purple/violet = red + blue). Intermediate colors are produced by mixing a primary and a secondary color (e.g., red-orange, yellow-orange, blue-green, yellow-green, blue-violet, or red-violet). Colors are arranged on the color wheel. Analogous colors are adjacent to each other on the wheel. Examples of analogous colors include yellow and orange, orange and red, blue and green, and green and yellow. Complementary colors are opposite each other on the color wheel. Examples of complementary colors include blue and orange, yellow and purple, and red and green. Mixing equal parts of two complementary colors produces brown. Blue and predominantly blue colors are cool. Red, yellow, and predominantly red/yellow colors are warm. Colors identify objects, evoke moods, and influence emotions.

BALANCE

Balance refers to how visual weight is distributed in a work of visual art. In two-dimensional art like paintings, balance is the visual equilibrium among the painting's elements, which make the entire picture look balanced. Balance can be symmetrical (both sides are equal) or asymmetrical, with shapes and spaces that are unequal and/or unevenly distributed. This produces psychological rather than physical balance, creating tension and suggesting movement. Radial balance/symmetry uses images radiating from a center, such as wheel spokes or ripples around a pebble thrown into water. An example of balance is seen in the painting "Dressing for the Carnival" (1877) by Winslow Homer. The central figure of a carnival performer putting on his costume is the focal point. The performer is surrounded by two adult assistants and a group of fascinated children who are watching him. The shapes, values, and colors are balanced to produce overall visual equilibrium and unity (another organizing principle of art).

VISUAL MOVEMENT

Artists create a visual sense of movement in paintings to direct the viewer's eyes. Direction is frequently toward a focal point or area within the painting. Artists can direct movement along lines, edges, shapes, and colors, but especially along parts with equal value (dark/light), which best facilitates the eyes' movement. For example, in "Liberation of the Peon" (1931), Diego Rivera depicts soldiers liberating a slave by cutting the ropes binding him while clothing his nakedness with a blanket or garment. Paths of movement in the painting all lead to the focal point of the knife cutting the ropes. (Emphasis, another art/design principle, is also seen in how the action of freeing the peon is made more important than the soldiers performing that action.) By painting all humans in the scene with their eyes focused on the slave, Rivera creates movement directing our view toward him. At the same time, he painted all horses with their eyes focused out at the viewer, drawing the viewer into the scene.

USING EMPHASIS

Artists use the design principle of emphasis to call attention to particular elements in their works. Emphasis directs the viewer's focus to certain parts of a painting, and makes certain components of a work dominant. Emphasis can be achieved in art by emphasizing various design elements like value (light/dark), color, shape, line, etc. Artists also use contrast (e.g., contrasting values, colors, shapes, etc.) to create emphasis. To emphasize a focal area, a center of interest which focuses on the most important part of a painting, an artist can create visual emphasis through extreme contrasts of light and dark values. Strongly contrasting shapes and/or marked contrasts in other design elements also create visual emphasis. As an example of visual emphasis, in the painting "At the Moulin Rouge" (1892/1895), Henri

166

Copyright © Mometrix Media. You have been licensed one copy of this document for personal use only. Any other reproduction or redistribution is strictly prohibited. All rights reserved.

de Toulouse-Lautrec emphasizes the focal area of a group of friends conversing in a cabaret through contrasting colors and values, as well as through movement directing the eye toward the group. His use of color, light, and shape also help create the scene's atmosphere.

UNITY

One of the most important characteristics of a well-developed work of visual art is its visual unity. When we view a painting without unity, we may see a collection of disconnected parts that do not come together to form a whole. We may perceive it as fragmentary, disorganized, and incomplete. When an artist achieves visual unity, all of the elements in a painting appear to belong together. Unity affords paintings the quality of cohesion that makes them look and feel finished and complete. For example, in the painting "Starry Night" (1889), Vincent Van Gogh used his characteristic large, visible brush strokes in a swirly pattern throughout the landscape, providing visual unity through the texture, rhythm, pattern, and movement of the lines and shapes. He used predominantly cool colors (blues and bluish browns), providing unity through color. (He also provided emphasis by adding contrasting yellow stars.) The result is a unified painting whose elements work together, strongly conveying the atmosphere, mood, emotion, and story that the artist wanted to express.

CONTRAST

Contrast refers to significant differences in the values (lights and darks), colors, textures, shapes, lines, and other elements of visual artworks. Visual contrast creates interest and excitement, and avoids monotony in art. For example, in the painting "Still Life with Apples and Peaches" (1905), Paul Cézanne combined all seven elements and all seven principles of design to create a unified composition. Among these, he used at least eight kinds of contrast:

1. unpatterned vs. intricately patterned surfaces (pattern contrast)
2. soft vs. hard/found edges (edge contrast)
3. dark vs. light vs. middle values (value contrast)
4. pure vs. muted/blended colors (intensity contrast)
5. cool vs. warm colors (temperature contrast)
6. textured vs. smooth surfaces (texture contrast)
7. organic vs. geometric shapes (shape contrast)
8. large vs. small objects/shapes (size contrast).

PATTERN

Pattern is the organized or random repetition of elements. Music is made up of sound patterns. Visual patterns often appear in nature. Artists frequently create works featuring repeated designs that produce patterns inspired by those seen in the natural world. Visual art is enhanced by pattern, which enriches surface interest to augment visual excitement. For example, in "Numbers in Color" (1958-59), the artist Jasper Johns created a regular pattern by assembling 11 rows of 11 stacked rectangles each. He painted various numerical digits from 0 to 9 within most of the rectangles. He made these numbers look irregular by irregularly distributing, varying, and applying the colors he used. Many patterned paintings do not include a focal point or area. This often makes them look more like designs—even when they include recognizable images—than portraits, landscapes, still-lifes, or other types of paintings that do not have such repetitive patterning.

PITCH, TEMPO, AND RHYTHM IN THE MUSICAL ARTS

Pitch is the frequency of a sound, such as a musical note. We hear high/middle/low frequency sound waves as high/middle/low pitched sounds. Various pitches are combined in musical compositions to create variety. A series of connected notes of different pitches creates a melody. Sounding (playing/singing) several pitches simultaneously and combining them produces harmonies and chords. Connected series of harmonies/chords in turn create harmonic/chord progressions. Tempo is the speed of music. Fast tempo can evoke happiness, excitement, fear, anger, or urgency. Slow tempo can evoke

Copyright © Mometrix Media. You have been licensed one copy of this document for personal use only. Any other reproduction or redistribution is strictly prohibited. All rights reserved.

serenity, grandeur, solemnity, sadness, or ominousness. Musical compositions commonly direct the tempo using terms like andante (walking speed), adagio (slow), allegro (happy/quick), lento (slow), largo (expansively slow), etc. Rhythm includes the overall beat/time signature (number of beats per measure) and the variations among note lengths that produce patterns (e.g., legato describes smoothly connected series of notes, while staccato describes sharply disconnected notes that are cut short and sounded separately). Composers combine pitch, tempo, and rhythm in music to create atmosphere and mood, and to evoke emotion in listeners. They also arrange these elements to construct/recall musical themes/motifs within compositions.

Copyright © Mometrix Media. You have been licensed one copy of this document for personal use only. Any other reproduction or redistribution is strictly prohibited. All rights reserved.

NBPTS Practice Test

Want to take this practice test in an online interactive format?
Check out the bonus page, which includes interactive practice questions and much
more: **http://www.mometrix.com/bonus948/nbptsgenec**

1. Which of these is NOT one of the major personality structures proposed by Sigmund Freud in his psychoanalytic theory of development?

   a. Id
   b. Ego
   c. Libido
   d. Superego

2. To support EC language development, experts advise which of the following teacher practices?

   a. Asking children linear or one-way questions
   b. Doing most of the talking in their classrooms
   c. Focusing on durations of verbal interactions
   d. Asking children more open-ended questions

3. According to Piaget's theory of cognitive development, _____ and _____ are processes included in the overall process of _____.

   a. Assimilation; accommodation; adaptation
   b. Adaptation; assimilation; accommodation
   c. Accommodation; adaptation; assimilation
   d. Adaptation; accommodation; equilibrium

4. Piaget coined the term "schema" to describe:

   a. Mental constructs for individual objects.
   b. Mental concepts of categories or classes.
   c. Mental programs only for motor actions.
   d. Mental ideas governing inborn reflexes.

5. The concept of object permanence is best characterized as:

   a. "Out of sight, out of mind."
   b. "Out of mind, out of sight."
   c. "Out of sight, still exists."
   d. "Out of sight, out of time."

6. According to Piaget's theory, in what age range do children begin representing things with symbols?

   a. Between birth and 6 months
   b. Between 6 and 12 months
   c. Between 12 and 18 months
   d. Between 18 and 24 months

Copyright © Mometrix Media. You have been licensed one copy of this document for personal use only. Any other reproduction or redistribution is strictly prohibited. All rights reserved.

7. A toddler sees a large brown dog and says, "Moo!" This is an example of:

a. Egocentrism.
b. Equilibrium.
c. Accommodation.
d. Assimilation.

8. According to Piaget's theory, the term *conservation* means which of these?

a. The idea that our natural resources are finite and hence, we must conserve them
b. The idea that amounts/numbers can be retained or conserved in one's memories
c. The idea that even when we cannot see an object, its existence is still conserved
d. The idea that amounts/numbers are the same regardless of shape or appearance

9. When a young child believes his/her thoughts caused something external to happen, which is the *most specific* Piagetian term to describe this phenomenon?

a. Animism
b. Centration
c. Egocentrism
d. Magical thinking

10. Which of the following processes occurs earliest in children?

a. Inductive logic
b. Conservation
c. Centration
d. Decentration

11. In which of the six stages of art growth and development do children begin to develop a visual schema?

a. Scribble
b. Preschematic
c. Schematic
d. Dawning Realism

12. Which of the following is most effective for teaching pre-math and manipulative skills to preschool children?

a. Giving them solid objects to manipulate physically
b. Giving them information for mental manipulation
c. Giving them math processes to memorize by rote
d. Giving them lessons to listen to while they sit still

13. At what age do children typically undergo the second of three periods of language/communication development?

a. From 0 - 6 months
b. From 6 - 18 months
c. From 8 - 12 months
d. From 18-24 months

14. Which of the following is most typical of the language development of a two-year-old?

a. Using three-word sentences with ease
b. Knowing and naming major body parts
c. Using at least two pronouns correctly
d. Using about three pronouns correctly

Copyright © Mometrix Media. You have been licensed one copy of this document for personal use only. Any other reproduction or redistribution is strictly prohibited. All rights reserved.

15. Which of these is more typical of the language development of a two to three year old than of a preschooler?

    a. Describing unseen objects
    b. Telling "make-believe" stories
    c. Speaking in complete sentences
    d. Expressing opinions/preferences

16. Which of these is correct about one-on-one vs. group conversations between adults and young children?

    a. Adults should discuss one on one during whole-group preschool activities.
    b. Adults can better reinforce what children say in group discussions.
    c. Adults have less chance to extend what children say in one on one context.
    d. Adults can better elicit children's abstract idea comprehension one on one.

17. Which of the following teacher actions is most effective for fostering greater depth of preschoolers' comprehension of word meanings?

    a. Focusing on one definition for a new vocabulary word
    b. Introducing new concepts separately from new words
    c. Limiting added information to simplify comprehension
    d. Giving multiple definitions and examples of new words

18. What is correct about how teachers can support young children's language development when the children tell stories?

    a. Teachers should not supply a vocabulary word if the child does not know it.
    b. When listening to children's storytelling, teachers should not ask questions.
    c. Storytelling permits young children to exercise their powers of imagination.
    d. Teachers should let children express their ideas without building onto them.

19. What is the most typical age for children to understand common opposites like big/little, hot/cold, etc.?

    a. Three years old
    b. Five years old
    c. Two years old
    d. Four years old

20. According to Roger Brown's (1973) Stage I sentence types, which of these is classified under "Operations of Reference"?

    a. A negation
    b. An action
    c. An agent
    d. An entity

21. In Brown's (1973) Stages of Syntactical and Morphological Development, which of these age ranges is associated with what he designated as Stage I?

    a. 12-26 months
    b. 15-30 months
    c. 24-36 months
    d. 27-30 months

Copyright © Mometrix Media. You have been licensed one copy of this document for personal use only. Any other reproduction or redistribution is strictly prohibited. All rights reserved.

22. A child who correctly uses irregular past tenses of verbs, e.g. *went, fell, froze,* etc., would be in which of Roger Brown's Stages of Syntactic and Morphological Development?

 a. Stage I
 b. Stage II
 c. Stage III
 d. Stage IV

23. According to Roger Brown, a child who indicates the regular plural by saying "My toys" is in which of his Stages of Syntactical and Morphological Development?

 a. Stage V
 b. Stage IV
 c. Stage III
 d. Stage II

24. When characterizing young children, what did Vygotsky mean by the term "private speech" that he coined?

 a. Speaking in private dialogue with another child
 b. Speaking in private conversations with an adult
 c. Speaking silently to themselves in their minds
 d. Speaking aloud to themselves during activities

25. Among the following auditory disabilities, which one does not involve any part of the hearing mechanism?

 a. Only sensorineural-type hearing loss
 b. The conductive form of hearing loss
 c. Central auditory processing disorder
 d. The condition of complete deafness

26. To promote young children's developing abstract thinking, which teacher technique(s) to use during and after shared readings is/are best suited for use with children in the younger, rather than older, ages of early childhood?

 a. Asking children to predict what they think will happen next in the story
 b. Asking children to imagine beyond the story: "What would you do if...?"
 c. Asking children to identify vocabulary words and describe story details
 d. Asking them to make conclusions about why characters do/feel things

27. When a student is able to consider whether an information source is reputable, has been proven objectively, and is accepted by experts in its discipline, which element of critical thinking does the student demonstrate?

 a. Evaluating supporting evidence
 b. Judging the quality of material
 c. Distinguishing fact from opinion
 d. Finding evidence/no evidence

28. What is true about the sequence that teachers should use for phonics instruction with young children?

 a. Teachers should introduce letters with similar sounds in separate lessons.
 b. Teachers should introduce stop consonants before continuous consonants.
 c. Teachers should introduce letters that look similar during the same lesson.
 d. Teachers should introduce low-utility before high-utility letters and sounds.

Copyright © Mometrix Media. You have been licensed one copy of this document for personal use only. Any other reproduction or redistribution is strictly prohibited. All rights reserved.

29. Which of these is correct regarding teacher assessment of early childhood print awareness using a storybook?

    a. Teachers can ask children to point out uppercase/lowercase letters and punctuation marks.

    b. It is not possible to conduct any accurate assessment of print awareness using a storybook.

    c. It is unnecessary to ask children to identify the front, back, spine, and title of the storybook.

    d. It does not inform assessment to have children show the first and last words in a sentence.

30. From birth to the age of 2 years, children typically grow to ___ times their newborn weights.

    a. Three

    b. Four

    c. Two

    d. Five

31. By the time they are two years old, children's brains typically have grown to ___ of their adult sizes.

    a. 90%

    b. 75%

    c. 55%

    d. 40%

32. What is true regarding children's motor development from infancy to preschool ages?

    a. Proprioception is established at birth and does not progress any further.

    b. The voluntary behaviors of newborns eventually progress into reflexes.

    c. Motor skills development involves learning of new physical movements over the course of time.

    d. Motor skills are largely known at infancy, but infants lack the strength to execute complex movements.

33. Which of these accurately reflects research findings on gender differences in early childhood motor development?

    a. Preschool girls are found to be equally muscular as, but more physically mature than, boys are in preschool.

    b. Preschool boys exhibit both more strength and coordination in large-muscle gross-motor skills than girls do.

    c. Preschool girls exhibit more fine-motor skills, but less gross-motor coordination, than boys do in preschool.

    d. Despite certain differences, preschool motor development between genders is more similar than different.

34. Regarding the three basic temperament types identified by psychologists in infants, which of these is true?

    a. There is no clear majority among infants having one of the types.

    b. The majority of babies are found to be of Difficult temperament.

    c. The majority of infants are found to be Slow to Warm Up types.

    d. The majority of infants are found to have the Easy temperament.

35. When a child gives reasons for succeeding at something, which of the following reflects an internal locus of control?

    a. "I did well because the teacher helped me."

    b. "I got a good mark because I was just lucky."

    c. "I did well because Danny showed me how."

    d. "I did a good job because I worked so hard."

Copyright © Mometrix Media. You have been licensed one copy of this document for personal use only. Any other reproduction or redistribution is strictly prohibited. All rights reserved.

36. For children with a primarily visual learning style, which material would be most effective to give them to help them understand abstract concepts and relationships?

    a.   Soft clay to sculpt
    b.   Dance movements
    c.   Multicolor graphics
    d.   Sporting activities

37. Which of Erikson's psychosocial stages of development corresponds to ages 2-3 years in early childhood?

    a.   Basic Trust vs. Mistrust
    b.   Autonomy vs. Shame
    c.   Initiative vs. Guilt
    d.   Industry vs. Inferiority

38. Which of the following reflects an adult expectation of a child that is developmentally appropriate?

    a.   Expecting a six-year-old to stay in-seat and attend to a first-grade lesson
    b.   Expecting a five-year-old to sit still and be quiet during long-term activity
    c.   Expecting a toddler to balance upon one foot and/or to hop on one foot
    d.   Expecting a four-month-old baby to sit up without any external support

39. According to Alfred Adler's theory about birth order, which of these applies to only or oldest children?

    a.   Only children tend to prefer the company of children to the company of adults.
    b.   Only children tend to prefer the company of adults to the company of children.
    c.   Only children tend to share things with other children more easily than others.
    d.   Older/oldest children never develop strict or authoritarian attitudes/behaviors.

40. Which of the following correctly reflects Adler's theory of birth order's influences on personality development?

    a.   The youngest children in families have no features in common with only children.
    b.   Twins are identical in activity and/or strength and parents perceive them as equal.
    c.   Some "babies" of the family grow to make grandiose plans, which never succeed.
    d.   Adler never noted any differences between twins as to personality development.

41. In Adler's psychoanalytic theory, which of these did he believe about male/female siblings in family birth orders?

    a.   An only boy with girl siblings will more likely behave effeminately than as overly masculine in the father's absence.
    b.   An only girl with boy siblings will more likely become a tomboy than become very feminine to differentiate herself.
    c.   Adler stated parents of all males/females wanting a child of the other sex never dress one child as the opposite sex.
    d.   Boy siblings of an only girl can behave protectively toward her; and she may make extra effort to please the father.

Copyright © Mometrix Media. You have been licensed one copy of this document for personal use only. Any other reproduction or redistribution is strictly prohibited. All rights reserved.

42. According to Murray Bowen's Family Systems Theory, which of the following accurately reflects what he called the Family Projection Process?

    a. A parent's fear about something being wrong with a child is based on a real problem in the child.

    b. The child's behavior confirms the parent's fears because something really is wrong with the child.

    c. In focusing on the child, parents' perceptions come to mirror the child's self-image and behaviors.

    d. Parental perception of child problems can become self-fulfilling prophecy in the child's self-image.

43. Typically, young children eat most of the same foods as adults by the age of ___.

    a. Five years old.

    b. Four years old.

    c. Three years old.

    d. Two years old.

44. Which of the following is most accurate about the sleep needs and behaviors of young children?

    a. Children typically need 9-11 hours of sleep from ages 2-5 years.

    b. Children typically need 7-9 hours of sleep at the ages 2-5 years.

    c. Children typically need 10-12 hours of sleep at ages of 2-5 years.

    d. Children typically need long daytime naps at the ages 2-5 years.

45. What is most true about hand-washing hygiene during early childhood?

    a. Parents continue to wash children's hands during the early childhood years.

    b. Young children are unlikely to wash their hands long or thoroughly enough.

    c. Toddlers are not exposed to more germs during the toilet-training process.

    d. Germ exposure in daycare/preschool is not a significant cause for concern.

46. Which of these most accurately reflects findings about mass media and other cultural influences on young children?

    a. Viewing video violence has been proven to increase young children's aggressive behaviors.

    b. Young children get more cognitive stimulation from watching TV than interactive activities.

    c. In larger families, children do not need 1:1 time with parents; group activities are as good.

    d. Parents should discourage playing "house" and other make-believe play as it is unrealistic.

47. Which of the following have research studies found regarding the relative individualism or collectivism of different world cultures?

    a. American culture has been found to be the most interdependent.

    b. Asian and Latin American cultures are both more interdependent.

    c. European cultures are found more individualistic than in the USA.

    d. European cultures are found more collectivistic than those in Asia.

48. What is true regarding survey findings about family differences among American socioeconomic and racial groups?

    a. Cultural and demographic factors influence disagreement styles more than parental stress does.

    b. Low-socioeconomic young children have no more development/behavior problems than others.

    c. Data have shown more violence in African-American families, then in Latino, then White families.

    d. Socioeconomically disadvantaged children have more problems and receive more help for these.

Copyright © Mometrix Media. You have been licensed one copy of this document for personal use only. Any other reproduction or redistribution is strictly prohibited. All rights reserved.

49. Which of these have researchers found about cultural and familial influences on school readiness and achievement?

   a. A national survey has not found significant differences in parenting practices among racial/ethnic groups.

   b. Varying degrees of early childhood development are unrelated to home routines, safety, and parenting.

   c. Researchers do not think racial and ethnic disparities in school achievement contribute to discrimination.

   d. American children in minority groups show lower average school readiness than American white children.

50. Which of the following reflects an early childhood application of Freud's psychoanalytic theory of development?

   a. Providing opportunities for children to "make believe"

   b. Providing models of behaviors children see and imitate

   c. Providing timely, consistent nursing/feeding to a baby

   d. Providing safe and sanitary objects for babies to mouth

51. Which of the following is an early childhood practice that best applies knowledge of Piaget's first stage of cognitive development?

   a. Introducing topics to children seen from others' perspectives

   b. Encouraging make-believe and pretend play that use symbols

   c. Introducing simple, basic arithmetic ideas as early as possible

   d. Providing many manipulable toys that move and make noises

52. The animation of letters and numbers in Sesame Street, or of objects in Spongebob Squarepants, appeals to children in Piaget's Preoperational stage of cognitive development because of their:

   a. Logical thinking.

   b. Magical thinking.

   c. Animistic thinking.

   d. Egocentric thinking.

53. Which of the following is NOT one of Bandura's conditions required for learning?

   a. Attention

   b. Cognition

   c. Retention

   d. Motivation

54. When a toddler begins to shout, "NO!" often, Erikson would characterize this behavior as:

   a. Developing autonomy

   b. Developing initiative

   c. Developing industry

   d. Developing mistrust

55. In Maslow's theory, which needs are at the base of the pyramid?

   a. Self-actualizing

   b. Physiological

   c. Security

   d. Esteem

Copyright © Mometrix Media. You have been licensed one copy of this document for personal use only. Any other reproduction or redistribution is strictly prohibited. All rights reserved.

56. According to Carl Rogers, a child who relies primarily on external locus of control demonstrates:

a. Incongruence
b. Conditions of worth
c. Conditional positive self-regard
d. Unconditional positive regard

57. A young child wakes up early one day and enjoys not being rushed by his mother in getting ready for preschool. This child then makes a point of waking up early again on subsequent days. According to behaviorist theory, this illustrates which principle?

a. Positive reinforcement
b. Positive punishment
c. Negative punishment
d. Negative reinforcement

58. Which statement is most accurate about the Montessori Method of education?

a. Practical skills and abstract concepts are taught via mental tasks.
b. Teachers observe and guide children but parents are uninvolved.
c. Learning environments are keyed to group developmental levels.
d. The self-direction and self-correction of children are emphasized.

59. Which of these correctly represents an element of the Bank Street Curriculum approach to early childhood education?

a. Children learn separate subjects, one at a time.
b. Children learn as individuals via 1:1 instruction.
c. Children learn in one type of childcare program.
d. Children learn at various developmental levels.

60. Which statement accurately reflects Friedrich Froebel's philosophy of early childhood education?

a. Froebel believed schools should not direct student will.
b. Froebel believed in group, not individual, attainments.
c. Froebel believed that nature is the heart of all learning.
d. Froebel believed instruction should not be play-based.

61. Of the following, which is true of Siegfried Engelmann's contributions to early childhood education?

a. The Bereiter-Engelmann Preschool Program tested teaching methods with affluent college faculty's children.
b. Engelmann demonstrated that Piaget's conservation of liquid volume did not depend only on a child's stage.
c. The philosophy and methodology of Direct Instruction were developed by somebody other than Engelmann.
d. Engelmann's research into curriculum and instruction excluded the study of children who had any disabilities.

Copyright © Mometrix Media. You have been licensed one copy of this document for personal use only. Any other reproduction or redistribution is strictly prohibited. All rights reserved.

62. The High/Scope Curriculum for preschoolers (Weikart et al) identifies 58 key developmental experiences for active learning, dividing them into 10 main categories. Which of the following does NOT correctly represent one of the first five of these 10 categories?

    a. Music, including being able to write musical notation and compositions
    b. Language/literacy including speaking, scribbling, describing, storytelling
    c. Creative representation; symbol recognition, imitation; and playing roles
    d. Initiative, social relations; problem-solving, decisions, and relationships

63. Which of these statements accurately reflects principles of emergent literacy theory?

    a. Children's first encounters with written language occur during early childhood.
    b. Young children learn reading and writing concurrently rather than sequentially.
    c. All young children's scribbles look similar regardless of native written language.
    d. Comprehension develops receptively before expressively with speech and print.

64. Which of the following is true about the whole language approach to early childhood literacy instruction?

    a. The whole language approach to literacy is very similar to phonics in their analytical nature.
    b. The whole language approach to literacy is quite similar in character to alphabetic learning.
    c. The whole language approach is based on the philosophy and psychology of constructivism.
    d. The whole language approach emphasizes the similarity of each child's learning experience.

65. What statement correctly represents how the whole language instructional approach addresses young children's mechanical errors in early literacy learning?

    a. Using printed language with technical correctness early is the priority in this method.
    b. Whole language teachers ignore young children's mechanical errors when they occur.
    c. Whole language teachers use only summative assessments of young children's errors.
    d. Children's overall engagement, comprehension, and appreciation precede correction.

66. When children construct meaning, they may address new information that does not fit into their existing concepts or schemes by either forming a new scheme or changing an existing one. What is this process called?

    a. Adaptation
    b. Assimilation
    c. Equilibration
    d. Accommodation

67. Which statement correctly describes some benefits to young children of the Language Experience Approach (LEA)?

    a. The LEA teaches beginning reading by using printed language apart from students' lives.
    b. With the LEA young students learn to use different words/language than they usually do.
    c. Instruction using the LEA enables the students to interact with text at one level at a time.
    d. Children realize they acquire knowledge and understanding from their own experiences.

68. Which of the following is correct regarding early childhood reading instruction using basal readers?

    a. Texts used for basal readers include children's literature rather than other genres.
    b. Basal reader texts graded by reading level use narrative instead of expository work.
    c. Instruction from smaller to larger skills helps student transitions from part to whole.
    d. Progressing in skills following a rigid, systematic sequence is less helpful to students.

Copyright © Mometrix Media. You have been licensed one copy of this document for personal use only. Any other reproduction or redistribution is strictly prohibited. All rights reserved.

69. Which of these helps young children to decode text in the basal reader approach to reading instruction?

    a. Precise control of word analysis skills
    b. All of these help for decoding of text
    c. Exactly controlling vocabulary items
    d. Included use of enlarged "big books"

70. What statement is accurate regarding the Directed Reading Activity (DRA) instructional practice using basal readers?

    a. Teachers first prepare students to read by introducing new concepts, words, and stimulating motivation.
    b. Before teachers give students motivation, vocabulary, and concepts, students silently do guided reading.
    c. When students are reading silently, teachers do not interfere by presenting any questions or statements.
    d. Student reading comprehension is developed by teacher actions rather than through student discussion.

71. Which best expresses what the Directed Reading-Thinking Activity (DR-TA) is intended to accomplish?

    a. To develop critical thinking through using individual 1:1 instruction
    b. To develop critical reading through teaching group comprehension
    c. To engage children in processing information without any feedback
    d. To engage children only by their asking questions about the reading

72. Which accurately reflects a contrast between the Directed Reading Activity (DRA) and the Directed Reading-Thinking Activity (DR-TA) as methods of reading instruction using basal readers?

    a. DR-TA only works with basal readers but DRA can work for other curriculum plans.
    b. The pre-teaching of new vocabulary is featured in DR-TAs but is absent from DRAs.
    c. DRA requires convergent thinking whereas DR-TA also requires divergent thinking.
    d. DR-TA approaches specify when to teach which skills, but DRA approaches do not.

73. What statement is most accurate about using manipulatives in preschool math instruction?

    a. Young children cannot understand abstract concepts at all.
    b. Young children can only understand solid, concrete objects.
    c. There are no early math curricula to require manipulatives.
    d. Manipulatives are proven to be effective learning devices.

74. Which of the following foundational science skills is best illustrated by an activity comparing non-standard measures, such as using scales to find the weight ratio when comparing apples and grapes.

    a. Observation
    b. Inference
    c. Communication
    d. Classifying

Copyright © Mometrix Media. You have been licensed one copy of this document for personal use only. Any other reproduction or redistribution is strictly prohibited. All rights reserved.

75. Which of the following is true about preschool activities to teach scientific inquiry and discovery?

    a. Exploring the solubility in water of various substances is not a scientific activity.
    b. Seeing what colors result from mixing other colors is strictly an art class activity.
    c. Comparing similarities and contrasting differences in objects are good activities.
    d. For a preschool teacher to create a science center is typically always expensive.

76. What statement is most appropriate regarding how teachers can help preschoolers learn to use scientific inquiry and discovery?

    a. Children learn best from age-appropriate science textbooks.
    b. Teachers can find materials in their everyday environments.
    c. Found objects from the natural world are not good materials.
    d. Teachers should not obtain materials from local businesses.

77. Which of these is accurate regarding physical and motor development in preschoolers?

    a. Preschool children's bodies have higher centers of gravity.
    b. Preschoolers are no more likely to fall than older children.
    c. Preschool teachers should not encourage children to hop.
    d. Balance/coordination exercises have no emotional benefit.

78. Of the following, which is true of teaching preschool children about the visual art element of color?

    a. Teachers cannot use stories or songs to teach children about colors.
    b. Children can learn color names, discrimination, and classification.
    c. There are no art museums that offer lessons for preschool ages.
    d. Preschool children cannot appreciate viewing works of fine art.

79. What can preschool children learn from lessons about the visual art element of line?

    a. This will not help them make better comparisons.
    b. Children's symbol recognition will not be affected.
    c. Children's ability to recognize shapes will develop.
    d. Preschoolers cannot distinguish among line types.

80. What is included in benefits of instructional activities teaching preschoolers about the visual art element of shape?

    a. These are unrelated to concept formation.
    b. Other elements help identify discrepancies.
    c. Creative thinking skills will not be affected.
    d. Early geometric math skills are developed.

81. What is the correct meaning of cognitive dissonance?

    a. A cognitive processing disorder affecting understanding
    b. A disruption of cognition caused by a sensory overload
    c. A feeling of discomfort due to contradictory information
    d. A lack of compatibility between instruction and learning

82. Of the following, which is true about providing affective learning experiences for preschoolers?

    a. Affective learning activities help children express, but not understand, emotions.
    b. Learning to understand their feelings will not help children with self-regulation.
    c. Affective activities cannot inform teachers of children's feelings or preferences.
    d. Children's social development and interactions require emotional development.

Copyright © Mometrix Media. You have been licensed one copy of this document for personal use only. Any other reproduction or redistribution is strictly prohibited. All rights reserved.

83. Giving preschool children an activity using different body postures and movements to portray different emotions can accomplish which of these?

a. Children understand their own emotions but not others'.
b. Children understand emotions, but do not express them.
c. Children participate in physical exercise while having fun.
d. Children use creative thinking without emotional benefit.

84. Which of the following most accurately describes aspects of early childhood social development?

a. Young children tend to use speech more than physical aggression.
b. Young children develop and apply motor skills before verbal skills.
c. Young children know constructive management of strong emotion.
d. Young children learn social skills directly rather than with puppets.

85. How much usable play space at a minimum do experts recommend for indoor and outdoor early childhood learning environments?

a. At least 35 sq. ft. indoors and 75 sq. ft. outdoors
b. At least 25 sq. ft. indoors and 50 sq. ft. outdoors
c. At least 50 sq. ft. indoors and 100 sq. ft. outside
d. At least 45 sq. ft. indoors and 85 sq. ft. outdoors

86. Which of these is correct regarding expert guidelines for indoor and outdoor spaces in EC learning environments?

a. Children's products and other visual elements should be put at adult eye level.
b. Spaces should be arranged for individual, small-group, and large-group activity.
c. Spaces should be organized to prohibit children from moving among activities.
d. Spaces should be arranged so children are not distracted by social interactions.

87. Of the following, which is correct about considerations in arranging indoor learning environments to fit with curriculum planning for toddlers and preschoolers?

a. Rooms should be arranged to limit activities to certain areas.
b. The floors in all the rooms should be covered with carpeting.
c. The rooms should be organized to enable different activities.
d. Math and science activities should be in one classroom area.

88. A teacher tells a class that anybody who gets 100 percent on the next quiz will be excused from doing homework for that day. According to behaviorist terminology relative to motivation theory, this incentive is an example of what technique?

a. Positive reinforcement
b. Primary reinforcement
c. Negative reinforcement
d. Secondary reinforcement

89. In indoor EC learning environments, which of the following is most related to providing for children's privacy needs?

a. Adult laps for cuddling
b. Pillows and soft upholstery
c. Areas of floor with thick carpets
d. Small inner rooms and partitions

Copyright © Mometrix Media. You have been licensed one copy of this document for personal use only. Any other reproduction or redistribution is strictly prohibited. All rights reserved.

90. Which statement is true regarding principles of early childhood behavior management?

- a. Punishing bad behaviors is more powerful.
- b. Punishments and rewards work equally well.
- c. Rewarding good behaviors is more powerful.
- d. Rewarding good behaviors should be occasional.

91. When considering behavior management with young children, which of these is most accurate?

- a. Behaviors can be replaced regardless of their function.
- b. To change a behavior, one must first know its function.
- c. Behaviors need no change if one knows their functions.
- d. The same consequences are applied for every function.

92. According to the provisions of FERPA, when can schools furnish student records without consent?

- a. To some doing studies, if on behalf of the school.
- b. Court orders and legal subpoenas are insufficient.
- c. Safety or health emergencies still require consent.
- d. To juvenile justice system authorities in all states.

93. How are teachers required to ensure educational equity?

- a. By delivering uniform instruction to all students
- b. By offering different opportunities to students
- c. By treating students less fairly if they deserve it
- d. By using materials reflecting multicultural views

94. What is the meaning of the "10:1 Rule" relative to early childhood behavior management?

- a. For every 10 negative comments/corrections, give 1 positive comment.
- b. For every 1 positive comment, give 10 negative comments/corrections.
- c. For every 1 new behavior to be learned, 10 repetitions are necessary.
- d. For every 1 negative comment/correction, give 10 positive comments.

95. Which statement is correct about managing young children's typical behaviors in care and educational settings?

- a. Adults do not need to do anything if children follow the rules.
- b. Withholding rewards for noncompliance needs no explanation.
- c. Once adults have stated rules, they need not constantly repeat.
- d. Children should be consistently rewarded for following the rules.

96. What applies for EC educators to include children's families in their educations?

- a. The family use of parenting skills is none of the educators' business.
- b. One-way educator communication to families periodically is enough.
- c. Educators should acknowledge parents' integral role in child learning.
- d. School staff should make parents feel welcome but not ask their help.

97. Which of these is most appropriate to EC educators for involving diverse families in children's educations?

- a. When educators design IFSPs for preschoolers, it is unnecessary to involve the family.
- b. Educators should ask families to develop their own goals for educational participation.
- c. Educators should create volunteer calendars and assign parents times for participating.
- d. It is not the educators' problem if families have difficulty with printed/written English.

Copyright © Mometrix Media. You have been licensed one copy of this document for personal use only. Any other reproduction or redistribution is strictly prohibited. All rights reserved.

98. Which of these should EC educators communicate to diverse families of the children they instruct?

    a. Information about their child instead of developmental milestones
    b. Information about developmental milestones rather than methods
    c. Information about development and methods for nurturing growth
    d. Information about class content but not developmental milestones

99. For teachers to make informal assessments of pre-K classes, which of these would apply?

    a. Teachers assess during small-group rather than whole-class activities.
    b. Teachers only make assessments during activities for the whole class.
    c. Teachers can organize assessments by using around ten themes a day.
    d. Teachers make classroom observations each targeting different skills.

100. Which of these is accurate concerning formal assessment instruments used in early childhood education?

    a. Formal assessment instruments cannot prevent administrator bias.
    b. Formal assessment instruments record more than child responses.
    c. Formal assessment data should not be compared by ages or levels.
    d. Formal assessments are typically standardized tests given to groups.

101. In his social learning theory, what does Bandura mean by reciprocal determinism?

    a. Learning mutually involves both the learner and the instructor.
    b. Learning mutually involves both the behavior and environment.
    c. Learning mutually involves both the individual and environment.
    d. Learning mutually involves individual, behavior, and environment.

102. What is accurate about different screening and assessment instruments used in EC education programs?

    a. All these instruments measure the same developmental domains.
    b. These instruments are all meant for use with the same applications.
    c. Not all of these are appropriate with ethnically diverse populations.
    d. The same methods of administration are used with all instruments.

103. Which statement is true about different screening and assessment instruments that can be used by educational programs for testing young children?

    a. These instruments are all comprehensive in assessing multiple domains.
    b. There are some instruments focusing on only one facet within a domain.
    c. Some instruments focus on a single domain but not on parts of domains.
    d. Tests measure developmental domains but not risk or resiliency factors.

104. Of the following, what is most accurate regarding ECE applications of screening and assessment instruments?

    a. Assessment instruments are used in planning curriculum and treatment programs.
    b. Screening instruments are routinely used for diagnosing developmental problems.
    c. It is inappropriate to use assessment instruments to develop or confirm diagnoses.
    d. ECE programs never use assessment instruments in determining a child's eligibility.

Copyright © Mometrix Media. You have been licensed one copy of this document for personal use only. Any other reproduction or redistribution is strictly prohibited. All rights reserved.

105. What is an accurate statement about selecting screening and assessment instruments according to the age ranges they cover for use in ECE programs?

- a. Tests covering the entire age range served in a program are less useful because they are not age-specific.
- b. Tests covering the entire age range served in a program can be used in mid-program to monitor progress.
- c. Tests that are separate and specific to different ages make it easier to compare before and after programs.
- d. Tests that cover the whole range of ages served in the program are not as accurate for all of the child ages.

106. Regarding paper-and-pencil reports for adults to provide screening and assessment of young children, which of these best reflects their characteristics?

- a. Such reports must be self-administered at respondents' reading levels in their native languages.
- b. These surveys or questionnaires must not be read to respondents even by trained interviewers.
- c. Self-reporting instruments have the advantage that they usually take shorter times to complete.
- d. ECE program personnel need relatively little training to administer, score, and interpret reports.

107. Adult interviews used to gather screening/assessment information about infants and young children:

- a. Are conducted in structured formats with assigned questions.
- b. Are in semi-structured formats using administrator judgment.
- c. Cover only the child's identified areas of strengths and needs.
- d. Are brief but usually still longer than self-reporting measures.

108. Which of the following screening and assessment methods yield the most comprehensive information for determining EC diagnoses and/or developing individualized plans for EC care or instruction?

- a. Self-reporting questionnaires/surveys
- b. Formal or informal observational tools
- c. Structured/semi-structured interviews
- d. Instruments that use multiple methods

109. Which of these is a correct definition of test-retest reliability?

- a. An instrument gives the same results for the same child at the same time and setting, by different persons.
- b. An instrument's individual items correlate highly with one another and with the overall instrument's score.
- c. An instrument includes individual items that cover the entire range of the content area that it claims to test.
- d. An instrument gets the same results when given twice or more to the same child within a short time period.

110. Of the following, which defines internal consistency in EC screening and assessment instruments?

- a. Two children score beyond a test's cutoff for assessment need, via different test items.
- b. A test's individual items are found to have low correlations with the test's overall score.
- c. Two children score past a test's cutoff for assessment need on most of the same items.
- d. The individual questions on a test are found to have low correlations with one another.

Copyright © Mometrix Media. You have been licensed one copy of this document for personal use only. Any other reproduction or redistribution is strictly prohibited. All rights reserved.

111. Which of these would apply to a test of EC social-emotional development with high content validity?

    a. A screening test screens for a child's interactions with caregivers and not those with the child's peers.

    b. A child's performance on the test can be used to generalize about how it predicts real-life functioning.

    c. A screening test screens for a child's social skills and does not screen for his/her communication skills.

    d. A screening test screens for a child's levels of attention and does not screen for his/her initiating play.

112. What is correct regarding predictive validity, sensitivity, specificity, and false-positive and false-negative errors in screening and assessment instruments used with preschool children?

    a. A screening tool identifies a potential mental health disorder which a complete evaluation then diagnoses.

    b. An instrument correctly identifying 6 of 10 children with disorders/delays is said to have a specificity of 60%.

    c. An instrument correctly identifying 8 of 10 children as not having disorders/delays shows sensitivity of 80%.

    d. A screening tool identifying delays or disorders in children where none exists contains false-negative errors.

113. How can assessment results be applied to instructional planning for ECE groups and individual children?

    a. If EC educators record careful anecdotal observations and authentic assessments, outlines are not necessary.

    b. Making organized outlines of developmental guidelines gives bases for anecdotal and authentic assessments.

    c. The extensive practice and review needed for young children to retain skills are outside of ECE program scope.

    d. Developmental sequences are irrelevant to systems that ECE programs utilize for tracking children's progress.

114. In a hypothetical scenario, an EC teacher sees injuries to a child in her class. She also has observed that this child's mother has a new boyfriend; behaves fearfully; and is evasive with the teacher's questions. Then the child tells this teacher that this new boyfriend hurt the child. Which description of the teacher's response would best meet legal responsibilities for a professional in the ECE setting?

    a. The teacher feels sorry for the mother and her situation and does not report suspicions she cannot prove.

    b. The teacher knows the mother depends on the boyfriend financially and emotionally and does not report.

    c. The teacher reports her suspicions because the law requiring it was made to stop violence against children.

    d. The teacher reports her suspicions regardless because the law requires it and penalizes her for not doing it.

Copyright © Mometrix Media. You have been licensed one copy of this document for personal use only. Any other reproduction or redistribution is strictly prohibited. All rights reserved.

115. Which of the following best reflects actions that enable and support positive interactions among adults within ECE settings?

    a.   EC educators should respect student privacy by not sharing anecdotal records and observations with colleagues.

    b.   Communicating to other adults about children and families is not positive interaction because of confidentiality.

    c.   EC educators should share their observations and records on students, but should not plan instruction together.

    d.   EC educators use problem-solving activities and dialogues to discern how to enhance child learning experiences.

116. Among the following, which is correct regarding legal regulations of records confidentiality in ECE settings?

    a.   The FERPA mandates student records confidentiality for every ECE program/facility/agency existing in the USA.

    b.   The special education laws of each U.S. state supersede the IDEA for confidentiality of disabled student records.

    c.   Laws penalize ECE employees for releasing records but require them to report suspected child abuse or neglect.

    d.   Laws require ECE employees to report suspected abuse/neglect and prevent liability for related records release.

117. What is true about guidelines for ECE personnel regarding medications administered to children in EC care and education settings?

    a.   ECE centers/programs should write their own policies and procedures, regardless of state licensing requirements.

    b.   ECE experts find it unnecessary for centers to require doctor and parent permission for giving medication to children.

    c.   If written parent consent to give medication is kept on file, separate charts for staff are redundant and enable errors.

    d.   Staff should label all medications by drug name, child name, doctor name and contact information, and instructions.

118. What is recommended for ECE settings regarding emergency first aid and medical treatment?

    a.   Written parental consent is unnecessary in real emergencies.

    b.   Centers need not file parental doctor or hospital preferences.

    c.   Information on family health insurance should be kept on file.

    d.   Notifying parents of emergencies is desired but not required.

119. Which of these accurately represents child custody issues affecting ECE facilities and types of custody?

    a.   Legal custody is an individual/agency's right and responsibility to give a child immediate care and housing.

    b.   One issue that affects ECE facilities is when state authorities have removed a child from parental custody.

    c.   Two parents' pursuing custody of a child but not living together will not have any impact on ECE facilities.

    d.   Physical custody is an individual/agency's right to decide for a child on housing, education, and medicine.

Copyright © Mometrix Media. You have been licensed one copy of this document for personal use only. Any other reproduction or redistribution is strictly prohibited. All rights reserved.

120. Of the following, which reflects recommend procedures for ECE facilities if non-custodial or non-authorized adults try to pick up children served at a facility?

    a. ECE administrators should inform unauthorized adults of policies and procedures, including custodial court orders.

    b. If an unauthorized adult refuses to leave, threatens/shows violence, or makes a scene, police should not be called.

    c. After an unauthorized adult leaves, the administrator must notify enrolling adults but need not file written reports.

    d. After an unauthorized adult leaves, the administrator must meet with the custodial adult without filing documents.

Copyright © Mometrix Media. You have been licensed one copy of this document for personal use only. Any other reproduction or redistribution is strictly prohibited. All rights reserved.

Answer Key and Explanations

1. C: The libido is part of the id according to Freud. It represents psychic energy as well as sex drive. Freud's three major personality structures are the id (A), which generates unconscious impulses; the ego (B), which realistically regulates acting on id impulses; and the superego (C), which morally regulates the id and ego.

2. D: Researchers advise EC teachers to ask children more open-ended questions, the kind that allow the children and the teacher to give two- and three-way responses in conversations, rather than the more common but less desirable practice of asking linear questions that demand one-way responses (A). They also criticize teachers' tendency to do most of the talking (B) in classrooms rather than encouraging children to use conversational language, which is preferable. Experts advise teachers not to focus only on the quantity of conversations (C), but equally on their quality.

3. A: Assimilation is fitting a new experience into an existing schema. Accommodation is altering an existing schema or forming a new schema to accommodate a new experience. These two processes are part of the overall process of adaptation, i.e. adjusting one's thinking to the environment via interacting with it. This adaptation process helps the individual to maintain equilibrium, or balance.

4. B: Schemata (plural of schema) are mental constructs or concepts of categories or classes of things, e.g. things I can suck on; things I can throw; furry four-legged animals, etc. They are not concepts of individual objects (A). They are not programs only for motor actions (C), but ideas for categorizing different components of the environment. Inborn reflexes are not governed by ideas (D) but are automatic reactions.

5. C: Object permanence, which babies develop during Piaget's first, Sensorimotor stage of cognitive development, is the realization that objects still exist even when they are out of sight. (A) is the opposite of this. The other choices are not related to the concept of object permanence.

6. D: Piaget theorized that children begin to use symbols to represent other things around the ages of 18-24 months. This is evident in their pretend play, when they might use a broom to represent a horse or a guitar, or a block to represent a phone; and pretend to be adults when playing "House," etc. Children are not observed to use symbols this way during the age ranges of (A), (B), or (C); and not doing so until later than 24 months would represent a cognitive developmental delay.

7. D: This is an example of assimilation. The toddler has a schema (concept) of large, brown, four-legged, furry animals as being cows. Seeing a large, brown, four-legged, furry dog, s/he fits it into the cow schema. When the child forms a new schema for dogs to include the different animal s/he saw, this would be an example of accommodation (C). Egocentrism (A) is Piaget's term for young children's inability to see things from another person's perspective, including from their physical position in space. Equilibrium (B) is the balance Piaget said children maintain through adaptation, the process of adjusting to the environment via assimilation and accommodation.

8. D: Piaget used the term *conservation* to mean the ability children develop in the stage of Concrete Operations to conserve the concept of the same quantity regardless of changes in appearance, shape, or arrangement. He did not use this term to refer to conserving natural resources (A) or retaining memories of quantities (B). (C) describes what Piaget termed object permanence.

9. D: The most specific description of this in Piaget's terms is magical thinking. Animism (A) is his term for ascribing human qualities to inanimate objects. Centration (B) is his term for focusing or centering on one quality of something, e.g. the height but not the width of a container. Egocentrism (C) is the

188

Copyright © Mometrix Media. You have been licensed one copy of this document for personal use only. Any other reproduction or redistribution is strictly prohibited. All rights reserved.

inability to see others' perspectives. Egocentrism also applies to viewing everything as revolving around oneself, of which magical thinking and animism are more specific phenomena.

10. C: Preoperational children centrate, or focus, on one attribute of an object to the exclusion of others. Thus they think, for example, that a tall, thin beaker contains more fluid than a short, wide one when both contain the same amount. Later, children achieve decentration (D), allowing them to include more than one attribute. Hence they are capable of conservation (B), the knowledge that the amount is the same despite different appearances or shapes. Children develop inductive logic (A), i.e. generalizing from specific events, in Piaget's stage of Concrete Operations, along with decentration and conservation.

11. B: During the Preschematic stage, around the ages of 4-6 years, children begin to develop a visual schema. In the Scribble (A) stage, which precedes the Preschematic, children first make uncontrolled scribbles; then controlled scribbles; and then name what their scribbles represent. In the Schematic (C) stage, around 7-9 years of age, following the Preschematic, children draw pictures more accurately reflective of real physical proportions, body parts, features, and colors. In the stage of Dawning Realism (D), around the ages of 9-11 years, children make increasingly representational drawings.

12. A: Young children must have concrete things they can see, touch, and manipulate. They are not yet cognitively capable of manipulating information mentally (B). They are not yet able to memorize math processes by rote (C), as older elementary-age children can memorize times tables, etc. They are too young to benefit from "sit still and listen" types of lessons (D).

13. B: Children to three developmental periods in language and communication. The first is using crying and eye contact for expressive behaviors from birth to six months. The second period, from 6-18 months, involves intentional communication. The third period is typically from the age of 18 months on, involving the use of language as the primary method of communicating.

14. C: Typically, a two-year-old's language development includes correctly using at least two pronouns (e.g. *me* and *you*). Using three-word sentences with ease (A), knowing and naming the major body parts (B), and using three pronouns correctly (D) in speech are characteristics typical of a three-year-old's language development.

15. D: The toddler years are typically when children begin to express their opinions, likes and dislikes as well as their feelings and ideas; and to ask questions. The early preschool years are typically when children are able to describe unseen objects (A), tell "make-believe" stories (B), and speak in complete sentences (C).

16. D: It is easier for adults to find out what young children understand about abstract concepts during one to one conversations than in group conversations. At preschools, adults should engage each child in one on one conversations at times like when children arrive and leave; during center time; and during shared reading activities with 1-2 children rather than during whole-group activities (A). 1:1 conversations enable adults to reinforce what children say by repeating it better in one on one than in group discussions (B). Adults also have *more* chance to extend what children say by adding to it in 1:1 conversations (C); and to restate what children say so they hear their own ideas reflected back to them one on one than in group conversations.

17. D: To deepen young children's comprehension of word meanings, teachers should provide them with multiple definitions and examples for each word rather than only one (A). They should introduce new concepts together with new vocabulary words (B) associated with the concepts. They should provide additional information to give children's comprehension of meanings more depth (C).

18. C: It is true that one benefit of children's storytelling is that it allows them to engage and exercise their imaginations. When young children tell stories and need a vocabulary word they do not know, their teachers *should* supply them with the word (A). Teachers *should* also ask children questions (B)

Copyright © Mometrix Media. You have been licensed one copy of this document for personal use only. Any other reproduction or redistribution is strictly prohibited. All rights reserved.

about their storytelling to model correct sentence structure and get children to elaborate on what they say. Teachers should not only let children express their ideas through storytelling; they should also build further upon these ideas (D) by asking them guiding questions to elicit more information.

19. B: Most children typically understand common antonyms around the age of five years. At three years (A), they understand simple questions and can answer what to do when they are hot or cold, hungry or thirsty, etc., but will not necessarily understand opposites. At two years (C), children typically can respond to some questions or directions, like "Where are your ears?" or "Show me your eyes," but cannot yet contrast opposing qualities. At four years (D), children can understand simple comparatives like "bigger" and "smaller" when given things of contrasting sizes, but do not necessarily have a consistent understanding of various common antonyms. By six years, children should have already achieved this understanding and been applying it in their speech for about a year.

20. A: Brown's "operations of reference" in Stage I sentence types include nomination (e.g. "this truck"), recurrence (e.g. "more juice"), and negation, which includes denial (e.g. "no drink"), rejection (e.g. "no more"), and nonexistence (e.g. "doggie go"). Actions (B), agents (C), entities (D), and objects are all classified under "semantic relations" and used in pairs, e.g. action + agent, action + object, agent + object, action + locative, entity + locative, possessor + object/possession, and demonstrative + entity.

21. A: Brown designated Stage I as typical of children 12 to 26 months old. 15-30 months (B) and 24-36 months (C) are not age ranges used by Brown for the developmental stages he defined. 27-30 months (D) is the age range Brown designated as associated with his Stage II of language development. 31-34 months is the age range Brown associated with his Stage III of language development.

22. C: Brown (1973) categorized correct use of irregular past tenses of verbs in his Stage III, associated with the age range of 36-42 months. Stage I (A) is associated with Stage I Sentence Types (Operations of Reference subtypes and Semantic Relations subtypes). Stage II (B) is associated with using the present progressive verb tense, regular –s plural endings, and the prepositions *in* and *on*. Stage IV (D) is associated with using articles, regular past tenses, and regular present tenses in the third person. Stage V is associated with using third-person irregular verbs, the uncontactable auxiliary form of "to be", the contractible copula form of "to be", and the contractible auxiliary form of "to be".

23. D: Brown classified use of the regular plural –s ending in his Stage II of Syntactical and Morphological Development. He defined his Stage V (A) with more advanced usages, like third-person irregular verbs and the uncontactable and contractible auxiliary and contractible copula forms of "to be". He identified his Stage IV (B) as using regular past tense, regular third-person present tense, and articles. He defined his Stage III (C) as using irregular past tense, possessive ('s) endings, and the uncontactable copula form of "to be". He associated his Stage I with use of the Stage I Sentence Types characterized by short utterances, usually 1 to 2 morphemes total and lacking usage of possessives and structured morphology.

24. D: By "private speech", Vygotsky meant the way that young children typically verbalize aloud to themselves while engaging in solitary activities. This helps them to think through their actions; make decisions; solve problems; and strengthen their knowledge of the correct sequences in activities with multiple steps. In using the term "private speech," Vygotsky was not referring to a private conversation with another child (A) or an adult (B); or silent mental speech (C)—which Vygotsky termed "inner speech." He said that children eventually internalized their external private speech: it progressed from overtly speaking aloud to oneself, to mentally speaking silently to oneself. Both private and inner speech serve the same functions at different ages.

25. C: Central auditory processing disorder is categorized as an auditory disability because it impairs the ability to understand spoken language received through the auditory sense (hearing). But it does not involve the outer, middle, or inner ear or auditory nerves. It involves a deficit in the brain's ability to

Copyright © Mometrix Media. You have been licensed one copy of this document for personal use only. Any other reproduction or redistribution is strictly prohibited. All rights reserved.

interpret the meanings and structures of speech sounds. Sensorineural hearing loss (A) involves the cochlea in the inner ear and/or auditory nerves leading to the brain. Conductive hearing loss (B) involves the outer and/or middle ear, where something obstructs conduction of sound, e.g., a deformed pinna/auricle, wax buildup, a closed or malformed or ear canal, fluid/pus buildup in the middle ear due to otitis media (middle ear infection), otosclerosis immobilizing the ossicles in the middle ear, etc. Complete deafness (D) most typically involves total sensorineural hearing loss.

26. C: Teachers can ask children at younger ages of early childhood to identify vocabulary words used in shared readings, e.g. "What was this called?"; and describe story details , e.g. "How did they do that?" Asking children to predict coming events in a story (A), to imagine applications of story situations beyond the story (B), and to conclude why story characters act/feel as they do (D) are all appropriate techniques to use during and after shared readings with children at older ages of early childhood. These elements of literature may be too abstract with the younger ages of early childhood.

27. A: Elements of critical thinking include distinguishing fact from opinion (C) in text or speech by looking for objectivity, facts, and proof vs. subjectivity, non-factual information, and absence of proof; finding evidence or no evidence (D) to support the writer or speaker's arguments by examining the text or speech; evaluating evidence used to support (A) arguments or statements by considering whether its source is reputable, proven, and accepted by authorities in the field; and judging the quality of material (B) or information by comparing it to other material/information, consulting one's own previous experience, and listening to one's own intuition.

28. A: Teachers should keep from confusing young children by introducing letters to them that have similar sounds in separate lessons. They should introduce continuous consonant sounds (f, r, s, m, n), which are easier to produce in isolation with less distortion, before they teach consonant sounds that are stops (p, b, t, d, k, g), which are more difficult for young children to produce, not vice versa (B). Letters with similar appearances should be presented during separate lessons, not the same one (C), also to prevent confusion. Teachers should introduce high-utility letters/sounds first, not low-utility (D), as the high-utility ones are those they will hear, see, and use most often.

29. A: Teachers can obtain a good assessment of the level of print awareness a young child has developed by using a storybook; hence (B) is incorrect. The teacher should first ask a young child to identify the front, back, spine, and title of the book; this is not unnecessary (C) because some children with undeveloped/less developed print awareness may not know these things, as well as where to start reading a book. Teachers should also ask children to point out a letter and a word in the book, and the first and last words in a sentence in the book, which does inform the assessment (D) by indicating whether they know how letters are combined to form words and words are arranged into sentences in books, and how they are separated by punctuation and spaces. They should also ask children to identify punctuation marks, uppercase letters, and lowercase letters. Teachers should not only praise children's correct responses; they should also correct wrong responses and review the corrections.

30. B: Typically, between birth and the age of two years, children grow to four times their newborn weights. This is the most rapid period of physical growth. After this, children's growth slows incrementally, decreasing between two and three years and decreasing even more between four and six years.

31. C: By the age of two years, children's brains have typically grown to 55% of their adult size. Their brains do not reach 90% (A) of adult size until they are around six years old. Their brains grow to 75% (B) of their adult sizes between the ages of approximately four and five years. Children's brains are 33% (E) and 40% (D) of their adult sizes before the age of two years.

32. C: The development of children's motor skills involves both learning new physical movements (C), and integrating previously learned motor movements into continuous, smooth patterns of combined

Copyright © Mometrix Media. You have been licensed one copy of this document for personal use only. Any other reproduction or redistribution is strictly prohibited. All rights reserved.

motions, as with learning to throw a ball with skill. Proprioception, i.e. knowing the size, shape, and position of their body parts and of their bodies in space and relative to other objects, progresses from infancy to become more accurate by preschool ages (A). Newborn motor movements are largely reflexive and progress to become voluntary movements by preschool years rather than vice versa (B). (D) is incorrect because there are several limiting factors in motor development, including coordination, muscular strength, and bone strength. As young children develop motor skills, each of these three categories are strengthened with time.

33. D: Researchers have observed consistent gender differences in preschool physical and motor development; however, they also observe that in spite of these differences, overall the physical and motor development of preschoolers is more similar than different between genders. In general, the differences are not significant enough to place any emphasis on motor development differences between preschool boys and girls. Some known differences, however, include that preschool boys are more muscular than preschool girls, but preschool girls are more physically mature than preschool boys (A). While preschool boys exhibit more strength in large-muscle, gross-motor skills, preschool girls exhibit more coordination in large-muscle, gross-motor skills (B and C). Additionally, preschool girls are superior to preschool boys in fine-motor skills as well as gross-motor coordination (C).

34. D: Psychologists studying infant behaviors have classified their basic temperaments into Easy, Difficult, and Slow to Warm Up. They find that the majority of babies have the Easy temperament. Thus (A) is incorrect, and babies with Difficult temperaments are not in the majority (B); neither are Slow to Warm Up types (C).

35. D: When a person attributes his/her success to internal attributes, like hard work or intelligence, psychologist Julian Rotter named this internal locus of control. He described external locus of control as attributing one's success to external factors outside of one's control, like getting help from the teacher (A) or a classmate/friend (C); or luck (B); or other factors, such as other peoples' efforts. Internal and external loci of control apply to people's attribution of causes for failures as well as successes.

36. C: Children with primarily visual learning styles focus on appearances and what they can see. They can understand and learn abstract concepts and relationships best when they are given visual stimuli like multicolor graphics, pictures, colorful objects, and other visual illustrations. Sculpting soft clay (A) would help a child who has a primarily haptic or tactile learning style, focusing on textures and movements. Dance movements (B) and sporting activities (D) are also stimuli that would help children with haptic learning styles to understand and learn abstract concepts and relationships. A primarily auditory learning style could be targeted with musical recordings, which can help a child to understand and learn abstract relationships and concepts.

37. B: Erikson saw infancy revolving around the nuclear conflict of Basic Trust vs. Mistrust. If a baby's needs are met, e.g. being fed timely, adequately, and consistently, s/he develops basic trust; if not, s/he develops basic mistrust. Autonomy vs. Shame (B) and Self-Doubt is Erikson's second stage, around the ages of 2-3 years. Children learn to walk and are toilet-trained, developing physical control. They feel autonomy/ independence through succeeding, and shame and self-doubt through failing. Initiative vs. Guilt (C) is Erikson's third stage, associated with the preschool years, around 3-5 years old. Children explore their environments, exercising power over them. Success results in a sense of purpose, disapproval for wielding excessive power in guilt. Industry vs. Inferiority (D) is Erikson's fourth stage during elementary school ages, around 6-11 years. Children adjust to new academic and social requirements. Success results in a sense of competence, failure in a sense of inferiority. Intimacy vs. Isolation is Erikson's sixth stage during young adulthood (the fifth is Identify vs. Role Confusion during adolescence).

38. A: The fact that most children are around six years old when they enter first grade is not a coincidence. This is the age when they are first able to stay in their seats, be quiet, and attend to a lesson

Copyright © Mometrix Media. You have been licensed one copy of this document for personal use only. Any other reproduction or redistribution is strictly prohibited. All rights reserved.

without getting up and running around, shouting out on impulse, and/or having their attention wander. Thus the expectations of first-graders are normally appropriate for most six-year-olds. However, kindergarten classes feature activities with shorter time spans and more physical activity to suit five-year-old developmental levels, so (B) is inappropriate. Similarly, toddlers have not yet developed steady gaits and cannot be expected to balance or hop on one foot (C). Babies younger than about five months cannot be expected to sit up unsupported (D) as they have not developed the strength to do so.

39. B: Adler observed that only children are likely to prefer the company of adults over that of children as their early experiences are with parents rather than siblings. Therefore, (A) is incorrect. Adler also found that only children have more difficulty sharing things with other children rather than finding it easier (C) because they have not had to share with siblings. He stated that older/oldest children may develop strict or authoritarian attitudes and behaviors (D) through feeling power over younger siblings; and that with encouragement, older/oldest children can develop helpful attitudes and behaviors.

40. C: One of the characteristics Adler described about the youngest siblings in families is that being the smallest, they often wish to be bigger than their older siblings; so as they grow, they may make grandiose plans which never succeed. Adler found that while youngest children, unlike only children, have multiple older siblings who "parent" them, they also have in common with only children (A) the fact that they are never displaced ("dethroned") by younger siblings. Adler observed that one twin is usually more active or stronger than the other and perceived by parents as older; and that the twin born a minute or more earlier may be perceived by the parents as more mature (B). Adler noted that one twin may develop a leadership role while the other may develop identity issues (D). Adler also commented that while some "babies" of the family may grow out of this role, others continue to feel and behave as the baby of the family indefinitely.

41. D: Adler observed that the boy siblings of the only girl in a family can behave overprotectively toward her, and that the only girl may go to more effort to please the father. He believed that an only boy among girl siblings was equally likely to behave effeminately to fit in with them, or to exhibit overly masculine behaviors to differentiate himself as the "man of the family" (A). Similarly, Adler believed that an only girl among boy siblings was equally likely to identify with her brothers by becoming a tomboy, or to adopt extremely feminine behaviors to differentiate herself from them (B). Adler believed parents of all boys or girls who wanted a child of the other sex might dress one child as the opposite sex (C); and that this child was equally likely either to object strongly to such a role reassignment, or to take advantage of it.

42. D: Bowen described how the parents' perception of a child can become self-fulfilling prophecies by influencing the child's self-image. For example, a child may not initially be helpless or dependent , but if the parents perceive and thus treat the child that way by helping her/him too much, the child can actually become helpless and dependent. Thus the child's self-image and behaviors come to mirror the parents' perceptions rather than vice versa (C). This process reflects parental fears that something is wrong with a child, not that there really is (A). The parents find the child's behavior to confirm their fears because they perceive the behavior through the distorting lens of their own anxiety, not because something is really wrong with the child's behavior (B). Bowen stated that the more intense this process is, the more the child develops relationship sensitivities beyond those of the parents.

43. D: Most children with typical development receive nourishment from mother's milk or infant formula during infancy, and then from baby foods until their teeth erupt. By the age of two years, young children eat most of the same foods that adults eat. Their nutritional needs at this age are similar to those of adults, though they eat smaller quantities of food. To begin eating the same foods as adults only by the age of three (C), four (B), or five (A) years is not developmentally typical.

44. C: At the ages of 2-5 years, young children typically need about 10-12 hours of sleep per 24 hours. They typically need 9-11 hours of sleep (A) at the ages of 5-7 years. Sleeping 7-9 hours (B) is generally inadequate during early childhood. While some young children sleep fewer nighttime hours and need long daytime naps (D) at the ages of 2-5 years, other children these ages need long, uninterrupted sleep at night but rarely take naps. This varies among individual children rather than one or the other being the rule for all young children.

45. B: Young children have short attention spans and tend to be impatient, so they are unlikely to wash their hands long enough or thoroughly enough. Parents and teachers must encourage them to do so by, for example, teaching them to sing "Happy Birthday" or songs/verses of similar duration while washing their hands, which makes it more fun while assuring they wash them for long enough times. A major transition of early childhood is that while parents washed their infants' hands for them, children learn to wash their own hands during toddlerhood and preschool years rather than parents continuing to do it for them (A). During the toilet-training process, toddlers get many more germs on their hands (C). Young children are also exposed to more unfamiliar germs in daycare and preschool (D).

46. A: Social psychologist Albert Bandura has proven that when children viewed videos with violent content, their aggressive behaviors increased. Hence adults must monitor and control what young children view. Intense and/or violent video content can frighten young children who cognitively cannot yet distinguish fantasy from reality In leisure activities, numerous studies show that children get more cognitive stimulation from interactive games, arts and crafts, music, puzzles, storytelling, and other activities than from watching TV for long time periods (B). In larger families, researchers find it is important for each individual child to have some 1:1 time with each parent, even during unstructured activities, rather than only interacting groups (C). Parents should encourage, not discourage children in playing "house", "dress-up", "auto shop", etc. as make-believe play is a significant developmental hallmark wherein children understand and use symbols (D), enabling them to learn to read and write the print language that symbolizes spoken language.

47. B: Research studies find that both Asian and Latin American cultures are more collectivist and interdependent than American and European cultures. American culture is found to be the most independent and individualistic, hence the *least* interdependent (A). European cultures are in the middle between the two extremes: they are *less* individualistic than in America (C), but also *less* collectivistic than Asian cultures (D).

48. C: Data collected from 2003 show that more than 15% of African-American families had violent conflicts; over 11% of Latino families did; and fewer than 9% of White families did. While researchers concede that cultural and demographic variables can influence styles of disagreement in families, they find parental stress the strongest influence on whether family conflicts become violent (A). The National Survey of Child and Adolescent Well-Being found that children of socioeconomically disadvantaged families have more developmental and behavioral problems than in other groups (B). However, these children were also less likely to receive help with their problems (D). For example, more than 40% of toddlers and more than 68% of preschoolers in contact with the child welfare system had high levels of developmental and behavioral needs; yet fewer than 23% of these children were receiving services to address those needs.

49. D: The National Survey on Early Childhood Health recently did find significant differences in parenting practices, as well as in home routines and home safety measures, of Latino and African-American families (A). The researchers associate these differences with different degrees of positive early childhood development (B). Researchers also believe that disparities among racial and ethnic groups in children's school readiness and ensuing school achievement may contribute to discrimination by teachers and other educational personnel against minority racial and ethnic groups (C). This survey found American minority children to have lower average school readiness than American white children. Moreover, most of these differences in school readiness are also associated with family income differences.

Copyright © Mometrix Media. You have been licensed one copy of this document for personal use only. Any other reproduction or redistribution is strictly prohibited. All rights reserved.

50. D: Freud's theory was that babies are in the first, Oral stage of development: because nursing is a primary need and activity, their attention is orally focused; they put everything in their mouths to explore and learn about the environment. In applying this theory, adults accept object-mouthing by babies; they prevent access to dangerous/unsanitary objects, providing safe and sanitary things they can mouth. Providing opportunities to "make believe" (A) reflects application of Piaget's theory of cognitive development, wherein children in his second, Preoperational stage develop symbolic representation. Modeling behaviors children can observe and imitate (B) reflects application of Bandura's Social Learning Theory, wherein children learn by seeing and imitating others' behaviors. Providing timely, consistent nursing/feeding to a baby (C) reflects application of Erikson's psychosocial theory: in his first, Basic Trust vs. Mistrust stage, babies develop trust when fed regularly, enough, and in time; or mistrust when feeding is late/irregular/inadequate.

51. D: Piaget's first stage is Sensorimotor, when infants learn about the world by receiving sensory input and engaging in motor activities to interact with the environment. Adults can apply knowledge of this stage by giving them a variety of toys babies can manipulate, and which spin, twirl, roll, bounce, fly, make noises, etc. and engage all of the sensory modalities. Introducing topics from others' perspectives (A) will not appeal to children this age, who are cognitively unable to understand others' points of view. Encouraging make-believe/pretend play (B) is inappropriate to this stage as children have not yet developed the ability to understand or use symbols. They are also not unable to understand logical operations like arithmetic (C). Adults understanding this stage should also not punish repeated throwing of objects out of the crib, a normal part of the learning process wherein babies observe what reactions their actions elicit, making cause-and-effect connections.

52. C: Piaget defined one characteristic of preschoolers' Preoperational thinking as animism, i.e. assigning human qualities to inanimate objects. Preoperational children do not yet think logically (A). Magical thinking (B), another characteristic Piaget defined of Preoperational children, means believing that one's thoughts or words cause external events to occur. Egocentric thinking (D), another Preoperational characteristic, means seeing things only from one's own viewpoint but not others'.

53. B: Cognition was not one of the conditions Albert Bandura has specified as requisite for learning in his theory. Bandura specified that first one must pay Attention (A) to another person's behavior in order to observe it, and also to observe reinforcement the other person may receive for performing it. One must then remember the behavior (and reinforcement when applicable), which is Retention (C). Bandura theorized that one must have the Motivation (D) to imitate the behavior, as well as the ability to imitate the observed behavior.

54. A: Toddlers are typically in Erikson's psychosocial stage centering on the nuclear conflict of Autonomy vs. Shame and Self-Doubt. The toddler who shouts "NO!" and has tantrums is exhibiting normal behaviors as s/he works to develop independence (autonomy). Children developing Initiative (B) vs. Guilt are in a later stage, as are children developing Industry (C) vs. Inferiority. Children developing Basic Trust vs. Mistrust (D) are typically the earlier stage of infancy.

55. B: Maslow conceived of human needs in a hierarchy, and visualized this hierarchy as a pyramid. At the base of this pyramid are physiological needs, which are the most fundamental. Above these are security (C) needs such as shelter and a safe environment. Above these are social needs like feeling loved and belonging to a group. Above these are esteem (D) needs like feeling personal value, social recognition, and accomplishment. At the top of the pyramid are self-actualizing (A) needs, i.e. realizing one's full potential and attaining optimal personal growth. Maslow theorized that lower levels of need must be met before any higher level(s) can be addressed; hence physiological needs must be met first.

56. C: Conditional positive self-regard was Rogers' term for self-esteem that depends on external standards. External locus of control was Julian Rotter's term for attributing one's own success or failure to external factors (e.g. "The teacher didn't explain it to me" for failure or "The teacher helped me" for

Copyright © Mometrix Media. You have been licensed one copy of this document for personal use only. Any other reproduction or redistribution is strictly prohibited. All rights reserved.

success). Conditional positive self-regard would be the equivalent in Rogers' theory. Rogers felt that children develop conditional positive self-regard when they are subjected to condition of worth (B), i.e. rewards based not on need but worthiness, as in behaviorism's contingencies of reinforcement. Rogers believed Incongruence (A) between one's ideal self and real self would cause neurosis. Unconditional positive regard (D) was what Rogers believed parents and therapists should give, i.e. unconditional love and acceptance, to children and all individuals.

57. D: This example illustrates the behaviorist principle of negative reinforcement: An aversive stimulus, i.e. something one does not like, is removed contingent on a behavior, increasing the probability one will repeat the behavior. In this example, being rushed by the mother is the aversive stimulus. Positive reinforcement (A) presents a desirable stimulus, i.e. something one likes, contingent on a behavior, increasing probability of repetition. For example, if the mother gave the child a favorite treat right after s/he woke up early, s/he would awaken early again for the treat. Positive punishment (B) presents an aversive stimulus contingent on a behavior to reduce probability of repetition. If the mother yelled at the child for awakening early, s/he would be less likely to awaken early again. Negative punishment (C) removes a desirable stimulus contingent on a behavior to reduce the probability of repetition; e.g. if the mother prohibited TV for awakening early.

58. D: The Montessori Method emphasizes children's self-direction in activities, while teachers make clinical observations and serve as guides; and self-correction via the use of autodidactic equipment. The Montessori Method teaches both practical skills and abstract concepts via physical activities, not just mental tasks (A). Montessori teachers make every effort to engage children's parents in their educations, rather than leaving them uninvolved (B). Learning environments in Montessori schools are adapted to the developmental levels of individual children rather than groups (C).

59. D: In the Bank Street approach, children can learn at different developmental levels appropriate for them. They typically learn multiple subjects together, not one at a time (A); and in groups rather than 1:1 as individuals (B). They engage in physical, cognitive, emotional, and social development through various types of childcare programs, not just one (C).

60. C: Froebel did believe that nature was the heart of all learning. He also believed that the role schools, among other things, was to direct the will of the students (A). He felt that human potential was defined through individual accomplishments (B). He not only believed in, but pioneered, play-based instruction (D) for young children; in fact, Froebel was the person who invented the original concept and practice of Kindergarten. He felt that the goals of education included the development of spirituality and self-control in students. Most of Froebel's philosophy and theory of education remain influential in early childhood education today.

61. B: Siegfried Engelmann collaborated with Carl Bereiter in experiments reexamining Piaget's theory of cognitive development. While Piaget had maintained that the ability to conserve liquid volume depended only on the child's level of cognitive development, Engelmann and Bereiter showed that this ability could also be taught to children before they reached the corresponding Piagetian stage. The Bereiter-Engelmann Preschool Program did not test teaching methods with affluent college faculty children (A); Piaget's case studies used such children, but the Bereiter'-Engelmann Program demonstrated the effectiveness of intensive instruction for enhancing cognitive skills in disadvantaged preschool-aged children. Engelmann did develop the philosophy and methodology of Direct Instruction (C), through his research into curriculum and instruction including children with Down syndrome (D) as well as children from impoverished backgrounds.

62. A: The High/Scope Curriculum for preschoolers does include music activities, but these do not include writing musical notation or music composition. They include listening to music, singing, and playing musical instruments. The other choices all represent activities included in each of four other out of 10 main categories of key experiences for preschool children's development and active learning.

Copyright © Mometrix Media. You have been licensed one copy of this document for personal use only. Any other reproduction or redistribution is strictly prohibited. All rights reserved.

63. B: One principle of emergency literacy theory is that young children learn to read and write concurrently, not in sequence, since reading and writing are integrally interrelated and cannot be separated. However, this theory does not find that children's first encounters with written language occur during early childhood (A); but rather that even infants encounter written language. Emergent literacy theorists also note that young children's scribbles do not all look the same (C) regardless of native language; rather, Egyptian children's scribbles resemble Egyptian writing more, American children's scribbles look more like English writing, etc. While receptive language comprehension develops before expressive comprehension with speech, this does not apply to print (D): preschoolers find early writing activities easier than early reading activities. In this theory, research finds that literacy does not involve abstract, isolated skills learned for their own sake, but rather authentic skills applied for real-life purposes, the same way children see adults use literacy.

64. C: The whole language approach to early childhood literacy instruction has its basis in the philosophy and psychology of constructivism. Hence it is not similar to the analytical nature of teaching phonics (A) or of alphabetical learning (B). It emphasizes the uniqueness of each child's cognitive experience, not similarity (D).

65. D: In the whole language approach, children's overall engagement, comprehension, and appreciation of reading, writing, and literature come before correction of mechanical errors. Therefore, (A) is incorrect. Whole language teachers do not ignore young children's mechanical errors (B). While they do not prioritize correction, they do use formative assessments, not only summative assessments (C) and then design learning activities that give children opportunities and help to acquire mechanically correct linguistic forms.

66. D: Like Darwin describing evolution before him, Piaget referred to adaptation (A) in describing how we adjust to our environment. We adapt not only to survive, but to establish, maintain, and restore equilibrium or balance. Piaget called this natural process of seeking balance equilibration (C). The process of adaptation seeks equilibrium. Components of adaptation are assimilation (B), i.e., fitting new but related information into an existing schema, and accommodation (D), i.e., forming a new schema or changing an existing one to fit new and related but very different information. For example, a young child assimilates a new food into his schema for "things I can eat." Encountering gum, the child accommodates to it by changing that schema to include "things I can chew but not swallow."

67. D: When teachers use the LEA with young children for learning beginning reading, children realize that they acquire knowledge and understanding through their own experiences as well as through instruction. This is because the LEA does connect printed language with the students' own personal life experiences (A). It has the children use their own language and words (B) to describe things. This enables them to interact with text on multiple levels at one time (C).

68. C: Instruction using basal readers goes from the bottom up, moving from smaller subsets of reading skills to larger ones. This helps students make transitions from each part to the whole. Basal readers use texts including children's literature *and* diverse other writing genres (A). Basal reader texts are graded by reading level, and include *both* narrative and expository writing (B). Instructional research finds that using rigid, systematic sequences in teaching from smaller to larger subsets of skills is *more* helpful to students (D).

69. B: All of these are techniques included in the basal reader approach to reading instruction. Young children are aided in decoding text through the precise control of word analysis skills, (A) as well as of vocabulary items (C), and by the use of enlarged "big books" (D).

70. A: During the DRA, teachers prepare students before they read by presenting them with new concepts and vocabulary words they will encounter in the text; and help them become more motivated to read. Only after this preparation by teachers do students read silently, guided by teacher questions

197

Copyright © Mometrix Media. You have been licensed one copy of this document for personal use only. Any other reproduction or redistribution is strictly prohibited. All rights reserved.

and statements (C); they do not read silently first (B). Student reading comprehension is developed not only by teacher actions but also through student discussions (D) of concepts, characters, plots, etc.

71. B: The DR-TA is meant to develop students' ability to read critically by teaching them reading comprehension as a group, not individually (A). It is meant to engage children's active participation in reading, not only by their processing information (C), but also by their asking questions (D) and receiving feedback as they are reading.

72. C: DRA manuals primarily use literal, factual questions that require only convergent thinking of students; whereas DR-TA questions require higher levels of reading comprehension and interpretation of students by demanding they engage in divergent or creative thinking. DRAs, having more specific materials, guidelines, and questions and being more manual-oriented and materials-oriented, are best suited specifically for use with basal readers; however, DR-TAs, having fewer directions and greater teacher flexibility and responsibility, can also be used for other curriculum and lesson planning (A) that involve reading. DRAs feature the pre-teaching of new vocabulary words, while DR-TAs do not (B), instead requiring more realistic during-reading decoding. While DRA manuals specify when to teach which skills, DR-TA approaches do not (D). Thus teachers need more expertise in asking questions and considering varied student answers when using DR-TAs than they do with DRAs.

73. D: Research with early childhood learning devices has proven that manipulatives are effective for helping young children to access abstract math concepts. It is not that they cannot understand these at all (A) or that they can only understand concrete objects (B); but rather that they cannot understand abstract concepts when these are presented only abstractly, but can understand abstract concepts when they are presented using concrete objects that young children can see, feel, and manipulate. Solid objects provide a bridge to abstract ideas for young children. Some early math curricula even require manipulatives (C), such as the Horizons curriculum.

74. A: An activity using non-standard measures two compare something like the weight of apples and grapes is helpful in learning inference skills, since students have to try out different combinations to find the balance. Students improve their inference skills by using the outcome of one attempt to inform their next through inference. Observation skills are also exercised in activities like these, as the students have to observe and operate the scales to find their answer, but it is not such a observationally focused activity as studying and describing physical traits of different objects. Communication would be a key feature if this type of activity were used in a group. Classification is not particularly exercised in this type of activity, since the only classifications would be the type of fruit, which is a given in this type of activity.

75. C: One way to engage preschoolers in scientific inquiry and discovery is to have them compare similarities and contrast differences among various objects, because observation and classification are scientific principles and process skills for children to develop. Exploring the solubility in water of various substances *is* a scientific activity (A) as it involves inquiring and discovering the properties of different forms of matter. Mixing colors is not strictly an art activity (B), but can be used equally well for scientific inquiry and discovery. Preschool teachers can create science centers inexpensively (D) by using common objects like magnets, mirrors, scales, magnifying glasses, prisms; by selecting books, games, puzzles, etc. related to various science themes; and using models, puppets, and other inexpensive, preschool-friendly objects and materials.

76. B: EC experts advise that teachers can and should find science teaching materials in their everyday environments, which cost nothing and appeal to children's natural curiosity and interests. Preschool children do not learn best from textbooks (A), even age-appropriate books; they enjoy learning with real-world materials. For example, found objects from nature like rocks, loose bird feathers, fallen leaves, etc. make good science materials (C). Teachers can also obtain animal fur from local groomers and turtle shells, snakeskins, etc. from local pet stores (D) are useful teaching materials.

Copyright © Mometrix Media. You have been licensed one copy of this document for personal use only. Any other reproduction or redistribution is strictly prohibited. All rights reserved.

Mometrix

77. A: Preschool children's upper bodies are typically more developed than their lower bodies, giving them higher centers of gravity. This makes them more likely to fall than older children (B). Preschool teachers can help them improve their balance and coordination by encouraging them to hop (C) and balance on one foot. Such exercises, including hopping races, can also enhance children's self-confidence, an emotional benefit (D).

78. B: In instruction about color as an element of visual art, preschool teachers can help children learn color names, sensory discrimination, and classification skills. Teachers can read children a story about colors, or sing/play a song about colors to introduce a lesson (A). Some art museums do offer pre-designed lessons in visual art elements for preschool ages (C), which teachers can use as models. After a story or song, teachers can present a painting or other artwork, which young children can appreciate (D) on their own levels.

79. C: Preschool children's ability to recognize shapes will develop through well-designed lessons focusing on line as an element of visual art. Such lessons will also help preschoolers to improve their ability to make comparisons (A) and expand their ability to recognize symbols (B). Teachers can help children identify different types of lines like straight, wavy, spiral, pointy, zigzag, etc., separately drawn on paper, which is within the abilities of preschoolers, and then ask them to find these line types in a work of art, (D), which they will be able to do after identifying them separately. Teachers can then have children draw the different line types themselves, and experiment with different line-drawing tools.

80. D: Teaching preschoolers about how shape is used in art helps develop their early geometric math skills as well as their understanding of visual art. It also helps them develop their ability to form concepts (A) and to identify discrepancies (B), as well as to stimulate their creative thinking skills (C). For example, teachers can read a story about shapes; then have children point to and name shapes they recognize in the story; then have them identify shapes in a work of art; and then have them arrange solid shapes into formations representing people, animals, houses, flowers, etc.

81. C: Cognitive dissonance is a term coined by psychologist Leon Festinger to describe the discomfort we feel when considering contradictory information. We resolve this discomfort by rejecting certain information, or forming new schemata or changing existing ones to accommodate some information. This term is not related to a disorder (A), sensory overload (B), or incompatible instructional and learning (D) processes.

82. D: Not only is emotional development necessary in itself; but it is also a prerequisite and a support for children's development of social interactions and social skills. Affective learning activities help children to express their emotions, and also to understand them (A). Understanding them will in turn help children to develop emotional self-regulation (B). In addition, affective learning activities can inform teachers about how children feel and which activities most interest them (C).

83. C: Giving preschoolers an activity wherein the teacher prompts them to use different body postures and movements to depict different emotions helps them to understand their own and others' emotions (A); express them as well as understand them (B), get physical exercise and have fun (C), and use creative thinking (D).

84. B: Children's motor skills typically develop sooner than their verbal skills. Hence young children are more likely to use physical aggression like kicking, biting, hitting, and pushing/shoving to get what they want rather than using speech (A). Young children have also not yet developed emotional self-regulation, so preschool teachers must help them learn how to manage their strong emotions constructively (C). Young children do not learn social skills only directly; teachers can help develop their social skills by demonstrating aggressive vs. proactive behaviors using puppets (D), which preschoolers find entertaining as well as concrete representations of emotions they can understand.

Copyright © Mometrix Media. You have been licensed one copy of this document for personal use only. Any other reproduction or redistribution is strictly prohibited. All rights reserved.

85. A: Early childhood education experts recommend providing at least 35 square feet indoors and 75 square feet outdoors of usable play space for learning environments. (B) would not be enough room for typical young children to engage in usual activities and avoid fighting or competing among age groups. (C) and (D) would be excellent but do not reflect the recommended *minimums*.

86. B: Indoor and outdoor spaces in EC learning environments should be arranged to allow individual, small-group, and large-group activities. Children's products and other visual elements should be placed at child eye level, not adult (A) when displayed. Spaces should be organized to allow, not prohibit, children's movement among activities (C) without unduly distracting other students. Spaces should also be arranged to promote children's positive social interactions (D) and behaviors, not to prevent these.

87. C: EC experts say that indoor learning environments for toddlers and preschoolers should have the rooms organized to enable a variety of activities, but not necessarily to limit the activities to certain areas (A). The floors in the rooms should include both hard and carpeted floors (B) to allow crawling, toddling, walking, etc., which should not be limited by insufficient space. Preschool math and science activities might occur in multiple areas of a classroom (D), while the room still should be laid out to facilitate their taking place.

88. C: Positive reinforcement (A) motivates the individuals by presenting something that increases the probability of a behavior's occurrence and/or recurrence. Primary reinforcement (B) is unconditioned, i.e., it naturally reinforces or increases a behavior's probability (e.g., food, water, sleep). Negative reinforcement (C) motivates the individuals by removing something whose removal reinforces or increases a behavior's probability. Secondary reinforcement (D) is conditioned, i.e., it did not originally reinforce the behavior but has been made to do so by pairing it with a primary reinforcement.

89. D: Small inner rooms and partitions in indoor environments provide ways for children to experience privacy and solitude when needed. Adult laps for cuddling (A), pillows and soft upholstery (B) and thickly carpeted floor areas (C) are all related to providing for children's sensory needs for softness, but not for privacy.

90. C: Behavioral principles have proven in many studies that it is more powerful to reward good behaviors than to punish bad behaviors (A); therefore, these are not equally effective (B). Good behaviors should be rewarded consistently, not occasionally (D). Positive reinforcement must be repeated consistently many times for young children to associate their behaviors with the rewards they receive as they will not instantly make this association.

91. B: Behaviors occur for reasons, to meet needs. Thus, one must know what function or purpose they serve before one can change them. An undesirable behavior can be replaced with a more desirable one, but the replacement behavior must serve the same purpose as the undesirable one, so (A) is incorrect. While knowing a behavior's function is necessary, this does not eliminate the need to change it (C). Knowing a behavior's function informs not only the choice of a replacement behavior, but also which consequences to apply to the undesired behavior. The same consequences will not work for every function (D) a behavior can serve. For example, a tantrum behavior the function of which is to get attention will not respond to a certain consequence the same as when its function is to express frustration.

92. A: FERPA provides that schools may furnish student records without prior consent to some researchers if they are conducting certain studies on behalf of the school; by court order or legal subpoena (B); to appropriate personnel in safety or health emergencies (C); and to juvenile justice system authorities, according to specific state laws (D).

93. D: Because of diverse student needs, teachers are required to ensure educational equity by differentiating their instruction accordingly with student abilities (A), offering equal opportunities to all

Copyright © Mometrix Media. You have been licensed one copy of this document for personal use only. Any other reproduction or redistribution is strictly prohibited. All rights reserved.

students (B), treating all students fairly (C), and choosing and/or adapting instructional materials to reflect multicultural perspectives (D) to which multicultural students can relate.

94. D: Relative to early childhood behavior management, the "10:1 Rule" means that for every 1 negative comment or correction one gives to a child, the adults should give that child at least 10 positive comments. Positive reinforcement for desired behaviors is proven to be always more powerful than punishment for undesired behaviors.

95. D: When young children follow adults' rules in care and educational settings, the adults should consistently reward them for doing so. Adults should never assume they can do nothing as long as children comply with rules (A): they will not continue without any positive reinforcement. When adults withhold rewards from children who do not follow rules, they cannot assume this needs no explanation (B): they must explain to young children why they did not get the reward by telling them which rule they did not follow. Initially stating the rules is not enough with young children; adults must repeat rules frequently and for a long time (C) before young children can remember and follow them.

96. C: One way EC educators can include families in children's education is to acknowledge the integral part that parents play in supporting their children's learning. Another way is for educators to promote and support parenting skills, their enhancement, and their application by parents (A). To include families, educators should work to achieve reciprocal and regular communication between the school and family (B). All school personnel should not only make parents feel welcome at the school; they should also seek out help and support from parents (D).

97. B: To involve families of diverse backgrounds, EC educators should ask them to develop their own goals for participating in their young children's educations since the family members know better how they are able and willing to participate. EC educators *must* involve families in designing IFSPs for preschoolers (A), since an IFSP is an Individualized FAMILY Service Plan. It is good for educators to create volunteer calendars; however, they should NOT assign parents times for participating (C), but rather should encourage them to collaborate with schools when they are able. If families have difficulty with printed/written English (or any printed/written language), educators should instead speak with them to promote regular communication (D). They should also get an interpreter if needed for parents who speak little or no English.

98. C: EC educators should frequently send communications to diverse families with information about their children (A); about important developmental milestones (A, B, and D); about methods they can use to nurture child growth and development (B and C); and about the content of their classes (D).

99. D: For informal assessments of pre-K classes, teachers can make classroom observations during story or circle times, each observation targeting different skills like math, alphabet knowledge, social-emotional skills, emergent writing, oral language, etc. They can make these observations during both small-group (A) and whole-class (B) activities. They should organize the assessments using around three themes per day (C).

100. D: Formal assessments are typically standardized tests administered to groups of students. They are designed to avoid administrator bias (A) and capture only the children's responses (B). They provide norms for age groups and/or developmental levels for comparison (C). Their data can be scaled and reported in aggregate to school and/or program administrators and policymakers.

101. D: By his term reciprocal determinism, Bandura means that learning involves the individual, the behavior, and the environment, all of which influence and are influenced by one another. This term does not specifically refer only to student and teacher (A), to behavior and environment only (B), or to individual and environment only (C).

Copyright © Mometrix Media. You have been licensed one copy of this document for personal use only. Any other reproduction or redistribution is strictly prohibited. All rights reserved.

102. C: Not all screening and assessment instruments used in EC education programs are appropriate for use with ethnically diverse populations. Depending on their authors and the populations samples used for norming, they may be culturally biased. Screening and assessment instruments used with EC students vary in which developmental domains they measure (A). Different tests are intended for use in different applications (B). The methods of administration also vary across instruments (D).

103. B: While some tests are comprehensive, assessing children's development in multiple domains, not all are (A). Some tests focus on a single domain (C), like language or emotional-social development, while others can even focus on one facet within a domain {(B), (C)}, like attachment or temperament within the emotional-social domain of development. In addition to developmental domains, some tests measure risk and resiliency factors (D) that influence developmental delays and disorders.

104. A: One application of assessment instrument results in ECE programs is for planning curriculum and treatment programs. However, screening instruments are used for identifying children who need further assessments rather than for diagnosing developmental problems (B). Assessment instruments are also applied in developing and/or confirming diagnoses (C) of developmental delays or disorders. An additional important application of assessment instruments is for determining a child's eligibility for a particular program (D).

105. B: It is more advantageous for ECE programs to use tests that cover the entire age range that their programs serve. This is because they not only can assess all ages of children in the program (A) with equal accuracy (D), but also because they are easier to administer and then re-administer later to monitor children's progress in the program than separate, age-specific tests are; they can also be administered during a program for progress monitoring (B); and they are easier to administer at the beginnings and ends of programs for comparison than separate, age-specific tests are (C).

106. C: Self-reporting instruments do have the advantage that they usually take fewer than 20 minutes for parents, caregivers, and teachers to complete. *If* they are self-administered, they must be at the respondents' reading levels and in their native language (A); but some of them *can* alternatively be read to respondents by interviewers who are trained in or familiar with the instrument's administration (B). While ECE program personnel need relatively little training to administer these assessments, they may need more training to score and interpret them (D); or in some cases, trained specialists may score and interpret them instead.

107. D: The interview method for gathering screening/assessment information from adults about infants and young children can involve brief interviews, but they typically still take longer than paper-and-pencil self-reporting questionnaires, surveys, or checklists. Interviews may be conducted in a structured format using the questions given (A); or in a semi-structured format wherein the administrator uses his/her judgment (B) in adding questions to those published to obtain complete enough information. Interview questions can cover not only the child's identified areas of strengths and needs (C), but also parental concerns, parent-child interactions, the child's behavior, and other subjects.

108. D: Instruments that use multiple methods, such as collecting data from a variety of respondents and settings, will yield the most comprehensive information for determining diagnoses and/or developing individualized care or instructional plans for EC populations. Self-reporting questionnaires and surveys (A) are more appropriate for use in screenings because they are usually short, need little administrator training and are easy to administer, are comparatively low in cost, and can be used in different settings like pediatricians' offices, homes, preschools, etc. Formal and informal observational tools (B) and structured and semi-structured interviews (C), while requiring more training, time, and expense, provide more detailed information for assessments to aid diagnoses and planning; however, multiple-method assessments still provide even more comprehensive information than these.

Copyright © Mometrix Media. You have been licensed one copy of this document for personal use only. Any other reproduction or redistribution is strictly prohibited. All rights reserved.

109. D: Test-retest reliability means that a test instrument will yield the same results when administered two or more times to the same child within a short period of time. (Developmental changes in early childhood occur too rapidly for this to apply if testing is done over a longer time period.) (A) is a definition of inter-rater reliability. (B) is a definition of internal consistency reliability. (C) is a definition of content validity.

110. C: If two children take the same test and both score beyond its cutoff score indicating need for assessment, and this results from their scoring the same on mostly the same test items, then the test's individual items correlate with one another and the overall test score, meaning the test has internal consistency. But if two children score past the cutoff but their scores result from completely different test items (A), then the test's items do not correlate with each other (D) or the overall test score (B), meaning the test does not have good internal consistency.

111. B: Content validity means that a test measures the entire content area it claims to measure. If a test does this, it can be used with more confidence to generalize about how its results predict a child's functioning levels in real life. However, if a test to screen for social-emotional development, for example, screens for a child's interactions with caregivers but not with peers (A); or screens for social skills but not communication skills (C); or screens for attention but not for initiation of play (D), the test would have low content validity by not screening for all elements of social-emotional development.

112. A: When a screening tool identifies a potential mental health disorder, and then a complete diagnostic evaluation confirms this prediction by diagnosing an actual mental health disorder, the screening tool has demonstrated good predictive validity. An instrument correctly identifying 6 of 10 children _with_ developmental disorders or delays is said to have a _sensitivity_ of 60%, not specificity (B). An instrument correctly identifying 8 of 10 children _without_ disorders or delays has 80% _specificity_, not sensitivity (C). Identification of delays/disorders where none exist constitutes false-_positive_ errors (D).

113. B: EC educators should make organized outlines of developmentally applicable guidelines for the children they serve. These outlines provide foundations for the anecdotal observations and authentic assessments they will use to track children's developmental progress; hence they are not unnecessary (A). ECE programs must include ample opportunities and activities for children to develop each individual skill, which includes all of the practice and review they need in order to retain what they learn (C). For tracking children's progress, ECE programs should use systems that follow developmental sequences (D). This helps teachers know whether they can advance some children to the next level, or need to reinforce some previously taught skills for other children.

114. C: The law stipulates that EC teachers and other professionals working with children and families are "mandated reporters" who are legally required to report any suspicions of child abuse or neglect. The teacher should report her suspicions to authorities because this law was enacted to stop violence against children, and not just because the law incurs penalties against professionals who do not comply with it (D). Even if the teacher feels sorry for the mother, and/or she cannot prove her suspicions, these are not reasons to refrain from reporting them (A). She should report seeing injuries to the child and hearing from the child that the boyfriend caused them, even though she knows the mother depends financially and emotionally on the boyfriend (B). Avoiding potentially harmful side effects for the mother is no justification for allowing suspected abuse to go unreported.

115. D: EC educators interact positively when they use problem-solving activities and dialogues to help them discover which learning experiences they can make more effective for children, and how to do this. Sharing anecdotal records and observations with other educators within the ECE program for the purpose of improving instruction does not disrespect privacy (A). Communicating with other adults within the ECE setting about the children and families they serve does not violate confidentiality (B) but does constitute positive interaction. EC educators within a program should not only share their

Copyright © Mometrix Media. You have been licensed one copy of this document for personal use only. Any other reproduction or redistribution is strictly prohibited. All rights reserved.

observations and records of their students, but should moreover use this shared information to collaboratively plan their instruction (C).

116. D: By law, ECE employees are both required to report suspected child abuse or neglect and are also immune from liability for releasing student records related to such reporting; therefore, (C) is incorrect. The Family Educational Rights and Privacy Act (FERPA) mandates student records confidentiality for every ECE program/facility/agency that receives federal funding, not every ECE program/facility/agency in the country (A): those NOT receiving any federal funding are not subject to this law. The IDEA (Individuals with Disabilities Education Act) is a federal law and hence not superseded by state special education laws (B).

117. D: Because of danger and liability issues, giving medication to children in ECE settings is controversial but often necessary. ECE staff should label children's medications with drug name, child's name, doctor's name and contact information, and dosage and administration instructions to prevent errors. ECE centers/programs must write and follow policies and procedures observing their state government's licensing requirements for medical care and treatment (A). ECE experts advise centers/programs require doctor and parent permission for giving children any prescription/non-prescription medication (B). In addition to keeping written parental consent on file, centers/programs should post separate charts for easy staff access with the child's name, medication, dosage, time to administer, and teacher initials. This does not induce redundancy or errors (C); rather, it documents that teachers follow physicians' and parents' directions, and can prevent errors.

118. C: ECE settings should keep certain things on file for medical emergencies, including detailed emergency treatment procedures; signed, written parent consent, which is necessary (A); parental preferences in doctors and hospitals (B); and information on the health insurance of children's families (C) as well as parent contact information. Notifying parents of emergencies is legally required (D) by licensing regulations; not notifying parents is subject to legal action.

119. B: One issue affecting ECE facilities is if state authorities remove a child from the parents' custody. Another issue that does affect ECE facilities is if two parents not living together are pursuing child custody (C), because parents frequently demand to visit with and/or take the child home even when they do not have custody, so ECE personnel must know this. (A) is the definition of physical custody, not legal custody. (D) is the definition of legal custody, not physical custody. Physical custody does not confer all the rights of full legal custody.

120. A: If an adult without custody or otherwise unauthorized attempts to pick up a child from an ECE facility, the administrator should inform the adult of the center's policies and procedures, including showing them their copy of the court's custody order (A) if needed. If the adult refuses to leave, threatens or shows violence or makes a scene, the ECE should call the police if necessary (B). If the adult leaves, the ECE administrator must not only notify the parents or other adult(s) who enrolled the child of the incident; s/he must also file a written report of it (C), meet with the custodial adult to review and/or update custody arrangements; document the meeting (D) including signatures and dates, and file the documentation in the child's center record.

Copyright © Mometrix Media. You have been licensed one copy of this document for personal use only. Any other reproduction or redistribution is strictly prohibited. All rights reserved.

Constructed Response

Read the scenario provided and answer each of the short answer sections with one or two paragraphs for each of the four sections.

CASE HISTORY

SCENARIO – MR. BANKS' CLASS

Jonathan is a seven-year-old student in Mr. Banks' class who is exhibiting difficulty in phonetic activities, such as breaking down words into correctly segmented syllables. Jonathan also seems to have difficulty paying attention in large-group activities and lessons, regardless of subject matter. After consultation with the school speech language pathologist, it was found that Jonathan is most likely struggling with hearing certain frequencies, which are inhibiting his ability to hear well in larger-class activities and are likely causing interference with his ability to tell the difference between specific sounds. At this time, Jonathan is not being given any hearing aids, but is recommended to be placed where he can hear better in class. Other recommendations include using phonics activities more targeted to Jonathan's specific needs.

CLASSROOM OBSERVATION NOVEMBER 13TH—FOCUS ON JONATHAN WILSON

In the first portion of observation, Mr. Banks was teaching a math lesson using manipulatives to perform addition. The classroom is arranged in 5 'islands' with 4 desks pushed together to form an island. Mr. Banks provides the instructions for students to work alone, and not to help each other with the assignment, despite being in groups of four. As the students begin working through their assignment, it is noted that Jonathan immediately started talking with the nearby students, seemingly trying to ask what the assignment was. Jonathan did not seem to be distracted, but was seemingly unaware of the task. Mr. Banks directly addressed Jonathan and provided him with more direct instructions, and class proceeded with no further incidents at this time. Jonathan seemed, at this time, to be a focused student, and not an intentional disruptor of the class. When the next portion of the lesson was explained and it was time to begin working on the next steps, Jonathan did not begin his work, but just sat looking around. It is assumed that Jonathan was afraid to disrupt the class again, as Jonathan is averse to drawing attention to himself in this way. Mr. Banks again went and provided direct instruction to Jonathan which seems to have resolved the current issue.

In another portion of the class, students are to listen to an audiobook reading of a story and answer questions following the story. Jonathan, who is normally very eager to participate in class activities, did not raise his hand or try to answer the questions. When asked for the answer to a specific question regarding the story, Jonathan did not have an answer. In reviewing Jonathan's grades on the reading portion of class, it is found that Jonathan has conspicuously inconsistent grades on assignments, including some perfect scores, and other non-passing scores, with notes that Jonathan did not participate fully. These trends seem to indicate that Jonathan's hearing is preventing him from having active participation in specific types of activities.

ESSAY QUESTIONS

1. Students as learners

- Identify two specific actions Mr. Banks should work to support Jonathan and his language and literacy development.
- Discuss the impact of language deficits on other areas of learning and development.
- Explain why each action will benefit Jonathan. Base your answer on understanding of principles of childhood development and the focus of students as learners.

205

Copyright © Mometrix Media. You have been licensed one copy of this document for personal use only. Any other reproduction or redistribution is strictly prohibited. All rights reserved.

2. Instructional Process

- Describe three ways in which Mr. Banks should alter his instructional processes to support Jonathan's areas of need. These modifications can be to curriculum, instructional practices, or to the classroom environment.
- Discuss how these modifications are designed with the whole class in mind.
- Explain why each modification is helpful in meeting Jonathan's specific needs.

3. Assessment

- Describe both formative and summative assessment processes Mr. Banks should employ to identify progress or lack of progress for Jonathan and other students with regards to material comprehension.
- Explain how each process Mr. Banks employs is a valid and reliable measure of student comprehension.
- Describe how these processes may inform future classroom practices as they indicate student comprehension deficits.

4. Professional Development, Leadership, and the Community

- Identify two ways in which Mr. Banks can promote awareness of Jonathan's needs to his educational community, including his family and other teachers.
- Explain how promoting professional development of this sort will benefit Jonathan and students like him.
- Describe what measures should be taken to ensure that the efforts are ethical.

Copyright © Mometrix Media. You have been licensed one copy of this document for personal use only. Any other reproduction or redistribution is strictly prohibited. All rights reserved.

Thank You

We at Mometrix would like to extend our heartfelt thanks to you, our friend and patron, for allowing us to play a part in your journey. It is a privilege to serve people from all walks of life who are unified in their commitment to building the best future they can for themselves.

The preparation you devote to these important testing milestones may be the most valuable educational opportunity you have for making a real difference in your life. We encourage you to put your heart into it—that feeling of succeeding, overcoming, and yes, conquering will be well worth the hours you've invested.

We want to hear your story, your struggles and your successes, and if you see any opportunities for us to improve our materials so we can help others even more effectively in the future, please share that with us as well. **The team at Mometrix would be absolutely thrilled to hear from you!** So please, send us an email (support@mometrix.com) and let's stay in touch.

> **If you'd like some additional help, check out these other resources
> we offer for your exam: http://MometrixFlashcards.com/NBPTS**

Copyright © Mometrix Media. You have been licensed one copy of this document for personal use only. Any other reproduction or redistribution is strictly prohibited. All rights reserved.

Additional Bonus Material

Due to our efforts to try to keep this book to a manageable length, we've created a link that will give you access to all of your additional bonus material.

Please visit http://www.mometrix.com/bonus948/nbptsgenec to access the information.

Copyright © Mometrix Media. You have been licensed one copy of this document for personal use only. Any other reproduction or redistribution is strictly prohibited. All rights reserved.

Copyright © Mometrix Media. You have been licensed one copy of this document for personal use only. Any other reproduction or redistribution is strictly prohibited. All rights reserved.